PERMANENTLY ONLINE, PERMANENTLY CONNECTED

Permanently Online, Permanently Connected establishes the conceptual grounds needed for a solid understanding of the permanently online/permanently connected phenomenon, its causes and consequences, and its applied implications. Due to the diffusion of mobile devices, the ways people communicate and interact with each other and use electronic media have changed substantially within a short period of time. This megatrend comes with fundamental challenges to communication, both theoretical and empirical. The book offers a compendium of perspectives and theoretical approaches from leading thinkers in the field to empower communication scholars to develop this research systematically, exhaustively, and quickly. It is essential reading for media and communication scholars and students studying new media, media effects, and communication theory.

Peter Vorderer is a professor of media and communication studies at the University of Mannheim. He served as president of the International Communication Association (ICA) from 2014 to 2015. His research focuses on media use and media effects with a special interest in entertainment research and new media and the question how does permanent connectedness with others via mobile devices change individuals and society at large.

Dorothée Hefner is a research associate at the Hanover University of Music, Drama and Media. Her research focuses on (permanent) mobile phone use and digital connectedness and their antecedents, as well as implications for interpersonal communication, political information, and individual well-being.

Leonard Reinecke is an associate professor at the Department of Communication at Johannes Gutenberg University Mainz, Germany. His research focuses on media uses and effects, media entertainment, and online communication. He has conducted research on various aspects of media use and well-being, including media-induced recovery from stress and strain and the interaction of media use and self-control.

Christoph Klimmt is a professor of communication at Hanover University of Music, Drama and Media. Beyond research on media entertainment, video games in particular, he is interested in media effects in news, advertising, risk, health, and science communication. Klimmt is currently serving as associate editor of the *Journal of Media Psychology*.

PERMANENTLY ONLINE, PERMANENTLY CONNECTED

Living and Communicating in a POPC World

Edited by Peter Vorderer, Dorothée Hefner, Leonard Reinecke, and Christoph Klimmt

Routledge
Taylor & Francis Group
NEW YORK AND LONDON

First published 2018
by Routledge
711 Third Avenue, New York, NY 10017

and by Routledge
2 Park Square, Milton Park, Abingdon, Oxon OX14 4RN

Routledge is an imprint of the Taylor & Francis Group, an informa business

© 2018 Taylor & Francis

The right of Peter Vorderer, Dorothée Hefner, Leonard Reinecke and Christoph Klimmt to be identified as the authors of the editorial material, and of the authors for their individual chapters, has been asserted by them in accordance with sections 77 and 78 of the Copyright, Designs and Patents Act 1988.

All rights reserved. No part of this book may be reprinted or reproduced or utilised in any form or by any electronic, mechanical, or other means, now known or hereafter invented, including photocopying and recording, or in any information storage or retrieval system, without permission in writing from the publishers.

Trademark notice: Product or corporate names may be trademarks or registered trademarks, and are used only for identification and explanation without intent to infringe.

Library of Congress Cataloging-in-Publication Data
Names: Vorderer, Peter, editor. | Hefner, Dorothée, editor. | Reinecke, Leonard, editor. | Klimmt, Christoph, editor.
Title: Permanently online, permanently connected / edited by Peter Vorderer, Dorothée Hefner, Leonard Reinecke, and Christoph Klimmt.
Description: New York and London : Routledge, Taylor & Francis Group, 2017.
Identifiers: LCCN 2017001816 | ISBN 9781138244993 (hardback) | ISBN 9781138245006 (pbk.) | ISBN 9781315276472 (ebk.)
Subjects: LCSH: Interpersonal relations. | Interpersonal relations—Technological innovations. | Internet—Social aspects. | Cell phones—Social aspects.
Classification: LCC HM1106 .P4354 | DDC 302.23—dc23
LC record available at https://lccn.loc.gov/2017001816

ISBN: 978-1-138-24499-3 (hbk)
ISBN: 978-1-138-24500-6 (pbk)
ISBN: 978-1-315-27647-2 (ebk)

Typeset in Bembo
by Apex CoVantage, LLC

CONTENTS

Contributors — *viii*
Acknowledgements — *xiv*

PART I
Introduction — 1

1 Permanently Online and Permanently Connected: A New Paradigm in Communication Research? — 3
  Peter Vorderer, Dorothée Hefner, Leonard Reinecke, and Christoph Klimmt

2 A Brief History of Individual Addressability: The Role of Mobile Communication in Being Permanently Connected — 10
  Rich Ling

3 The Permanently Online and Permanently Connected Mind: Mapping the Cognitive Structures Behind Mobile Internet Use — 18
  Christoph Klimmt, Dorothée Hefner, Leonard Reinecke, Diana Rieger, and Peter Vorderer

4 Methodological Challenges of POPC for Communication Research — 29
  Frank M. Schneider, Sabine Reich, and Leonard Reinecke

PART II
POPC and Decision-Making: Selecting, Processing, and Multitasking — 41

5 Reconceptualizing Uses and Gratifications vis-à-vis Smartphone Applications: The Case of WhatsApp — 43
  Vered Malka, Yaron Ariel, Ruth Avidar, and Akiba A. Cohen

6 Always On? Explicating Impulsive Influences on Media Use 51
   *Guido M. van Koningsbruggen, Tilo Hartmann,
   and Jie Du*

7 Permanence of Online Access and Internet Addiction 61
   Christoph Klimmt and Matthias Brand

8 Multitasking: Does It Actually Exist? 72
   Shan Xu and Zheng Wang

9 Threaded Cognition Approach to Multitasking and Activity
   Switching in a Permanently Online and Permanently
   Connected Ecosystem 83
   Prabu David

PART III
Social Dynamics of POPC: Self, Groups, and Relationships **95**

10 Living in the Moment: Self-Narratives of Permanently Connected
   Media Users 97
   Thilo von Pape

11 Getting the Best Out of POPC While Keeping the Risks in Mind:
   The Calculus of Meaningfulness and Privacy 107
   Sabine Trepte and Mary Beth Oliver

12 The Experience of Narrative in the Permanently Online, Permanently
   Connected Environment: Multitasking, Self-Expansion, and
   Entertainment Effects 116
   *Kelsey Woods, Michael D. Slater, Jonathan Cohen, Benjamin K. Johnson,
   and David R. Ewoldsen*

13 Being POPC Together: Permanent Connectedness and Group
   Dynamics 129
   Katharina Knop-Huelss, Julia R. Winkler, and Jana Penzel

14 POPC and Social Relationships 140
   Sonja Utz

15 Between Surveillance and Sexting: Permanent Connectedness
   and Intimate Relationships 149
   Diana Rieger

PART IV
Socialization in a POPC Environment: Development, Skill Acquisition, and Cultural Influences — 163

16 Growing Up Online: Media Use and Development in Early Adolescence — 165
    Amy B. Jordan

17 Being Mindfully Connected: Responding to the Challenges of Adolescents Living in a POPC World — 176
    Dorothée Hefner, Karin Knop, and Christoph Klimmt

18 Permanent Connections Around the Globe: Cross-Cultural Differences and Intercultural Linkages in POPC — 188
    Hartmut Wessler, Diana Rieger, Jonathan Cohen, and Peter Vorderer

PART V
The POPC Citizen: Politics and Participation — 197

19 The POPC Citizen: Political Information in the Fourth Age of Political Communication — 199
    Dorothée Hefner, Eike Mark Rinke, and Frank M. Schneider

20 The Networked Young Citizen as POPC Citizen — 208
    Ariadne Vromen, Michael A. Xenos, and Brian D. Loader

21 Permanent Entertainment and Political Behavior — 220
    R. Lance Holbert, Carina Weinmann, and Nicholas Robinson

PART VI
Brave New World: Networked Life and Well-Being — 231

22 POPC and Well-Being: A Risk–Benefit Analysis — 233
    Leonard Reinecke

23 Being Permanently Online and Being Permanently Connected at Work: A Demands–Resources Perspective — 244
    Sabine Sonnentag

24 The Dose Makes the Poison: Theoretical Considerations and Challenges of Health-Related POPC — 254
    Jutta Mata and Eva Baumann

Index — *265*

CONTRIBUTORS

Yaron Ariel is on the faculty of the Communication Department at the Max Stern Yezreel Valley College, Israel. His areas of expertise include new media, interactivity, and computer-mediated communication. He studies mobile media and social media from a user-centered perspective. He published chapters in the *Oxford Handbook of Internet Psychology* and *Psychological Aspects of Cyberspace* and articles in journals including *Telematics and Informatics*, *Media, War and Conflict*, and the *Atlantic Journal of Communication*.

Ruth Avidar is on the faculty of the Communication Department at the Max Stern Yezreel Valley College, Israel. Her research focuses on online public relations, social media, marketing communications, computer-mediated communication, and new technologies. Her publications appear in leading refereed journals. She spent two years working as a policy advisor in the Israeli Knesset (parliament) and almost a decade as a spokesperson in various Israeli commercial companies and nonprofit organizations.

Eva Baumann is Professor of Communication at Hanover University of Music, Drama and Media and head of the Hanover Center for Health Communication. Her research interests focus on health and risk communication strategies, health information seeking, eHealth, and sociocontextual factors of health-related attitudes and behaviors. Baumann is currently serving as vice president of the German Communication Association (DGPuK).

Matthias Brand is Professor of General Psychology at the University of Duisburg-Essen, Germany, and director of the Erwin Hahn Institute for Magnetic Resonance Imaging in Essen, Germany. He is interested in research on behavioral addictions, including Internet addiction, as well as in processes of human decision-making. Brand has established and is head of the Center for Behavioral Addiction Research (CeBAR) at the University of Duisburg-Essen.

Akiba A. Cohen is Professor (Emeritus) of Communication at Tel Aviv University. He is a fellow of the International Communication Association and a former president of the association. His main research interests are comparative study of news, iconic images, and mobile communication. Among his books is *The Wonder Phone in the Land of Miracles: Mobile Telephony in Israel* (with Dafna Lemish and Amit Schejter, Hampton Press, 2008).

Jonathan Cohen is Associate Professor in the Department of Communication, University of Haifa, Israel. His research and teaching focus on narrative persuasion, audience relationships with media characters, and perceptions of media influence. His recent publications on these topics have appeared in such journals as the *Journal of Communication*, *Media Psychology*, and *Communication Research*, among others.

Prabu David is Professor of Communication at Michigan State University, USA. His research focuses on mobile phone use, multitasking, health outcomes through mobile media, and the effects of mobile media on children.

Jie Du is a PhD student in the Department of Communication Science at the Vrije Universiteit Amsterdam. Her research interests concern self-control and social media use.

David R. Ewoldsen is Professor in the Department of Media and Information at Michigan State University. His research focuses on media psychology, including the study of stereotyping, cooperative video game play, comprehension processes, and adolescent risk behavior. He is currently the editor of the *Annals of the International Communication Association*. He also edited *Media Psychology* (1999–2007) and *Communication Methods and Measures* (2006–2010).

Tilo Hartmann is Associate Professor at the Department of Communication Science, Vrije Universiteit Amsterdam. His research focuses on psychological mechanisms underlying media use and effects. He is editor of the book *Media Choice: A Theoretical and Empirical Overview* and served as editorial board member of *Journal of Communication*, *Human Communication Research*, and *Media Psychology*.

Dorothée Hefner is a research associate at the Hanover University of Music, Drama and Media. Her research focuses on (permanent) mobile phone use and digital connectedness and their antecedents, as well as implications for interpersonal communication, political information, and individual well-being.

R. Lance Holbert is Professor and Chair of the Department of Strategic Communication, School of Media and Communication, Temple University (Philadelphia, PA, USA). His research interests include political communication, entertainment media, and persuasion.

Benjamin K. Johnson is Assistant Professor of Communication Science at Vrije Universiteit Amsterdam. His research examines selective exposure in new media settings, especially the ways that media choice relates to impression management, social comparison, and self-regulation processes. His publications have investigated media selection, processing, and effects in the contexts of political news, health news, science news, social media, e-commerce, and entertainment narratives.

Amy B. Jordan is Associate Dean for Undergraduate Studies at the Annenberg School for Communication, University of Pennsylvania. She is past president (2015–2016) of the International Communication Association, coeditor of the *Journal of Children and Media*, and author or editor of five books related to media and the well-being of children and adolescents. Her research has been funded by the Centers for Disease Control and Prevention, the National Institutes of Health, and the Robert Wood Johnson Foundation, and her work has been featured in, among others, *The Economist*, *The New York Times*, CNN, National Public Radio, and numerous parenting magazines.

Christoph Klimmt is a professor of communication at Hanover University of Music, Drama and Media. Beyond research on media entertainment, video games in particular, he is interested in media effects in news, advertising, risk, health, and science communication. Klimmt is currently serving as associate editor of the *Journal of Media Psychology*.

Karin Knop is Research Assistant at the Institute for Media and Communication Studies at the University of Mannheim. Her current research focuses on opportunities and risks of mobile phone use and new media literacy.

Katharina Knop-Huelss is Junior Researcher and PhD candidate at the Hanover University of Music, Drama and Media. Her work addresses media use and effects on social groups in the context of being permanently online and permanently connected, as well as entertainment research with a focus on morality, information processing, and learning outcomes.

Rich Ling is the Shaw Foundation Professor at Nanyang Technological University, Singapore. He also works closely with Telenor Research and has an adjunct position at the University of Michigan. He has written *The Mobile Connection* (Morgan Kaufmann, 2004), *New Tech, New Ties* (MIT, 2008), and *Taken for Grantedness* (MIT, 2012). He is a founding coeditor of *Mobile Media and Communication* and the Oxford University Press series on mobile communication.

Brian D. Loader is a Political Sociologist at the University of York, UK. His academic interests are focused around social relations of power in a digitally mediated world, including social media and citizenship participation. More specifically, his research interest is in young citizens, civic engagement, and social media; social movements and digital democracy; community informatics; and the digital divide. He is the editor-in-chief of the international journal *Information, Communication and Society*. Recent books include *Young Citizens in the Digital Age* (Routledge, 2007), *Social Media and Democracy* (Routledge, 2012), and *The Networked Young Citizen: Social Media, Political Participation and Civic Engagement* (edited with Ariadne Vromen and Mike Xenos, New York: Routledge, 2014).

Vered Malka is on the faculty of the Communication Department at the Max Stern Yezreel Valley College, Israel. Her areas of expertise are political communication, journalism in the new media era, and the roles of new media in contemporary society. She recently studied smartphones and Twitter as a new journalistic working tool. She has published in several journals, including *Media, War, and Conflict*, *Howard Journal of Communications*, and *Public Relations Review*.

Jutta Mata is Professor of Health Psychology at the University of Mannheim. Previous affiliations include the Max Planck Institute for Human Development, Stanford University, Technical University of Lisbon, and University of Basel. Her research focuses on determinants of long-term health behavior change and the effects of health behaviors on well-being. She has a special interest in how individual, psychological factors interact with environmental characteristics (including online, social, information, or built environments) in determining health and health behaviors.

Mary Beth Oliver is Distinguished Professor of Communications and Co-Director of the Media Effects Research Laboratory at the Pennsylvania State University. Her research focuses on entertainment psychology and on social cognition and the media. She is specifically interested in how media can be used for purposes of social good, including meaningfulness, connectedness, and well-being.

Thilo von Pape is Postdoctoral Researcher at Hohenheim University in Stuttgart, Germany. His research interests are media use, online communication, mobile communication, and media innovation. He is cofounder and editor-in-chief of the journal *Mobile Media and Communication*.

Jana Penzel studied Media and Communication Studies at the University of Mannheim. She has conducted research on various aspects of privacy and self-disclosure on social networking sites and in mobile messaging apps, as well as on the use and effects of self-tracking apps and wearable devices. She is now working as an online merchandiser of a German fashion company.

Sabine Reich is Research Associate at the Hanover University of Music, Drama and Media. Her research focuses on the use and effects of entertaining media, online communication, and music. She is interested in the media's role in social identity work, achieving well-being, and in advocating pro-social (e.g., health) and anti-discriminatory messages (e.g., gender, racism).

Leonard Reinecke is an assistant professor at the Department of Communication at Johannes Gutenberg University Mainz, Germany. His research focuses on media uses and effects, media entertainment, and online communication. He has conducted research on various aspects of media use and well-being, including media-induced recovery from stress and strain and the interaction of media use and self-control.

Diana Rieger is Postdoctoral Researcher at the Institute of Media and Communication Studies at the University of Mannheim. Her research focuses on the intersection between media effects and media psychology. She investigates media effects of mass communication (movies, computer games), online propaganda (right-wing extremist and Islamic extremist), and interpersonal communication (smartphones) on well-being-related outcomes and resilience.

Eike Mark Rinke is Research Associate in the Mannheim Centre for European Social Research at the University of Mannheim. His research focuses on political communication and media effects and examines these from international and individual as well as normative perspectives.

Nicholas Robinson is a PhD student at Temple University (Philadelphia, PA, USA). His research focuses on the relationship between evolving media technologies and political movements, including protest organizations and anti-establishment political parties and candidates.

Frank M. Schneider is Postdoctoral Researcher at the Institute for Media and Communication Studies, University of Mannheim, Germany. His research interests concern communication processes and effects with a focus on online communication, entertainment research, and political communication, as well as methodological advances in communication science.

Michael D. Slater is Social and Behavioral Science Distinguished Professor at the School of Communication, Ohio State University. His research includes theory-building efforts in narrative processing and impact and in dynamic processes of media use and identity formation and maintenance, and he has undertaken an extensive research program in the use of mediated communication to influence health attitudes and behavior.

Sabine Sonnentag is Professor of Work and Organizational Psychology at the University of Mannheim, Germany. Her research addresses the question of how employees can achieve sustainable high job performance and remain healthy at the same time. She studies recovery from job stress, proactive work behavior, and self-regulation at work—mainly in connection to individual well-being. Recently, she became more and more interested in employees' experiences of being permanently online and permanently connected to others at work.

Sabine Trepte is Professor of Media Psychology at the University of Hohenheim, Germany. Her research focuses on online disclosure and privacy from a psychological perspective.

Sonja Utz is Professor for Communication via Social Media at the University of Tübingen. She is head of the research lab Social Media at Leibniz-Institut für Wissensmedien in Tübingen. Her current research focuses on the emotional and informational benefits of social media use in the interpersonal and the professional domain. She is also the vice chair of the division of media psychology of the German Psychological Society.

Guido M. van Koningsbruggen is Assistant Professor in the Department of Communication Science at the Vrije Universiteit Amsterdam. Beyond research on the self-regulation of media use, he is interested in the media effects in health communication and the self-regulation of health behavior.

Peter Vorderer is a professor of media and communication studies at the University of Mannheim. Previous affiliations include the University of Toronto, Hanover University of Music, Drama and Media, the University of Southern California, and the VU University of Amsterdam. He served as president of the International Communication Association (ICA) from 2014 to 2015. His research focuses on media use and media effects with a special interest in entertainment research and new media and the question how does permanent connectedness with others via mobile devices change individuals and society at large.

Ariadne Vromen is Professor of Political Sociology in the Department of Government and International Relations, University of Sydney, Australia. Her research interests include political participation, social movements, advocacy organizations, digital politics, and young people and politics. She has completed extensive research on young people's political engagement, and her new book, *Digital Citizenship and Political Engagement*, looks at the emergence and effects of online advocacy organizations.

Zheng Wang is Associate Professor in the School of Communication and the Center for Cognitive and Brain Sciences at the Ohio State University. She directs the Communication and Psychophysiology research laboratory. One of her research foci is to study how people process and use media. In particular, she is interested in the dynamic reciprocal influences between media choice/use behavior and media information processing over time. She coedited *The Oxford Handbook of Computational and Mathematical Psychology* (2015).

Carina Weinmann is a PhD student and Research Associate at the Institute for Media and Communication Studies, University of Mannheim. Her main research interests concern political communication and entertainment research, with a specific focus on the connection of both areas. She studied media and communication, German language, and psychology at the University of Mannheim from 2007 to 2013.

Hartmut Wessler is Professor of Media and Communication Studies and a member of the Mannheim Center for European Social Research (MZES) at the University of Mannheim. Previous affiliations include the Free University of Berlin and Jacobs University Bremen. His research focuses on the intersection of political communication and transnational communication, with a particular focus on cultural differences in how global problems are discussed through mass and network media.

Julia R. Winkler is Research Assistant at the Institute for Media and Communication Studies at the University of Mannheim. Her research interests include group-based norms, representations, and perceptions in various media contexts, as well as media entertainment and its implications for psychological well-being, self-concepts, and pro-social outcomes.

Kelsey Woods is a PhD student and Graduate Research Associate at The Ohio State University. Her research focuses on how information is processed during media multitasking, particularly as it relates to narrative engagement and persuasion, health communication, and adolescent/young adult media use.

Michael A. Xenos is Communication Arts Partners Professor and also serves as Chair of the Department of Communication Arts at the University of Wisconsin-Madison. He also serves as editor-in-chief of the *Journal of Information Technology & Politics*, also published by Taylor & Francis. His research focuses on how individuals, political candidates, journalists, and other political actors adapt to changes in information and communication technologies, and how these adaptations affect broader dynamics of political communication and public deliberation.

Shan Xu is a PhD student in the School of Communication at The Ohio State University. She is interested in media technology, media processing, and media effects, especially their effects on well-being and health communication.

ACKNOWLEDGEMENTS

The editors would like to thank Sarah von Hören for her contribution to the volume's artwork. Furthermore, they appreciate the continuous support for research on "POPC" by the University of Mannheim. Finally, the editors express their gratitude to Autumn Spalding at Apex CoVantage, to the entire publishing team at Routledge, and to Linda Bathgate for their engaged, kind, and patient collaboration in completing this book project.

PART I
Introduction

1
Permanently Online and Permanently Connected

A New Paradigm in Communication Research?

Peter Vorderer, Dorothée Hefner, Leonard Reinecke, and Christoph Klimmt

Talking to students in a class, meeting with friends at a restaurant, working with associates in a small group, discussing with your own children the schedule for any given day, even being intimate with your romantic partner: No matter how such an interpersonal communication situation is specifically shaped, the chances are pretty good nowadays that the person you are facing is dividing his or her attention between you and the device she holds in her hand. This person is involved and actively participating in some form of interpersonal communication with you and with somebody else he or she is connected to via a smartphone. Or, equally possible, he or she is being exposed to news sites, blogs, electronic magazines, television, video clips, or even movies. In other words, this person participates in online exchange or attends to mass communication while simultaneously communicating face-to-face with you.

While until recently communication scholars have systematically distinguished between mass communication and interpersonal communication (the latter being face-to-face or mediated), such classifications have become fuzzy, as different forms of communication are about to merge. More and more often, we socialize with peers, work on a task, or engage in some other activity while allocating (some of) our attention to the messages that appear on the screens of our smartphones, wearables, or other online devices. Despite the fact that we are socially involved with others who are physically present or engaged in a task in the offline setting, we are additionally and simultaneously retrieving information from the Internet (being almost permanently online [PO]) and we are yet connected to other individuals via any form of online communication (being almost permanently connected [PC]).

Such forms of POPC behavior of course also require a certain POPC mindset. A POPC mindset, we believe, is more or less constantly oriented toward digital communication content, be that in the form of possible interactions with friends and peers, new posts on social network sites, public information via newsfeeds, or new decisions and moves of co-players in an online game, to name just a few examples. The POPC mindset refers to (a) the close and intense relationship with the smartphone and its communication ecology to which it grants permanent access and (b) the communication-related expectations that are brought forth with one's own and others' permanent connectedness. These expectations play a key role in how users approach and interpret situations, solve problems, regulate their emotions, interact with others, make decisions, and many other fundamentally important domains of behavior and social life (see Chapter 3 by Klimmt, Hefner, Reinecke, Rieger, and Vorderer).

The Present Volume

To digitally communicate or at least to be (permanently) accessible seems to be the "new normal" of our time. It appears as the default mode, whereas abstaining from the digital communication ecology needs to be justified among peers, friends, and colleagues. We believe that this shift from the "offline world" to the "online world" constitutes a disruptive change that affects individuals in their thinking, feeling, and behavior. Historically, one may compare the availability of such permanent communication opportunities with the advent of new infrastructures in earlier times: To be permanently online and permanently connected could have a similar impact on individual and social processes as had the installation of electricity nets or the mass availability of mobility enabled by cars, urban streets, and long-distance roads in the late 19th and early 20th centuries. The new permanence in communication has a significant impact on the individual users, on dyadic relationships, on social groups, and on society and culture at large. With this volume, we aim at describing and—if already possible—explaining the diverse manifestations, implications, and consequences of the new and permanent opportunities of mobile online communication. Our focus lies on the individual processes and effects of being POPC, knowing well that POPC will also have a profound impact on macro-level processes, such as economic value generation or the formation of public opinion.

In order to address the great diversity of manifestations and implications of POPC, the present volume consists of six sections. Next to this kick-off chapter, the "Introduction" section explains the phenomenon of POPC from a historical (see Chapter 2 by Ling) and a theoretical (see Chapter 3 by Klimmt, Hefner, Reinecke, Rieger, and Vorderer) point of view and discusses methodological challenges of POPC for communication research (see Chapter 4 by Schneider, Reich, and Reinecke).

The second section, "POPC and Decision-making: Selecting, Processing, Multitasking," is dedicated to the perspective of message choices and decision-making in permanent digital communication. In the first chapter within this section, Chapter 5 by Malka, Ariel, Avidar, and Cohen, the relevance of the uses-and-gratifications approach in the POPC context is demonstrated by explicating the use of "WhatsApp" in times of crisis. It then discusses how today's media-rich environment can be a strong trigger of impulsive media use that may be in conflict with other goals and obligations (see Chapter 6 by van Koningsbruggen, Hartmann, and Du) and how the new permanence in online communication affects the development, but also the prevention and treatment, of pathological Internet use (see Chapter 7 by Klimmt and Brand). Finally, the increasingly important phenomena of multitasking and task switching are reviewed and discussed in light of the opportunities in a POPC environment (see Chapter 8 by Xu and Wang and Chapter 9 by David).

The third section, "Social Dynamics of POPC: Self, Groups, and Relationships," addresses the consequences of POPC in the context of social and self-related processes. The first three chapters of this section address self-relevant processes in a POPC world, such as new forms of narrating the self and its consequences for well-being (see Chapter 10 by von Pape), potential conflicts of experiencing meaningfulness in a POPC world and protecting privacy simultaneously (see Chapter 11 by Trepte and Oliver), and how being POPC affects narrative engagement (see Chapter 12 by Woods, Slater, Cohen, Johnson, and Ewoldsen). The last three chapters are dedicated to the effects of POPC on social relationships. Their authors elaborate on how POPC affects group processes and dynamics (see Chapter 13 by Knop-Huelss, Winkler, and Penzel), how permanence in connectedness and interstitial communication in particular make a difference for social relationships (see Chapter 14 by Utz), and how being POPC alters beginnings, maintenance, and dissolutions of intimate relationships (see Chapter 15 by Rieger).

Section four, "Socialization in a POPC Environment: Development, Skill Acquisition, and Cultural Influences," discusses factors of influence that affect socialization processes under the conditions of POPC. The first two chapters in this section are focused on the developmental phase in adolescence. While Chapter 16 by Jordan elaborates on the question of what it means to grow up "online" in a POPC world, Chapter 17 by Hefner, Knop, and Klimmt introduces a conceptualization of important competencies that help today's adolescents respond to the challenges of living in a POPC environment. Chapter 18 by Wessler, Rieger, Cohen, and Vorderer discusses cultural influences on POPC behavior and how cultural identities are renegotiated in permanent cross-border POPC linkages between people from different cultural backgrounds.

Section five, "The POPC Citizen: Politics and Participation," discusses deployments that (possibly) result from today's media ecology and its opportunities for political communication and participation. Chapter 19 by Hefner, Rinke, and Schneider elaborates on how the POPC environment as a high-choice, high-stimulation media ecology shapes exposure to and processing of political information. Chapter 20 by Vromen, Xenos, and Loader deals with young citizens and their new forms of participation under conditions of POPC. Chapter 21 by Holbert, Weinmann, and Robinson is dedicated to the intersection of political communication and entertainment and discusses how the POPC environment affords citizens with new opportunities to combine entertainment and politics.

In the last section of the book, "Brave New World: Networked Life and Well-Being," the affordance and obligations of a POPC environment and the resulting implications for different facets of health and the quality of life are discussed: Chapter 22 by Reinecke provides an overview of potential consequences of POPC behavior and a POPC mindset for psychological health and well-being. Chapter 23 by Sonnentag is dedicated to the role of today's media and communication affordances at the intersection of work and private life and discusses the effects of POPC in work–life balance. Finally, Chapter 24 by Mata and Baumann addresses the question of how the POPC environment interacts with physical health and health behavior.

Open Questions and Future Challenges

The various chapters in this volume are meant to describe and analyze the most relevant manifestations, implications, and consequences of mobile online communication for individuals and for societies at large. Most of the ideas presented in this volume refer to individual processes and effects of being permanently online and/or permanently connected, and this perspective alone comes with an impressive number of research challenges for communication studies, media psychology, and their neighboring fields. Conclusions on where to direct future efforts in our discipline will therefore build on basically all chapters collected here and will most likely emphasize individual or psychological perspectives. Yet, we argue that the POPC phenomenon is also of great importance for other, namely more global, perspectives and approaches in communication. One example is the well-elaborated reflections on how the online infrastructure and its use by significant parts of a population affect society at large (e.g., Castells, 2001). We suggest developing new research programmatics that will eventually connect current observations of individual POPC mindsets and behaviors with more global developments that are located and have been identified on a group, organization, and societal level. To illustrate what we have in mind, we would like to very briefly highlight a few examples and expectations and need to start, one more time, at the individual level.

At the level of individual processes, we believe that POPC is a phenomenon that holds the potential to radically affect perceptions of social reality, identity processes, motivational structures and needs, health behavior, and the striving for well-being (Vorderer, 2016), to name just a few. Individuals who are practicing and relying on permanence in communication are likely to develop new perspectives and viewpoints on their (networked) self, new strategies for problem solving and self-regulation, and new desires and preferences for social interactions, romantic relationships, and their links to organizations and to society at large. They will simultaneously face new challenges for their health and well-being and experience new threats to and opportunities for their happiness, cognitive functioning, and their social capital. A POPC lifestyle may question traditional roles, such as the role of a citizen, an employee, a parent, or a partner. POPC individuals will likely hold alternative views, attitudes, expectations, and fears concerning loneliness, geographic distances to relevant others, traveling, and mobility in general. New sources of meaning and a specific purpose of life may emerge from living POPC, as well as new modes of experiencing and expressing aversive conditions such as personal loss, divorce, or depression. If this will be the case—and we believe that the collected chapters in this volume provide much evidence for this expectation—the permanence of communication will also challenge our scholarly theories, models, explanations, and predictions of many individual behaviors, experiences, expectations, emotions, and decisions.

One example of this is the often found and confirmed result that POPC behaviors both serve a person's needs while simultaneously challenging and stressing out this same individual (Vorderer, 2016; Vorderer, Krömer, & Schneider, 2016). The most recent trend of tailoring and customizing apps so that they can serve an individual's interests most effectively (Sundar, 2015) may exemplify this: Individually tailored or customized apps have become extremely popular despite the fact that media users are also concerned about the protection of their privacy when interacting with these programs. But the promise to be supported, helped, and relieved by a system that seems to understand oneself better than any real human being is apparently too tempting, so that many users more and more rely on such sources of support. This may go so far as to let an app make major personal decisions, not only by providing the "best and most relevant information" for oneself but also by telling, if not coercing, the individual to work out at a certain time, to eat more healthy, or to date somebody else. While in the history of our discipline we have always believed that most individuals want to keep agency about their lives as much as possible, today we observe the advent of more advanced technology to make these decisions more frequently than ever, hence relieving the individual from the strain of permanent decision-making.

At the level of dyadic relationships, mobile phones and their apps enable individuals to easily and constantly stay in contact independent from geographic distances. This yields many advantages, particularly for romantic partners, as being in touch certainly can create a sense of togetherness and stimulate new forms of intimate interactions over distance that might intensify relationships (Hassenzahl, Heidecker, Eckoldt, Diefenbach, & Hillmann, 2012). At the same time, it must be questioned if these new kinds of communication incidences can replace longer phone calls—that might become rare—with continuous interaction instead of often interrupted interaction threads via communication apps (cf. Rieger, this volume; Utz, this volume).

Another ambiguous facet of permanent digital connectedness in dyadic relationships concerns the dichotomy between perceiving social support from close others on the one side and—on the other side—insufficient opportunities or necessities to get along alone, resulting in fewer opportunities to experience successful coping competencies and self-efficacy. Of course, it can be comforting to permanently have the partner, best friend, or mother "in the pocket" and in constant readiness to help out in new and unfamiliar situations. Particularly in parent-child relationships, the temptation is high for both parties to be constantly on "stand-by," so that parents can always check if their children are well and children can always ask their parents for advice or support. However, adolescents need to learn to master challenges without their parents, and constant parental support can adversely affect necessary, emancipatory processes of becoming independent (e.g., Schiffrin et al., 2014).

At the meso or group level, the fact that individuals are often acting in a POPC-specific way when it comes to interactions with groups may also come with profound changes to common practices. POPC, it seems, could lend more stability and cohesion to (some types of) groups and teams, but may also generate higher volatility and speed in alterations of group structure, membership, productivity, mutual trust, and overall social capital (cf. Knop-Huelss et al., this volume). Groups will become more visible and more easily accessible to members, because they now appear as virtual entities and through technologically defined "locations" and "headquarters," such as stable chat rooms or WhatsApp channels. Perceived boundaries of groups, such as sharp distinctions of who belongs to the group and who does not, or the predefined mission or shared interest of a group, are likely to lose stability and rise in ambiguity. For instance, groups that originated at work may lose their focus on work-related issues, because the permanence of member communication will infuse other topics, discussions, conflicts, and contributions into the group's proceedings (cf. Marwick, 2011). The POPC phenomenon may thus transform existing groups, their social architecture and their informal hierarchies, as the negotiation of within-group social status and leadership will be affected by new rules and alternative pathways to reputation (e.g., through strategic self-presentation, Krämer & Haferkamp, 2011). Likewise, the development and formation of new social groups is likely to follow new laws and complexities under the condition of POPC. Creating new groups is apparently a lot easier given the permanent availability of possible partners for communication. However, given the many communication opportunities and obligations that POPC brings to each possible member, important ingredients for group sustainability, such as reliable commitment and active contributions of members, may become more difficult to secure. Similarly to the proposed implications of POPC at the individual level (see above), then, group processes and dynamics affected by members' POPC behavior are possibly more diverse, unpredictable, and both desirable and undesirable, depending on the goals and normative standpoints of the individuals involved.

At the macro level, finally, it is particularly interesting to debate possible changes that can be derived from the already postulated shifts at the lower levels of analysis. The POPC trend seems to be in synchronicity with other macro developments. Among them are those that sociologists have outlined as manifestations of radical change, for example, the general, multifaceted acceleration of life (Rosa, 2013) and the increased demands and burdens that advanced, knowledge-based economies impose on workers, employees, executives, and entrepreneurs (most importantly, permanent, life-long flexibility and uncertainty of the future, cf. Sennett, 1998, 2006). With regard to social cohesion and social capital, there is an interesting co-occurrence of POPC and increased polarization or (even extreme) diversification of political and normative points of view. These developments, we believe, have become visible, for instance, in the support for extremist political parties in many countries around the globe as well as in various backlashes—and, sometimes, surprising successes—for endorsers of civil rights, social equality, protection of minorities' and citizens' freedom, and democratic structures (e.g., Rød & Weidmann, 2015). Reconstructing possible bidirectional connections between POPC as a common practice of many individuals and these macro trends (acceleration, flexibilization, polarization) is an ambitious intellectual challenge and offers exciting new chances of understanding and predicting global change. For agents of social change—activists, legislators, NGOs, and many more—POPC may turn out as a pathway to understanding social dynamics and as an instrument to influence these dynamics at the same time.

The conviction that POPC is and will be a source of radical, disruptive change (with only a few historically comparable predecessors) calls for substantial effort by communication scholars to study this phenomenon much further, in other words, more systematically and empirically. Some of the already existing individual studies and a few concepts, terms, and theoretical models related to the permanence in online communication have been discussed in the present volume. This diverse and inspiring work by many scholars should not only continue, but also grow further. What is needed is a common understanding of the permanence in communication and connectedness as a key element of defining the ontological nature of the field's very object of inquiry. Past propositions of the discipline's identity were often bound to either a specific (new or particularly important) part of the communication and media landscape (e.g., newspaper or television) or to the application of more tradition-rich philosophies and methodologies, such as sociology, psychology, political science, cultural studies, and media and communication (Craig, 1999). The powerful, multidirectional force of change that the new permanence in communication is creating will require communication scholars to integrate it into their definition of what the field is about, interested in, and responsible for within the family of academic disciplines. Communication of the future—private and public, entertaining and informing, persuasive and educational—will be *permanent* communication. And communication scholarship will thus have to take this permanence into account: In the future, we believe that we will have to study individuals, groups, and societies that are permanently online and permanently connected.

We would like to conclude with a piece of advice, if we may: We suggest turning off all other devices now and exclusively allocating your attention to the content of the various chapters in this book. We hope and quite honestly believe that it will be worthwhile to interrupt being online and connected otherwise and to deliberate the ideas, arguments, and suggestions of the authors collected in this volume. Technological as well as human developments are rarely straightforward but rather complex and multifaceted, if not oblique. Even in a dominantly POPC world, there will be islands of activities that stick out from the rest. Reading a book may—if only sometimes—be one of them.

References

Castells, M. (2001). *The Internet galaxy: Reflections on the Internet, business, and society*. Oxford: Oxford University Press.
Craig, R. T. (1999). Communication theory as a field. *Communication Theory, 9*(2), 119–161.
Hassenzahl, M., Heidecker, S., Eckoldt, K., Diefenbach, S., & Hillmann, U. (2012). All you need is love: Current strategies of mediating intimate relationships through technology. *ACM Transactions on Computer-Human Interaction, 19*(4), 1–19. http://doi.org/10.1145/2395131.2395137
Krämer, N. C., & Haferkamp, N. (2011). Online self-presentation: Balancing privacy concerns and impression construction in social networking sites. In S. Trepte & L. Reinecke (Eds.), *Privacy online: Perspectives on privacy and self-disclosure in the social web* (pp. 127–141). Heidelberg: Springer.
Marwick, A. E. (2011). I tweet honestly, I tweet passionately: Twitter users, context collapse, and the imagined audience. *New Media & Society, 13*(1), 114–133.
Rød, E. G., & Weidmann, N. B. (2015). Empowering activists or autocrats? The Internet in authoritarian regimes. *Journal of Peace Research, 52*(3), 338–351.
Rosa, H. (2013). *Social acceleration: A new theory of modernity*. Columbia: Columbia University Press.
Schiffrin, H. H., Liss, M., Miles-McLean, H., Geary, K. A., Erchull, M. J., & Tashner, T. (2014). Helping or hovering? The effects of helicopter parenting on college students' well-being. *Journal of Child and Family Studies, 23*(3), 548–557.
Sennett, R. (1998). *The corrosion of character: The personal consequences of work in the new capitalism*. New York: Norton.
Sennett, R. (2006). *The culture of the new capitalism*. New Haven, CT: Yale University Press.
Sundar, S. S. (Ed.). (2015). *The handbook of the psychology of communication technology*. Malden, MA: Wiley Blackwell.

Vorderer, P. (2016). Communication and the good life: Why and how our discipline should make a difference. *Journal of Communication, 66*, 1–12.

Vorderer, P., Krömer, N., & Schneider, F. M. (2016). Permanently online—permanently connected: Explorations into university students' use of social media and mobile smart devices. *Computers in Human Behavior, 63*, 694–703. http://dx.doi.org/10.1016/j.chb.2016.05.085

2
A Brief History of Individual Addressability

The Role of Mobile Communication in Being Permanently Connected

Rich Ling

Introduction

In the past decades, we have experienced a fundamental transition in interpersonal communication that can be characterized as keeping us permanently online, permanently connected (Vorderer, Krömer, & Schneider, 2016). An important part of this in the area of telephony is that we have moved from relying on geographically fixed telecommunication devices to mobile devices through which we are individually addressable (Ling, 2008). Currently, we are also seeing the extension of wireless-based connectivity being further developed in the internet of things. This chapter will largely focus on human-based connectivity and the social consequences of mobile communication. In the latter part of the chapter, I will also consider some future directions.

It is perhaps easiest to see the development of individual addressability where it is the most temporally compressed. The adoption of mobile communication in the Global South provides one such lens. In 1982, in an era where notions of telephony were firmly rooted in the geographically fixed terminals, the International Telecommunications Union held a conference with the fetching title the "International Telecommunication Union Plenipotentiary Conference." At this conference, a commission was established to examine worldwide telecommunication needs. The commission was chaired by Donald Maitland and it produced what is perhaps our best benchmark of telecommunication development in the 1980s, *The Missing Link: Report of the Independent Commission for World Wide Telecommunications Development* (Maitland, 1984). The report examined the global availability of telecommunications. However, it went further and related telephonic accessibility to the potential for economic growth. Not surprisingly, the report cast a particular focus on telephony in the Global South. The report famously found that there were more phones in Tokyo than in all of Africa. The authors noted:

> The situation in the developing world is in stark contrast. In a majority of developing countries the telecommunications system is inadequate to sustain essential services. In large tracts of territory there is no system at all. Neither in the name of common humanity nor on grounds of common interest is such a disparity acceptable.
>
> *(Maitland, 1984, p. 1)*

Looking at Tanzania, the authors found that there were about 41,000 working lines in 1981; that is one telephone line for approximately 400 people. In the rural areas, there was one telephone line for every 1,000 people (Maitland, 1984, p. 107).

In these settings, there was poor information flow. The work of the commission provides insight into the communication issues and the logic of the era predating the adoption of mobile communication. The report paints scenarios of bureaucrats without access to crucial information; bankers unable to process loans because they lack the credit ratings of eventual customers; healthcare workers unable to know the dimensions of epidemics; food producers unable to check on the status of the farmers supplying them; and families unable to stay in touch with one another.

The authors wrote that telecommunications would facilitate business, health care, emergency services, agricultural production, and social caregiving. The commission noted, however, that it was economically difficult to develop (largely landline) telecommunication systems that would provide adequate service. The authors note that the average investment needed to add an additional landline was about $2,800 (approximately $6,500 in 2015, accounting for inflation); in Ethiopia it was $36,400 ($84,000). The technologies envisioned to address these issues included wire-based landline connections, radio-based backbone services, and eventually satellite links with geographically fixed terminals.

At the time of the report, mobile phones were only starting to be commercially available in the Global North. According to Kelly (2005), it took the industry 20 years to reach their first one billion mobile subscriptions. However, the second billion came in four years and, as of 2016, there are more than 7.6 billion mobile subscriptions. That is, there are more subscriptions than there are people in the world.[1]

Looking back at the situation in, for example, Tanzania as described in the Maitland Report, how has this played out? Did the Maitland Commission get it right? As noted, the authors failed to see the role of mobile communication. Indeed, it is mobile and not satellite or landline telephony that took the day. In Tanzania, the number of mobile subscriptions went from less than one per 100 people in 2000 to approximately 63 per 100 in 2014.[2] As has been seen in a variety of studies, mobile communication is easily adaptable to, and strongly desired in the Global South (Donner & Escobari, 2010; Jensen, 2007). A mobile communication base station can provide connections to a large number of people, whereas the construction of a wire-based landline system is far more resource intensive.

That said, the work of Jensen (2007) and Donner and Escobari (2010) support the idea that telephony facilitates various types of development. As they note, access to reliable point-to-point communication often has the effect of supporting various types of entrepreneurship (Ling, Oreglia, Aricat, Panchapakesan, & Lwin, 2015). Experience shows that there is indeed a strong desire to have this type of access.

Simple numbers of devices, however, does not begin to describe the social consequences of the mobile communication. For many of the Tanzanians who now have a mobile phone, this is often the first time that they have experienced electronically mediated communication of any type. They are using it to facilitate many aspects of their lives. It is being used to work out the logistics of commerce and to stay in touch with family and friends (Stark, 2013).

These effects are particularly dramatic in the Global South, but they are seen around the world. Indeed, the ability to better coordinate and interact are a part of mobile communication in Atlanta just as they are in Accra, London as in Lagos, and Chicago as in Chennai. The fact that we carry a device in our pocket that perpetually tethers us to one another, regardless of where we might be, is truly phenomenal. It is this permanent personal access to others, and their access to us, that is the basis of individual accessibility. Others can immediately reach out to us regardless of where we may be. They can call for a chat or send a text message, photo, or voice message. It is used for business, for logistics to gather information, and to touch bases with friends. The bureaucrat, the banker, the farmer, the parent, or the lover are all quickly accessible. They can send us information of any type, ranging from a cooing missive between lovers to a hot-headed demand from a boss, to the location for a coffee chat. In short, individual addressability has restructured coordination, logistics, information sharing, and expressive interaction.

The Progression From Geographic to Individual Addressability

The Logic of Geographic (Landline) Addressability

The landline phone brought with it a logic of geographically fixed locations that afforded communication. These locations could be extended in various ways. In the public realm, this was by deploying telephone booths or public phones or by granting a person in need of making a call access to an office phone. In the private sphere, extension phones were seen as a way to extend the reach of the landline phone. These might be simply a second (or third or fourth) terminal. For example, a study done in 1966 for the Norwegian Televerket indicated that 8% of homes had a secondary terminal and 1% had several secondary terminals (Johannesen, 1981).

At its core, landline telephony assumed the fixed location of the telephone. This was seen in a variety of ways. Phrases such as "he cannot come to the phone" were used to indicate that an individual was not disposed to talk. The phrase implicitly assumes that the phone is in a fixed location and it is the people who are moving in relation to the phone. The fixed nature of the phone was also seen in various types of furniture. This included telephone chairs that included a seat, a small table for the terminal, and a drawer in which to keep the phone book and perhaps items with which to write down a message.

Written phone messages are another lost practice/artifact. These were developed in an era when it was assumed that the telephone terminal occupied a fixed place. The caller was, in effect, taking a chance that they would "catch" their intended interlocutor at a particular location. If the callee was not there, or if they were unable to be summoned to the phone, there was the need to take a message. The messages were often noted on a dedicated paper notepad that allowed the person who took the message to note the name of the caller, their phone number, and the time, date, and the nature of the call. Paper, and later recorded messages, time shift the interaction in anticipation that the person receiving the message will call back when they returned. All of this assumed that the locus of the calling/messaging was within the radius of the fixed location phone. While recorded "voice mail" has made the transition to the mobile era, it is perhaps only harried executives who still receive paper-based messages.

Other landline-era services, such as call forwarding and eventually paging systems, also pushed in the direction of matching individual mobility with the ability to communicate. Call forwarding moved the call from one fixed telephone to another, thus still assuming the fixity of the telephone terminal. Pagers, and particularly the early one-way systems, were able to alert a person that they had received a call. However, to return the call, the individual again needed to find a fixed-line telephone. Clearly, with the development of cellular telephony and permanent availability, these systems lost their position in the market.

The Logic of Individual Addressability

The ubiquity of the mobile phone exposed the limitations of the geographically fixed landline phone. It replaced the logic of fixed terminals with a logic of individual addressability. At the point of departure, it eliminated the need for extension phones, call forwarding, and paging systems. It allowed us to directly call (or text) each other, thus eliminating the need for written messages. While these functionalities were implied by the adoption of the mobile phone, the lag between the technical potential of the mobile phone and its realization in cultural adoption took some time (Ogburn, 1922, p. 200). There was a sense that it was a blessing to not be continually available. Indeed, early in the adoption phase of mobile communication, people such as Karen, interviewed in Norway in 1997, noted, "I am glad that I am not available all the time." She was evoking the landline-era standard of being able to put distance between oneself and the telephone in a period when this possibility was being challenged. Interviewees noted the stress associated with being continually available. Another person, Kari, saw the implicit tension associated with mobile telephony when she said that "it helps but it also stresses." She suggests that the phone simplified navigating through the various errands and tasks of quotidian life, just as it granted others access and thus made her vulnerable to their sometimes capricious needs.

The Social Consequences of Individual Addressability

With time, we have worked out how mobile communication and individual availability play out. One important thing is that individual availability facilitates fine-grained interaction. Since we are continually accessible, we can interact and microcoordinate, as needed. Following the notion of Licoppe (2004), there is an ambient "connected presence" between people. This is seen most intensely among members of the intimate sphere, where it has become structured into our expectations of one another. Another dimension of the technology is that smartphones facilitate a variety of location-based services where we use the functionality of the device at locations where heretofore there have not been communication possibilities.

Microcoordination and the Structuring of Mobile Availability

The individual addressability of mobile communication makes possible microcoordination (Ling & Yttri, 2002). That is, the mobile phone supports instantaneous and nuanced coordination that was not possible with the landline telephone. The mobile phone facilitates dynamic planning, midcourse adjustments, and the "softening" of schedules (Ling, 2004). It allows us to iteratively work out the time and place of social interaction. If one location or time for a meet-up is not viable ("The restaurant is full, do you want to meet at the café around the corner?") we can, on the fly, contact the other participants and develop an alternative plan. This can be done even as the participants are en route to the eventual location. In addition, we can adjust the timing of the event as needed ("I am running a bit late, you can wait in my office."). This function is seen in, for example, the way that teens work out their various encounters (Ling, 2005), how lovers "link up" in locations such as Jamaica (Horst & Miller, 2005), and how trishaw operators in Myanmar organize their trips (Ling et al., 2015).

One aspect of microcoordination is that it makes us continually available to one another. This in turn facilitates sociation and the development of social cohesion. Analysis has shown that this sociation occurs within a relatively tight core of individuals. Indeed, half of all texts and calls go to just four or five others (Ling, Bertel, & Sundsøy, 2012). This is a core social group with which there is often a high degree of reciprocity. The mobile phone and individual addressability often mean that we are more closely tied to the flux of this group of intimates. It accelerates the exchange of communications just as it lowers the threshold for interaction. The motivation to call, text, or message need not be a major issue, but rather it can be to discuss a minor point.

The mobile phone not only changes the potential for social cohesion, but also the expectations regarding one another's availability. Since the device has been freed from the geographical hobbling of landline phones, we are continually available and our availability has become an ambient expectation. If we do not take the phone, or if for some reason our phone is inoperative or forgotten at home, it becomes more difficult for us to operate socially. Others are not able to reach us with updates and information on coordination, just as we cannot work out day to day logistics. In sum, we have structured the device into our daily lives. This has taken on dimensions of what Durkheim called social facts, that is, "manners of acting, thinking and feeling external to the individual, which are invested with a coercive power by virtue of which they exercise control over him" (Durkheim, 1938, p. 52). The system of interaction enabled by the mobile phone is located outside the exclusive agency of the individual. Further, ignoring it is increasingly not an option. To not be available, or to not have an operational phone, is in a small way shirking our social responsibility.

The Smartphone Turn

The major transition in mediated interpersonal communication came with the development of mobile telephony. As 2G and 3G phones were adopted in the 1990s and the first decade of the new millennium, we began to abandon the logic of landline telephony and to adopt microcoordination. Until approximately 2007, and for some time after that, the form of interaction via mobile phones was based on one-to-one communications using either text or mobile voice. This meant that if there were several people trying to coordinate an interaction, there was the need for one person to act as a hub for all the messages, since interlocutors could only text or talk with one other person at a time.[3]

The development of the 3G network and its focus on the mobile internet, as well as the 2007 deployment of the iPhone, opened the way for alternative forms of mediated interaction. With the development of messaging apps, there was no longer a reliance of the hub-and-spoke topology of the earlier one-to-one communication forms. This allowed for multisided interactions. Indeed, mobile communication and microcoordination could take on new dimensions (Ling & Lai, 2016). Messaging apps such as WhatsApp, Facebook Messenger, MXit, Line, and BlackBerry Messenger overcame the limitations of SMS and mobile voice communication. Smartphones and the enhanced capacity of the net meant that many individuals could discuss and make plans.

Bringing this back to the issue of individual addressability, messaging groups are yet a new reason to be permanently available (Vorder & Kohring, 2013). Rather than only being accessible to individual members of one's social sphere one at a time, there is the implicit motivation to be available to both individuals and various chat groups as plans for social interaction are being developed or as expressive discussions are taking place. The fact that we are persistently available facilitates these types of interaction.

Moving Beyond Availability to the Closest Social Sphere

Sharing Economy and Crowd Sourcing

It can be asserted that mobile communication and individual addressability empower portions of the so-called sharing economy (Allen, 2015; Owyang, n.d.). The sharing economy is seen in, for example, the context of services such as Uber and Airbnb. In many ways, these services are premised on the pooling of information via the internet. The mobile phone, and the ubiquitous connectivity that it affords, adds an important dimension to these types of services. This can be seen in services that link users together in various ways to, for example, enhance transportation systems or share information on local conditions.

Various real-time ride-sharing, ride-pooling, and taxi-like services allow the individual to broadcast their location and their desired destination (Alexander & González, 2015). These apps then seek out others who are willing to transport them either for free, for a donation, or as a quasi-formalized business. These services employ the GPS functionality and mapping functions of smartphones along with the ability for the rider and the driver to interact when working out the details of the pick-up and the trip. In addition, when considering the commercial services, there is often a payment function that allows for the direct transfer of funds. Finally, each actor can often evaluate the quality and trustworthiness of the other. The individual addressability of the rider and the driver enable these types of services, just as the advanced location-based functionality of smartphones makes it easy to arrange the geographical and the financial logistics of the arrangement. The provision of evaluations means that later users make a more reasoned choice in their selection of riders/drivers.[4]

In other applications that facilitate mobility, location-based services again employ the direct accessibility associated with mobile communication. In these cases, rather than the consumer coming to the service provider, it is the opposite. Indeed, one of the earliest functions of mobile telephony was to summon help when needed. In the initial period of mobile telephony, people noted buying phones in case "something happens" (Ling, 2004, p. 42). Common scenarios were getting stuck in winter weather and having health-related issues. Early users had made the connection between the accessibility provided by the device and being able to call for assistance. In these early days, the individual would need to tell their interlocutor where they were. There was no ability to transmit location information. With time, the development of smartphones with GPS functionality has meant that direct location information can be transmitted. This means that the person delivering the service can more easily find the person seeking the assistance. Based on this, services have been developed that aid motorists when their car breaks down or, for example, when they run out of fuel.[5]

Other location-based applications facilitate other types of actionable information. These can include apps to record urban problems, such as various forms of blight (potholes, trash dumping, etc.).[6] In some cases, these applications rely on the individual noting the problem, perhaps taking a photo and sending it in. In other cases, such as in the case of Bump, the application uses the accelerometer on the phone to note where potholes are found. These are then geotagged for eventual entry into authorities' street repair "to do" list. In yet other cases, the real-time individual addressability of the phone allows users to "crowdmap" various phenomena (Furtado, Caminha, Ayres, & Santos, 2012). The application Ushahidi[7] has been used, for example, to trace violence against women and minorities (Bahree, 2008), the ravages of environmental disasters such as the Deepwater Horizon explosion (Louisiana Bucket Brigade, n.d.), flooding in Queensland, Australia (Ross & Potts, 2011), and a large number of other applications.

The development of the mobile internet and smart terminals has pushed the process further. Rather than simply being two individuals interacting, we are able to gather information from cloud-based services. We can order services and we are able to report various types of information in real time and also alert others (both known and unknown) as to the new developments. Apps that allow drivers to report accidents that are again sent to the devices of other drivers on the same stretch of highway illustrate this.[8] The only common point shared between the users is their simultaneous use of a portion of the highway. Nonetheless, their individual access to the network allows them to share important information.

Internet of Things

A continuation of individual addressability is the further extension of communication into objects is seen in the internet of things (Atzori, Iera, & Morabito, 2010). Where mobile telephony made individual persons addressable, the internet of things extends the capacity to various objects in our environment. Just as new forms of interaction and logistics were made possible with mobile telephony and later smartphones and the mobile internet, we can expect the same transitions associated with the internet of things.

This development, along with the development of neural networks (Schmidhuber, 2015), will likely be seen in the development of smart infrastructure, healthcare, supply chains/logistics, and various other social applications (Li, Da Xu, & Zhao, 2015). Just as the mobile telephony facilitated logistics and coordination, the internet of things takes this same phenomenon to a machine level.

Conclusion

This discussion began by examining the problems experienced by people in the Global South before they had reliable access to telephony. The work of the Maitland Commission showed the awkwardness of social interactions, work, and commerce. With the development of first landline phones and then mobile communication, there has been an increasing ability to interact with others in real time and directly.

Indeed, it is the transition to mobile communication that has allowed for the individual addressability. This has provided the ability to always contact one another as needed (Vorderer et al., 2016). Rather than relying on geographic proximity to a landline phone, we have moved to an era of ubiquitous and permanent mediated availability. Research has shown that this accessibility has facilitated coordination, and it has allowed us to maintain fine-grained contact with our immediate social sphere. It has enhanced social cohesion and, indeed, it has resulted in the social expectation of availability.

We are now moving into an era when it is not simply one-to-one interaction, nor even person-to-person interaction, that is being channeled through our devices. We are interacting with groups and we are accessing various cloud-based services. Finally, our devices are also starting to link up with other devices to, we hope, serve the needs of their owners.

Notes

1. GSMA Intelligence. https://gsmaintelligence.com/
2. See the ITU website: www.itu.int/en/ITU-D/Statistics/Pages/stat/default.aspx
3. Granted, if one was technically deft, it was possible to have multisided communications, but it was not a common skill set. Setting up a multisided call often required keying in long series of numbers and special codes.
4. These systems can, however, be gamed in some cases.
5. Wefuel. www.wefuel.com/
6. See, for example, ichangemycity (www.ichangemycity.com/) or Bump (http://bu.mp/)
7. Ushahidi. www.ushahidi.com/
8. Waze. www.waze.com/

References

Alexander, L. P., & González, M. C. (2015). Assessing the impact of real-time ridesharing on urban traffic using mobile phone data. Presented at the *UrbComp'15*, Sydney, Australia. Retrieved from http://humnetlab.mit.edu/wordpress/wp-content/uploads/2014/04/sig-alternate.pdf

Allen, D. (2015). The sharing economy. *Review—Institute of Public Affairs, 67*(3), 24–27.
Atzori, L., Iera, A., & Morabito, G. (2010). The internet of things: A survey. *Computer Networks, 54*(15), 2787–2805.
Bahree, M. (2008, November 29). Citizen voices. *Forbes*. https://www.forbes.com/global/2008/1208/114.html
Donner, J., & Escobari, M. X. (2010). A review of evidence on mobile use by micro and small enterprises in developing countries. *Journal of International Development, 22*(5), 641–658.
Durkheim, E. (1938). *The rules of the sociological method*. New York: The Free Press.
Furtado, V., Caminha, C., Ayres, L., & Santos, H. (2012). Open government and citizen participation in law enforcement via crowd mapping. *IEEE Intelligent Systems, 27*(4), 63–69. http://doi.org/10.1109/MIS.2012.80
Horst, H. A., & Miller, D. (2005). From kinship to link-up: Cell phones and social networking in Jamaica. *Current Anthropology, 46*(5), 755–778.
Jensen, R. (2007). The digital provide: Information (technology), market performance and welfare in the South Indian fisheries sector. *The Quarterly Journal of Economics, 122*(3), 879–924.
Johannesen, S. (1981). *Sammendrag av markedsundersøkelser gjennomført for televerket i tiden 1966–1981*. Kjeller: Televerkets Forskninginstitutt.
Kelly, T. (2005). Twenty years of measuring the missing link. In G. Milward-Oliver (Ed.), *Maitland+20: Fixing the missing link* (pp. 23–33). Bradford on Avon: Anima Centre Limited.
Li, S., Da Xu, L., & Zhao, S. (2015). The internet of things: A survey. *Information Systems Frontiers, 17*(2), 243–259.
Licoppe, C. (2004). Connected presence: The emergence of a new repertoire for managing social relationships in a changing communications technoscape. *Environment and Planning D: Society and Space, 22*(1), 135–156.
Ling, R. (2004). *The mobile connection: The cell phone's impact on society*. San Francisco, CA: Morgan Kaufmann.
Ling, R. (2005). Mobile communications vis-à-vis teen emancipation, peer group integration and deviance. In R. Harper, A. Taylor, & L. Palen (Eds.), *The inside text: Social perspectives on SMS in the mobile age* (pp. 175–194). London: Klewer.
Ling, R. (2008). *New tech, New ties: How mobile communication is reshaping social cohesion*. Cambridge, MA: MIT Press.
Ling, R., Bertel, T. F., & Sundsøy, P. R. (2012). The socio-demographics of texting: An analysis of traffic data. *New Media & Society, 14*(2), 281–298. http://doi.org/10.1177/1461444811412711
Ling, R., & Lai, C.-H. (2016). Microcoordination 2.0: Social coordination in the age of smartphones and messaging apps. *Journal of Communication, 66*(5), 834–856.
Ling, R., Oreglia, E., Aricat, R. G., Panchapakesan, C., & Lwin, M. (2015). The use of mobile phones among trishaw operators in Myanmar. *International Journal of Communication, 9*(18).
Ling, R., & Yttri, B. (2002). Hyper-coordination via mobile phones in Norway. In J. E. Katz & M. Aakhus (Eds.), *Perpetual contact: Mobile communication, private talk, public performance* (pp. 139–169). Cambridge: Cambridge University Press.
Louisiana Bucket Brigade. (n.d.). iWitness pollution map. http://map.labucketbrigade.org/
Maitland, D. (1984, December). The missing link. *Independent Commission for Worldwide Telecommunications Development Report*.
Ogburn, William Fielding. 1922. *Social change with respect to culture and original nature*. New York: BW Huebsch, Inc.
Owyang. (n.d.). *The mobile technology stack for the collaborative economy*. Retrieved January 28, 2016, from http://venturebeat.com/2015/02/17/the-mobile-technology-stack-for-the-collaborative-economy/
Ross, N., & Potts, M. (2011, January 13). ABC's crowdsourced flood-mapping initiative. *ABC Technology and Games*. www.abc.net.au/technology/articles/2011/01/13/3112261.htm
Schmidhuber, J. (2015). Deep learning in neural networks: An overview. *Neural Networks, 61*, 85–117.
Stark, L. (2013). Transactional sex and mobile phones in a Tanzanian slum. *Suomen Antropologi: Journal of the Finnish Anthropological Society, 38*(1), 12–36.
Vorder, P., & Kohring, M. (2013). Permanently online: A challenge for media and communication research. *International Journal of Communication, 7*, 1–20.
Vorderer, P., Krömer, N., & Schneider, F. M. (2016). Permanently online—permanently connected: Explorations into university students' use of social media and mobile smart devices. *Computers in Human Behavior, 63*, 694–703. http://doi.org/10.1016/j.chb.2016.05.085

3

The Permanently Online and Permanently Connected Mind

Mapping the Cognitive Structures Behind Mobile Internet Use

Christoph Klimmt, Dorothée Hefner, Leonard Reinecke, Diana Rieger, and Peter Vorderer

High-performance smartphones and the virtually ubiquitous availability of mobile Internet access have profound consequences for the daily lives of countless people around the globe. Many of these consequences seem to be intensified, accelerated, or elsewise continued developments already known from earlier stages of modern societies' digitalization. However, this book suggests that with the mass proliferation of "always online" technologies, an almost disruptive change in the mindset of many users is underway or has occurred already. At the center of this change is the acknowledgment of *permanence* in communication ("permanently online," Vorderer, 2016; Vorderer & Kohring, 2013, p. 190; Vorderer, Krömer, & Schneider, 2016). It is only a few years ago that connecting to the Internet, using media fare, and communicating with others via technology were actions that required individual intentions, planning, and spatial arrangements of specific hardware and devices. Through "always on" technologies, that is, primarily smartphones with Internet connection, the situation most recently has inversed: Being involved in mediated communication and maintaining availability to communicate is now the norm for many people for most of the day (Ling, 2012). And *abstaining* from media use and communication access is now an action that requires intentions, planning, and specific arrangements. Clearly, this development has put communicative behavior, like individuals' media use and mediated exchange with others, into the position of primary importance in everyday life management and lifestyle (Mihailidis, 2014; Quinn & Oldmeadow, 2013).

This trend has many individual and societal implications, and we firmly believe that they need to be studied systematically: Among them are, to name just a few, the consequences for the composition of public spheres and the opportunities for political debate, for market communications and consumers' behavior, for interpersonal relationships, for children's and adolescents' individual development, for health in general and for stress in particular, for media users' entertainment and well-being, and many more. But what is required above and before such domain-specific inquiries is a theoretical understanding of what exactly the experience of permanence in communication does to individuals: How can we describe the mindset of a person who is permanently online and permanently connected? What are the cognitive structures that seem to lead to new forms of behavior, such as people staring at or swiping on their smartphones while walking, talking with friends, driving cars, sitting on the toilet, lying in bed, or even being intimate with their partners (Vorderer et al., 2016; David, this volume; Xu and Wang, this volume)?

This chapter deals with the question of how habitual, frequent, almost permanent use of smartphones and their functionalities in daily life affects and is affected by cognitive structures and mindsets of individuals. It aims at explicating the psychological condition of being *permanently online and permanently connected* (POPC). To this end, we start with differentiating two levels of smartphone-related habitual cognitions that we believe constitute the POPC mindset. The first level refers to the close, intense, even intimate relationship users often experience with their smartphone and the communication environment to which it grants permanent access. At this level, three components define the POPC mindset, which constitute the concept of *online vigilance*: a preoccupation with smartphone functions and mobile online communication (*salience*), responsiveness to smartphone events and mobile online communication (*reactibility*), and continuous observation of one's digital communication environment (*monitoring*).

The second level of cognitive structures that we assume to coevolve with intense smartphone use pertains to communication-related *expectations*, that is, specific hypotheses that heavy smartphone users hold and apply to guide their behavior in many (routine, but also novel) situations (Bayer, Campbell, & Ling, 2016). While the first level of cognitive structures points to the connection between the user's inner self and the smartphone (and its options for various communications), the second level represents the link between the heavy smartphone user and the outer social sphere. These expectations play a key role in how users approach and interpret situations, solve problems, regulate their emotions, interact with others, make decisions, and act in many other fundamentally important domains of behavior and social life. We argue that through these expectations, the core elements of the POPC mindset (salience, reactibility, monitoring) become potentially powerful factors in many contexts of individual behavior and social interaction. With the explication of these expectations, we hope to open up this field of POPC to future theorizing and empirical research in various academic communities, within and beyond the communication discipline.

How the Smartphone in the Pocket Shapes Human Reasoning: Online Vigilance as the Core of the POPC Mindset

Descriptive studies on smartphone use reveal that many users have already developed rather strong habits of frequently checking their devices for relevant communication—text messages, social media posts, news, etc.—throughout the day, and that specific applications and functionalities, like, for example, sports apps or the device's camera, further add to the overall time spent with the smartphone (Oulasvirta, Rattenbury, Ma, & Raita, 2012; Rosen, Carrier, & Cheever, 2013). Particularly, adolescents have acquired routines of active participation in social media; they post text messages, images, videos, and web discoveries and share them with friends, classmates, and other followers on a regular basis, which triggers further episodes of smartphone usage throughout the day (e.g., Mihailidis, 2014; Lenhart, 2015; Quinn & Oldmeadow, 2013). We propose that many (heavy) users have thereby developed new cognitive structures in their mindsets that rest on the assumption that attending to one's smartphone is *possible and goal-serving* virtually everywhere and anytime. Smartphone use, we believe, appears to them to be legitimate, effective, and necessary, even natural and common sense across many situations. In other words, in many cognitive scripts of routine activities, measures of specific smartphone use have been included. The routine of taking photos of fancy meals and sharing them online, for example, seems to have been added by many individuals to their cognitive script of visiting a restaurant (Diehl, Zauberman, & Barasch, 2016).

How can these cognitive traces that habitual smartphone use (being POPC) seem to leave in people's mindsets be systematized? We suggest three dimensions to constitute online vigilance, that is, the permanent representation of partners, services, and possibilities for online communication in everyday thinking. Or, in other words, the POPC mindset and the daily self-experience of heavy smartphone users are composed of the dimensions salience, reactibility, and monitoring.

Salience

The many modes through which online and offline settings become intertwined, due to mobile online communication, are most likely to shape heavy smartphone users' thinking. The invisible but permanently accessible presence of one's personal online sphere has already become part of many individuals' routine information processing. Online content and personal connections have become highly salient at least for heavy users, even when and while they are involved in activities in which they are *not* using the smartphone or any other online device (Cheever, Rosen, Carrier, & Chavez, 2014). Salience means that users who are embedded in a given situation—at work, at home, doing sports, meeting friends, waiting for somebody or something, being in line, etc.—will cognitively be online and process additional information and reflect on what is happening beyond the given social situation in which they currently are. It means to devote parts of one's thinking to what one believes is currently going on in one's online environment while *not* actively or physically being connected to it: What are my friends talking about right now? Which important public or social events are happening in my online media environment? What do I miss out on (Przybylski, Murayama, DeHaan, & Gladwell, 2013)? Should I post something about my current situation? Would it be useful to activate my location-based game at this particular place? Salience implies that individuals perceive their online environment as an additional, invisible layer of their reality in any offline setting, because it is accessible (and appealing) anywhere and anytime (e.g., Lee, 2013). Manifestations of salience of the online sphere need not necessarily be conscious thoughts; rather, the permanent awareness of online friends, services, or resources may also be existent in automatic or implicit cognitions. Salience is the cognitive foundation for the ease with which many users switch from an offline setup (e.g., a face-to-face meeting, or the use of a word processing program) to an online context anytime and with great fluency—the people, the contents, the functions that they can and want to access are psychologically near, as users think about them virtually anywhere and anytime.

Whether salience comes with the risk of distraction from ongoing offline activities (e.g., Rosen et al., 2013), reduced mental capacity (e.g., Stothart, Mitchum, & Yehnert, 2015), tendencies to procrastinate offline tasks (e.g., Meier, Reinecke, & Meltzer, 2016), and other risks outlined in the literature or in the public debate about new technologies, certainly requires systematic empirical exploration. And even if most heavy smartphone users would still be capable of maintaining a good performance in their respective offline setting, we propose that their mindset will comprise a default element of including the personal online sphere into perceptions and interpretations of their current offline reality. The users stay, we assume, cognitively connected to the online sphere to which their smartphone serves as a portal they can always open.

Reactibility

We assume that many individuals develop rather strong habits of using their smartphones because they generate a lot of positive experiences when used (Oulasvirta et al., 2012, Wang & Tchernev, 2012). Smartphones most often deliver and transport messages by and to relevant others, providing access to various sources of social support and other helpful knowledge resources; they (can) assist in self-optimization (e.g., in sports, dieting, sleep, and stress management), and they are versatile entertainers. The bundling of so many appealing functions or, to use a communication term, the reliable and frequent delivery of diverse *gratifications*, is a feature that lets smartphones earn recognition, valuation, and the assignment of primary importance in the daily life of their users (de Reuver, Nikou, & Bouwman, 2016). In addition to many gratifying episodes of mobile Internet attendance, many users know circumstances under which they feel social obligations or even pressure to process and deal with incoming online communication, for example, to comply with job demands or to avoid conflicts with family members. From positive and negative past experiences, many users extrapolate that whatever happens on the smartphone—be that incoming messages, social media notifications, alerts by a pervasive game, etc.—*deserves immediate attention*. Consequently, the mindset of a POPC user includes an element of willingness and preparedness to respond to incoming and/or automatic smartphone activities. This refers both to episodes of nonusage when a beep tone or the vibrating of the device calls for a user's attention and to episodes when a user is already attending to her/his smartphone and has to decide whether to respond to displayed information (e.g., a new social media post by a friend) or to deal with the current offline environment first.

Most individuals are connected to many friends, relatives, and colleagues, and the large community of connected others inevitably produces a great number of interpersonal and intragroup messages (LaRose, Connolly, Lee, Li, & Hales, 2014; Utz, this volume). This way, the device and the online services it hosts generate socially relevant affordances; habitualized reactibility implies that the user "has to" respond quite often and—if at all possible—immediately to these affordances simply because this behavior has been trained and reinforced so many times before. To understand the core mindset of the heavy smartphone user, it is important to acknowledge that smartphone signals serve as cues that trigger highly automatized, positively or negatively reinforced responses of immediate attention and readiness to answer incoming communication (Bayer et al., 2016).

The strong tendency to prioritize smartphone communication and to react to incoming messages and notifications almost immediately implies that users with a high level of reactibility are willing to interrupt non-smartphone activities and to turn away from offline contexts for the purpose of going or staying online. This may, but does not necessarily, lead to undesirable consequences, such as impoliteness toward face-to-face encounters ("phubbing"), distraction, or fragmentation of focused offline activities (Chotpitayasunondh & Douglas, 2016; David, Kim, Brickman, Ran, & Curtis, 2015). There is presumably a great deal of variance between individuals and situations concerning these potential conflicts in allocating one's attention. Concepts such as media multitasking (Wang & Tchernev, 2012; also see the chapters by Xu and Wang and by David, this volume) suggest that a high level of reactibility to smartphone signals may not necessarily lead to cognitive-perceptual withdrawal from the offline sphere; the reality of intense smartphone use seems to be more complex than being mentally present in either the online or the offline ecology.

For example, younger individuals seem to be more tolerant when it comes to interruptions of interpersonal communication by a conversation partner's immediate turning away from oneself to his or her smartphone (e.g., Gonzales & Wu, 2016). They seem to apply new conversation rules that permit reactibility to the smartphone, so that either the smartphone communication is actively integrated into the interpersonal conversation or the remaining participants of the conversation continue without the one person who becomes involved in a smartphone communication. Sometimes, the other conversation partners will respond to this situation by also turning to their devices and, as a consequence, negative outcomes of high smartphone reactibility might be smaller than often assumed. However, in order to better understand this communicative situation and to judge whether reactibility causes desirable versus undesirable effects, empirical research is required.

Monitoring

Salience and reactibility describe a smartphone user's mindset as being permanently intruded by the online world. This intrusion affects not only the actual perception but also the felt experience and the behavior of an individual when acting in the offline world. An important third element of online vigilance is the habitualized active monitoring of the online sphere. Mobile social media such as WhatsApp, Instagram, or Facebook do not only operate with push messages that trigger smartphone signals such as beeps or blinking diodes. Rather, they also channel the majority of information that a user's online social sphere is producing and circulating in "threads," "feeds," and "timelines," that is, repositories for communication incidents (postings, shared rich media assets, etc.). These repositories archive the recent "proceedings" of the community—messages, images, videos, etc.—and hence offer a (near-)live view on what is happening in the user's online environment(s).

Heavy users will routinely monitor these online proceedings and maintain a frequently updated, near-live state of knowledge about their online social sphere. Oftentimes, episodes of just a few seconds of smartphone exposure suffice to complete such updates (Oulasvirta et al., 2012). Heavy smartphone users are characterized by the habit of staying vigilant for new developments in their online ecology similar to how they scan offline contexts for relevant information or changes. Living POPC, hence, does not only mean to think of the online sphere very often (salience) and to react to cues sent out by the online world (reactibility), but also to enter the online sphere on a regular basis in order to keep track of recent developments in preferred online channels and with relevant others to whom one is connected (monitoring). The high usability and efficient performance of popular smartphone apps bring down the barriers to entering the online world and hence allow checking behaviors at very low costs of time and effort. As a consequence, frequent checking behaviors or monitoring of this type maintain the sense of permanence in connectedness, as heavy smartphone users will make sure they are aware of the proceedings of their online community at short intervals (e.g., Mascheroni & Vincent, 2016). This provides them with a sense of experientially "sharing" the social life of their online friends in (near) real time. Of course, these patterns of behavior imply that heavy smartphone users have already acquired a routine of observing their online ecology with similar efforts as they keep track of their current offline setting. Online vigilance includes a sense of participating in two layers of social reality (virtually) simultaneously (e.g., Burchell, 2014).

Intermediate Summary

The sense of having a smartphone in the pocket and the experience and lived routines of using it in manifold situations form a specific POPC mindset, that is, a cognitive structure and (a readiness for) behavioral patterns that add the aspect of permanent connectedness to the perception and processing of day-to-day reality. With salience, reactibility, and monitoring, we propose three dimensions that constitute the POPC mindset and describe how heavy, experienced smartphone users approach their inner and outer world. Manifestations of salience, reactibility, and monitoring may vary between users and between situations; these variations are likely to affect many other dimensions of communication and social life, for instance, the search for information, someone's responding to stress, his or her decision-making in respect to consumption choices, or problem solving, to name just a few. In general, however, it is these three characteristics that we assume to fundamentally differ between the mindset of heavy smartphone users and those individuals who are either light users or nonusers of mobile online devices. Individuals scoring high on one or more of these dimensions will display a stronger affinity for using the smartphones in different contexts and situations, and will consider smartphone use a default, "normal" mode of everyday behavior that is as useful and common as is talking with other people, eating, drinking, or putting clothes on. Their experience of normality includes a high level of online vigilance.

Everybody I Know Has a Smartphone, So . . . Default Expectations Nurtured by Living POPC

A great deal of the appeal and the felt utility of heavy smartphone use originates presumably from the fact that many individuals can afford and now own such a device and have established dense networks of communication connections among each other (Foucault Welles, Vashevko, Bennett, & Contractor, 2014). Heavy users of smartphones typically communicate with many other heavy users, and sharing permanent access to the mobile Internet infrastructure is the key prerequisite for many of the new phenomena we observe in the context of POPC (e.g., microcoordination among group members, Ling & Lai, 2016). From the perspective of the individual user, the experience and knowledge that relevant communication partners out there will act similarly to oneself—that is, exhibit comparable levels of salience, reactibility, and monitoring to the shared online sphere—will bring about specific expectations about how relevant others and the social groups to which one belongs will communicate and act in specific situations (Ling, 2012). For instance, from the assumption that all members of one's inner circle of online friends practice high reactibility, the expectation follows that (at least some) online friends are accessible as a source of advice or social support at any time and independently from where they are (currently) located. This expectation of permanent availability of social capital, we believe, will make a profound difference in many situations, for instance, with regard to somebody's sense of security, fear, self-efficacy, and other high-level cognitions and affective states. Hence, to complete our explorations about the POPC user's mindset, we will outline those types of expectations that seem to be most common among heavy smartphone users and that hold important conceptual implications for studying intense mobile online communication.

Permanent Accessibility of One's Social Networks and Required Information

The primary and most obvious expectation that "always online" users are likely to hold is that those resources the Internet world usually has to offer will be available to them at any time and under any circumstances. This refers to all kind of information that one may need to retrieve, be it news, academic knowledge, business-related advice, or practical guidance in unfamiliar situations and locations. But the expectation of permanent accessibility also applies to the network of individuals with whom the user is connected. Social media and chat applications such as Facebook and WhatsApp seem to keep the entire group of friends, family members, colleagues, and teammates, as well as less well-connected individuals ("weak ties"), available to a user, both for initiating new and for continuing previous threads of communication. Through the smartphone in the pocket, the assumption of "They are with me, all the time" may and most likely will often emerge (e.g., Mascheroni & Vincent, 2016), an expectation with far-reaching motivational consequences.

Permanent Observation by the Social Network

Because mobile Internet devices are mostly used for interpersonal communication (Quinn & Oldmeadow, 2013; Vorderer et al., 2016), many individuals are participating in very active networks of daily information exchange, often with high frequencies of contact. From observing online "friends" and receiving feedback from them, users are likely to conclude that their own online activities will be observed permanently by others. An active social network may cause users to perceive their digitally connected life as happening on a virtual stage on which they have to perform (Hogan, 2010): Relevant others are assumed to follow the (social) media traces one is leaving through permanent communication and self-presentation. This sense of a "permanent audience" for one's own communication may be gratifying at some times and stressful at other times. But either way, heavy smartphone users will likely form an expectation of being observed online by others and that their own communication behavior therefore needs to be adjusted.

Permanent Communication Among Network Members

In addition to the sense of being observed by others online, the perception of active others in the smartphone network is also likely to foster the assumption that these others will communicate with each other frequently, without necessarily including all members of the group. New instant messaging circles can be formed quickly, hence, one can never know whether some "friends" are running separate communications. Because many smartphone owners have experiences with multiple streams of communication in which they are involved (Wang, Irwin, Cooper, & Srivastava, 2015), the extrapolation of this experience to other users may foster the expectancy that some communication among one's friends or colleagues is happening without oneself. This might cause fears of "missing out" (Przybylski, Murayama, DeHaan, & Gladwell, 2013) or of being "cyber-ostracized" (Vorderer & Schneider, 2017) and lead to the intensified motivation to be particularly active within this network of friends. More generally speaking, the experience of participating in a communication swarm will probably come with an understanding that one is not necessarily included in all activities of this swarm.

Real-Time Notification of Relevant (Public) Events

Another important facet of the perceived permanence of communication (possibilities) is the immediacy of information flow and the expectation that one will learn about important events in (near) real time. Because the device is permanently online, it is continuously retrieving updated information, which in turn enables the user to learn about important news—be that public events, such as disasters or diplomatic breakthroughs in international crises, or private events, such as the split-up of a befriended couple—almost at the very moment they are occurring. "Always online" users will likely hold the expectation of permanent receptiveness to important notifications by news media and interpersonal contacts alike (Turcotte, York, Irving, Scholl, & Pingree, 2015); staying permanently informed and becoming aware of important events quickly are thus further expectations of heavy users of mobile Internet devices.

Avoidability of Aversive States

Among the most popular functionalities of smartphones are various diverse manifestations of entertainment. Games, (funny) online videos, memes, and other forms of social media humor are examples of frequently used "mood managers" (Zillmann, 2000) that mobile online devices hold available for spontaneous and/or continuous consumption. The permanent accessibility of a multitude of entertainment options seems to be particularly valuable to users in situations that are associated with aversive states, most importantly, waiting periods, commuting with public transport, (boring) lectures in educational settings, and other contexts that constrain appealing activities. The smartphone seems to be the ultimate remedy for boredom (Matic, Pielot, & Oliver, 2015) and maybe further aversive emotional states such as sadness or anger. We believe that instant and permanent access to fun will make heavy users develop the expectancy that typically aversive states in everyday life can reliably be avoided through smartphone use and that the emotional consequences of aversive events ("daily hassles") can be healed quickly.

Intermediate Summary

The new permanence in communication that many smartphone users have internalized will also shape their communication-related expectations. Compared to the times preceding the "always online" era, we argue that five new types of expectations have become common sense and prototypical for mobile media users: permanent access to other individuals as well as to information, permanent observation of oneself by one's social network, permanent communication among one's network members, real-time reception of push information about relevant events, and avoidability of aversive affective states. One or several of these expectations are likely to be relevant in virtually any given communication situation during the course of a day of a (heavy) smartphone user. Certainly, further cognitive structures or expectancies may also be affected by such frequent smartphone use, but with regard to our present purpose of understanding "always online" communication, we argue that these five types are most important, as they shape the motivational state of users and, in turn, affect their actual choices of communication behavior and action.

Conclusion: The POPC Mindset Between Empowerment and Being Overpowered

The present explication of how we believe heavy smartphone use is shaping the mindset of individuals points very generally to the importance of mediated communication in daily life. We believe that past experiences with and the expectation of permanent connectedness in the future comes with multiple routines in individuals' mindsets, both in respect to one's own and others' smartphone and online sphere, as well as to the respective behavior (Bayer et al., 2016). In the self-experience of a heavy user, permanent connectedness establishes a new layer of social reality; invisible to others, yet highly salient and important to oneself. Always accessible, and with manifold implications for one's thinking, feeling, and behavior (Figure 3.1).

We therefore conclude that heavy smartphone use simultaneously feeds both a sense of empowerment and a sense of being overpowered. Impressions of empowerment originate from positive experiences with gratifications obtained from permanent connectedness, such as an increased capacity for problem solving, reduced feelings of loneliness, or achievements of overcoming aversive states. We believe that heavy smartphone users will anticipate such empowerment for future situations, novel or routine, in which they will be carrying their smartphone with them.

However, at the same time, these cognitive structures may also lead to a sense of being overwhelmed, for instance, by a large number of incoming messages that are felt to make almost immediate responses necessary (Mai, Freudenthaler, Schneider, & Vorderer, 2015), by high communication demands from

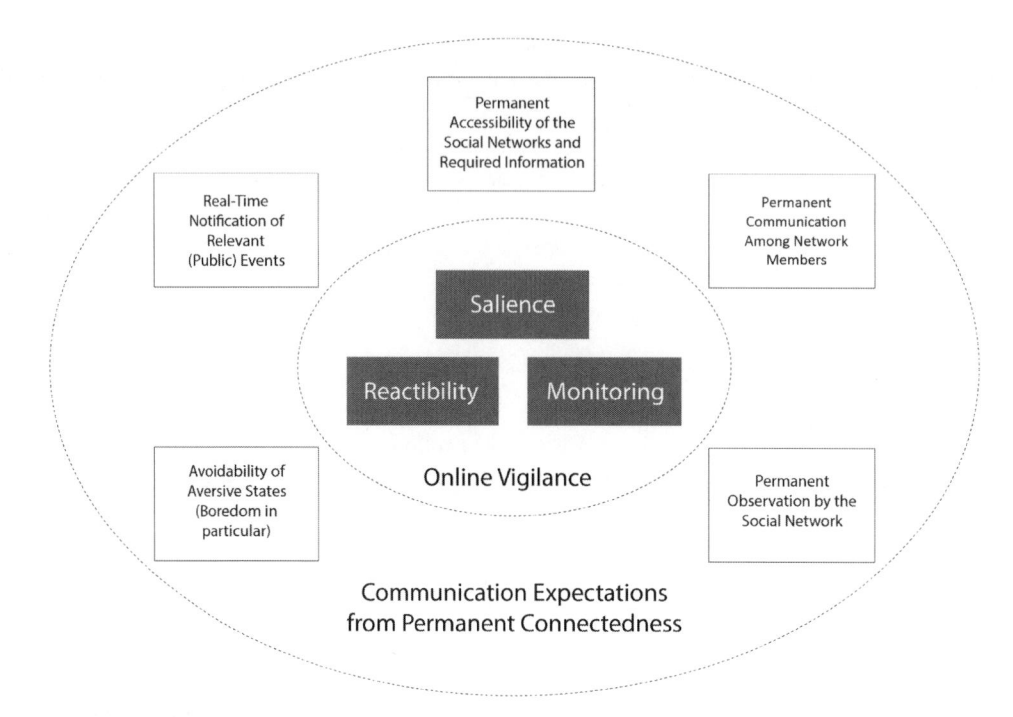

FIGURE 3.1 The POPC Mindset: Habits and Cognitive Structures That Characterize Heavy Users of the Mobile Internet.

online friends and groups (Reinecke et al., 2017), and by social stress that stems from the knowledge of being observed online (e.g., Hefner & Vorderer, 2016). It is possible that some heavy smartphone users, maybe depending on their age, personality, or history with the online world, underestimate the probability of undesirable consequences of such a POPC lifestyle for most of the time. Therefore, the risks of these undesirable consequences deserve as much scholarly attention as the benign implications.

From the proposed outline of the POPC mindset, a broad research agenda for the field of communication can be derived. Many related topics have already been addressed in individual studies; particularly, surveys on motivations and experiences for and with smartphone use have already been published extensively. We suggest to extend these research activities by looking at the question of what smartphones do to individuals in times when they are actually *not* using them (e.g., Cheever et al., 2014). What are the empirical manifestations of the proposed POPC mindset or online vigilance? How much variance is there between individuals and situations, and even between owners of different types of smartphones?

The consequences of a POPC mindset for the psychological functioning and the social behavior of a user also need to be addressed empirically. And here, virtually all domains of communication can benefit from such a perspective, for example, by asking, How does online vigilance affect consumption, involvement, and comprehension of and with daily news (Hefner, Rinke, and Schneider, this volume)? How does the POPC mindset affect preferences for and experiences with mediated entertainment? Which consequences do living POPC cause for persuasion, be it with advertising, propaganda, or political campaigning? How does the POPC mindset relate to psychological health, stress, and well-being (Reinecke, this volume; Mata and Baumann, this volume)? While these questions relate to some of the core issues in communication, a myriad of psychological perspectives needs to be addressed as well: What does a POPC mindset do to the self-concept (von Pape, this volume), authenticity (Trepte and Oliver, this volume), self-esteem, self-confidence, self-efficacy, empathy, the readiness for experiential engagement, and social behavior in intimate relationships (Rieger, this volume), among work teams (Sonnentag, this volume), and among any other social groups (Knop-Huelss, Winkler, and Penzel, this volume)? Given the importance of the various components of this mindset, a remarkable array of research lines in communication and other social sciences may gain fresh impulses from including the perspective of the POPC mindset and the common expectations held by heavy smartphone users.

References

Bayer, J. B., Campbell, S. W., & Ling, R. (2016). Connection cues: Activating the norms and habits of social connectedness. *Communication Theory, 26*, 128–149. doi:10.1111/comt.12090.

Burchell, K. (2014). Tasking the everyday: Where mobile and online communication take time. *Mobile Media & Communication, 3*, 36–52. doi:10.1177/2050157914546711

Cheever, N. A., Rosen, L. D., Carrier, L. M., & Chavez, A. (2014). Out of sight is not out of mind: The impact of restricting wireless mobile device use on anxiety levels among low, moderate and high users. *Computers in Human Behavior, 37*, 290–297. doi:10.1016/j.chb.2014.05.002.

Chotpitayasunondh, V., & Douglas, K. M. (2016). How "phubbing" becomes the norm: The antecedents and consequences of snubbing via smartphone. *Computers in Human Behavior, 63*, 9–18. doi:10.1016/j.chb.2016.05.018

David, P., Kim, J.-H., Brickman, J. S., Ran, W., & Curtis, C. M. (2015). Mobile phone distraction while studying. *New Media & Society, 17*, 1661–1679. doi:10.1177/1461444814531692

de Reuver, M., Nikou, S., & Bouwman, H. (2016). Domestication of smartphones and mobile applications: A quantitative mixed-method study. *Mobile Media & Communication, 4*, 347–370. doi:10.1177/2050157916649989

Diehl, K., Zauberman, G., & Barasch, A. (2016). How taking photos increases enjoyment of experiences. *Journal of Personality and Social Psychology, 111*, 119–140. doi:10.1037/pspa0000055

Foucault Welles, B., Vashevko, A., Bennett, N., & Contractor, N. (2014). Dynamic models of communication in an online friendship network. *Communication Methods and Measures, 8*(4), 223–243.

Gonzales, A. L., & Wu, Y. (2016). Public cellphone use does not activate negative responses in others ... Unless they hate cellphones. *Journal of Computer-Mediated Communication, 21*, 384–398. doi:10.1111/jcc4.12174

Hefner, D., & Vorderer, P. (2016). Digital stress: Permanent connectedness and multitasking. In L. Reinecke & M.-B. Oliver (Eds.), *Handbook of media use and well-being* (pp. 237–249). New York: Routledge.

Hogan, B. (2010). The presentation of self in the age of social media: Distinguishing performances and exhibitions online. *Bulletin of Science, Technology & Society, 30*(6), 377–386. doi:10.1177/0270467610385893

LaRose, R., Connolly, R., Lee, H., Li, K., & Hales, K. D. (2014). Connection overload? A cross cultural study of the consequences of social media connection. *Information Systems Management, 31*, 59–73. doi:10.1080/10580530.2014.854097

Lee, D. H. (2013). Smartphones, mobile social space, and new sociality in Korea. *Mobile Media & Communication, 1*, 269–284. doi:10.1177/2050157913486790

Lenhart, A. (2015). *Teens, social media & technology overview 2015*. Retrieved from www.pewinternet.org/2015/04/09/teens-social-media-technology-2015/

Ling, R. (2012). *Taken for grantedness: The embedding of mobile communication into society*. Cambridge, MA: MIT Press.

Ling, R., & Lai, C. H. (2016). Microcoordination 2.0: Social coordination in the age of smartphones and messaging apps. *Journal of Communication, 66*(5), 834–856. doi:10.1111/jcom.12251

Mai, L. M., Freudenthaler, R., Schneider, F. M., & Vorderer, P. (2015). "I know you've seen it!" Individual and social factors for users' chatting behavior on Facebook. *Computers in Human Behavior, 49*, 296–302. doi:10.1016/j.chb.2015.01.074

Mascheroni, G., & Vincent, J. (2016). Perpetual contact as a communicative affordance: Opportunities, constraints, and emotions. *Mobile Media & Communication, 4*, 310–326. doi:10.1177/2050157916639347

Matic, A., Pielot, M., & Oliver, N. (2015). Boredom-computer interaction: Boredom proneness and the use of smartphone. In *Proceedings of the 2015 ACM International Joint Conference on Pervasive and Ubiquitous Computing* (pp. 837–841). ACM.

Meier, A., Reinecke, L., & Meltzer, C. E. (2016). "Facebocrastination"? Predictors of using Facebook for procrastination and its effects on students' well-being. *Computers in Human Behavior, 64*, 65–76. doi:10.1016/j.chb.2016.06.011

Mihailidis, P. (2014). A tethered generation: Exploring the role of mobile phones in the daily life of young people. *Mobile Media & Communication, 2*, 58–72. doi:10.1177/2050157913505558

Oulasvirta, A., Rattenbury, T., Ma, L., & Raita, E. (2012). Habits make smartphone use more pervasive. *Personal and Ubiquitous Computing, 16*(1), 105–114. doi:10.1007/s00779-011-0412-2

Przybylski, A. K., Murayama, K., DeHaan, C. R., & Gladwell, V. (2013). Motivational, emotional, and behavioral correlates of fear of missing out. *Computers in Human Behavior, 29*(4), 1841–1848.

Quinn, S., & Oldmeadow, J. (2013). The Martini effect and social networking sites: Early adolescents, mobile social networking and connectedness to friends. *Mobile Media & Communication, 1*, 237–247. doi:10.1177/2050157912474812

Reinecke, L., Aufenanger, S., Beutel, M. E., Dreier, M., Quiring, O., Stark, B., . . . Müller, K. W. (2017). Digital stress over the life span: The effects of communication load and Internet multitasking on perceived stress and psychological health impairments in a German probability sample. *Media Psychology, 20*, 90–115. doi:10.1080/15213269.2015.1121832

Rosen, L. D., Mark Carrier, L., & Cheever, N. A. (2013). Facebook and texting made me do it: Media-induced task-switching while studying. *Computers in Human Behavior, 29*(3), 948–958. doi:10.1016/j.chb.2012.12.001

Stothart, C., Mitchum, A., & Yehnert, C. (2015). The attentional cost of receiving a cell phone notification. *Journal of Experimental Psychology: Human Perception and Performance, 41*(4), 893–897. doi:10.1037/xhp0000100

Turcotte, J., York, C., Irving, J., Scholl, R. M., & Pingree, R. J. (2015). News recommendations from social media opinion leaders: Effects on media trust and information seeking. *Journal of Computer-Mediated Communication, 20*(5), 520–535. doi:10.1111/jcc4.12127

Vorderer, P. (2016). Communication and the good life. Why and how our discipline should make a difference. *Journal of Communication, 66*, 1–12.

Vorderer, P., & Kohring, M. (2013). Permanently online: A challenge for media and communication research. *International Journal of Communication, 7*, 188–196.

Vorderer, P., Krömer, N., & Schneider, F. M. (2016). Permanently online—permanently connected: Explorations into university students' use of social media and mobile smart devices. *Computers in Human Behavior, 63*, 694–703. doi:10.1016/j.chb.2016.05.085

Vorderer, P., & Schneider, F. (2017). Social media and ostracism. In K. D. Williams & S. A. Nida (Eds.), *Ostracism, exclusion, and rejection* (pp. 240–257). New York: Psychology Press.

Wang, Z., Irwin, M., Cooper, C., & Srivastava, J. (2015). Multidimensions of media multitasking and adaptive media selection. *Human Communication Research, 41*, 102–127. doi:10.1111/hcre.12042

Wang, Z., & Tchernev, J. M. (2012). The "myth" of media multitasking: Reciprocal dynamics of media multitasking, personal needs, and gratifications. *Journal of Communication, 62*(3), 493–513.

Zillmann, D. (2000). Mood management in the context of selective exposure theory. In M. E. Roloff (Ed.), *Communication Yearbook 23* (S. 123–145). Thousand Oaks: Sage.

4

Methodological Challenges of POPC for Communication Research

Frank M. Schneider, Sabine Reich, and Leonard Reinecke

The world of smart devices has inspired communication research and neighboring disciplines. In the Communication and Mass Media Complete (CMMC) database alone, 1,816 results come up in a Boolean keyword search for ("smartphone" OR "smart phone" OR "mobile phone") from January 2015 to May 2016. This development is paralleled by the growth of online social networks and communication apps (5,986 hits for ["social networking site" OR "social media"] alone in CMMC), which have caused similar research commotion and still do. Smart mobile online devices and their communicative options have become a permanent presence in our everyday lives (e.g., Vorderer & Kohring, 2013). This ubiquity is methodologically challenging, because it includes not only multi-platform behaviors, like receiving push messages from social network sites (SNS) and sports or health apps on the mobile phone, but also multiple devices that can facilitate these information streams, such as notebooks, tablets, smartphones, and wearable devices like smart watches. Empirical investigations of permanent or extremely frequent multi-platform communication—its antecedents, contexts, contents, dynamics, and short-term and long-term consequences—are facing substantial difficulties in obtaining complete, reliable, and valid information. For instance, the numerous episodes of interstitial communication that many smartphone users experience (Utz, this volume) challenge the validity of self-report measures of frequency, sequence, and psychological relevance of this communication, as users are likely to fail in remembering and summarizing their fragmented messaging history.

In this chapter, we review the existing methodological approaches to the permanently online (PO)/permanently connected (PC) phenomenon (POPC), discuss the challenges that come with it, and review possible solutions. We consider the seemingly endless possibilities of the new technologies themselves as an aid in research, as well as the capable catalogue of established social science methods.

Methods for Researching POPC: The State of the Art

What Is POPC and What Is It Not?

Although different observations and conceptualizations of the phenomenon termed POPC exist, they all have the notion in common that the considered behavior and/or state is present *constantly*, *always*, or *permanently*. Furthermore, it is helpful to consider two prevalent aspects of the POPC construct, namely (a) the *behavior* of constantly using mobile online devices (including entertainment, news, or interpersonal communication) and (b) the *psychological state of vigilance* (see also Klimmt, Hefner, Reinecke, Rieger, and Vorderer, this volume) about the device and the potential interactions it holds, to react to incoming information and/or awareness about possible interactions with other people and available content (e.g., Bayer, Campbell, & Ling, 2016; Vorderer, Krömer, & Schneider, 2016; Walsh, White, & Young, 2010). To investigate these phenomena, they need to be theoretically differentiated from neighboring concepts like habits, multitasking, and addiction, to separate POPC processes from their antecedences and consequences. Without a doubt, the overt behaviors through which being PO manifests itself have the potential to become habitual (e.g., checking behaviors, Oulasvirta, Rattenbury, Ma, & Raita, 2012, or phantom phone signals, Tanis, Beukeboom, Hartmann, & Vermeulen, 2015). These habits can become potentially problematic, to the extent that individuals lose their ability to effectively self-regulate these behaviors (LaRose, Lin, & Eastin, 2003). Yet, the permanent quality of the enclosed behaviors itself is separated from habitual use or potentially addictive behavior (see also Klimmt and Brand, this volume). Similarly, multitasking—performing two behaviors at seemingly the same time (see also the chapters by Xu and Wang and by David, this volume)—is rather a possible consequence of POPC than a requirement or manifestation. Other consequences of POPC would include situations when permanent online vigilance is experienced as stress (see also Reinecke, this volume; Hefner & Vorderer, 2017). The communicative options of mobile online media and their availability could satisfy social and informational needs alike. Also, the user's mobile phone involvement (Walsh et al., 2010) could increase with heightened POPC. Dispositions that support PO behavior could include insufficient self-control and impulse control (see van Koningsbruggen, Hartmann, and Du, this volume), but also communication styles or attachment styles are likely factors. Additionally, PO and PC possibly determine each other in a way that communicative vigilance may result in checking behaviors, in initiating communication, or pulling communication streams. Then again, these behaviors could facilitate a constant activation of the interaction possibilities and therefore vigilance for incoming communication (PC). Individual propensities in the area of social relationships (e.g., need to belong, communication styles and willingness, attachment styles, reassurance seeking; see the chapters by Utz and by Rieger, this volume) would further influence how prone an individual is to PC. Finally, environmental and situational factors would influence PO and PC (e.g., norms and technological abilities that allow for using one's smartphone constantly). In sum, all these neighboring concepts are part of the nomological network in which the POPC construct is situated. However, using them as simple proxies for assessing POPC might fall short of the prevalent aspects of POPC.

After providing a short concept explication of POPC and its potential antecedents and effects, we will proceed by discussing the methodological challenges involved in measuring POPC phenomena but also the methodological challenges the discipline of communication research as a whole is facing due to the new usage patterns associated with POPC.

Measuring POPC: Obstacles and Opportunities

To grasp what POPC is really about, we need to move beyond the mere description of this phenomenon and put our methodological toolkit to the test: What kind of methods are available to measure POPC and which have already been applied successfully? Are we well equipped with instruments that are suitable to support our new endeavors? Or do we need to newly develop, refine, or dismiss specific methods when we want to measure POPC? What are the disadvantages of traditional and innovative methods?

Different challenges and opportunities are associated with the measurement of POPC behavior and the psychological state of online vigilance, respectively. As on overt behavior, POPC activities are accessible for measurement through both self-report and observation. Prior research has made first attempts to explicate POPC behavior through self-report measures. In a survey study exploring the POPC behavior of German students, Vorderer, Krömer, and Schneider (2016) measured the frequency of POPC activities in various social situations and contexts of life. While the results clearly underline the general feasibility of operationalizing POPC behavior via self-reports, the specific characteristics of media use in a POPC environment may call the validity of self-report measures into question. The methodological limitations of self-report measures of media exposure have been critically discussed long before the advent of mobile media use and with regard to traditional forms of media exposure (e.g., Prior, 2009). The available evidence suggests that questions pertaining to media use put respondents under considerable cognitive strain, and due to inaccurate recall, biased heuristics, or a lack of motivation, may result in inaccurate estimates of media exposure (De Vreese & Neijens, 2016; Prior, 2009). These traditional challenges of self-report measures of media use are multiplied in a POPC environment: Not only do mobile devices vastly increase the opportunities for media use over the day, mobile media use also typically consists of a large number of short usage episodes (Oulasvirta et al., 2012) and often represents a habitual and automatic behavior, rather than conscious media exposure decisions (Bayer, Dal Cin, Campbell, & Panek, 2016). The mere frequency of POPC behavior, the superficiality of use, and the lack of conscious awareness should make accurate self-reports of POPC particularly difficult (De Vreese & Neijens, 2016).

Fortunately, the POPC phenomenon does not only create new methodological difficulties but also provides fascinating new opportunities for the *unobtrusive* assessment of usage behavior. The fact that the vast majority of POPC activities unifies the use of multiple online platforms on a central device (i.e., the smartphone) makes it easier than ever before to track the digital traces of user behavior and create rich datasets of behavioral observations. For example, specific smartphone apps are able to record smartphone or app usage (e.g., iYouVU, Asselbergs et al., 2016; Menthal, applied in Montag et al., 2015). In fact, prior research clearly demonstrates the superiority of log data over self-report, regarding both Internet use in general (Scharkow, 2016) and mobile phone use in particular (Boase & Ling, 2013). Furthermore, a growing number of studies have successfully applied tracking data in the context of POPC. For instance, Kobayashi, Boase, Suzuki, and Suzuki (2015) used a specifically developed app to collect data from smartphone address books and log communication data (e.g., voice calls, text messages, Gmail messages) to investigate the strength of relationships (ties) and the communication with weak ties. Oulasvirta and colleagues (2012) examined smartphone users' checking behavior and how they respond to awareness cues using a custom software.

In addition, smartphones are equipped with a variety of sensors that are helpful for further *behavioral observations*. For example, the Global Positioning System (GPS) and assisted GPS (i.e., combination of signals from satellites, nearby cell towers, and WLAN) can help to investigate daily activities (e.g., Wolf, Figueredo, & Jacobs, 2013), built-in smartphone accelerometers can detect movements (e.g., how fast users pick up their phones to answer incoming messages; for further examples, see e.g., Miller, 2012), and the microphone can be used for sound tracking of the aural POPC environment (e.g., Lacour & Vavreck, 2014). Even the smartphones' front and rear cameras and flashlight could be used for assessing heart and breathing rates (Nam, Kong, Reyes, Reljin, & Chon, 2016) as possible physiological indicators of POPC. All of these behavioral and physiological observations could help to measure indicators of POPC or describe POPC environments more exactly (i.e., conditions under which POPC occurs).

However, given that our conceptualization of POPC also includes a psychological state of vigilance, the behavioral traces that can be found in server- or client-based log-file data cannot record whether individuals watch their smartphones' screens for any signals or alerts, pay attention to them after receiving such signs of smartphone activity, or think and feel about it. A combination of self-report and log data thus appears to be a particularly fruitful measurement approach in the POPC context.

Whilst the *behavioral component* of POPC has received some attention (see above), the *psychological state* of being POPC, that is, staying ready and awaiting incoming communication, has received honorable mentions at best. However, prior research has established operationalizations for many of the potential antecedents and consequences of POPC. While these measures do not provide direct and explicit measures of the POPC concept, they can function as empirical proxies of POPC behavior and of online vigilance. In this line of research, *standardized psychological tests or scales* have been applied to measure especially trait-like constructs, such as the Big Five, the need to belong, or self-esteem as predictors of POPC-related outcome variables (e.g., Facebook use; for an overview, see Nadkarni & Hofmann, 2012). With regard to PO, *self-report questionnaires* have been used to measure the respondents' online media use (Vorderer et al., 2016) or the use of platform-specific features (e.g., Facebook features, Smock, Ellison, Lampe, & Wohn, 2011). Concerning PC, prior research has measured individuals' swiftness of reacting to smartphone prompts (Mai, Freudenthaler, Schneider, & Vorderer, 2015), or their experienced involvement with mobile online devices (Walsh et al., 2010). Other approaches to self-reports target related or consequential POPC experiences and behaviors. For example, Tanis et al.'s (2015) research suggests that a sizeable population experiences phantom phone signals that trigger the behavioral schema of checking one's phone when experiencing environmental cues similar to mobile phone signals. Other indicators could include an uncomfortable feeling when not having a mobile online device available (Sapacz, Rockman, & Clark, 2016) or the individual's social accessibility (Quan-Haase & Collins, 2008).

Most of these studies are based on cross-sectional survey designs. That is, predictor and outcome variables are assessed in a specific situation at one and the same time, thereby making causal inferences and generalizations (e.g., to other situations, times, or settings) hardly possible. Thus, electronic diaries and experience sampling have been proposed to monitor experiences and behaviors more accurately across different contexts and multiple measurement occasions in daily life. For example, the *experience sampling method* (ESM) allows collecting self-report data in everyday life situations. Although this approach has been rarely applied in communication research, the ubiquity of smartphone use and online access in the POPC environment may help to overcome technical obstacles. For instance, the ESM has been used to investigate the antecedents and consequences of daily recreational and procrastinatory media use (Reinecke & Hofmann, 2016) or the relationship between Facebook use and subjective well-being (Kross et al., 2013). In such studies, the smartphone can be used to deliver prompts to fill out (online) surveys or diaries immediately or within a given time limit. This can be triggered by text messages (via Short Message Service [SMS]; e.g., using the SurveySignal software, Hofmann & Patel, 2015), by e-mails (e.g., administered via online survey tools such as SoSci Survey, Leiner, 2014), or by installed applications that send reminders (e.g., movisensXS, http://xs.movisens.com). In contrast to traditional ESM research, extra devices are no longer necessary (Hofmann & Patel, 2015), and research can make use of the fact that the smartphone is in everyone's pocket anyway. In addition, cell phone surveys achieved higher response rates compared to web surveys in countries with high cell phone coverage (Woo, Kim, & Couper, 2015).

Although our focus on approaches to collect data in the field clearly reflects the vast amounts of highly externally and ecologically valid opportunities the smartphones offer to communication researchers, the traditional experimental setting in the laboratory should not go unmentioned. Not only does the lab equipment often provide the chance to measure constructs that cannot be assessed via mobile technologies in a satisfactory way yet (e.g., attention via eye-tracking, Vraga, Bode, & Troller-Renfree, 2016, or defensive responses to smartphone signals via physiological measures, Clayton, Leshner, & Almond, 2015), but it also enables secure high internal validity by keeping contextual factors constant (e.g., screen size, connectivity, etc.) and applying techniques to control third variables (e.g., randomization, parallelization). On the one hand, these examples show that the drawbacks of experimental settings also apply here: Holding some constituents of POPC or features of communication via smartphone constant may be highly artificial, and the results are neither generalizable from these specific circumstances to everyday life situations nor might they take the natural dynamics of online communication situations into account. On the other hand, the benefits of experimental settings are vital to further elaborate the POPC construct and to allow for causal interpretations. Alternatively, whenever experimental designs are not feasible or possible, one might consider longitudinal approaches as alternatives, in which not all third variables can be controlled, but the determinants would precede the consequential effects. Besides the diary, ESM, and tracking studies mentioned above, there are only rare examples with regard to self-reports that apply longitudinal designs with more than two measurement occasions in POPC-related research areas (e.g., Bødker, Gimpel, & Hedman, 2014).

In sum, our review of POPC measures suggests that the research field lacks a coherent measurement standard. Prior research provides numerous operationalizations for related concepts, antecedents and effects of POPC, whereas instruments that explicitly measure behavioral or psychological components of POPC are rare exceptions. Furthermore, the frequency, subtleness, and high degree of automaticity that is typical for POPC behavior makes its accurate assessment particularly difficult. Besides these methodological challenges, however, the measurement of POPC also benefits from new opportunities, such as access to behavioral tracking data, big data, and innovative forms of ESM data collection.

POPC as a Methodological Challenge for the Discipline

In addition to the methodological problems associated with operationalizing the behavioral and psychological components of POPC, the new usage patterns resulting from the POPC lifestyle have methodological implications that go well beyond the POPC context and affect the discipline of media uses and effects research as a whole (Vorderer et al., 2015).

Many of the problems caused by the new communication patterns discussed above do not only complicate the measurement of POPC behavior per se, but equally apply to the work of communication researchers outside the POPC research field. Just like the validity of self-report measures in the POPC context, the ubiquity of mobile communication and the prevalence of media multitasking also challenge the usefulness of traditional self-report measure of media exposure in virtually all other fields of communication research (DeVreese & Neijens, 2016). The necessity of making increased use of new combinations of self-report and behavioral tracking data is thus not only a pressing challenge for researchers interested in the phenomenon of POPC or online communication specifically, but to all fields of our discipline (e.g., public opinion research, political communication) that rely on media use (e.g., news exposure) as a central variable of interest. The methodological challenges discussed in this chapter thus do not exclusively apply to the measurement of POPC. Rather, the new patterns of

POPC behavior will likely call for a new era of alternative and additional measures of media use in all contexts of communication research.

In addition to challenges with regard to measuring media exposure, POPC phenomena also present new challenges to media effects research, as they lead to an exponential growth in contextual factors that need to be accounted for. The advent of smartphones has resulted in a plethora of new technical infrastructures and software interfaces that interact with media uses and effects. In contrast to the pre-POPC era, when the technical contexts of media use were relatively stable—a TV series was watched on a TV set, Facebook was used in a web browser—smartphones with their different technical features (e.g., screen size) and software architecture (e.g., apps vs. browser) add a whole new layer of technical complexity and affordances that make generalizations across users populations increasingly difficult (Boase, 2013). Besides the growing number of technical contextual factors, the fast-increasing mobility of media use introduces a multitude of additional situational influences. Media use is no longer restricted to a relatively small number of typical settings (e.g., watching TV in the living room) but takes place anytime and anywhere—on the train, in the bathroom, during conversations. This explosion in the number of contextual factors has crucial implications for media effects research, because we cannot expect that a media message has the same impact on media users irrespective of the context of use. In fact, a growing number of studies suggest that important processes, such as persuasion (Kim & Sundar, 2016) or self-disclosure (Murthy, Bowman, Gross, & McGarry, 2015), work differently in the context of mobile media use. This growing importance of contextual factors is a challenge for traditional research methods in media effects studies: The many contextual factors that are potentially relevant and need to be assessed go beyond the scope of traditional survey research. They also challenge the external validity of traditional experimental designs that treat contextual factors as a source of error that needs to be eliminated or at least kept constant. The situation is further complicated by the growing prevalence of media multitasking that is associated with the POPC lifestyle (see the chapters by Xu and Wang and by David, this volume). When two media messages are consumed simultaneously or in fast succession, their respective effects on the media user are hard to differentiate. Overall, these methodological challenges resulting from POPC phenomena strongly underline the necessity to make use of the new opportunities that mobile devices provide for in situ assessment of media uses and effects, such as the mobile ESM.

Ethical Concerns

As suggested above, although POPC makes the life of media uses and effects researchers more difficult, it also introduces fascinating new methodological resources. However, the brave new world of technological possibilities of smart devices comes with a growing responsibility for social scientists. Wrzus and Mehl (2015, pp. 263–264) discuss four ethically and legally risky kinds of information—"information about participants that they did not want to reveal is obtained, information about others is unintentionally obtained, information about medical illnesses or criminal acts is obtained and any of the before mentioned information becomes available to third persons"—researchers have to be made aware of, so they can deal with them. Especially with regard to big data, this becomes more and more important. As boyd and Crawford (2012, p. 671) put it: "just because it is accessible does not make it ethical." An already well-known illustrative example is the Facebook "emotional contagion" study (Kramer, Guillory, & Hancock, 2014), in which the newsfeeds of 689,003 Facebook users were experimentally manipulated to only show positive or negative emotional content. This publication has caused an outbreak of ethical discussion among researchers (e.g., Schroeder, 2014, or the recent special issue in *Research Ethics*, Hunter & Evans, 2016), because the participants were not informed about their participation and had no possibility to opt out—both are standard requirements with regard to participants' rights in social science research. Nevertheless, everything was in accordance with the data use policy of Facebook with which the researchers were cooperating. What is new here is not the thin line between academic institutions and for-profit companies with regard to research ethics or consent and privacy policies, but the power with which knowledge is generated and how big data permeates our daily lives (cf. Schroeder, 2014). For instance, Google data sources like Google Search, Gmail, Google Calendar, Google+, Google Drive, YouTube, Google Maps, Google Play Store, etc. may be linked to provide accurate individual profiles. In light of this powerful knowledge, new ethical guidelines need to be developed and, as Miller (2012, p. 232) proposed, "Ideally, the new rules would apply equally to corporate researchers and academic researchers, holding Facebook to the same standard as Harvard."

Remedies and Promising Solutions

Given the limited space of this chapter, we finally want to highlight four aspects that might advance our knowledge and overcome some obstacles in POPC research: interdisciplinary collaboration, multi-methodological designs, cross-validations and replications, and meta-analyses.

First, as communication scholars, we are interested in the uses, processes, and effects of POPC and their contextual and social dependencies. We are trained in social scientific research methods. Rarely, we are also specialists in computer science and engineering. Thus, the only way to keep pace with the rapid technological developments in the field lies in the collaboration between disciplines (e.g., communication, computer science, computational social science, etc.; cf. Weller, 2015) and with commercial institutions that provide access to large-scale data (Taneja, 2016). With regard to big data and theory-driven or hypothetico-deductive approaches to test theories (e.g., Landers, Brusso, Cavanaugh, & Collmus, 2016), all the data gathered from smartphone sensors or social media platforms might be useless for measuring POPC, unless they are underpinned by theoretically sound assumptions and operationalizations. In contrast, large-scale databases allow also for data mining and machine learning—in other words, data-driven or inductive approaches to explore and detect patterns and build theories (e.g., Lazer et al., 2009; Stopczynski et al., 2014). By combining both ways of thinking, all disciplines would benefit and extend their scientific techniques—especially in such a fast-evolving field. Of course, when it comes to cooperation with business companies, standards common to academic research have to be met (e.g., consultation of ethical committees) or new guidelines have to be created.

Second, such collaboration certainly calls for multi-methodological approaches to data collection, at least to establish the construct validity of the applied measures. For instance, to examine whether a GPS-based measure is indicative of an active lifestyle (i.e., compared to a sedentary lifestyle), Wolf et al. (2013) used a self-report diary, a Google Maps task, and GPS data to measure the number of places a participant has been and investigated the correlation of these measures with standardized scales and tests that assess individual differences (e.g., satisfaction with life, depression, the Big Five). Other examples include the combination of data gained from the billing system of mobile network operators with self-reports (Gerpott, 2010), or self-report, smartphone calls and SMS, Bluetooth proximity, and weather data (Bogomolov, Lepri, Ferron, Pianesi, & Pentland, 2014). We conclude that multi-methodological designs should be the gold standard to study POPC.

Third, by conducting not only one single multi-method study but combining it with (large-scale) replications, the importance of multi-method findings can be increased. Cross-validations and replications are standard procedures while constructing and validating measures but are particularly helpful to reduce biases and flaws in large-scale social media data. For instance, platform-specific findings or populations (e.g., concerning Facebook) might not generalize to other SNS; the features and algorithms of one platform might have changed over time (e.g., storage or privacy policies), thereby changing user behavior; or overfitted models might not perform well with alternative data sets. Ruths and Pfeffer (2014) provide some fundamental discussion and recommendations for these and related issues. It is also obvious that this makes multi-study papers and well-documented method sections as recommendable as open data strategies.

Finally, although much research on POPC—operationalized as constant online media use and a constant psychological state of vigilance—is yet to come, insights from the vast amount of studies on related concepts, such as social media and instant messaging use (e.g., Facebook, Twitter, WhatsApp), can help to discuss alternative explanations for the uses and effects of smart devices. To bundle these myriad findings, we advocate meta-analysis, a statistical way of summarizing empirical results (e.g., Schmidt & Hunter, 2015). Meta-analyses are useful tools because—if they are carefully conducted—they help to estimate generalizable and more precise magnitudes of an effect, to increase the power, to paint an integrative picture if results are conflicting, and to provide more detailed analyses (e.g., moderators, subgroup analyses). Some examples from POPC-related research topics include mobile Internet use (Gerpott & Thomas, 2014), social media use and participation (Boulianne, 2015), Facebook use and loneliness (Song et al., 2014), online media use and perceived social capital/support (Domahidi, 2016), texting effects on driving (Caird, Johnston, Willness, Asbridge, & Steel, 2014), problematic Internet use (Tokunaga & Rains, 2016), and use of mobile devices and learning performance (Sung, Chang, & Liu, 2016).

Concluding Remarks

> If psychology had no history—if it was invented today and had no methodological inertia—what research methods would we use for gathering behavioral data? I think that we would use smartphones, because they are ubiquitous, unobtrusive, intimate, sensor-rich, computationally powerful, and remotely accessible.
>
> (Miller, 2012, p. 221)

From Miller's (2012) encomium on smartphones, the reciprocal relationship between POPC and smartphones as research tools becomes obvious. POPC research is in need of appropriate methods and measures and thus might rely on the smartphone as the ultimate methodological toolkit. At the same time, the smart mobile devices as omnipresent research instruments pave our irrevocable way to being even more than permanently online, permanently connected—we will also be permanently measured. Whether we will be increasingly aware of being permanently measured, and if so, whether this will change the way we use our mobile devices and the corresponding psychological mechanisms, time will tell.

References

Asselbergs, J., Ruwaard, J., Ejdys, M., Schrader, N., Sijbrandij, M., & Riper, H. (2016). Mobile phone-based unobtrusive ecological momentary assessment of day-to-day mood: An explorative study. *Journal of Medical Internet Research*, *18*, e72. http://dx.doi.org/10.2196/jmir.5505

Bayer, J. B., Campbell, S. W., & Ling, R. (2016). Connection cues: Activating the norms and habits of social connectedness. *Communication Theory*, *26*, 128–149. http://dx.doi.org/10.1111/comt.12090

Bayer, J. B., Dal Cin, S., Campbell, S. W., & Panek, E. (2016). Consciousness and self-regulation in mobile communication. *Human Communication Research*, *42*, 71–97. http://dx.doi.org/10.1111/hcre.12067

Boase, J. (2013). Implications of software-based mobile media for social research. *Mobile Media & Communication*, *1*, 57–62. http://dx.doi.org/10.1177/2050157912459500

Boase, J., & Ling, R. (2013). Measuring mobile phone use: Self-report versus log data. *Journal of Computer-Mediated Communication*, *18*, 508–519. http://dx.doi.org/10.1111/jcc4.12021

Bødker, M., Gimpel, G., & Hedman, J. (2014). Time-out/time-in: The dynamics of everyday experiential computing devices. *Information Systems Journal*, *24*, 143–166. http://dx.doi.org/10.1111/isj.12002

Bogomolov, A., Lepri, B., Ferron, M., Pianesi, F., & Pentland, A. (2014). Daily stress recognition from mobile phone data, weather conditions and individual traits. In K. A. Hua, Y. Rui, R. Steinmetz, A. Hanjalic, A. Natsev, & W. Zhu (Eds.), *The 22nd ACM International Conference on Multimedia* (pp. 477–486). Retrieved from http://arxiv.org/abs/1410.5816

Boulianne, S. (2015). Social media use and participation: A meta-analysis of current research. *Information, Communication & Society*, *18*, 524–538. http://dx.doi.org/10.1080/1369118X.2015.1008542

boyd, d. m., & Crawford, K. (2012). Critical questions for big data: Provocations for a cultural, technological, and scholarly phenomenon. *Information, Communication & Society*, *15*, 662–679. http://dx.doi.org/10.1080/1369118X.2012.678878

Caird, J. K., Johnston, K. A., Willness, C. R., Asbridge, M., & Steel, P. (2014). A meta-analysis of the effects of texting on driving. *Accident Analysis & Prevention*, *71*, 311–318. http://dx.doi.org/10.1016/j.aap.2014.06.005

Clayton, R. B., Leshner, G., & Almond, A. (2015). The extended iSelf: The impact of iPhone separation on cognition, emotion, and physiology. *Journal of Computer-Mediated Communication*, *20*, 119–135. http://dx.doi.org/10.1111/jcc4.12109

De Vreese, C. H., & Neijens, P. (2016). Measuring media exposure in a changing communications environment. *Communication Methods and Measures*, *10*, 69–80. http://dx.doi.org/10.1080/19312458.2016.1150441

Domahidi, E. (2016). *Online-Mediennutzung und wahrgenommene soziale Ressourcen: Eine Meta-Analyse* [Online media use and perceived social resources. A meta-analysis]. Wiesbaden: Springer VS.

Gerpott, T. J. (2010). Impacts of mobile Internet use intensity on the demand for SMS and voice services of mobile network operators: An empirical multi-method study of German mobile Internet customers. *Telecommunications Policy*, *34*, 430–443. http://dx.doi.org/10.1016/j.telpol.2010.06.003

Gerpott, T. J., & Thomas, S. (2014). Empirical research on mobile Internet usage: A meta-analysis of the literature. *Telecommunications Policy*, *38*, 291–310. http://dx.doi.org/10.1016/j.telpol.2013.10.003

Hefner, D., & Vorderer, P. (2017). Digital stress: Permanent connectedness and multitasking. In L. Reinecke & M. B. Oliver (Eds.), *The Routledge handbook of media use and well-being* (pp. 237–249). New York: Routledge.

Hofmann, W., & Patel, P. V. (2015). SurveySignal: A convenient solution for experience sampling research using participants' own smartphones. *Social Science Computer Review*, *33*, 235–253. http://dx.doi.org/10.1177/0894439314525117

Hunter, D., & Evans, N. (Eds.). (2016). Facebook special issue. *Research Ethics*, *12*(1).

Kim, K. J., & Sundar, S. S. (2016). Mobile persuasion: Can screen size and presentation mode make a difference to trust? *Human Communication Research*, *42*, 45–70. http://dx.doi.org/10.1111/hcre.12064

Kobayashi, T., Boase, J., Suzuki, T., & Suzuki, T. (2015). Emerging from the cocoon? Revisiting the tele-cocooning hypothesis in the smartphone era. *Journal of Computer-Mediated Communication*, *20*, 330–345. http://dx.doi.org/10.1111/jcc4.12116

Kramer, A. D. I., Guillory, J. E., & Hancock, J. T. (2014). Experimental evidence of massive-scale emotional contagion through social networks. *PNAS Proceedings of the National Academy of Sciences of the United States of America*, *111*, 8788–8790. http://dx.doi.org/10.1073/pnas.1320040111

Kross, E., Verduyn, P., Demiralp, E., Park, J., Lee, D. S., Lin, N., . . . Ybarra, O. (2013). Facebook use predicts declines in subjective well-being in young adults. *PLoS ONE*, *8*, e69841. http://dx.doi.org/10.1371/journal.pone.0069841

Lacour, M. J., & Vavreck, L. (2014). Improving media measurement: Evidence from the field. *Political Communication*, *31*, 408–420. http://dx.doi.org/10.1080/10584609.2014.921258

Landers, R. N., Brusso, R. C., Cavanaugh, K. J., & Collmus, A. B. (2016). A primer on theory-driven web scraping: Automatic extraction of big data from the Internet for use in psychological research. *Psychological Methods, 21*, 475–492. http://dx.doi.org/10.1037/met0000081

LaRose, R., Lin, C. A., & Eastin, M. S. (2003). Unregulated Internet usage: Addiction, habit, or deficient self-regulation? *Media Psychology, 5*, 225–253. http://dx.doi.org/10.1207/S1532785XMEP0503_01

Lazer, D., Pentland, A., Adamic, L., Aral, S., Barabási, A.-L., Brewer, D., . . . van Alstyne, M. (2009). Computational social science. *Science, 323*, 721–723. http://dx.doi.org/10.1126/science.1167742

Leiner, D. J. (2014). *SoSci survey* (Version 2.5.00-i). [Computer software]. Retrieved from www.soscisurvey.de

Mai, L. M., Freudenthaler, R., Schneider, F. M., & Vorderer, P. (2015). "I know you've seen it!" Individual and social factors for users' chatting behavior on Facebook. *Computers in Human Behavior, 49*, 296–302. http://dx.doi.org/10.1016/j.chb.2015.01.074

Miller, G. (2012). The smartphone psychology manifesto. *Perspectives on Psychological Science, 7*, 221–237. http://dx.doi.org/10.1177/1745691612441215

Montag, C., Błaszkiewicz, K., Sariyska, R., Lachmann, B., Andone, I., Trendafilov, B., . . . Markowetz, A. (2015). Smartphone usage in the 21st century: Who is active on WhatsApp? *BMC Research Notes, 8*, 331. http://dx.doi.org/10.1186/s13104-015-1280-z

Murthy, D., Bowman, S., Gross, A. J., & McGarry, M. (2015). Do we tweet differently from our mobile devices?: A study of language differences on mobile and web-based Twitter platforms. *Journal of Communication, 65*, 816–837. http://dx.doi.org/10.1111/jcom.12176

Nadkarni, A., & Hofmann, S. G. (2012). Why do people use Facebook? *Personality and Individual Differences, 52*, 243–249. http://dx.doi.org/10.1016/j.paid.2011.11.007

Nam, Y., Kong, Y., Reyes, B., Reljin, N., & Chon, K. H. (2016). Monitoring of heart and breathing rates using dual cameras on a smartphone. *PLoS ONE, 11*, e0151013. http://dx.doi.org/10.1371/journal.pone.0151013

Oulasvirta, A., Rattenbury, T., Ma, L., & Raita, E. (2012). Habits make smartphone use more pervasive. *Personal and Ubiquitous Computing, 16*, 105–114. http://dx.doi.org/10.1007/s00779-011-0412-2

Prior, M. (2009). The immensely inflated news audience: Assessing bias in self-reported news exposure. *Public Opinion Quarterly, 73*, 130–143. http://dx.doi.org/10.1093/poq/nfp002

Quan-Haase, A., & Collins, J. L. (2008). 'I'm there, but I might not want to talk to you'. *Information, Communication & Society, 11*, 526–543. http://dx.doi.org/10.1080/13691180801999043

Reinecke, L., & Hofmann, W. (2016). Slacking off or winding down? An experience sampling study on the drivers and consequences of media use for recovery versus procrastination. *Human Communication Research, 42*, 441–461. http://dx.doi.org/10.1111/hcre.12082

Ruths, D., & Pfeffer, J. (2014). Social media for large studies of behavior. *Science, 346*, 1063–1064. http://dx.doi.org/10.1126/science.346.6213.1063

Sapacz, M., Rockman, G., & Clark, J. (2016). Are we addicted to our cell phones? *Computers in Human Behavior, 57*, 153–159. http://dx.doi.org/10.1016/j.chb.2015.12.004

Scharkow, M. (2016). The accuracy of self-reported Internet use—a validation study using client log data. *Communication Methods and Measures, 10*, 13–27. http://dx.doi.org/10.1080/19312458.2015.1118446

Schmidt, F. L., & Hunter, J. E. (2015). *Methods of meta-analysis: Correcting error and bias in research findings* (3rd ed.). Los Angeles, CA: Sage.

Schroeder, R. (2014). Big data and the brave new world of social media research. *Big Data & Society, 1*(2). http://dx.doi.org/10.1177/2053951714563194

Smock, A. D., Ellison, N. B., Lampe, C., & Wohn, D. Y. (2011). Facebook as a toolkit: A uses and gratification approach to unbundling feature use. *Computers in Human Behavior, 27*, 2322–2329. http://dx.doi.org/10.1016/j.chb.2011.07.011

Song, H., Zmyslinski-Seelig, A., Kim, J., Drent, A., Victor, A., Omori, K., & Allen, M. (2014). Does Facebook make you lonely? A meta analysis. *Computers in Human Behavior, 36*, 446–452. http://dx.doi.org/10.1016/j.chb.2014.04.011

Stopczynski, A., Sekara, V., Sapiezynski, P., Cuttone, A., Madsen, M. M., Larsen, J. E., & Lehmann, S. (2014). Measuring large-scale social networks with high resolution. *PLoS ONE, 9*, e0095978. http://dx.doi.org/10.1371/journal.pone.0095978

Sung, Y.-T., Chang, K.-E., & Liu, T.-C. (2016). The effects of integrating mobile devices with teaching and learning on students' learning performance: A meta-analysis and research synthesis. *Computers & Education, 94*, 252–275. http://dx.doi.org/10.1016/j.compedu.2015.11.008

Taneja, H. (2016). Using commercial audience measurement data in academic research. *Communication Methods and Measures, 10*, 176–178. http://dx.doi.org/10.1080/19312458.2016.1150971

Tanis, M., Beukeboom, C. J., Hartmann, T., & Vermeulen, I. E. (2015). Phantom phone signals: An investigation into the prevalence and predictors of imagined cell phone signals. *Computers in Human Behavior, 51*, 356–362. http://dx.doi.org/10.1016/j.chb.2015.04.039

Tokunaga, R. S., & Rains, S. A. (2016). A review and meta-analysis examining conceptual and operational definitions of problematic Internet use. *Human Communication Research, 42*, 165–199. http://dx.doi.org/10.1111/hcre.12075

Vorderer, P., Klimmt, C., Rieger, D., Baumann, E., Hefner, D., Knop, K., . . . Wessler, H. (2015). Der mediatisierte Lebenswandel: Permanently online, permanently connected [The mediatized lifestyle]. *Publizistik, 60*, 259–276. http://dx.doi.org/10.1007/s11616-015-0239-3

Vorderer, P., & Kohring, M. (2013). Permanently online: A challenge for media and communication research. *International Journal of Communication, 7*, 188–196.

Vorderer, P., Krömer, N., & Schneider, F. M. (2016). Permanently online—permanently connected: Explorations into university students' use of social media and mobile smart devices. *Computers in Human Behavior, 63*, 694–703. http://dx.doi.org/10.1016/j.chb.2016.05.085

Vraga, E., Bode, L., & Troller-Renfree, S. (2016). Beyond self-reports: Using eye tracking to measure topic and style differences in attention to social media content. *Communication Methods and Measures, 10*, 149–164. http://dx.doi.org/10.1080/19312458.2016.1150443

Walsh, S. P., White, K. M., & Young, R. M. (2010). Needing to connect: The effect of self and others on young people's involvement with their mobile phones. *Australian Journal of Psychology, 62*, 194–203. http://dx.doi.org/10.1080/00049530903567229

Weller, K. (2015). Accepting the challenges of social media research. *Online Information Review, 39*, 281–289. http://dx.doi.org/10.1108/OIR-03-2015-0069

Wolf, P. S. A., Figueredo, A. J., & Jacobs, W. J. (2013). Global positioning system technology (GPS) for psychological research: A test of convergent and nomological validity. *Frontiers in Psychology, 4*, 315. http://dx.doi.org/10.3389/fpsyg.2013.00315

Woo, Y., Kim, S., & Couper, M. P. (2015). Comparing a cell phone survey and a web survey of university students. *Social Science Computer Review, 33*, 399–410. http://dx.doi.org/10.1177/0894439314544876

Wrzus, C., & Mehl, M. R. (2015). Lab and/or field? Measuring personality processes and their social consequences. *European Journal of Personality, 29*, 250–271. http://dx.doi.org/10.1002/per.1986

PART II
POPC and Decision-Making
Selecting, Processing, and Multitasking

5
Reconceptualizing Uses and Gratifications vis-à-vis Smartphone Applications
The Case of WhatsApp

Vered Malka, Yaron Ariel, Ruth Avidar, and Akiba A. Cohen

In their classic volume *Pragmatics of Human Communication*, Watzlawick, Bavelas, and Jackson (1967) proposed several axioms of communication. The first stated, in part: "behavior has no opposite. In other words, . . . one cannot *not* behave . . . it follows that no matter how one may try, one cannot *not* communicate" (pp. 48–49). Thus, communication takes place all the time, in dyads and groups, verbally or nonverbally, in both active and immobile states. This nontrivial conception can be seen as a foundation for the notion that people are incessantly in a state of communication.

Perhaps the best exemplification of this phenomenon was the early generations of mobile phones and the current ubiquity of smartphones. But it is not only the ability of these devices to connect people anytime and anywhere. They also represent a change in usage patterns, as many people utilize them for entertainment and information seeking via the web, for navigating space, and purchasing goods and services, all in addition to interpersonal communication. In short, people are constantly online and connected to others (Vorderer & Kohring, 2013; Vorderer, Krömer, & Schneider, 2016).

Considerable research has been conducted during the past two decades on the worldwide adoption of these technologies and the versatility of their features and usage. In this chapter, we summarize two research trends and provide a case study of Israeli smartphone usage during wartime as an illustration of our argument about the need for a new line of research: understanding smartphones beyond their revolutionary technology and the multifaceted uses and gratifications they afford and enable.

The Prevalent Research on Mobile Phones and Smartphones in Society

The study of mobile telephony and its users has expanded since the late 20th century (Campbell, 2013; Cohen, Lemish, & Schejter, 2008; Katz & Aakhus, 2002). While the present chapter focuses on smartphones and some of their distinctive features, it is impossible to disregard the earlier research on the "traditional" mobile phone, much of which was conducted in similar venues and using similar methodologies. Scholars have been interested in various aspects of mobile telephony. These include motivations for mobile phone use (Lim & Shim, 2016; Wei et al., 2014); actual usage patterns and practices (Ha, Kim, Libaque-Saenz, Chang, & Park, 2015; Katz & Aakhus, 2002; Kongaut & Bohlin, 2016); psychological consequences (Bianchi & Phillips, 2005; Castells, Fernandez-Ardevol, Qiu, & Sey, 2007); sociological impacts of using mobile phones (Hislop & Axtell, 2011; Wajcman, Bittman, & Brown, 2008); and technology acceptance and smartphone usage (e.g., Joo & Sang, 2013; Kim, 2008; Park & Chen, 2007).

Early uses and gratifications (U&G) research (Katz, Blumler, & Gurevitch, 1974) sought to identify the sources of social and psychological needs that create expectations from the media. In the domain of mass communication, U&G studies typically identified five generic clusters of needs that media can fulfill: cognitive, affective, personal integrative, social integrative, and diversion (Katz, Haas, & Gurevitch, 1973). Fast forward to the end of the 20th century, when research on new media, including mobile telephony, also often employed the U&G paradigm. Studies probing the main needs that new media fulfill revealed some of the same functions but added others. Leung and Wei (2000) as well as Wei and Lo (2006) conducted some of the earliest U&G studies relating to mobile phones. Most pertinent to our discussion were their findings regarding two functions: "to be always accessible to anyone no matter where you are" and "to provide immediate access to others anywhere anytime." These are clearly along the lines of the notion of being permanently connected (although this was before the smartphone era that also enables one to be permanently online).

Other early studies on mobile telephony also employed the U&G approach, focusing on the rapid adoption of mobile phones and their unique communication technology. These studies revealed three paramount factors: concern for safety, security, and accessibility (Palen, Salzman, & Youngs, 2000; Schejter & Cohen, 2002). More recently, studies were conducted that explored the general uses of smartphones (Joo & Sang, 2013) and the use of specific applications, such as social networking by adolescents (Sanz-Blas, Ruiz-Mafé, Martí-Parreño, & Hernández-Fernández, 2013). Studies also found smartphones fulfilling users' needs, such as learning, safety, and social interaction (Campbell, 2007; Petrie, Petrovcic, & Vehova, 2011), while Park and Lee (2012) found that they help users maintain human relations and develop feelings of belongingness. Additional studies found that the mobility factor contributed to the development of personal or social well-being (Macario, Ednacot, Ullberg, & Reichel, 2011). In addition, smartphone features, such as social media apps and games, were found to have contributed to users' satisfaction with life (Ellison, Steinfield, & Lampe, 2007; Shen & Williams, 2011). Sundar and Limperos (2013), however, caution against certain methodological artifacts in some U&G studies and call for more refined definitions of gratifications of smartphones in order to detect and distinguish among them vis-à-vis other media platforms.

So far, we have provided a cursory view of the U&G research on mobile telephony in "normal" times. We now turn to the examination of the role of mobile telephony—both "traditional" (mobile phones) and "new" (smartphones)—during crisis situations in general and war in particular, both of which would be particularly amenable to be permanently online and permanently connected.

Schejter and Cohen (2013) evaluated the use of mobile phones by Israelis during the Second Lebanon War in 2006 and "Operation Cast Lead" in the Gaza District in 2009. They asserted that during these periods, the use of cell phones increased, thanks to their most elementary feature—their mobility—that made them usable at all times, everywhere. Bracken, Jeffres, Neuendorf, Kopfinan, and Moulla (2005) also highlighted the importance of the mobile phone in times of crisis and contended that cell-phone-based interpersonal communication networks, in combination with television, constituted the main source of information during the 9/11 terror attack in New York as far back as 2001. They argued that the relatively extensive use of the mobile phone is, among others, a product of the timing of the event, which took place in the morning—when people are in transit on their way to work, often without access to regular or stationary media.

As noted above, considerable research has been conducted during the past two decades on the worldwide adoption of early models of mobile phones—later on smartphones—and the versatility of their usage. Nevertheless, it seems that from a communicative perspective, researchers have been trying to comprehend this new phenomenon by comparing smartphones to other media and by exploring the uses and gratifications attributed to them. While media scholars recognize several communication revolutions, all of which were based on the introduction, adoption, and penetration of new media technologies, we argue that smartphones should be assessed differently, notwithstanding their revolutionary nature. In order to illustrate this claim, we present an Israeli case study involving the use of WhatsApp during wartime.

WhatsApp in Wartime

Ever since their appearance on the scene, smartphones have been very popular among Israelis (Cohen, Lemish, & Schejter, 2008; Malka, Ariel, & Avidar, 2015; Ariel et al., forthcoming). Enabling via various applications a constant flow of interpersonal and group communication, as well as news updates and significant information, smartphones are omnipresent and invaluable in a society typified by an unstable security situation, strong family bonds, an obsession with news consumption, and a fascination with technological innovations (Avidar, Ariel, Malka, & Levy, 2013; Cohen & Lemish, 2003; Schejter & Cohen, 2002, 2013). In the Israeli situation, Mesch and Talmud (2010), as well as more generally elsewhere (Ling, 2008; Wellman, 2001; Helles, 2013), scholars have noted that new state-of-the-art mobile media can support traditional social interactions as well as reconfigure the social networking structure of social groups, even when their members are not in physical proximity.

In recent years, WhatsApp has become one of the most popular smartphone applications both in Israel and globally (Richter, 2016). WhatsApp enables its users to send and receive text messages, video, and audio files free of charge and with no limit. Among its unique features is the ability to enable group communication with no substantial restrictions regarding the number of group participants, the number of groups in which an individual can be a member, and the volume of activity and content transferred. A telephone survey with a representative sample of 500 Israeli smartphone owners conducted in 2014 (Avidar, Ariel, Malka, & Levy, 2015; Malka, Ariel, Avidar, & Levy, 2014) revealed an impressive rate of WhatsApp adoption in Israeli society: 69% of the respondents reported using WhatsApp in order to send personal messages on a daily basis, and 52% of respondents reported sending group messages daily. Additionally, in-depth interviews based on a convenience sample of 60 smartphone users aged 21–30 supported the quantitative evidence regarding the centrality of WhatsApp in the lives of young people (Malka et al., 2014). Most interviewees reported changes in their patterns of creating, managing, and preserving romantic, social, family, and professional relationships ever since they downloaded the application. When describing their perspective of the characteristics of WhatsApp, the respondents indicated that the application enables effective group activities for diverse needs—family, social, and professional—as well as for ad hoc and prolonged management of projects and preserving relationships with friends and family. In other words, WhatsApp provides a convenient and user-friendly platform for different types of content in various contexts.

During the nearly two-month war in the summer of 2014 (known as "Operation Protective Edge") between Israel and Hamas, research was conducted by Malka, Ariel, and Avidar (2015) in an attempt to determine if and to what extent the unique circumstances of the war led to distinctive usage patterns of WhatsApp. The study examined the modes and purposes for which WhatsApp was used during the military campaign, as well as users' perceptions and evaluations of the application. In order to answer these questions, a second telephone survey with a representative sample of 500 Israelis, aged 16 to 75, who own smartphones was conducted during the third week of the military operation, in July 2014.

The survey indicated that various media were used for news consumption during the war: browsing websites was done several times a day by 75% of Israelis; 68% of the respondents reported catching up on the news several times a day via television, and 45% were updated similarly via radio. And yet, while "traditional" media continued to play an important role as information providers, WhatsApp, as a new platform, also had a conspicuous presence on the news scene: nearly 47% of Israelis used it at least once a day to be kept abreast of the situation.

Assuming that the notion of being permanently online and connected implies that media users have learned and become used to being constantly connected with numerous people and sources of information (Vorderer & Kohring, 2013), let alone in wartime, users who directly experienced the erosion of the distinction between the home front and battle zone (mainly residents in southern Israel where the war was most intense) used WhatsApp more than in any other geographic region of the country. Thus, the situation enabled or compelled them to be more online and connected than usual. An evaluation of the application's usage among individuals shows the types of interaction performed by users—as individuals and as group members—and the types of content that they sent. The findings show that 49% of Israelis that used their smartphones on a daily basis sent and received personal messages via WhatsApp at least once a day in order to keep apprised of the news related to the military campaign, and 40% did so via group messaging. Another type of information disseminated via WhatsApp were "rumors"—reports that turned out in retrospect to be true but had not yet been published by the media, as well as false reports—all dealing with different aspects of the campaign. Indeed, 38% of the respondents admitted to having been involved in passing on rumors at least once during the fighting. Humorous and satirical messages were also very popular: 85% of the respondents said they had sent such war-related texts at least once and 50% did so at least once each day.

Another key role filled by WhatsApp was keeping people updated about the safety of family members and friends: 49% of Israelis used personal messages to find out about the welfare of relatives at least once a day, while 44% did so via group messaging. In addition, the use of WhatsApp during Operation Protective Edge was very apparent as a platform for various initiatives to promote civic engagement, volunteerism, and mobilization: 45% of the respondents reported having been involved in sending such messages at least several times a week in order to encourage volunteering, make donations, and organize and/or participate in protests, while 68% did so at least once during the operation.

Respondents also evaluated the use of WhatsApp as making a real contribution to their lives. First, its frequent use during the war was credited with cognitive effects, identified for the most part with the consumption of news in the various media: 42% of Israelis agreed or strongly agreed that WhatsApp helped them to stay current about the situation; 30% agreed or strongly agreed that the application helped them to better understand the news; and 21% agreed or strongly agreed that the application helped them to form an opinion with respect to what was happening.

Interestingly, alongside the application's functioning as a source of information for news about the fighting, ramifications were attributed to the use of WhatsApp that are seemingly inconsistent with the flow of news from the front. An analysis of the survey findings shows that 28% of the respondents agreed or strongly agreed with the statement that WhatsApp helped them to relax and assuage stress. Similar findings came to light in Israel during previous national emergencies, such as the functioning of online platforms (including blogs, electronic mail lists, citizens' reports, users' comments) during the 2006 Second Lebanon War (Naveh, 2008). It is possible that strengthening the sense of knowing what was happening, which the respondents associated with the use of WhatsApp, led to a subjective feeling that the application has the ability to alleviate stress, despite the grim nature of many news stories at the time.

Other significant effects attributed to the use of WhatsApp during the campaign may be described as "integrative effects": 31% of the respondents agreed or strongly agreed that using the application reinforced their sense of belonging to the state, while 41% agreed or strongly agreed that it strengthened their sense of belonging to the community. The same proportion of respondents (41%) agreed or strongly agreed that the use of WhatsApp during the fighting inspired them to want to do "something" for the fighters and/or citizens.

Conclusions

Analyzing the patterns of usage of WhatsApp, as well as users' perceptions of its influences on them during a time of national crisis in Israel, may be considered a good illustration of what living permanently online and permanently connected actually means: using a single application in multiple ways (for both personal and group communication) and for an extremely varied set of functions and purposes, simultaneously satisfying different types of needs.

This case study demonstrates that the traditional direct bond between a medium and its related uses and gratifications has become less relevant. New communication technologies such as smartphones seem to be amenable to modification and adjustment by users in order for them to suit constantly changing needs, such as turning a social-oriented application into a news medium. Furthermore, WhatsApp is a perfect example of Jenkins's (2006) theory regarding the consolidation of culture and convergence of media modes, as well as the creation of a new hybrid medium that does not correspond to the conventional dichotomy of mass vs. interpersonal media. We therefore suggest a reevaluation of certain media theories, most notably the uses and gratifications paradigm, that draws a clear distinction among different traditional mass media (such as television, radio, and newspapers) based on peoples' needs. As Lim and Kim (2007) argue:

> As the media system becomes more complex owing to the emergence of new media such as the internet, uses and gratifications researchers show a great interest in the different uses of different media. They often question, "What kind of people use what kind of media more frequently?" and "Do different uses of media lead to differential social behavior?" (p. 321).

It seems that some current studies regarding new media uses make an attempt to reconceptualize the core questions in relation to media–audience interactions. Thus, they reevaluate traditional top-down or bottom-up perspectives of these interactions, taking into account the versatile users' experiences. Probing for the nature of sociability, interactivity, and information within online social networks, Ariel and Avidar (2015) suggest that "not solely the technological features of a platform determine its level of interactivity and sociability but the actual performances of its users" (p. 28). Similarly, we argue that current research on new technologies such as smartphones and applications such as WhatsApp seems to indicate that scholars tend to be confined to searching for perpetual functions-uses-appraisals of media.

Much of the previous correlational research based on survey data conducted in several countries has led to weak predictions at best regarding cognitive, affective, and behavioral effects of smartphones. As the availability of applications for smartphones keeps growing at an incredible rate, so do the number of functions and options at users' fingertips keep increasing and changing. Thus, any attempt to predict user behavior, especially over time, should be carefully considered. At the very least, it seems crucial at this point to avoid broad predictions with regard to patterns of usage and gratifications.

In conclusion, we suggest that research on smartphones ought not to focus on their technological characteristics, but rather on the functional compatibility of smartphones to the specific time, situation, or user. This might suggest an important theoretical linkage between the U&G paradigm, discussed briefly in this chapter within the prism of mobile media, and the notion of "permanently online/ permanently connected." Several studies have been carried out within the U&G paradigm to explain why people make use of mobile communication technologies and the gratifications they seek in using them (e.g., Peters & Ben Allouch, 2005). Even so, the conceptualization of "uses" and "gratifications" is challenged by the growing phenomena of user-generated content/media. This phenomena has blurred the traditional distinction between sender/recipient and producer/consumer due to the dynamic supplanting role of each player in the online environment (Örnebring, 2008; Shao, 2009). Thus, drawing a distinction between "permanently online" and "permanently connected" could be beneficial for an enhanced conceptualization of "uses" and "gratifications," by considering uses as actual activities that were performed and gratifications as a psychological state. Vorderer, Krömer, and Schneider (2016) suggest that being permanently online and connected should be defined along two dimensions: (a) as an overt behavior in the form of the use of online services and information technology, and (b) as a psychological state of permanent communicative vigilance, by referring to the subjective feeling of permanent availability and connectedness.

Nearly 40 years ago, Gibson (1977) coined the term "affordance" in the context of ecological psychology. Gibson's conception refers to humans and animals that attribute to various objects in the world the potential for action. Hutchby (2001) suggested a closely related definition for the term affordance vis-à-vis technology. The term "media affordance" has also been referred to in the context of research on mobile phones usage (Schrock, 2015). Utilizing the concept of affordance to describe mobile media technologies, "uses" should draw scholars' attention to users' changing experiences, rather than to the characteristics of the technologies or their content producers and designers. The nature of the technological mediators of human communication has clearly altered the ways in which humans interact. Thus, scrutiny of mobile media technologies in general—and smartphones in particular—raises the issue of technology affordances. Tsai and Ho (2013) suggest scholars should look deeper into the cultural and situational aspects of smartphone affordances. Indeed, our current work points to the versatility of smartphones' affordances by looking at the WhatsApp application as an exemplar of the different uses, gratifications, and perceptions of mobile technology.

References

Ariel, Y., & Avidar, R. (2015). Information, interactivity, and social media. *Atlantic Journal of Communication, 23*(1), 19–30.
Avidar, R., Ariel, Y., Malka, V., & Levy, E. C. (2013). Smartphones and young publics: A new challenge for public relations practice and relationship building. *Public Relations Review, 39*(5), 603–605.
Avidar, R., Ariel, Y., Malka, V., & Levy, E. C. (2015). Smartphones, publics, and OPRs: Do publics want to engage? *Public Relations Review, 41*(2), 214–221.
Ariel, Y., Elishar-Malka, V., Avidar, R., & Levy, E.C. (forthcoming). Smartphone's usage among young adults: A combined quantitative and qualitative approach. *Israel Affairs*.
Bianchi, A., & Phillips, J. G. (2005). Psychological predictors of problem mobile phone use. *CyberPsychology & Behavior, 8*(1), 39–51.
Bracken, C., Jeffres, L., Neuendorf, K., Kopfman, J., & Moulla, F. (2005). How cosmopolites react to messages: America under attack. *Communication Research Reports, 22*(1), 47–58.
Campbell, S. W. (2007). A cross-cultural comparison of perceptions and uses of mobile telephony. *New Media & Society, 9*(2), 343–363.

Campbell, S. W. (2013). Mobile media and communication: A new field, or just a new journal? *Mobile Media and Communication, 1*(1), 8–13.

Castells, M., Fernandez-Ardevol, M., Qiu, J. L., & Sey, A. (2007). *Mobile communication and society: A global perspective.* Cambridge, MA: MIT Press.

Cohen, A. A., & Lemish, D. (2003). Real time and recall measures of mobile phone use: Some methodological concerns and empirical applications. *New Media and Society, 5*(2), 176–183.

Cohen, A. A., Lemish, D., & Schejter, A. M. (2008). *The wonder phone in the land of miracles: Mobiletelephony in Israel.* Cresskill, NJ: Hampton Press.

Ellison, N. B., Steinfield, C, & Lampe, C. (2007). The benefits of Facebook friends: Social capital and college students' use of online social network site. *Journal of Computer-Mediated Communication, 12*(4), 1143–1168.

Gibson, J. (1977). The theory of affordances. In R. Shaw & J. Bransford (Eds.), *Perceiving, acting, and knowing: Toward an ecological psychology* (pp. 67–82). Hillsdale, NJ: Lawrence Erlbaum.

Ha, Y. W., Kim, J., Libaque-Saenz, C. F., Chang, Y., & Park, M. (2015). Uses and gratifications of mobile SNSs: Facebook and KakaoTalk in Korea. *Telematics & Informatics, 32*(3), 425–438.

Helles, R. (2013). Mobile communication and intermediality. *Mobile Media and Communication, 1*(1), 14–19.

Hislop, D., & Axtell, C. (2011). Mobile phones during work and non-work time: A case study of mobile, non-managerial workers. *Information and Organization, 21*(1), 41–56.

Hutchby, I. (2001). Technologies, texts and affordances. *Sociology, 35*(2), 441–456.

Jenkins, H. (2006). *Convergence culture: Where old and new media collide.* New York: New York University Press.

Joo, J., & Sang, Y. (2013). Exploring Koreans' smartphone usage: An integrated model of the technology acceptance model and uses and gratifications theory. *Computers in Human Behavior, 29*(6), 2512–2518.

Katz, E., Blumler, J. G., & Gurevitch, M. (1974). Utilization of mass communication by the individual. In J. G. Blumler & E. Katz (Eds.), *The uses of mass communications: Current perspectives on gratifications research* (pp. 19–32). Beverly Hills: Sage.

Katz, E., Haas, H., & Gurevitch, M. (1973). On the use of the mass media for important things. *American Sociological Review, 38*(2), 164–181.

Katz, J. E., & Aakhus, M. (Eds.). (2002). *Perpetual contact: Mobile communication, private talk, public performance.* Cambridge: Cambridge University Press.

Kim, S. H. (2008). Moderating effects of job relevance and experience on mobile wireless technology acceptance: Adoption of a smartphone by individuals. *Information and Management, 45*(6), 387–393.

Kongaut, C., & Bohlin, E. (2016). Investigating mobile broadband adoption and usage: A case of smartphones in Sweden. *Telematics and Informatics, 33*(3), 742–752.

Leung, L., & Wei, R. (2000). More than just talk on the move: Uses and gratifications of the cellular phone. *Journalism and Mass Communication Quarterly, 77*(2), 308–320.

Lim, S., & Shim, H. (2016). Who multitasks on smartphones? Smartphone multitaskers' motivations and personality traits. *Cyberpsychology, Behavior & Social Networking, 19*(3), 223–227.

Lim, T., & Kim, S. (2007). Many faces of media effects. In R. W. Preiss., B. M. Gayle, N. Burrell, M. Allen, & J. Bryant (Eds.), *Mass media effects research: Advances through meta-analysis* (pp. 315–325). Mahwah, NJ: Lawrence Erlbaum Associates.

Ling, R. (2008). *New tech, new ties: How mobile communication is reshaping social cohesion.* Cambridge, MA: The MIT Press.

Macario, E., Ednacot, E. M., Ullberg, L., & Reichel, I. (2011). The changing face and rapid pace of public health communication. *Journal of Communication in Healthcare, 4*(2), 145–150.

Malka, V., Ariel, Y., & Avidar, R. (2015). Fighting, worrying and sharing: Operation "protective edge" as the first WhatsApp War. *Media, War and Conflict, 8*(3), 329–344.

Malka, V., Ariel, Y., Avidar, R., & Levy, E. C. (2014). What's up in WhatsApp world? The role of a popular smartphone application in the lives of Israeli users. In *The 16th International Conference of General Online Research,* Cologne University of Applied Sciences, Cologne, Germany, March 5–7.

Mesch, G. S., & Talmud, I. (2010). *The wired youth: The social world of youth in the information age.* Oxford: Routledge.

Naveh, C. (2008). *The Internet as an environment of encouragement and civilian consolidation during the Second Lebanon War.* Tel-Aviv: Chaim Herzog Institute for Media, Politics and Society (In Hebrew).

Örnebring, H. (2008). The consumer as producer—of what? User-generated tabloid content in the Sun (UK) and Aftonbladet (Sweden). *Journalism Studies*, *9*(5), 771–778.

Palen, L., Salzman, M., & Youngs, E. (2000). Going wireless: Behavior and practice of new mobile phone users. Paper presented at the *ACM 2000 Conference on Computer Supported Cooperative Work (CSCW '00)*, Philadelphia.

Park, N., & Lee, H. (2012). Social implications of smartphone use: Korean college students' smartphone use and psychological well-being. *Cyberpsychology, Behavior, and Social Networking*, *15*(9), 491–497.

Park, Y., & Chen, J.V. (2007). Acceptance and adoption of the innovative use of smartphone. *Industrial Management & Data Systems*, *107*(9), 1349–1365.

Peters, O., & Ben Allouch, S. (2005). Always connected: A longitudinal field study of mobile communication. *Telematics and Informatics*, *22*(3), 239–256.

Petrie, G., Petrovcic, A., & Vehovar, V. (2011). Social uses of interpersonal communication technologies in a complex media environment. *European journal of Communication*, *26*(2), 116–132.

Richter, F. (2016, January 18). *WhatsApp approaches 1 billion users*. Retrieved from www.statista.com/chart/4245/whatsapp-user-growth.

Sanz-Blas, S., Ruiz-Mafé, C., Martí-Parreño, J., & Hernández-Fernández, A. (2013). Assessing the influence of motivations and attitude on mobile social networking use. *Global Business Perspectives*, *1*(2), 164–179.

Schejter, A., & Cohen, A. A. (2002). Israel: Chutzpah and chatter in the Holy Land. In J. Katz & M. Aakhus (Eds.), *Perpetual contact: Mobile communication, private talk and public performance* (pp. 30–41). New York: Oxford University Press.

Schejter, A., & Cohen, A. A. (2013). Mobile phone usage as an indicator of solidarity: Israelis at war in 2006 and 2009. *Mobile Media & Communication*, *1*(2), 174–195.

Schrock, A. R. (2015). Communicative affordances of mobile media: Portability, availability, locatability, and multimediality. *International Journal of Communication*, *9*, 1229–1246.

Shao, G. (2009). Understanding the appeal of user-generated media: A uses and gratification perspective. *Internet Research*, *19*(1), 7–25.

Shen, C., & Williams. D. (2011). Unpacking time online: Connecting Internet and massively multiplayer online game use with psychosocial wellbeing. *Communication Research*, *38*(1), 123–149.

Sundar, S. S., & Limperos, A. M. (2013). Uses and Grats 2.0: New gratifications for new media. *Journal of Broadcasting and Electronic Media*, *57*(4), 504–525.

Tsai, J. P., & Ho, C. F. (2013). Does design matter? Affordance perspective on smartphone usage. *Industrial Management & Data Systems*, *113*(9), 1248–1269.

Vorderer, P., & Kohring, M. (2013). Permanently online: A challenge for media and communication research. *International Journal of Communication*, *7*, 188–196.

Vorderer, P., Krömer, N., & Schneider, F. M. (2016). Permanently online—permanently connected: Explorations into university students' use of social media and mobile smart devices. *Computers in Human Behavior*, *63*, 694–703. doi:10.1016/j.chb.2016.05.085

Wajcman, J., Bittman, M., & Brown, J. E. (2008). Families without borders: Mobile phones, connectedness and work-home divisions. *Sociology*, *42*(4), 635–652.

Watzlawick, P., Bavelas, J. B., & Jackson, D. D. (1967). *Pragmatics of human communication: A study of interactional patterns, pathologies and paradoxes*. New York: W. W. Norton & Company.

Wei, R., & Lo, V.H. (2006). Staying connected while on the move: Cell phone use and social connectedness. *New Media & Society*, *8*(1), 53–72.

Wei, R., Lo, V.H., Xu, X., Chen, Y.N.K., & Zhang, G. (2014). Predicting mobile news use among college students: The role of press freedom in four Asian cities. *New Media & Society*, *16*(4), 637–654.

Wellman, B. (2001). Physical place and cyber-place: Changing portals and the rise of networked individualism. *International Journal for Urban and Regional Research*, *25*(2), 227–252.

6

Always On? Explicating Impulsive Influences on Media Use

Guido M. van Koningsbruggen, Tilo Hartmann, and Jie Du

Many people, especially in industrialized countries, live in a media-rich environment where media content and mediated communication options are easily accessible and almost always available independent from time and place. The widespread use of mobile Internet connections and portable devices, in particular, appear to induce many people to be permanently online and permanently connected (POPC; Vorderer & Kohring, 2013) and to develop an always-on mentality (Hefner & Vorderer, 2017). Such a POPC media-rich environment that constantly confronts people with—often attractive—media-related stimuli may trigger media use in a rather impulsive fashion (e.g., Bayer, Campbell, & Ling, 2016; Hofmann, Reinecke, & Meier, 2017; LaRose, 2010; Naab & Schnauber, 2016). By impulsive media use, we refer to media use that is facilitated by automatic positive affective (e.g., because of the rewarding properties of media) and behavioral approach reactions (e.g., because of media habits) to media-related stimuli. This can be opposed to reflective media use that is facilitated by both reasoned judgments and evaluations, and conscious goal-directed planning (e.g., one's deliberate intention to watch a YouTube video to be entertained). In the present chapter we propose that, in addition to investigating reflective influences on media use, investigating impulsive influences by adopting a process-oriented approach provides a more complete understanding of people's media use and media-related behaviors in our current permanently online media-rich environment.

We believe that impulsive influences on media use deserve more research attention for several reasons. First, despite growing interest on media habits (e.g., LaRose, 2010), traditionally, research and theories in communication science and media psychology emphasized reflective determinants and processes by which people deliberately decide to use media (e.g., reasoned attitudes, behavioral intentions, expected gratification). Examples (for an overview, see, e.g., Hartmann, 2009) include studies in the tradition of the uses-and-gratification approach (e.g., Katz, Blumler, & Gurevitch, 1974; Ruggiero, 2000; see also Malka, Ariel, Avidar, and Cohen, this volume) and of the information utility model (e.g., Atkin, 1972), or applications of the theory of reasoned action to media choice like the technology acceptance model (e.g., Davis, Bagozzi, & Warshaw, 1989). However, dual-systems models of behavior, such as the reflective-impulsive model (Strack & Deutsch, 2004), suggest that behavior can also be determined by more automatic, impulsive determinants and processes (Hofmann, Friese, & Strack, 2009).

Second, even though other lines of research and theorizing provided important insights into how media users' *tendencies* to act without much deliberation are related to their media use (e.g., media habits, trait impulsivity, or low trait self-control; Bayer et al., 2016; LaRose, 2010; Minear, Brasher, McCurdy, Lewis, & Younggren, 2013; Panek, 2014), they usually do not directly measure the automatic, impulsive processes that are assumed to play a role in this. Thus, from studies adopting such an approach that also predominantly used explicit self-report measures, we can only draw indirect conclusions regarding the influence of impulsive processes on media use. Thus, a more direct, *process-oriented* approach measuring automatic, impulsive processes may advance our knowledge regarding the impulsive influences on media use (cf. Hofmann, Friese, & Wiers, 2008, who made a similar argument in the context of health behavior).

Third, our POPC media-rich environment appears to pose a big challenge for media users' self-control, as recent research suggests that media users frequently give in to the temptation to use media despite their intentions to do other things (Du, Van Koningsbruggen, & Kerkhof, 2016; Hofmann, Vohs, & Baumeister, 2012; Reinecke & Hofmann, 2016). Since automatic, impulsive processes play an important role in understanding self-control failures (Hofmann et al., 2009), it seems timely to pay more research attention to the automatic, impulsive processes that influence media use.

We begin this chapter by considering impulsive influences on media use from the perspective of the reflective-impulsive model (Strack & Deutsch, 2004); a frequently used dual-system model of behavior from social psychology proposing that behavior is determined by both a reflective and an impulsive system. We will review arguments and research suggesting the relevance of studying automatic, impulsive processes in the context of media use in media-rich environments in general, and in the context of media-related self-control dilemmas in particular. Next, we review a number of specific media-related behaviors, often involving a self-control dilemma, that have received increasing attention among scholars examining the permanently online-environment and that may particularly benefit from adopting a process-oriented focus on impulsive influences. Finally, we raise some further issues for consideration of studying impulsive influences in a media-rich environment.

Impulsive Influences on Media Use

The reflective-impulsive model (Hofmann et al., 2009; Strack & Deutsch, 2004) suggests that behavior is guided by two different systems: the reflective and the impulsive. This model assumes that impulsive, automatic forms of behavior result from an impulsive system in which people quickly and effortlessly process stimuli in terms of their affective and motivational significance through the spreading of activation in an associative network. In contrast, deliberate, controlled forms of behavior are assumed to originate from a slow-acting, low-capacity reflective system in which people effortfully process stimuli in terms of their significance for long-term goals and personal standards through syllogistic reasoning (for an overview of reflective influences on media choice, see, e.g., Hartmann, 2009). Because the processes of behavior determination differ between the two systems, it has been proposed that different measurement strategies should be used to capture either reflective or impulsive influences on behavior (Hofmann et al., 2009).

Hofmann and colleagues suggest that *explicit* self-report measures are appropriate for assessing reflective influences on behavior because "the symbolic content in the reflective system forms the basis of conscious experiences that can be communicated to others" (Hofmann et al., 2009, p. 167). Thus, by employing explicit self-report measures of constructs associated with the deliberate use of a particular medium (e.g., attitudes, gratifications, behavioral intentions), for instance, one taps into the reflective precursors of media behavior. In contrast, the use of *implicit* measures is recommended for capturing impulsive precursors of behavior. According to Hofmann et al., measures like the implicit association test (Greenwald, McGhee, & Schwartz, 1998) and the affect misattribution procedure (Payne, Cheng, Govorun, & Stewart, 2005) are particularly suitable to assess people's automatic *affective* reactions to particular stimuli of interest. To assess people's automatic *behavioral* reactions, in addition, procedures that assess approach-avoidance reactions to stimuli, such as the stimulus-response compatibility task (e.g., Field, Mogg, & Bradley, 2005) or the approach avoidance task (e.g., Peeters et al., 2012) could be used. These implicit measurement procedures are deemed appropriate to capture impulsive precursors of behavior as they tap into the associative structure underlying hedonic or behavioral reactions in response to stimuli, assess spontaneous (as opposed to more consciously controlled) reactions, and are sensitive to detect state influences in addition to stable trait influences (Hofmann et al., 2009).

Returning to the reflective-impulsive model, impulses are thus proposed to emerge in the impulsive system from the activation of associative clusters in long-term memory (Hofmann et al., 2009; Strack & Deutsch, 2004). Founded on the learning history of the individual, these associative clusters have been created from the joint activation of external stimuli, the individual's affective reactions to these stimuli, and the behavioral tendencies associated with these stimuli (Hofmann et al., 2009). For instance, through repeated Facebook use, the concept of Facebook may become associated with both positive affective reactions to the Facebook experience and the behavior that caused the positive affective reaction (e.g., tapping on the Facebook app icon on your smartphone). As a result, a "Facebook cluster" can be created in the individual's long-term memory. Once created, it can easily be reactivated by perceptual input (e.g., seeing the Facebook logo) or internal triggering conditions (e.g., the thought of checking Facebook; Hofmann et al., 2009; Strack & Deutsch, 2004). It is argued that these associative clusters enable individuals to quickly evaluate and respond to the environment following one's needs and previous learning experiences (Hofmann et al., 2009). This means that for a frequent Facebook user, exposure to a Facebook cue (perceptual or internal) in a future situation is likely to reactivate the "Facebook cluster." This, in turn, is proposed to automatically trigger the associated positive affect and behavioral tendency to approach it, resulting in an impulse to use Facebook (Hofmann et al., 2009).

Because our media-rich environment and certain features of information and communication technologies (ICTs; e.g., instant messages, push notifications) provide constant reminders of media, we propose that many everyday media uses are likely to be driven by the above-described automatic, impulsive processes (also see Hofmann et al., 2017). Furthermore, as argued by Hofmann and colleagues (2017), previous literature is consistent with the idea that people form automatic affective and approach reactions to media and ICTs. Specifically, they propose that the immediate gratifications associated with the habitualized usage of media and ICTs makes it highly likely that people possess such automatic, impulsive reactions. We will now consider these arguments and describe some initial empirical evidence in support of this reasoning.

Hofmann et al. (2017) propose that people learn to associate positive affective states with certain media behaviors because they frequently use media to fulfill various psychological and social needs. Indeed, a large literature suggests that people frequently use media because they provide numerous immediate gratifications (e.g., Błachnio, Przepiórka, & Rudnicka, 2013; Katz et al., 1974; Reinecke, Vorderer, & Knop, 2014). In addition, Hofmann et al. note that, through operant conditioning, media users learn to approach media that can improve their current mood (Zillmann, 1988). Social media users, for instance, may learn that they can improve their mood by browsing a social network site (Johnson & Knobloch-Westerwick, 2014). Other findings indicate that media use provides a reliable source of pleasure (e.g., Vorderer, Klimmt, & Ritterfeld, 2004), has been associated with increases in subjective well-being (see Reinecke, this volume), and is viewed as a highly desirable activity (Hofmann et al., 2012). Accordingly, Hofmann et al. (2017) propose that it is likely that people form strong and positive automatic affective reactions to media and ICTs. Indeed, recent research appears to provide initial support for this idea (Van Koningsbruggen, Hartmann, Eden, & Veling, 2017).

In their research, Van Koningsbruggen et al. (2017) employed the affect misattribution procedure (AMP; Payne et al., 2005)—an implicit measure—to assess social media users' automatic affective reactions to social media cues. In this procedure, participants complete a series of trials in which they are first presented with a picture containing a social media or control cue (prime stimulus; 75 ms), followed by a blank screen (125 ms) and a Chinese pictograph (100 ms). Participants have to rate the pleasantness of the Chinese pictograph, and their ratings are assumed to reflect the (misattributed) affective reaction to the prime stimulus (i.e., the social media or control cue) presented at the start of the trial. The social media cues were Facebook-related pictures (e.g., the Facebook logo) and the control cues were pictures of office supplies (e.g., a stapler). Results demonstrated an interaction between prime stimulus and social media use on the proportion of pleasant responses to the primes. Specifically, frequent Facebook users showed more favorable affective reactions to the Facebook (vs. control) cues, while occasional Facebook users' affective reactions did not differ between Facebook and control cues. In a second study, this effect was replicated, and in addition, the positive affective reactions to the Facebook cues appeared to be meaningfully related to Facebook cravings experienced by the participants. This research thus supports the proposition that media users possess strong and positive automatic affective reactions to media content.

Based on the literature suggesting that media use is often highly habitualized (Bayer et al., 2016; LaRose, 2010; Naab & Schnauber, 2016), Hofmann et al. (2017) further propose that it is likely that media users possess strong automatic approach reactions to media content and ICTs. Through repeated use of media in similar situations, media users learn to associate a certain context with using particular media and the expected outcomes of this media use, herewith developing a mental script (Naab & Schnauber, 2016). The behavioral response in this mental script—the habit—might be activated automatically when media users find themselves again in that situation (Naab & Schnauber, 2016). Think of, for instance, a person who more or less automatically checks his or her Facebook account when having breakfast as a result of performing this behavior since that person bought a smartphone. While this indeed makes it likely that people possess strong automatic approach reactions to media content and ICTs, this has not yet empirically been demonstrated as far as we know. Research could test this proposition by following a similar setup as Van Koningsbruggen et al. (2017), but instead of measuring automatic affective reactions, include a task that captures participants' spontaneously activated behavioral reactions to media stimuli. This could, for instance, be done by using a joystick task that measures automatic approach-avoidance tendencies via push and pull reactions to stimuli (e.g., Peeters et al., 2012).

When do these automatic, impulsive processes with regard to media and ICTs influence media users' behavior? The reflective-impulsive model proposes that the reflective and impulsive systems both determine behavior by the activation of behavioral schemas (Hofmann et al., 2009; Strack & Deutsch, 2004). Often, the behavioral schemas activated in the impulsive and reflective systems are compatible. For instance, acting on the impulse to watch a YouTube video can concur with one's deliberate plan to look for entertainment. In many other situations, however, the behavioral schema activated in the impulsive system is incompatible with the schema activated in the reflective system, for instance, when the strong impulse to watch a YouTube video conflicts with one's deliberate plan to study for an important exam. In situations like this, the reflective-impulsive model suggests that the schema that is activated most strongly eventually determines the individual's course of action (Hofmann et al., 2009; Strack & Deutsch, 2004).

Importantly, the reflective system requires a high amount of control resources to determine behavior (i.e., people have to be able and motivated to engage the reflective system), while the impulsive system only requires relatively few resources (Hofmann et al., 2009). Thus, in general, when sufficient motivation and control resources are available, the reflective system (e.g., one's reasoned actions) is assumed to determine behavior. However, when people are unmotivated or control resources are low, the automatic, impulsive processes are assumed to guide behavior. Both situational (e.g., ego depletion, cognitive load, or alcohol intoxication) and dispositional factors (e.g., working memory capacity, trait self-control) can reduce the individual's available control resources (e.g., Hofmann et al., 2009).

Given that people frequently make media choices when control resources are low (e.g., Hofmann et al., 2012; Reinecke, Hartmann, & Eden, 2014) and live in an environment where they are constantly exposed to media-related stimuli that likely trigger strong and automatic affective and approach reactions, investigating impulsive processes will provide a more complete understanding of media use in our current POPC media-rich environment. This will be particularly true for media choices made in situations in which the media-related behavioral schemas activated in the impulsive and reflective systems are incompatible. Under these circumstances, the stronger the impulsive reaction, the more likely impulsive processes drive people's media use, particularly when their control resources are low.

Conflicts Between the Impulsive and the Reflective System in Media Behaviors

Recent findings suggest that the media-related behavioral schemas activated in the impulsive and reflective systems indeed often appear to be incompatible. For instance, experience sampling research showed that people's media use conflicted most often with efficient time use, not delaying things, and professional and educational achievements (Hofmann et al., 2012, see also supplementary material; Reinecke & Hofmann, 2016). In another study, daily social media users reported that goals, tasks, or activities related to school/study, work, and doing things at home (housework) were most in conflict with their social media use (Du et al., 2016). These conflicts between media use and other important goals might in part be a reflection of incompatible behavioral schemas activated in the impulsive and reflective systems. When the two systems are in conflict, that is, when our impulses are in conflict with reasoned actions, media users face a prototypical self-control dilemma that requires choosing between an immediately rewarding behavior (e.g., watching an entertaining YouTube video) and a behavior that results in a more valuable yet delayed reward (e.g., studying to pass an exam). To resist their impulses, people need to exert self-control, which can be defined as "the ability to override or change one's inner responses, as well as to interrupt undesired behavioral tendencies (such as impulses) and refrain from acting on them" (Tangney, Baumeister, & Boone, 2004, p. 274).

Unfortunately, media users appear to frequently fail in exerting self-control. Experience sampling research, for instance, showed that in almost half of the instances, people give in to their desires to use media despite their willingness to resist them (Hofmann et al., 2012). Another survey among college students revealed that visiting social network sites and online video viewing were negatively related to self-control, and that online video viewing was associated with less time spent on schoolwork (Panek, 2014). Additionally, it has been found that daily social media users estimated that about one-third of their time spent on social media during a typical day was perceived as giving in to temptation (Du et al., 2016). Together, these findings suggest that despite their intentions to do other things (i.e., the behavioral schema activated in the reflective system), people often find themselves using media (i.e., the behavioral schema activated in the impulsive system).

Media use thus appears to be a seductive temptation in everyday life that people often cannot resist. Research and theorizing on impulse and self-control suggest that such self-control failures are driven by automatic, impulsive processes that override the influence of the reflective system (e.g., Hofmann et al., 2009). Hence, a process-oriented approach in which these impulsive processes are directly measured can increase our understanding of media-related self-control failures. Intriguingly, conflicts between the impulsive and reflective system appear to underlie many media-related behaviors that have received increasing attention among scholars examining the permanently online environment. The predictive validity of research and theory related to these specific behaviors may thus be further improved by paying more attention to automatic, impulsive processes. In the next section, we will describe some examples of media-related behaviors we potentially might better understand by including measurements of impulsive processes.

Many Permanently Online Phenomena May Be Impulsive

Many phenomena that are associated with our media-rich environment reveal typical characteristics of impulsive behavior, including online procrastination or "cyberloafing" (Lavoie & Pychyl, 2001; Vitak, Crouse, & LaRose, 2011), mobile phone checking ("phubbing"; Roberts & David, 2016), media multitasking (Van der Schuur, Baumgartner, Sumter, & Valkenburg, 2015; also see David, this volume, and Xu and Wang, this volume), and guilty media pleasures (Panek, 2014), including binge watching (Pena, 2015). However, although these POPC behaviors received increasing attention among scholars, their explanation has not, to the best of our knowledge, been thoroughly based on theorizing on and directly investigating the role of impulsive influences.

Online procrastination, for example, can be defined as "the act of needlessly delaying tasks to the point of experiencing subjective discomfort" (Solomon & Rothblum, 1984, p. 503) by engaging in online use. Typically, the primary task at hand is perceived as aversive, because it seems effortful or potentially frustrating—like writing an article. Procrastinators revert from tackling the primary task (often despite better knowledge) by consecutively engaging for short intervals in non-task-related behaviors that are more pleasurable, like using media (Reinecke & Hofmann, 2016). While procrastinating, these unrelated activities are rationalized as preparatory steps toward the main task. For example, "quickly checking Facebook" may be considered a preparatory step toward writing an article. However, such perceptions may only represent reflective efforts to justify the unrelated media use. This typical characteristic of online procrastination reminds one of underlying goal conflicts commonly observed in impulsive behavior.

Similarly, cyberloafing, that is, engaging in non-work-related media activities at work (Vitak et al., 2011), may often result from impulsive processes. This should be particularly true if people engage in cyberloafing simply because they perceive non-work-related media options as more pleasurable than the primary working task. The idea that cyberloafing resembles impulsive behavior is also consistent with the finding that the behavior is more common among people with low trait (Restubog, Garcia, Wang, & Cheng, 2010) or state self-control (e.g., due to insufficient sleep, Wagner, Barnes, Lim, & Ferris, 2012). People that generally score low on self-control or momentarily lack the resources to engage in self-control are less likely to successfully regulate an impulse (Hofmann et al., 2009).

Characteristics of impulsive processes can also be identified in media multitasking, that is, "simultaneously engaging in two or more types of media or using media while engaging in non-media activities" (Van der Schuur et al., 2015, p. 205), and interruptive mobile phone use (Brown, Manago, & Trimble, 2016). Multitasking implies that people switch back and forth their attentional focus on several available options (van der Schuur et al., 2015). As a variant of multitasking, people may also interrupt an ongoing face-to-face conversation by shifting their attentional focus, for instance, to their mobile phone (Humphreys, 2005; also see Rieger, this volume). A few studies show that media multitasking is linked to trait impulsivity (Minear et al., 2013; Sanbonmatsu, Strayer, Medeiros-Ward, & Watson, 2013). In addition, media multitasking is often characterized by goal conflicts like attending to a tedious primary task in the presence of more pleasurable options. For example, in a study by Calderwood, Ackerman, and Conklin (2014), students were more inclined to engage in media multitasking if they were less motivated to complete their homework (as a primary task). Apparently, less-motivated students found available media options relatively more tempting and were, thus, more inclined to impulsively engage in multitasking. Furthermore, individuals that are particularly sensitive to notice available media options in their environment and that struggle to filter out their presence as "irrelevant information" may be more prone to engage in media multitasking, although existing evidence regarding this assumption is mixed (e.g., Van der Schuur et al., 2015). The idea, however, fits to the notion that media multitasking is guided by impulsive influences, because the disability in executive functioning to neglect irrelevant cues seems closely linked to impulsivity (e.g., in ADHD disorder; Kenemans et al., 2005).

Further Considerations of Studying Impulsive Influences in a Media-Rich Environment

The emphasis of this chapter on impulsive processes should not be mistaken as a call to solely focus on impulsive influences triggering POPC behavior. Rather, as the prior discussion of goal conflicts and self-regulatory demands arising in the face of impulses already shows, to gain a complete picture, parallel reflective processing and self-control capacity must be examined, too. According to dual-systems perspectives on self-control (Hofmann et al., 2009), impulsive and reflective precursors, as well as situational and dispositional boundary conditions, need to be taken into account for a comprehensive study of behavior. For example, reflective precursors like deliberate and critical evaluations of a situation (e.g., "using Facebook now may distract me for a longer time than I think") and existing standards to restrain behavior in accordance with one's long-term goals (e.g., "I told myself to not use Facebook before finishing homework") may effectively shield individuals against "acting on impulse." Furthermore, to what extent an arising impulse eventually guides behavior also depends on the situational capacity of the reflective system to regulate the impulse. According to Hoffmann et al., with diminished capacity of the reflective system (e.g., due to momentary depletion or cognitive load), "impulse-triggered behavioral schemas are more likely to exert an influence on overt behavior" (2009, p. 166). Accordingly, only a more holistic examination of impulsive processes and their interplay with reflective processes allows one to illuminate under which conditions POPC behavior is truly guided by impulses. Similarly, directly measuring these different influences in joint examinations promises a better understanding of media use in the current permanently online media-rich environment.

Milyavskaya, Inzlicht, Hope, and Koestner (2015) provide another example of why scholars should not neglect reflective processing if studying impulsive POPC behavior. They show that the *magnitude* of impulses may vary—depending on whether people follow autonomously chosen or externally imposed long-term goals. Specifically, their studies reveal that want-to goal pursuit (e.g., "I *want* to become a better student and study hard") may diminish impulses as compared to have-to goal pursuit (e.g., "I *have* to become a better student and study hard"). Similarly, Gillebaart and De Ridder (2015) find that people with higher (vs. low) dispositional self-control capacity may perceive identical options as less tempting. Together, these findings suggest that higher-order cognitive processing and the capacity of the reflective system not only affect regulatory efforts, but also the actual magnitude of arising impulses. Accordingly, people that freely commit themselves to long-term goals and that score high on self-control seem better prepared to not act on impulse in face of pleasurable media options, also because they perceive them as less tempting.

Conclusion

In many societies around the globe, media and ICTs have become ubiquitous options in everyday life. People navigate through a media-rich environment that constantly offers incentives for action. The main implication of this media-rich environment resembles that of a nutrition-rich environment like a luxurious buffet: It provides a lot of tempting options whose indulgence may conflict with relevant long-term goals, but impulses arising from a sudden craving may override any reflective restraints. Consistent with this idea (and with similar thoughts expressed by others, e.g., Hofmann et al., 2017), in this chapter we argued that a media-rich environment is cluttered with media options that, by their sheer presence (e.g., the smartphone on the table), people may constantly become aware of, and which, once their presence is noted, may trigger impulses in the form of strong and automatic affective and behavioral reactions. Impulses, however, may often be incompatible with one's reasoned actions (e.g., intention to complete a primary task) and, thus, result in goal conflicts. Depending on various situational (e.g., fatigue), motivational (e.g., external goal pursuit), and dispositional (e.g., low trait self-control) precursors, impulses to use a media option may override competing reflective self-regulatory processes.

In the present chapter, we highlighted some striking similarities in the psychological characteristics of many permanently online phenomena and impulsive behaviors. However, to the best of our knowledge, past conceptualizations of these phenomena were not thoroughly based on impulsive processes. Accordingly, the central take-home message of the present chapter is that the application of theory and methods of impulsive processes that guide behavior to the study of permanently online media use in a media-rich environment is a promising avenue for future research. Such an application may add further substance to existing explanations of POPC phenomena and their underlying mechanisms, and help improving theorizing.

To conclude, while much remains to be discovered about how, when, and to what extent automatic affective and approach reactions influence people's media choices, we hope to have motivated readers to take the impulsive system into account when trying to make sense of what drives media use in our media-rich environment.

References

Atkin, C. K. (1972). Anticipated communication and mass media information-seeking. *Public Opinion Quarterly, 36,* 188–199. http://doi.org/10.1086/267991

Bayer, J. B., Campbell, S. W., & Ling, R. (2016). Connection cues: Activating the norms and habits of social connectedness. *Communication Theory, 26,* 128–149. http://doi.org/10.1111/comt.12090

Błachnio, A., Przepiórka, A., & Rudnicka, P. (2013). Psychological determinants of using Facebook: A research review. *International Journal of Human-Computer Interaction, 29,* 775–787. http://doi.org/10.1080/10447318.2013.780868

Brown, G., Manago, A. M., & Trimble, J. E. (2016). Tempted to text: College students' mobile phone use during a face-to-face interaction with a close friend. *Emerging Adulthood, 4,* 440–443. http://doi.org/10.1177/2167696816630086

Calderwood, C., Ackerman, P. L., & Conklin, E. M. (2014). What else do college students "do" while studying? An investigation of multitasking. *Computers & Education*, *75*, 19–29. http://doi.org/10.1016/j.compedu.2014.02.004

Davis, F. D., Bagozzi, R. P., & Warshaw, P. R. (1989). User acceptance of computer technology: A comparison of two theoretical models. *Management Science*, *35*, 982–1003. http://doi.org/10.1287/mnsc.35.8.982

Du, J., Van Koningsbruggen, G. M., & Kerkhof, P. (2016). A brief measure of social media self-control failure. *Manuscript in Preparation*.

Field, M., Mogg, K., & Bradley, B. P. (2005). Craving and cognitive biases for alcohol cues in social drinkers. *Alcohol and Alcoholism*, *40*, 504–510. http://doi.org/10.1093/alcalc/agh213

Gillebaart, M., & de Ridder, D. T. D. (2015). Effortless self-control: A novel perspective on response conflict strategies in trait self-control. *Social and Personality Psychology Compass*, *9*, 88–99. http://doi.org/10.1111/spc3.12160

Greenwald, A. G., McGhee, D. E., & Schwartz, J. L. K. (1998). Measuring individual differences in implicit cognition: The implicit association test. *Journal of Personality and Social Psychology*, *74*, 1464–1480. http://doi.org/10.1037/0022-3514.74.6.1464

Hartmann, T. (2009). *Media choice: A theoretical and empirical overview*. New York: Routledge.

Hefner, D., & Vorderer, P. (2017). Digital stress: Permanent connectedness and multitasking. In L. Reinecke & M. B. Oliver (Eds.), *The Routledge handbook of media use and well-being: International perspectives on theory and research on positive media effects* (pp. 237–249). New York: Routledge.

Hofmann, W., Friese, M., & Strack, F. (2009). Impulse and self-control from a dual-systems perspective. *Perspectives on Psychological Science*, *4*, 162–176. http://doi.org/10.1111/j.1745-6924.2009.01116.x

Hofmann, W., Friese, M., & Wiers, R. W. (2008). Impulsive versus reflective influences on health behavior: A theoretical framework and empirical review. *Health Psychology Review*, *2*, 111–137. http://doi.org/10.1080/17437190802617668

Hofmann, W., Reinecke, L., & Meier, A. (2017). Of sweet temptations and bitter aftertaste: Self-control as a moderator of the effects of media use on well-being. In L. Reinecke & M. B. Oliver (Eds.), *The Routledge handbook of media use and well-being: International perspectives on theory and research on positive media effects* (pp. 211–222). New York: Routledge.

Hofmann, W., Vohs, K. D., & Baumeister, R. F. (2012). What people desire, feel conflicted about, and try to resist in everyday life. *Psychological Science*, *23*, 582–588. http://doi.org/10.1177/0956797612437426

Humphreys, L. (2005). Cellphones in public: Social interactions in a wireless era. *New Media & Society*, *7*, 810–833. http://doi.org/10.1177/1461444805058164

Johnson, B. K., & Knobloch-Westerwick, S. (2014). Glancing up or down: Mood management and selective social comparisons on social networking sites. *Computers in Human Behavior*, *41*, 33–39. http://doi.org/10.1016/j.chb.2014.09.009

Katz, E., Blumler, J. G., & Gurevitch, M. (1974). Utilization of mass communication by the individual. In J. G. Blumler & E. Katz (Eds.), *The uses of mass communication: Current perspectives on gratifications research* (pp. 19–32). Beverly Hills, CA: Sage.

Kenemans, J. L., Bekker, E. M., Lijffijt, M., Overtoom, C. C. E., Jonkman, L. M., & Verbaten, M. N. (2005). Attention deficit and impulsivity: Selecting, shifting, and stopping. *International Journal of Psychophysiology*, *58*, 59–70. http://doi.org/10.1016/j.ijpsycho.2005.03.009

LaRose, R. (2010). The problem of media habits. *Communication Theory*, *20*, 194–222. http://doi.org/10.1111/j.1468-2885.2010.01360.x

Lavoie, J. A. A., & Pychyl, T. A. (2001). Cyberslacking and the procrastination superhighway: A web-based survey of online procrastination, attitudes, and emotion. *Social Science Computer Review*, *19*, 431–444. http://doi.org/10.1177/089443930101900403

Milyavskaya, M., Inzlicht, M., Hope, N., & Koestner, R. (2015). Saying "no" to temptation: Want-to motivation improves self-regulation by reducing temptation rather than by increasing self-control. *Journal of Personality and Social Psychology*, *109*, 677–693. http://doi.org/10.1037/pspp0000045

Minear, M., Brasher, F., McCurdy, M., Lewis, J., & Younggren, A. (2013). Working memory, fluid intelligence, and impulsiveness in heavy media multitaskers. *Psychonomic Bulletin & Review*, *20*, 1274–1281. http://doi.org/10.3758/s13423-013-0456-6

Naab, T. K., & Schnauber, A. (2016). Habitual initiation of media use and a response-frequency measure for its examination. *Media Psychology*, *19*, 126–155. http://doi.org/10.1080/15213269.2014.951055

Panek, E. (2014). Left to their own devices college students' "guilty pleasure" media use and time management. *Communication Research, 41*, 561–577. http://doi.org/10.1177/0093650213499657

Payne, B. K., Cheng, C. M., Govorun, O., & Stewart, B. D. (2005). An inkblot for attitudes: Affect misattribution as implicit measurement. *Journal of Personality and Social Psychology, 89*, 277–293. http://doi.org/10.1037/0022-3514.89.3.277

Peeters, M., Wiers, R. W., Monshouwer, K., Van de Schoot, R., Janssen, T., & Vollebergh, W. A. M. (2012). Automatic processes in at-risk adolescents: The role of alcohol-approach tendencies and response inhibition in drinking behavior. *Addiction, 107*, 1939–1946. http://doi.org/10.1111/j.1360-0443.2012.03948.x

Pena, L. (2015). Breaking binge: Exploring the effects of binge watching on television viewer reception. *Dissertations—ALL*, Paper 283.

Reinecke, L., Hartmann, T., & Eden, A. (2014). The guilty couch potato: The role of ego depletion in reducing recovery through media use. *Journal of Communication, 64*, 569–589. http://doi.org/10.1111/jcom.12107

Reinecke, L., & Hofmann, W. (2016). Slacking off or winding down? An experience sampling study on the drivers and consequences of media use for recovery versus procrastination. *Human Communication Research, 42*, 441–461. http://doi.org/10.1111/hcre.12082

Reinecke, L., Vorderer, P., & Knop, K. (2014). Entertainment 2.0? The role of intrinsic and extrinsic need satisfaction for the enjoyment of Facebook use. *Journal of Communication, 64*, 417–438. http://doi.org/10.1111/jcom.12099

Restubog, S. L. D., Garcia, P. R. J. M., Wang, L., & Cheng, D. (2010). It's all about control: The role of self-control in buffering the effects of negative reciprocity beliefs and trait anger on workplace deviance. *Journal of Research in Personality, 44*, 655–660. http://doi.org/10.1016/j.jrp.2010.06.007

Roberts, J. A., & David, M. E. (2016). My life has become a major distraction from my cell phone: Partner phubbing and relationship satisfaction among romantic partners. *Computers in Human Behavior, 54*, 134–141. http://doi.org/10.1016/j.chb.2015.07.058

Ruggiero, T. E. (2000). Uses and gratifications theory in the 21st century. *Mass Communication and Society, 3*, 3–37. http://doi.org/10.1207/S15327825MCS0301_02

Sanbonmatsu, D. M., Strayer, D. L., Medeiros-Ward, N., & Watson, J. M. (2013). Who multi-tasks and why? Multi-tasking ability, perceived multi-tasking ability, impulsivity, and sensation seeking. *PLOS ONE, 8*, e54402. http://doi.org/10.1371/journal.pone.0054402

Solomon, L. J., & Rothblum, E. D. (1984). Academic procrastination: Frequency and cognitive-behavioral correlates. *Journal of Counseling Psychology, 31*, 503–509. http://doi.org/10.1037/0022-0167.31.4.503

Strack, F., & Deutsch, R. (2004). Reflective and impulsive determinants of social behavior. *Personality and Social Psychology Review, 8*, 220–247. http://doi.org/10.1207/s15327957pspr0803_1

Tangney, J. P., Baumeister, B., R. F., & Boone, A. L. (2004). High self-control predicts good adjustment, less pathology, better grades, and interpersonal success. *Journal of Personality, 72*, 271–324. http://doi.org/10.1111/j.0022-3506.2004.00263.x

Van der Schuur, W. A., Baumgartner, S. E., Sumter, S. R., & Valkenburg, P. M. (2015). The consequences of media multitasking for youth: A review. *Computers in Human Behavior, 53*, 204–215. http://doi.org/10.1016/j.chb.2015.06.035

Van Koningsbruggen, G. M., Hartmann, T., Eden, A., & Veling, H. (2017). Spontaneous hedonic reactions to social media cues. *Cyberpsychology, Behavior, and Social Networking, 20*, 334–340. http://doi.org/10.1089/cyber.2016.0530

Vitak, J., Crouse, J., & LaRose, R. (2011). Personal Internet use at work: Understanding cyberslacking. *Computers in Human Behavior, 27*, 1751–1759. http://doi.org/10.1016/j.chb.2011.03.002

Vorderer, P., Klimmt, C., & Ritterfeld, U. (2004). Enjoyment: At the heart of media entertainment. *Communication Theory, 14*, 388–408. http://doi.org/10.1111/j.1468-2885.2004.tb00321.x

Vorderer, P., & Kohring, M. (2013). Permanently online: A challenge for media and communication research. *International Journal of Communication, 7*, 188–196.

Wagner, D. T., Barnes, C. M., Lim, V. K. G., & Ferris, D. L. (2012). Lost sleep and cyberloafing: Evidence from the laboratory and a daylight saving time quasi-experiment. *Journal of Applied Psychology, 97*, 1068–1076. http://doi.org/10.1037/a0027557

Zillmann, D. (1988). Mood management through communication choices. *The American Behavioral Scientist, 31*, 327–340. http://doi.org/10.1177/000276488031003005

7
Permanence of Online Access and Internet Addiction

Christoph Klimmt and Matthias Brand

Concerns about problematic, excessive, and unhealthy uses of the Internet emerged soon after online technologies had begun to proliferate beyond expert circles into larger user communities (Young, 1996). As Internet access, broadband connections, and advanced online services became increasingly available to and popular among many people across the world, parents, educators, therapists, and researchers warned that some users face severe troubles in controlling the amount of time they spend online and display behavioral symptoms known from addictive disorders such as alcoholism (e.g., Griffiths, 2000). Such problematic Internet use increases the risk for undesirable critical circumstances in life, such as job loss, academic failure, or divorce (e.g., Lortie & Guitton, 2013). After two decades of research and interdisciplinary terminological debate, the use of "Internet addiction" (IA) has been receiving acceptance and practical use among large parts of the involved research and intervention communities (Brand, Laier, & Young, 2014).

The present contribution examines the implications of the new developments in mobile Internet use and permanent connectedness (permanently online, permanently connected or POPC, cf. Klimmt, Hefner, Reinecke, Rieger, and Vorderer, this volume) for the explanation, prevention, and therapy of IA. Various aspects of the phenomena summarized as POPC relate to the complex set of variables that are considered causes or manifestations of (subtypes of) IA. Some of them originate in new possibilities for online use enabled by technological progress, for instance, the permanent and virtually ubiquitous accessibility of online services provided by smartphones. Others are rooted in the (expected) shifts in users' cognitive structures caused by habitualized use of technical features, for example, the assumption that permanent communication among peers would continue if one would disconnect from one's circle of "online friends" ("fear of missing out", cf. Przybylski, Murayama, DeHaan, & Gladwell, 2013).

For our analysis, we differentiate common subtypes of IA and introduce a state-of-the-art model of the psychological causes of IA. We then discuss how specific aspects of the POPC complex relate to this theoretical account of IA. While this reflection will focus on how POPC thinking and behavior increase the risks of developing or maintaining IA, the subsequent section will reason about the chances of POPC technology and habits for IA-related prevention and intervention. We conclude with suggestions for future research that could contribute to a better understanding of both the influences of POPC as mainstream communication behavior on IA and new opportunities to counteract undesirable manifestations and consequences of heavy online use.

Understanding Internet Addiction

Describing, defining, and detecting addictive use of the Internet have turned out to be major challenges for researchers and therapists. These difficulties closely relate to the two terms that "Internet addiction" is composed of. First, the "Internet" is a multifunctional communication infrastructure that provides access to manifold platforms, services, and media. If somebody is addicted "to the Internet", this typically means he or she displays addiction-like patterns of using several online applications, such as games or pornography. The Internet merely serves as a technology of delivery for the actual object of addiction, but the net is not the addictive "substance" itself. Second, because in behavioral addictions, such as excessive and uncontrolled online use, there is no physiological agent or substance that triggers addictive body responses such as craving and withdrawal symptoms known from alcoholism or other drug addictions, a long debate has taken place among experts about whether and how to apply the concept of addiction to online use at all. Both terminological complexities have caused substantial variation in the concepts and phrases used to address Internet addiction, and in the present chapter, several of these, such as "problematic Internet use" and "excessive Internet use" appear interchangeably with "Internet addiction." Internet addiction is currently the most frequently used term in publications (see Brand, Laier et al., 2014, for an overview), while recently, the term Internet use disorder has also become prominent.

Contemporary research on Internet addiction differentiates between five subtypes that refer to specific online services or types of content to which users have been shown to maintain addictive consumption patterns. The most prominent subtype is Internet gaming disorder (APA, 2013). While the first cases had been reported from the earlier era of offline gaming, new features of the gaming experience bound to the mode of online play caused the number of patients to rise substantially and hence attracted the attention of addiction researchers (e.g., Dong & Potenza, 2014, 2016; Fauth-Bühler & Mann, 2017; Kuss, 2013; Thalemann, Wölfling, & Grüsser, 2007). More recently, other subtypes of Internet addiction have been discussed as well; they mirror addictions known from the offline sphere, namely addictive use of online pornography, social networking sites, shopping sites, and gambling (Brand, Young, & Laier, 2014; Griffiths, 2012; Kuss & Griffiths, 2011; Müller, Brand, Mitchell, & de Zwaan, in press; Müller et al., 2016; Young, Pistner, O'Mara, & Buchanan, 1999). With regard to the present context, it is worthwhile noting that all identified subtypes of Internet addiction are bound to online services and media that are widely used today via mobile devices such as smartphones (e.g., mobile gaming, cf. Bowman, Jöckel, & Dogruel, 2015).

While understanding the particularities of each subtype of Internet addiction is key to explaining the emergence and identifying the risk factors of the disorder, recent theoretical advances in modelling the causes and pathways of excessive online use allow explicating the phenomenon independently from specific subtypes. Integrated models of "general Internet addiction" (GIA) offer a comprehensive account of explaining why some people drift into addictive online behavior (and how), whereas most other users stay within the limits of "normal," healthy, nonproblematic Internet attendance (e.g., LaRose & Eastin, 2004). Because reviewing and comparing different models of GIA is beyond the scope of the present contribution, we focus on one contemporary approach, the integrated model proposed by Brand, Laier, and Young (2014), which has received both substantial empirical support and wide acknowledgment within the research community. This model has been revised and specified recently (Brand, Young, Laier, Wölfling, & Potenza, 2016) and is now termed the I-PACE (interaction of person-affect-cognition-execution) model. The I-PACE model, however, only focuses on specific

Internet addictions (e.g., gaming, gambling, cybersex, online shopping, and communication) and not on what is frequently called GIA.

The model on GIA (Brand, Laier et al., 2014) operationally defines Internet addiction as a combination of several behavioral phenomena known from or similar to conventional, substance-bound addictions, namely loss of control/time management, craving, and social problems caused by online use. These dimensions have been established by previous conceptual work (i.e., the components model: Griffiths, 2005). The dimension "loss of control/time management" relates to how strongly a person suffers from time management problems in everyday life due to her or his Internet use, such as neglecting household chores or experiencing sleep problems. It also includes negative consequences caused by the excessiveness of the Internet use (e.g., low school performance) and failures to actively reduce Internet use in the past. The second dimension, "craving/social problems," addresses aversive effects of excessive Internet use on social interactions and preoccupation with the medium (e.g., the frequency of fantasizing about connecting to the Internet). Further included aspects of this dimension are interpersonal problems (e.g., antisocial behavior when being disturbed during online use) and usage of the Internet for the purpose of mood regulation (which is expressed empirically in questionnaire items such as "How often do you feel depressed, moody, or nervous when you are offline, which goes away once you are back online?").

The model traces the origins of addictive Internet use back to a set of individual difference variables. If a person scores high on one or several of these predispositions, she or he is more likely to develop GIA. According to the model, psychopathological symptoms, most importantly, depression and social anxiety, dysfunctional personality factors such as low self-efficacy, shyness, stress vulnerability, and procrastination tendencies, and social isolation or lack of social support (Brand, Laier et al., 2014, p. 2) represent such psychological burdens that drive the affinity to Internet addiction. All of them have been demonstrated empirically as relevant determinants of excessive online use in past studies (see Brand, Laier et al., 2014, for a review). The model suggests that two types of specific Internet-related cognitions that result from these predispositions mark the pathway that leads into GIA. One type of such addiction-facilitating cognitions is Internet-related *expectancies*. Individuals who assume, have learned, and/or have been reinforced in their expectation that using the Internet brings about desirable, positive consequences that immediately or directly ease the psychological troubles they are facing, such as loneliness, sadness, or feelings of emptiness, are strongly motivated to maintain or repeat online use, which renders drifting into uncontrolled, excessive consumption much more likely. A parallel set of relevant cognitions refers, according to this model, to *coping behaviors*. If people tend to cope with the stressors they are confronted with (again, for example, loneliness or sadness) in dysfunctional ways, that is, suppressing aversive experiences, avoiding active reflection of the problem, or maladaptive coping such as mere mood improvement, and consider the Internet as a valuable tool for such dysfunctional coping, such Internet-related cognitions will also pave the way into addictive use.

In sum, the model explains Internet addiction as a result of interacting undesirable personal characteristics and Internet-related cognitions. The latter are partially fueled by appealing technical features and attractive characteristics of online media that reinforce expectations and afford frequent use, which then drive habitualization as well as chronification of expectancies and other dysfunctional cognitive structures. Consequently, a stable pattern of addictive Internet use will emerge that is hard to change, relevant to daily behavior, and severe in its consequences. In this sense, the model converges with alternative approaches (e.g., Dong & Potenza, 2014; LaRose & Eastin, 2004). From past survey research, the prevalence of such severe forms of Internet addiction has been estimated between 1% and 8% of the population (Weinstein & Lejoyeux, 2010).

Conceptual Connections Between POPC and Internet Addiction

Based on the explication of "how Internet addiction works," we now discuss how the recent developments labeled as POPC interrelate to excessive online use. If many people are (expecting to be) online permanently and ubiquitously, what does that mean for the likelihood of emerging Internet addiction? We discuss four points of connection between POPC and Internet addiction: the permanence of availability and appeal, the strong drive to habitualize online use, the experience of social normality of heavy online use, and the collective stabilization of online use through social network effects.

Permanence of Availability and Appeal

The core characteristic of the POPC phenomenon, that is, the possibility to connect to the Internet virtually anytime and anywhere, also has direct implications for Internet addiction. First, we adopt a perspective on individuals who already display addictive online behavior. These people face severe difficulties in regulating the amount of time spent online and in deciding autonomously and with effective goal orientation about the timing, location, content, and activity of being online. Prior to the POPC era, such individuals experienced solid barriers to (continued, repeated) online use caused by technical and situational circumstances. For example, a desktop computer or laptop that was formerly required to go online was not available in all possible situations an addicted person would find herself or himself in, or specific applications associated with the addiction (e.g., an online game, an online shop) were not reliably available on the hardware the person had access to. Such external barriers thus supported addicted users in maintaining a certain (maybe very low) level of everyday functioning, as they forced the individual to adapt, at least for brief episodes, to circumstances where going online was impossible and the fulfillment of the addictive desire was blocked. The "accessibility" has been already suggested as a core factor contributing to the development of Internet addiction in general and Internet sex addiction in particular (Young, 2008). The accessibility has become increasingly important in the age of mobile devices. Accessibility represents a key technical fact contributing to the permanence of being online and consequently Internet addiction.

With the advent and mass proliferation of mobile broadband Internet access and ultrafunctional devices such as high-end smartphones, the number of such forced-offline situations that an addicted individual has to endure during an average day is declining toward zero. There are virtually no technical barriers any more that could prevent the addicted individual from going and staying online. Even at extreme or remote locations, such as on high-speed trains or in public parks, the Internet is now reliably accessible, and the same applies to any online service of desire, including games, social media, pornography, or shopping platforms. This implies that addicted individuals are confronted with the appealing call of their object of desire permanently. With a smartphone in one's pocket, there is no possibility any more to keep a distance—voluntarily or involuntarily—from the Internet. This permanent availability and the perception of continued closeness of the object of addiction is likely to overwhelm addicted users with their notorious problems of self-regulation and self-directedness, which are main factors in explaining Internet addiction (Sariyska et al., 2014). The configuration of POPC for the smartphone user with Internet addiction is comparable to a person suffering from alcoholism who is granted access to a huge liquor store where she or he is permitted to take any bottle from the shelves at any time without paying. Under such conditions of permanent, massive "seduction," it is unlikely that addicted individuals will find any means of resilience, self-control, and autonomy in deciding about going online. Under the condition of POPC, the behavioral execution of Internet addiction is also likely to become permanent, and severe aversive consequences must be expected in the sense that well-known negative long-term outcomes of Internet addiction, such as school or job failure, sleep problems, or family conflicts (e.g., Weinstein & Lejoyeux, 2010), will emerge with greater probability and within shorter periods of time.

In a similar vein, the new permanence of availability and appeal of the Internet caused by POPC technology and behavior is a fundamental threat to individuals who are not yet addicted to the Internet, but are at risk for developing an Internet addiction. These people score high on some personological risk factors, and if being online is a behavioral option at any time and any place, these undesirable predispositions are confronted with self-regulation challenges at high frequency. For example, individuals who display strong procrastination tendencies (Thatcher, Wretschko, & Fridjhon, 2008) now find effective means to procrastinate permanently and reliably by using their smartphone (Reinecke & Hofmann, 2016). Likewise, depressive individuals will value the permanent availability of mood-improving contents and services they can access via their smartphone and are likely to make frequent use of these highly available options (see Reinecke, this volume). A third example are individuals confronted with high loads of daily stress who turn to online services for coping purposes; the permanent accessibility of their preferred (and often dysfunctional) coping technique will stabilize their stress-induced online use behavior (Kardefelt-Winther, 2014; Tang et al., 2014). Thus, from the perspective of the outlined model (Brand, Laier et al., 2014), at-risk individuals are much more likely to develop addiction-facilitating Internet-specific cognitions under the condition of POPC, such as Internet-related expectancies and dysfunctional Internet-related coping cognitions (see also van Koningsbruggen, Hartmann, and Du, this volume).

These problematic amplification dynamics of POPC are likely to play out with different power for the differentiated subtypes of IA. Specifically, for those subtypes that typically require long, continuous online "sessions," that is, Internet gaming and Internet pornography addiction, the permanence and ubiquity of Internet access is probably less relevant. Playing or watching videos for hours is typically not very satisfying when one is using the small display of a smartphone. In contrast, those IA subtypes that typically manifest themselves in spontaneous, impulsive, short episodes of consumption, such as online shopping addiction, and to some extent, social media and online gambling addiction, are more likely to become dynamized through POPC technologies and behavior. The reason for this assumption is that permanent availability of online services implies the permanent presence of those behavior options toward which the individual's impulse control is constrained (van Koningsbruggen et al., this volume). Whenever an individual suffering from one of these subtypes of IA enters a situation with a new powerful impulse to go online, the possibility to respond immediately to this impulse is always given, thanks to smartphones and the POPC environment. Over time, then, the massively increased number of episodes in which the urge to go online can be satisfied immediately will result in the development, maintenance, and fortification of addiction-facilitating cognitive structures—POPC is argued to function as an amplifier and stabilizer to IA dynamics.

Habitualization of Online Use as Precedent of Internet Addiction

The basic observation of the POPC phenomenon—a growing number of people are using their smartphones in a growing number of situations for a growing number of purposes—means that many people have developed a strong *habit* to take out their smartphone frequently for solving many different tasks and without necessarily planning each action of usage consciously (Oulasvirta, Rattenbury, Ma, & Raita, 2012). To many "small" problems that occur in daily life, the smartphone and the online services it makes accessible offer fast and effective solutions, including information search, entertainment needs when facing boredom and waiting periods, and communication requirements in situations of loneliness or other needs to connect socially (Klimmt et al., this volume). Taking out and using the mobile device has become, for many people at least, a *default* response to a large array of affordances and requirements.

From the perspective of the outline model of GIA, smartphones and their multi-functionality facilitate not only the habitualization of using the smartphone frequently and for many diverse purposes, but they also foster the forming of Internet-related expectancies and chronify cognitive structures related to coping with (aversive, challenging) daily experiences. If individuals with problematic personological configurations (in the sense of the GIA model, see above) develop strong habits of using their smartphone—which may happen independently from a specific addictive tendency—this "general" habitualization of going online for any purpose may push the individual toward addictive usage patterns, because the default reaction to those problems that an individual is facing due to her or his personal background (e.g., lack of social support, depressive symptoms, etc.; see the model explication above) will then also "go online." People who have learned that using the smartphone is most often an effective behavior will apply this knowledge also to addiction-related situations and problems, which may start the chronification cycle for Internet-related expectancies and dysfunctional coping that the outlined model proposes to cause addictive online usage. By nesting itself in cognitive structures of the digital lifestyle of POPC, the smartphone may thus open a (partially) new pathway toward Internet addiction by forming a powerful habit of using the smartphone as the default response to (virtually) any challenging circumstance. This proposition converges with current research on the habitualization in substance dependency (Everitt & Robbins, 2016; Piazza & Deroche-Gamonet, 2013).

Normalization of Heavy Online Use

The observation that many people use their smartphone in situations and at locations that were unlikely to enable media use before is changing the impression of what people do in the public arena. Well-known episodes discussed in the media underline the high visibility of smartphone use by pedestrians, car drivers, guests in restaurants, and clients in waiting lines, to name just a few examples. An average smartphone user will be able to observe hundreds of other people each day who are also looking at, swiping on, speaking into, or doing something else with their smartphone. Seeing people interacting with their mobile Internet device has become a very common, "normal" experience.

The trend of permanent smartphone use as mainstream, everyday behavior has implications for the development of Internet addiction that can be explained through social learning theory (Bandura, 1986). People who are at risk to acquire IA and people who would already be classified as suffering from IA are, under the condition that virtually everybody is/does POPC, less likely to recognize their problem through social comparison. Rather, observing other people's daily behavior will leave them with the impression that their own problematic or even highly dysfunctional way of using the Internet is pretty normal, usual, certainly not newsworthy, and probably (because so many people seem to do it) rational. This does not only refer to observing strangers interacting with their smartphones at public places, but also to the lessons one can learn from the communication behavior of one's online contacts. Some online friends are always available, respond extremely quickly to messages, and seem to never log out of messenger and social media services. Many people interact at least sometimes with individuals who enact, even celebrate, an "always on" digital lifestyle in which accessibility and permanent connection seem to be important goals of living per se (Bayer, Campbell, & Ling, 2016). Individuals with addictive tendencies will hence rarely experience situations in which they would recognize their highly unusual, extreme pattern of Internet consumption. The perceived normality of being and behaving POPC is, again from the perspective of the outlined model of GIA, likely to undermine individuals' willingness and ability to find alternative coping strategies and reinforce their proclivity to find solutions to their psychological problems by going and staying online.

Collective Self-Stabilization: Permanent Social Dynamics Maintain Addictive Usage

Much use of the mobile Internet in daily life serves social and communication goals (Bayer et al., 2016; Bayer, Ellison, Schoenebeck, & Falk, 2016). From the perspective of an individual user, this implies that she or he is connected via the smartphone to several, if not many, other users who are displaying similar routines of (heavy) smartphone communication (see above). Users do not only produce and send messages, obviously, they are "invited" (or urged) to respond to incoming communication frequently. Many users seem to run several streams of interpersonal or intragroup communication using messenger apps in parallel or have developed other routines of handling large amounts of messages during a normal day (Malka, Ariel, Avidar, and Cohen, this volume).

From an Internet addiction perspective, the social function of smartphone communication (e.g., Valkenburg & Peter, 2011) is highly interesting and relevant, because it adds to the individual psychological and technological factors that are often considered to be fundamental ingredients to IA (Kuss & Griffiths, 2011). If other users invite, urge, or even press—through communication—an at-risk person or someone who is already suffering from addictive online behavior to stay online, to continue a conversation, or to participate in an ever-new round of playing, these social dynamics will inevitably put severe (additional) stress on the self-regulation capacities of that person. Depending on the individual predisposition, the wish not to disappoint relevant others by logging out, quitting a game, or delaying a response may turn out as a particularly relevant force that overrides a user's self-control and lets him drift into addictive tendencies. For example, a person who is desperately needing social support from her or his online friends due to a lack of social integration in the offline sphere may be highly susceptible to social cues (or urges) to stay online in order not to jeopardize this only and valuable source of social connection ("fear of missing out"; cf. Przybylski et al., 2013). In turn, other users who may face similar problems will then be affected by this individual's online communication; this way, entire networks of online friends may stabilize each other's addictive online behavior patterns simply by responding to previous communication and by preventing others from exiting networks of joint online activity (Wu, Ko, Wong, Wu, & Oei, 2016). If POPC means a permanently active and present online network of "friends," the collective self-stabilization of heavy Internet use may represent a completely new facilitator of addictive online use that expands the set of Internet-specific expectancies and dysfunctional coping behaviors outlined in the model of GIA by Brand, Laier et al. (2014; see above).

POPC and Chances for Prevention and Intervention

So far, we have discussed pathways of how POPC technology and behavior may amplify risks or existing problems of Internet addiction. The same phenomena may, however, also bring about new opportunities and chances for counteracting Internet addiction.

One of these chances is related to the fact that POPC behavior leaves many data traces and recordings of usage times and attendance to services and applications. These data could provide individual users with feedback information on their online consumption. Various smartphone apps serve this purpose of measuring a user's online behavior and offer tips on improving, optimizing, or simply reducing (online) use. One example is the app Menthal, which tracks various parameters of smartphone uses for scientific research (Markowetz, Błaszkiewicz, Montag, Switala, & Schlaepfer, 2014) but also enables users to keep an overview of their patterns of online consumption.

Such applications, for which the label "quantified self" is used frequently, may turn out as effective means to support users at risk of developing IA. The permanent availability of metrics on one's own (mobile) online usage is a valuable information source to increase awareness for (high) consumption patterns during daily living. Not being aware of one's actual online consumption may lead to problematic Internet-related expectancies and may legitimate dysfunctional coping cognitions, which would, according to the outlined model, increase the risk of developing or maintaining IA. With a permanent automatic observer of online behavior installed on the smartphone, users can be reminded on a regular basis about how they are doing in managing and limiting their Internet behavior, which may serve as valuable support for those individuals with self-regulation problems.

A more advanced utilization of the data traces generated and recorded by smartphones would be the implementation of smartphone-based prevention and intervention measures that help users to actually modify their online behavior step by step on a daily basis. Applying principles of behavioral therapy, such technology-based approaches would analyze a client's patterns of online usage according to definitions of addiction and with regard to changes in usage patterns in the past. Based on these results, the smartphone would indicate specific and individualized behavioral recommendations to the user, such as to become more aware of smartphone usage at certain times of the day, or reflecting on the actual value of those online games with which a person has been spending so much time recently. Because of the permanent availability and obtrusiveness of thematic notifications, the potential for modifying online behavior in a sustainable way may be relatively large (Bakker, Kazantzis, Rickwood, & Rickard, 2016). From the perspective of the model of GIA, the value of such smartphone-based intervention strategies would be the permanent activity and availability of observation and behavioral feedback to the user, which could not be achieved through conventional, offline counselling. Many single messages of feedback and behavioral recommendation that are grounded on actual usage data will improve the chances of modifying cognitive structures, such as habits, but also Internet-related expectancies so that there is a realistic chance of altering online behavior itself.

Conclusion: Research Challenges at the Intersection of POPC and Internet Addiction

The present contribution has reviewed multiple connections between the observational syndrome labeled POPC and Internet addiction. Departing from a state-of-the-art model of Internet addiction, various dimensions of how these two concepts may be causally connected have been identified, both with aversive, risk-increasing outcomes and with benign implications for prevention and intervention. Because the POPC issue is so new, not much of our reflection can be based on empirical data, so the research agenda that follows from our review could simply be described along all the issues brought up before. However, four domains of inquiry seem to be of particular importance in our view.

First, the conceptual understanding and empirical measurement of Internet addiction seem to be challenged by POPC as a mass phenomenon. Due to habits and cognitive structures of permanent smartphone usage, an increasing number of people seem to display some of the defining elements of Internet addiction. For instance, loss of control over Internet use, which is one symptom of Internet addiction, seems to occur quite frequently among POPC users ("online procrastination," Reinecke & Hofmann, 2016; van Koningsbruggen et al., this volume). Likewise, the symptom of negative consequences of heavy online use, such as damage to intimate relationships (Rieger, this volume) or reduced well-being due to communication stress (Reinecke, this volume; Hefner & Vorderer, 2016), may be on the rise in the general population because of POPC behaviors. These developments increase the difficulties to isolate actual symptoms of Internet addiction against "normal" online use. As a consequence, future research will have to revisit the conceptual definition and measurement indicators for Internet addiction in order to maintain a viable, comprehensive understanding that can be reliably operationalized in spite of the fact that POPC behavior is becoming "normal" and many users seem to display some characteristics of addiction.

Second, it is crucial to better understand how technology and software features of smartphones, their online connection, and their apps interact with personality variables in bringing about known and maybe not-yet-known Internet-related cognitions. Understanding these cognitions, expectancies in particular (Brand, Laier et al., 2014), is key to tracing the pathways and dynamics of emerging IA, and as the present chapter has argued, technology and behavior labeled as POPC is likely to affect these cognitions in sustainable, lasting ways. Empirical data is urgently needed in order to enable additional research to respond appropriately to the new challenges that the POPC trend may impose. For instance, do smartphones enlarge the part of the population who is at risk of developing IA, because POPC technology is also "seductive" for people who are not susceptible on the personality dimensions known as risk factors so far (depression, lack of social support, etc.)?

Third, much past research and theorizing has considered IA as a stable disorder that is not going to disappear once it has emerged. However, at least for the case of excessive online gaming, several longitudinal studies suggest that there is only limited temporal stability in Internet addiction (Rothmund, Klimmt, & Gollwitzer, in press). If the amplification effects of POPC on Internet addiction that have been assumed here can be substantiated empirically, it would therefore be important to investigate also whether these influences are temporally stable or whether excessive POPC behavior is a transition behavior that disappears with ongoing development. For example, patterns of addictive smartphone use might dissolve as a user undergoes the transition from late adolescence to early adulthood, or through appropriation and adaptation effects (Wirth, von Pape, & Karnowski, 2008).

Finally, the outlined idea of "technological homeopathy" for prevention and intervention needs empirical examination. Is it really possible to support users in handling their smartphone and online use effectively using tools installed on the same device that represents the source, origin, and object of addiction (Kwon et al., 2013)? Is there a risk of boomerang effects in smartphone-based prevention? Which kind of (at-risk) users will benefit from such support, and which subtype of IA may be easier to counteract this way than other subtypes?

Clearly, the emerging developments named POPC are not only altering daily life for many people fundamentally, but also have the potential to affect the risks, pathways, experiences, and outcomes of Internet addiction for today's and future generations. Advancing our theoretical understanding and investigating the intersections of POPC and IA empirically will therefore contribute to minimizing the harmful effects of the modern online world and to informing the entire field of behavioral addictions, their prevention and intervention alike.

References

APA (2013). *Diagnostic and statistical manual of mental disorders* (5th ed.). Arlington, VA: American Psychiatric Publishing.

Bakker, D., Kazantzis, N., Rickwood, D., & Rickard, N. (2016). Mental health smartphone apps: Review and evidence-based recommendations for future developments. *JMIR Mental Health*, *3*(1), e7. http://doi.org/10.2196/mental.4984

Bandura, A. (1986). *Social foundations of thought and action: A social cognitive theory.* Englewood Cliffs, NJ: Prentice Hall.

Bayer, J. B., Campbell, S. W., & Ling, R. (2016). Connection cues: Activating the norms and habits of social connectedness. *Communication Theory, 26*, 128–149.

Bayer, J. B., Ellison, N. B., Schoenebeck, S. Y., & Falk, E. B. (2016). Sharing the small moments: Ephemeral social interaction on Snapchat. *Information, Communication & Society, 19*(7), 956–977.

Bowman, N. D., Jöckel, S., & Dogruel, L. (2015). "The app market has been candy crushed": Observed and rationalized processes for selecting smartphone games. *Entertainment Computing, 8*, 1–9.

Brand, M., Laier, C., & Young, K. S. (2014). Internet addiction: Coping styles, expectancies, and treatment implications. *Frontiers in Psychology, 5*, 1256.

Brand, M., Young, K. S., & Laier, C. (2014). Prefrontal control and Internet addiction: A theoretical model and review of neuropsychological and neuroimaging findings. *Frontiers in Human Neuroscience, 8*, 375. doi:10.3389/fnhum.2014.00375

Brand, M., Young, K. S., Laier, C., Wölfling, K., & Potenza, M. N. (2016). Integrating psychological and neurobiological considerations regarding the development and maintenance of specific Internet-use disorders: An Interaction of Person-Affect-Cognition-Execution (I-PACE) model. *Neuroscience & Biobehavioral Reviews, 71*, 252–266. doi:0.1016/j.neubiorev.2016.08.033

Dong, G., & Potenza, M. N. (2014). A cognitive-behavioral model of Internet gaming disorder: Theoretical underpinnings and clinical implications. *Journal of Psychiatric Research, 58*, 7–11. doi:10.1016/j.jpsychires.2014.07.005

Dong, G., & Potenza, M. N. (2016). Risk-taking and risky decision-making in Internet gaming disorder: Implications regarding online gaming in the setting of negative consequences. *Journal of Psychiatric Research, 73*, 1–8. doi:10.1016/j.jpsychires.2015.11.011

Everitt, B. J., & Robbins, T. W. (2016). Drug addiction: Updating actions to habits to compulsions ten years on. *Annual Review of Psychology, 67*, 23–50. doi:10.1146/annurev-psych-122414-033457

Fauth-Bühler, M., & Mann, K. (2017). Neurobiological correlates of Internet gaming disorder: Similarities to pathological gambling. *Addictive Behaviors, 64*, 349–356. doi:10.1016/j.addbeh.2015.11.004

Griffiths, M. D. (2000). Does Internet and computer "addiction" exist? Some case study evidence. *CyberPsychology & Behavior, 3*, 211–218. doi:10.1089/109493100316067

Griffiths, M. D. (2005). A "components" model of addiction within a biopsychosocial framework. *Journal of Substance Use, 10*, 191–197. doi:10.1080/14659890500114359

Griffiths, M. D. (2012). Internet sex addiction: A review of empirical research. *Addiction Research and Theory, 20*, 111–124. doi:10.3109/16066359.2011.588351

Hefner, D., & Vorderer, P. (2016). Digital stress: Permanent connectedness and multitasking. In L. Reinecke & M.-B. Oliver (Eds.), *Handbook of media use and well-being* (pp. 237–249). New York: Routledge.

Kardefelt-Winther, D. (2014). A conceptual and methodological critique of Internet addiction research: Towards a model of compensatory Internet use. *Computers in Human Behavior, 31*, 351–354. doi:10.1016/j.chb.2013.10.059

Kuss, D. J. (2013). Internet gaming addiction: Current perspectives. *Psychology Research and Behavior Management, 6*, 125–137.

Kuss, D. J., & Griffiths, M. D. (2011). Online social networking and addiction: A review of the psychological literature. *International Journal of Environmental Research and Public Health, 8*, 3528–3552. doi:10.3390/ijerph8093528

Kwon, M., Lee, J. Y., Won, W. Y., Park, J. W., Min, J. A., Hahn, C., . . . Kim, D. J. (2013). Development and validation of a smartphone addiction scale (SAS). *PlOS One, 8*(2), e56936.

LaRose, R., & Eastin, M. S. (2004). A social cognitive theory of Internet uses and gratifications: Toward a new model of media attendance. *Journal of Broadcasting & Electronic Media, 48*(3), 358–377.

Lortie, C. L., & Guitton, M. J. (2013). Internet addiction assessment tools: Dimensional structure and methodological status. *Addiction, 108*, 1207–1216. doi:10.1111/add.12202

Markowetz, A., Błaszkiewicz, K., Montag, C., Switala, C., & Schlaepfer, T. E. (2014). Psycho-informatics: Big data shaping modern psychometrics. *Medical Hypotheses, 82*(4), 405–411.

Müller, A., Brand, M., Mitchell, J. E., & Zwaan, M. de (in press). Pathological online shopping. In M. Potenza (Ed.), *Online addiction.* Oxford: Oxford University Press.

Müller, K. W., Dreier, M., Beutel, M., Duven, E., Giralt, S., & Wölfling, K. (2016). A hidden type of Internet addiction? Intense and addictive use of social networking sites in adolescents. *Computers in Human Behavior, 55*, 172–177. doi:10.1016/j.chb.2015.09.007

Oulasvirta, A., Rattenbury, T., Ma, L., & Raita, E. (2012). Habits make smartphone use more pervasive. *Personal and Ubiquitous Computing, 16*, 105–114. doi:10.1007/s00779-011-0412-2

Piazza, P. V., & Deroche-Gamonet, V. (2013). A multistep general theory of transition to addiction. *Psychopharmacology, 229*, 387–413.

Przybylski, A. K., Murayama, K., DeHaan, C. R., & Gladwell, V. (2013). Motivational, emotional, and behavioral correlates of fear of missing out. *Computers in Human Behavior, 29*(4), 1841–1848.

Reinecke, L., & Hofmann, W. (2016). Slacking off or winding down? An experience sampling study on the drivers and consequences of media use for recovery versus procrastination. *Human Communication Research, 42*, 441–461.

Rothmund, T., Klimmt, C., & Gollwitzer, M. (in press). Low temporal stability of excessive video game play in German adolescents. *Journal of Media Psychology*.

Sariyska, R., Reuter, M., Bey, K., Sha, P., Li, M., Chen, Y. F., . . . Montag, C. (2014). Self-esteem, personality and Internet addiction: A cross-cultural comparison study. *Personality and Individual Differences, 61–62*, 28–33.

Tang, J., Yu, Y., Du, Y., Ma, Y., Zhang, D., & Wang, J. (2014). Prevalence of Internet addiction and its association with stressful life events and psychological symptoms among adolescent Internet users. *Addictive Behaviors, 39*, 744–747. doi:10.1016/j.addbeh.2013.12.010

Thalemann, R., Wölfling, K., & Grüsser, S. (2007). Specific cue reactivity on computer game-related cues in excessive gamers. *Behavioral Neuroscience, 121*(3), 614–618.

Thatcher, A., Wretschko, G., & Fridjhon, P. (2008). Online flow experiences, problematic Internet use and Internet procrastination. *Computers in Human Behavior, 24*, 2236–2254. doi:10.1016/j.chb.2007.10.008

Valkenburg, P. M., & Peter, J. (2011). Online communication among adolescents: An integrated model of its attraction, opportunities, and risks. *Journal of Adolescent Health, 48*(2), 121–127.

Weinstein, A., & Lejoyeux, M. (2010). Internet addiction or excessive Internet use. *American Journal of Drug and Alcohol Abuse, 36*, 277–283. doi:10.3109/00952990.2010.491880

Wirth, W., von Pape, T., & Karnowski, V. (2008). An integrative model of mobile phone appropriation. *Journal of Computer-Mediated Communication, 13*(3), 593–617.

Wu, J. Y. W., Ko, H. C., Wong, T. Y., Wu, L. A., & Oei, T. P. (2016). Positive outcome expectancy mediates the relationship between peer influence and Internet gaming addiction among adolescents in Taiwan. *Cyberpsychology, Behavior, and Social Networking, 19*(1), 49–55.

Young, K. S. (1996). Addictive use of the Internet: A case that breaks the stereotype. *Psychological Reports, 79*, 899–902. doi:10.2466/pr0.1996.79.3.899

Young, K. S. (2008). Internet sex addiction: Risk factors, stages of development, and treatment. *American Behavioral Scientist, 52*, 21–37. doi:10.1177/0002764208321339

Young, K. S., Pistner, M., O'Mara, J., & Buchanan, J. (1999). Cyber disorders: The mental health concern for the new millennium. *Cyberpsychology & Behavior, 2*, 475–479. doi:10.1089/cpb.1999.2.475

8
Multitasking
Does It Actually Exist?

Shan Xu and Zheng Wang

Multitasking is broadly defined as engaging in two or more activities at the same time. That involving at least one form of media is called media multitasking. Humans multitasked long before media technologies were invented (Smith, 2010). After our ancestors developed the ability to stand and walk on feet, their hands became available to engage in other tasks, such as tool making and fruit picking. These are the earliest multitasking activities. However, electronic media technologies invented in the past century have enabled multitasking in an unprecedented way. In the 1930s, it was already noted that two-thirds of a radio audience were involved in some other activities while listening to the radio, and among those under 30, the proportion approached three-quarters (Cantril & Allport, 1935). In the 1960s when television became the entertainment center for families in the United States, substantial percentages of audiences would "eat, drink, sleep, play, argue, fight, and occasionally make love" in front of the TV set rather than giving undivided attention to television programming (Allen, 1965, p. 6).

Over the past decade, multitasking with media has reached a new record as the versatility and accessibility of mobile devices, such as laptops, tablets, and smartphones, rapidly increased, allowing for integration of work, play, and social interaction everywhere and anytime (e.g., Rosen, Mark, & Cheever, 2013; Srivastava, 2013; David, Kim, Brickman, Ran, & Curtis, 2014). The prevalence of media multitasking is related to the emerging phenomena called permanently online and permanently connected (POPC; Vorderer & Kohring, 2013; Vorderer, Krömer, & Schneider, 2016). For example, in a recent investigation in the United States (Common Sense Census, 2015), teens reported that they "often" or "sometimes" use social media (50%) while doing homework, and even more say so about texting (60%) and listening to music (76%). Another study conducted in the United Kingdom reveals that 16- to 24-year-olds use media for 9.5 hours a day, of which 52% involves media multitasking (Ofcom & GfK, 2010). Similar prevalence of media multitasking has been documented across ages, countries, and cultures (e.g., Moisala et al., 2016; Xu, Wang, & David, 2016). The technology availability and the overt behavior of multitasking—often involving online media—agrees with the first dimension of POPC: permanently online, an overt behavior of constantly using online communication. The second dimension of POPC: permanently connected, a psychological state of wanting to connect via media technology with other people, places, and activities outside the immediate spatial context, has also been demonstrated in studies that explored multitasking's effect on social well-being (Pea et al., 2012; Misra,

Cheng, Genevie, & Yuan, 2014). Unsurprisingly, *Time* magazine has labeled young people today the "generation M"—the multitasking generation (Wallis, 2006).

However, does "multitasking" actually exist? With increasing attention on the phenomenon from the press and the public, as well as flourishing research from various perspectives using a myriad of methods, it is time to reflect on the concept of multitasking. If you are a media researcher, you probably have encountered situations when a news reporter or one of your aunts at a family gathering asks for your expert opinions, "Is multitasking so harmful?" Likely, the first sentence of a long answer goes, "It depends." Indeed, it depends on many factors, including what specific outcomes we are evaluating. For example, multitasking impairs cognitive and behavioral task performance, but may have some emotional benefits in certain contexts (e.g., Wang & Tchernev, 2012). So, we cannot draw simple conclusions on the effects of multitasking. However, first and foremost, the answer depends on how we define "multitasking" in the question.

In existing research, multitasking refers to engaging in two or more activities at the same time, and that involving media is called media multitasking. However, the terms "multitasking" and "media multitasking" cover numerous different types of specific behaviors that can vary dramatically in their nature, features, and effects. What is multitasking? Can we really do two things at once? How can we better define media multitasking? This chapter discusses the different types of multitasking behaviors and specifically the continuum of multitasking behaviors that ranges from serial to concurrent multitasking. Then it reviews the central bottleneck theories, multiple resource theories, and threaded cognition theory, all of which shed light on whether we can truly multitask. Finally, the concept of media multitasking is discussed in terms of a multidimensional framework and the level of analysis that can help us compare and synthesize the myriad media multitasking studies.

The Continuum of Multitasking Behaviors

Two types of multitasking behaviors have been identified (Lang & Chrzan, 2015): (1) task switching, or serial multitasking, such as switching back and forth between texting on a cell phone and reading a book, and (2) concurrent processing, or simultaneous multitasking, such as listening to music while reading a book. Actually, these two types of behaviors represent two ends of a continuum of multitasking behaviors. Essentially, the multitasking continuum can be defined in terms of "the time spent on one task before switching to another" (Salvucci, Taatgen, & Borst, 2009, p. 1819). For example, at one end of the continuum, reading a book and checking text messages on a cell phone from time to time involve relatively long intervals between task switches—perhaps minutes, or even hours. At the other end of the continuum are tasks perceived to be carried out simultaneously, such as listening to music while reading a book, and talking on a cell phone while walking.

The two ends of the multitasking continuum, or the two types of multitasking behaviors, both have stimulated a rich history of research. Typical task-switching paradigms require participants to perform tasks of short duration and switch between tasks, and the research has focused on the switch cost in response time and task performance (Salvucci, Taatgen, & Borst, 2009). Some studies along this line have examined real-world human-computer interaction tasks and evaluated the cost of interruptions and the resumption of tasks across different contexts, such as how the incoming instant messaging and emails impacted primary task performance (e.g., Cutrell, Czerwinski, & Horvitz, 2000).

Extensive research has been conducted on concurrent multitasking as well. For example, the well-known dual-task paradigm was developed in the 1930s to examine the cognitive process and response time needed to identify two simultaneously presented stimuli (Stroop, 1935; Telford, 1931). Meanwhile, research has tested concurrent multitasking performance in more applied, real-world contexts, including piloting (Jones et al., 1999) and driving (Strayer & Johnston, 2001).

Can We Do Two Things at Once? Competing Theories

Of the two types of multitasking behaviors, serial multitasking is common in our daily observation and practice, and is intuitive to understand. In contrast, simultaneous multitasking has provoked debate among scholars. Can we really do two things at once? Is simultaneous multitasking actually possible? Several theoretical perspectives provided insights into these questions.

According to the *central bottleneck theories*, multitasking is fundamentally sequential, as the human cognitive processing is confined by a single-channel structure, called processing central bottleneck (Welford, 1952; Pashler, 1998). The singular cognitive structure cannot handle two processes at the same time (Marois & Ivanoff, 2005). Consequently, during multitasking, the different tasks have to be lined up to be managed by the central cognitive structure. The information modalities involved in the tasks would not make any difference in this process, since the tasks requiring different modalities (auditory, visual, and motor) are in the same queue waiting to be processed by the central cognitive structure. Therefore, performance decrements in multitasking is an inevitable outcome. The central bottle theories have been supported by many empirical findings, including the well-known psychological refractory paradigm (PRP) and attentional blinks studies (e.g., Marois & Ivanoff, 2005). Functional magnetic resonance imaging (fMRI) research suggests that the posterior lateral prefrontal cortex and the superior medial frontal cortex regions may act as the central cognitive structures (Dux, Ivanoff, Asplund, & Marois, 2006).

However, *multiple resources theories* disagree with the central bottleneck theories and suggest that our minds can concurrently or simultaneously process several tasks, as long as they use separate resources (Navon & Gopher, 1979; Wickens, 2002). Multiple resources theories assume that there are different resource pools available for different cognitive functions, and different resource pools typically handle different modalities (Basil, 1994; Salvucci & Taatgen, 2008). When it comes to multitasking, the more similar the two tasks are in terms of their modalities, the more likely they are to compete for resources from the same pool and interfere with one another. Conversely, two tasks could be performed simultaneously as long as they draw primarily from separate resource pools. For instance, when music was introduced as a distraction in a reading task, there was no significant drop in performance compared with the control conditions without music (Pool, Koolstra, & van der Voort, 2003). Based on multiple resources theories, a plausible explanation for the benign effect of music on the reading task is that music primarily draws upon a resource pool for processing auditory information, and typically it does not compete for the visual resource pool being consumed by the reading task. However, in comparison, checking social media websites via smartphone requires the same visual attention and cognitive resources as those demanded by reading, thus it is expected to interfere with reading because of the direct competition for resources.

Threaded Cognition: A Theory of Multitasking

Threaded cognition theory (Salvucci & Taatgen, 2008) integrates central bottleneck theories and the multiple resources theories to explain when and how simultaneous processing and serial processing occur during multitasking. It posits the following assumptions. Cognitive resources have two components: a module "that performs the processing related to that resource" and a buffer associated with the module that serves as a communication channel between the module and a procedural module. Some modules deal with specific perceptions or motor activities, such as the visual module, the aural module, the manual module, and the vocal module, and others are central cognitive modules: (1) the declarative module refers to the storage of memory for information or knowledge including task instructions and (2) the procedural module connects and coordinates all other modules, integrates information, and directs new processing among modules. This procedural module has a goal buffer that stores information about the current goal and keeps track of the process.

In essence, the threaded cognition theory suggests that all modules can operate in parallel, but each module can serve only one task at a time. During multitasking, multiple tasks, or threads, are activated to execute simultaneously across modules, and these threads are coordinated by the procedural module. In dealing with competing requests or goals for the same module during task switching, the theory proposes that different threads share available modules through a greedy/polite policy: If a module is not in use, any of the threads can claim it (greed); however, once a thread is done with a module, it releases the module immediately for other threads to use (politeness).

Specifically, the theory posits that simultaneous processing of multiple tasks can happen if those tasks involve threads that utilize resources in different modules. Consider a common instance of a person jogging in the street while listening to music from his/her smartphone. This set of behaviors triggers several threads directed by the procedural resource pool to draw resources from multiple pools (motor, visual, and aural) to accomplish multiple goals (jogging, monitoring the traffic, and listening to music). The person can move legs, encode visual information of the traffic, and process the auditory information of the music at the same time without interference. Then, when the person suddenly thinks about what to cook for dinner, it adds one more thread in the procedural module to retrieve information from the declarative module. This new thread in the procedural and declarative resources is not in conflict with the existing threads that guides jogging, traffic monitoring, and music listening, and all these threads can be processed in parallel as long as the other threads involve tasks that are skilled and do not require declarative resources for task instruction.

However, sequential processing occurs at the level of a single type of resource. That is, each module (including the perceptual module, the motor module, and the central cognitive modules) can only execute one request at a time. If multiple requests are placed on the same module, only one thread can be processed at a time. Returning to the jogging and music example, if a notification sound rings on the phone indicating an incoming text message, this new environmental stimulus fires a new goal to the procedural module: Attend to the text message. However, there is already a thread in the procedural module demanding the resources in the visual module for traffic monitoring. The procedural resource only processes one request for the same resources at a time and similarly the visual module only processes one request at a time: either reading the text message or monitoring the traffic. If the text message takes a higher priority, this goal proceeds in the procedural resource, which guides the new thread to put new commands on the visual module besides a new thread to the motor module to take out the phone and read the text message. Perhaps another thread is added on the declarative module as well to query information related to the text message. Hence, the person shifts from monitoring the traffic to attending to the text message on the phone. In this case, the procedural module and the visual module can only process one request at a time and thus sequential multitasking is performed. In other cases, the declarative module can lead to sequential multitasking when two tasks both use memory for information retrievals or for retrievals of task instructions.

The Multidimensional Framework to Conceptualize Media Multitasking

Along the continuum of multitasking, there are literally numerous different multitasking behaviors. The terms "multitasking" and "media multitasking" are overly general and vague. It becomes problematic to synthesize the results of multitasking and media multitasking because of the great variety of multitasking behaviors covered by empirical studies. It is also challenging to make useful predictions of multitasking behaviors since new types of tasks and task combinations are enabled by the evolving media technologies at an unprecedented speed.

For example, one study tested three types of smartphone multitasking behavior when studying: texting, checking social media, and listening to music (David et al., 2014). Not surprisingly, the results found different impacts of these behaviors on the study performance: some (social media and texting) significantly jeopardize study outcome but some (music) do not. Even media multitasking behaviors with the same primary task (studying) and in the same context can result in diverging results, let alone those engaged in distinct task combinations and contexts. Thus, a more specific and systematic conceptualization of media multitasking behaviors is needed to delineate numerous media multitasking behaviors.

It is with this motivation that a multidimensional framework was proposed to help conceptualize media multitasking behaviors and help synthesize the large body of studies examining a myriad of different behaviors (Wang, Irwin, Cooper, & Srivastava, 2015). Based upon resourced theories and threaded cognition theory, as well as a large body of empirical research on information processing and multitasking, the authors have identified 11 cognitive dimensions in four categories: task relations, task inputs, task outputs, and individual differences. These dimensions can predict media multitasking choices in everyday life (Wang et al., 2015) and distinguish the effects of different media multitasking on cognition, attitudes, and psychological and social well-being (Jeong & Hwang, 2016). The specific 11 dimensions in four categories are summarized below.

The task relations category refers to how the tasks relate to each other within a certain multitasking activity. Five dimensions have been identified in this category. (1) *Task hierarchy*: whether a task is considered more important than others are, or if multiple tasks are relatively equal in significance. Goal regulation determines the allocation of mental resources to the tasks. (2) *Task switch*: the extent of control a person has in switching between or among tasks. For example, in the case of multitasking with a smartphone, texting allows more control on when to attend and respond to messages, while phone conversations dictate immediate attention and response from the users (Wang et al., 2012). (3) *Task relevance*: How do the multiple tasks relate to each other? Are they serving the same or a different purpose? Irrelevant tasks lead to greater performance impairment (e.g., Jeong & Hwang, 2016). (4) *Shared modality*: the degree of shared sensory modalities, such as auditory, visual, and motor modalities. A multitasking behavior should be less demanding and cause less performance deterioration when tasks are spread across multiple modalities, avoiding competing for resources in the same modality pools (e.g., Salvucci & Taatgen, 2008; Wang et al., 2012). (5) *Task contiguity*: the physical proximity of the multiple tasks. The task-switching cost will be reduced if relevant tasks are physically close to each other (e.g., Mayer & Moreno, 2002).

The task inputs category identifies three dimensions of the format and content of the multitasking stimuli. (1) *Information modality* refers to the type and number of modalities engaged by the stimuli of each task. Studies suggest that the more sensory modalities engaged, the more likely the interference will occur between tasks that share a common resource pool, and the greater mental load on the central procedural pool (e.g., Salvucci & Taatgen, 2008). (2) *Information flow* concerns the rate at which the stimulus information is presented to the user. This can range from static (e.g., text) to transitory (e.g., moving images and sound), and more specifically, can vary in pacing (e.g., slow-paced documentary, fast-paced music videos). Video and audio media content provide a lot of production features (e.g., camera changes, sound effects) that can elicit attentional orienting responses, and typically require more mental resources than static content does (Lang, 2000). (3) Lastly, *emotional content* refers to the valence and intensity of stimuli that can motivate resources allocation. Positive or negative emotional content can trigger activation of the appetitive and/or aversive systems, allocating cognitive resources toward or away from the content (Lang, 2006; Wang, Lang, & Busemeyer, 2011).

The third category is task outputs. Two dimensions have been identified. (1) *Behavioral responses* distinguish tasks that require a person to provide behavioral responses (e.g., responding to a phone conversation or playing video games) from those that do not (e.g., listening to music or watching a video). Tasks that require behavioral responses demand additional cognitive and motor resources. (2) *Time pressure* refers to whether a behavioral response is required within a short period of time. As time pressure increases, stress and arousal levels would increase, which will influence resource allocation.

Finally, a large number of individual differences have been identified that can influence multitasking choices and effects, such as mindfulness (i.e., Haller, Langer, & Courvoisier, 2012), content expertise (Lin, Robertson, & Lee, 2009), attentional styles (Hawkins et al., 2005), extraversion and neuroticism (Wang & Tchernev, 2012), and sensation seeking (Jeong & Fishbein, 2007). These variables can help predict both the likelihood and performance outcomes of media multitasking behaviors.

This multidimensional conceptualization of media multitasking allows us to better recognize media multitasking for the complex phenomenon that it is. It provides a theoretical structure upon which media multitasking research can be compared and synthesized, and predictions of the numerous media multitasking behaviors on cognition and well-being can be drawn (e.g., Jeong & Hwang, 2016; Xu et al., 2016). Let us return to the example showing inconsistent results of different media multitasking behaviors (music, social media, and texting) on study performance (David et al., 2014). The multidimensional framework would have predicted the diverging effects observed in the study. First, in terms of *task relations*, unlike texting and checking social media, listening to music does not compete for visual resources required for studying (i.e., low on shared modality). In addition, with regard to *task output*, compared with texting and checking social media that usually require interactive communication, listening to music does not demand behavioral responses (i.e., no behavioral responses and no time pressure). Thus, listening to music taxes fewer mental resources than do the other two media activities, allowing more resources to be allocated to studying. In addition, this dimensional framework can also help predict the multitasking choices. Evidence shows that people typically avoid more cognitive-demanding task combinations and favor easier ones (Wang et al., 2015). This suggests that self-selected media multitasking in daily life may be adaptive to our increasingly media-saturated environments.

The Level of Analysis

The multidimensional framework has provided a theory-based conceptualization of media multitasking. It points out how one multitasking behavior can dramatically differ from another. Related to the multidimensional framework is the level of analysis, which can also help us think about the concept of media multitasking. Consider a scenario where two activities are aligned under the same goal: A student is listening to the teacher's lecture and looking at the lecture slides at the same time. Is this multitasking or not? Again, it depends. It depends on at what level of analysis we are talking about the behavior.

Goals

Some research has defined multitasking as the performance of two or more tasks with separate, unique goals (Sanbonmatsu, Strayer, Medeiros-Ward, & Watson, 2013). This notion agrees with our intuitions about multitasking activities in everyday life. For example, a driver talks with a friend over the phone (for social purposes) while driving to the friend's home (for transportation purposes). Television viewers watch the news (for information-seeking purposes) and share the news with their social media friends using a tablet (for social purposes). These activities can be defined as multitasking at the level of different goals as pointed out, although these goals can be viewed as contributing to a bigger common goal (i.e., social). At the higher level of goals (e.g., visiting friends, sharing information), they also can be viewed as a single task. Similarly, the constituent tasks, such as driving, can be further reduced into a series of tasks, and can be analyzed as multitasking as well.

A large number of communication studies have examined multitasking activities that serve distinct goals. In particular, experimental research often uses the different goals to manipulate multitasking behaviors. For example, in one experiment, participants were instructed to achieve two distinct goals at the same time by carrying out a cognitive task (visual pattern matching) on a computer while having a social interaction with a peer by communicating either via instant messaging or voice chat on the computer (Wang et al., 2012). In another study (Jeong & Hwang, 2012), participants were reading persuasive arguments in print while using entertainment media (watching a movie).

Modalities and Features

Some activities are considered to be multitasking at the level of modalities. Returning to the example of a student listening to a lecture and reading the lecture presentation slides at the same time. These two activities serve the same goal of learning the lecture content, and thus can be considered a single task. However, they can also be considered multitasking at the level of modalities: auditory resources are directed to listening to the lecture, whereas visual resources are allocated to reading the slides. Similarly, replying to a text message, typically viewed as a single task in communication research, can be considered multitasking: Reading the message mainly involves the visual resources and comprehension processes while typing a response requires visual motor integration. Research on multimedia learning typically considers multitasking behaviors at the level of modalities (e.g., Moreno & Mayer, 1999).

Related to the level of task modality is the level of task features, such as the color, shape, moving direction, emotion, and semantics of the task objects or inputs. For example, in a singleton experimental paradigm in psychology, participants are asked to search for a singleton target among a number of distractors, where for example, target singletons are distinct from distractors in terms of their colors (e.g., van Zoest, Donk, & Theeuwes, 2004). At the level of specific features, participants need to examine all the singletons in different colors on a screen, either simultaneously or serially, to search for the target. Similarly, in an emotional Stroop task, neutral or fearful words are presented on top of neutral or fearful face images, and participants are asked to judge whether faces are neutral or fearful in expression while ignoring congruent or incongruent words (e.g., Krug, 2011). At the level of different visual presentations (text vs. image), participants have to focus on the emotional expression of the face and suppress their response to the distracting emotional words. As a feature can be further divided into subfeatures, and a cognitive process can be further defined by multiple subprocesses, a single-tasking behavior can be viewed as multitasking at a lower level of analysis.

An interesting example is facial processing. Looking at a face can be viewed as concurrent multitasking. Facial features are not perceived and analyzed separately, but processed as a whole unit or as a Gestalt (Galton, 1883). Through two widely used experimental paradigms, the composite face paradigm and the whole–part paradigm, researchers found that participants recognize facial features better when these features are embedded in the whole face stimulus than when they are presented separately (Tanaka & Farah, 1993), thus providing evidence for the argument that facial features are processing simultaneously. Thus, even for such a quick and simple task, at the level of facial features, the processing can be thought of as concurrent multitasking.

Time

Orders of magnitude being considered for the time scale in the analysis also determine whether an activity can be categorized as multitasking or not. Some task switching is fast, such as rapid switches between monitoring traffic and checking GPS maps during driving that occur at the subsecond to second time scale, and neurological sensory processing of multiple sensory modality inputs (e.g., visual, auditory, tactile, olfactory, taste) that occurs at the millisecond time scale. They can be viewed as either single-tasking at a higher level of time scale or as multitasking at a lower level of time scale.

Activities that take longer intervals (e.g., days, hours) to switch between tasks can be viewed as multitasking or single-tasking, depending on the time scale. For example, a student who multitasks between two course projects may focus on one project for hours or days before switching to the other. This may be viewed as single-tasking—that is, completing course projects—as well if the time scale being considered is the entire work time (for example, when examining how the students' work time affects their entertainment media use). Another typical example is multitasking "soccer moms." In North America, people call a mother who spends a lot of her time transporting her children to their sporting events and other extracurricular activities a soccer mom. They need to juggle their children's extracurricular activities, housework, and their own professional lives. If the level of analysis of the time is the period of being a soccer mom, then "being a soccer mom" may be considered a single task (for example, when comparing soccer moms' media use with that of career women without children).

Most multitasking studies, especially lab experiments, focus on rapid-switching multitasking, and only a paucity of research has investigated multitasking over longer intervals. This, at least partially, is because of the challenges associated with data collection of the latter. Newer methods in communication research, such as computer surveillance programs and experience sampling methods (e.g., Wang & Tchernev, 2012), have emerged to overcome the challenges. For example, a screenshot application was used to record participants' computer screens to monitor their multitasking behavior, and results showed that there were 1,584 switches across the 28 hours of time spent at the computer (Yeykelis, Cummings, & Reeves, 2014).

Concluding Comments

Media multitasking behaviors, most involving online media, is a manifestation of POPC, and probably both the means and consequences of POPC: always online, and always seeking for information, craving for entertainment, and longing for connectedness. On the one hand, multitasking is an adaptive function that enables organisms to survive and thrive in a complex environment that constantly imposes multiple demands on the organisms. In the past decade, the unprecedented development of and access to media technologies have enabled the unprecedented media multitasking trends. Based on the review of theories and empirical studies in this chapter, we can safely conclude that multitasking, including concurrent multitasking, indeed is possible. On the other hand, however, multitasking can be maladaptive. Multitasking can be an agent of its own, that is, multitasking itself can provide the contentment (or illusion) of time maximization resulted from simultaneous execution of more than one activity and accomplishing more than one goal. When the total demand of various tasks exceeds one's cognitive resources and such information overload may lead to a decrease in task performance, anxiety, and even depression (Becker, Alzahabi, & Hopwood, 2012), let alone life-threatening consequences such as car crashes caused by texting and driving.

It is worth pointing out that research on media multitasking's effect on social and psychological well-being have yielded inconsistent results (e.g., Pea et al., 2012; Xu et al., 2016). One reason could be that the terms "multitasking" and "media multitasking" are overly general and vague (Wang et al., 2015; Xu et al., 2016). They often refer to different behaviors in different empirical studies, which makes comparison and synthesis of the findings difficult. A multidimensional framework for conceptualizing the concepts can help overcome the challenge. Probably more importantly, the framework also offers a systematic, theory-guided way to help develop strategies to promote better, more mindful design and choices of media multitasking (Wang et al., 2015).

For example, exchanging text messages with friends during class can be detrimental for the comprehension of lecture material, as the two activities compete for the same visual resource, and the social interaction with friends is probably more stimulating than listening to a lecture and thus automatically attracts more attention. Hence, such multitasking activity could be maladaptive. However, the dimension of emotional content of multitasking behavior can be utilized for its motivational benefits. For example, listening to music while doing homework may increase enjoyment (Wang & Tchernev, 2012) and thus may motivate students to work longer and be more productive in the long run, especially if the media task is strategically designed to minimize its competition for the mental resources needed by the homework. In addition, based on the dimensions of task inputs and relations, we can design the media task to be relevant and contiguous to the homework task and to require different modality resources from those needed by the homework (Moreno & Mayer, 1999; David et al., 2014).

With emerging new media technologies, it becomes even more important to extend cognitive and communication theories to the exploding multitasking and POPC phenomena (e.g., Vorderer, 2016). How can media multitasking, under certain contexts, serve as a way to cope with the emerging social norms and personal needs of POPC? How does POPC determine media multitasking behaviors, and vice versa? Guided by the theories of multitasking and POPC, media multitasking research can inform practitioners and the public on how to safely and efficiently interact with environmental demands, including those imposed by media, and how to utilized media to make life and work safer, more efficient, and more enjoyable.

References

Allen, C. L. (1965). Photographing the TV audience. *Journal of Advertising Research*, *5*(1), 2–8.
Basil, M. D. (1994). Multiple resource theory I application to television viewing. *Communication Research*, *21*(2), 177–207.
Becker, M. W., Alzahabi, R., & Hopwood, C. J. (2012). Media multitasking is associated with symptoms of depression and social anxiety. *Cyberpsychology, Behavior, and Social Networking*, *16*(2), 132–135.
Cantril, H., & Allport, G. W. (1935). *The psychology of radio*. New York: Harper & Brothers.
Common Sense Census. (2015). *The common sense census: Media use by tweens and teens*. Retrieved from www.commonsensemedia.org/census.

Cutrell, E. B., Czerwinski, M., & Horvitz, E. (2000). Effects of instant messaging interruptions on computing tasks. In *CHI '00 Extended Abstracts on Human Factors in Computing Systems* (pp. 99–100). New York: ACM.

David, P., Kim, J.-H., Brickman, J. S., Ran, W., & Curtis, C. M. (2014). Mobile phone distraction while studying. *New Media & Society, 17*(10), 1661–1679. https://doi.org/10.1177/1461444814531692

Dux, P. E., Ivanoff, J., Asplund, C. L., & Marois, R. (2006). Isolation of a central bottleneck of information processing with time-resolved FMRI. *Neuron, 52*(6), 1109–1120.

Galton, F. (1883). *Inquiries into human faculty and its development*. London: Macmillan.

Haller, C. S., Langer, E. J., & Courvoisier, D. S. (2012). Mindful multitasking: The relationship between mindful flexibility and media multitasking. *Computers in Human Behavior, 28*, 1526–1532.

Hawkins, R. P., Pingree, S., Hitchon, J., Radler, B., Gorham, B. W., Kahlor, L., . . . Kolbeins, G. H. (2005). What produces television attention and attention style? *Human Communication Research, 31*, 162–187.

Jeong, S.-H., & Fishbein, M. (2007). Predictors of multitasking with media: Media factors and audience factors. *Media Psychology, 10*, 364–384.

Jeong, S.-H., & Hwang, Y. (2012). Does multitasking increase or decrease persuasion? Effects of multitasking on comprehension and counterarguing. *Journal of Communication, 62*(4), 571–587.

Jeong, S., & Hwang, Y. (2016). Media multitasking effects on cognitive vs. attitudinal outcomes: A meta-analysis. *Human Communication Research, 42*(4), 599–618. https://doi.org/10.1111/hcre.12089

Jones, R. M., Laird, J. E., Nielsen, P. E., Coulter, K. J., Kenny, P., & Koss, F. V. (1999). Automated intelligent pilots for combat flight simulation. *AI Magazine, 20*(1), 27.

Krug, M. K. (2011). *Cognitive control of emotion and its relationship to trait anxiety*. Unpublished dissertation. University of California, Davis, CA. Retrieved from http://search.proquest.com/docview/872842676/abstract

Lang, A. (2000). The limited capacity model of mediated message processing. *Journal of Communication, 50*, 46–70.

Lang, A. (2006). Using the limited capacity model of motivated mediated message processing to design effective cancer communication messages. *Journal of Communication, 56*, S57–S80.

Lang, A., & Chrzan, J. (2015). Media multitasking: Good, bad, or ugly? *Annals of the International Communication Association, 39*(1), 99–128.

Lin, L., Robertson, T., & Lee, J. (2009). Reading performances between novices and experts in different media multitasking environments. *Computers in the Schools, 26*, 169–186.

Marois, R., & Ivanoff, J. (2005). Capacity limits of information processing in the brain. *Trends in Cognitive Sciences, 9*, 296–305.

Mayer, R. E., & Moreno, R. (2002). Aids to computer-based multimedia learning. *Learning and Instruction, 12*(1): 107–119.

Misra, S., Cheng, L., Genevie, J., & Yuan, M. (2014). The iPhone effect the quality of in-person social interactions in the presence of mobile devices. *Environment and Behavior*, 1–24.

Moisala, M., Salmela, V., Hietajärvi, L., Salo, E., Carlson, S., Salonen, O., . . . Alho, K. (2016). Media multitasking is associated with distractibility and increased prefrontal activity in adolescents and young adults. *NeuroImage, 134*, 113–121.

Moreno, R., & Mayer, R. (1999). Cognitive principles of multimedia learning: The role of modality and contiguity. *Journal of Educational Psychology, 91*, 358–368.

Navon, D., & Gopher, D. (1979). On the economy of the human-processing system. *Psychological Review, 86*(3), 214–255.

Ofcom and GfK. (2010). *The consumer's digital day*. Retrieved from http://stakeholders.ofcom.org.uk/binaries/research/811898/consumers-digital-day.pdf

Pashler, H. (1998). *The psychology of attention*. Cambridge, MA: MIT Press.

Pea, R. Nass, C. Meheula, L., Rance, M., Kumar, A., & Bamford, H. (2012). Media use, face-to-face communication, media multitasking, and social well-being among 8- to 12-year-old girls. *Developmental Psychology, 48*(2), 327–336.

Pool, M. M., Koolstra, C. M., & van der Voort, T. (2003). The impact of background radio and television on high school students' homework performance. *Journal of Communication, 53*, 74–87.

Rosen, L. D., Mark Carrier, L., & Cheever, N. A. (2013). Facebook and texting made me do it: Media-induced task-switching while studying. *Computers in Human Behavior, 29*(3), 948–958.

Salvucci, D. D., & Taatgen, N. A. (2008). Threaded cognition: An integrated theory of concurrent multitasking. *Psychological Review, 115*, 101–130.

Salvucci, D. D., Taatgen, N. A., & Borst, J. P. (2009). Toward a unified theory of the multitasking continuum: From concurrent performance to task switching, interruption, and resumption. In *Proceedings of the SIGCHI Conference on Human Factors in Computing Systems* (pp. 1819–1828). New York: ACM.

Sanbonmatsu, D. M., Strayer, D. L., Medeiros-Ward, N., & Watson, J. M. (2013). Who multi-tasks and why? Multitasking ability, perceived multi-tasking ability, impulsivity, and sensation seeking. *PLoS ONE, 8*(1), e54402.

Smith, M. L. (2010). *A prehistory of ordinary people*. Tucson, AZ: University of Arizona Press.

Srivastava, J. (2013). Media multitasking performance: Role of message relevance and formatting cues in online environments. *Computers in Human Behavior, 29*(3), 888–895.

Strayer, D. L., & Johnston, W. A. (2001). Driven to distraction: Dual-task studies of simulated driving and conversing on a cellular telephone. *Psychological Science, 12*(6), 462–466.

Stroop, J. R. (1935). Studies of interference in serial verbal reactions. *Journal of Experimental Psychology, 18*, 643–662.

Tanaka, J. W., & Farah, M. J. (1993). Parts and wholes in face recognition. *The Quarterly Journal of Experimental Psychology Section A, 46*(2), 225–245.

Telford, C. W. (1931). The refractory phase of voluntary and associative responses. *Journal of Experimental Psychology, 14*, 1–36.

van Zoest, W., Donk, M., & Theeuwes, J. (2004). The role of stimulus-driven and goal-driven control in saccadic visual selection. *Journal of Experimental Psychology: Human Perception and Performance, 30*(4), 746–759.

Vorderer, P. (2016). Communication and the good life: Why and how our discipline should make a difference. *Journal of Communication, 66*, 1–12.

Vorderer, P., & Kohring, M. (2013). Permanently online: A challenge for media and communication research. *International Journal of Communication, 7*, 188–196.

Vorderer, P., Krömer, N., & Schneider, F. M. (2016). Permanently online—permanently connected: Explorations into university students' use of social media and mobile smart devices. *Computers in Human Behavior, 63*, 694–703.

Wallis, C. (2006). genM: The multitasking generation. *Time*. Retrieved from http://content.time.com/time/magazine/article/0,9171,1174696,00.html

Wang, Z., David, P., Srivastava, J., Powers, S. R., D'Ángelo, J., Brady, C., & Moreland, J. (2012). Behavioral performance and visual attention in communication multitasking: A comparison between instant messaging and online voice chat. *Computers in Human Behavior, 28*, 968–975.

Wang, Z., Irwin, M., Cooper, C., & Srivastava, J. (2015). Multi-dimensions of media multitasking and adaptive media selection. *Human Communication Research, 41*, 102–127.

Wang, Z., Lang, A., & Busemeyer, J. R. (2011). Motivational processing and choice behavior during television viewing: An integrative dynamic approach. *Journal of Communication, 61*, 71–93.

Wang, Z., & Tchernev, J. (2012). The "myth" of media multitasking: Reciprocal dynamics of media multitasking, personal needs, and gratifications. *Journal of Communication, 62*, 493–513.

Welford, A. T. (1952). The "psychological refractory period" and the timing of high-speed performance—a review and a theory. *British Journal of Psychology. General Section, 43*(1), 2–19.

Wickens, C. D. (2002). Multiple resources and performance prediction. *Theoretical Issues in Ergonomics Science, 3*, 159–177.

Xu, S., Wang, Z., & David, P. (2016). Media multitasking and well-being of university students. *Computers in Human Behavior, 55*, 242–250.

Yeykelis, L., Cummings, J. J., & Reeves, B. (2014). Multitasking on a single device: Arousal and the frequency, anticipation, and prediction of switching between media content on a computer. *Journal of Communication, 64*(1), 167–192.

9
Threaded Cognition Approach to Multitasking and Activity Switching in a Permanently Online and Permanently Connected Ecosystem

Prabu David

If mobile technology is the vehicle for a permanently online and permanently connected (POPC) life, multitasking is the road we take to cope with its demands. Being permanently on and connected requires allocation of attention to various activities that occur concurrently. At coffee shops near a university campus, we see students doing homework, listening to music, interacting via social media and at the same time chatting face to face with a friend. Likewise, at work, we see employees responding to emails, browsing the web, and taking meeting notes at the same time. In both scenarios, our POPC culture has invaded human interactions that for centuries had no competition.

It would be reasonable to think of POPC as the cause and multitasking as the symptom. Spurred by mobile media, it seems we are permanently on and connected. As a consequence, we are permanently multitasking as well (Carrier, Cheever, Rosen, Benitez, & Chang, 2009; David, Kim, Brickman, Ran, & Curtis, 2015). Multitasking involves pursuing multiple activities concurrently, and researchers have examined the motivations of multitasking (Kononova & Chiang, 2015; Wang & Tchernev, 2012) and its effects on learning (Rosen, Carrier, & Cheever, 2013), cognition (Ophir, Nass, & Wagner, 2009), work performance (Garrett & Danziger, 2007), and persuasion (Jeong & Hwang, 2016).

Despite the interest in POPC multitasking, because it is a relatively new phenomenon, psychological models of multitasking have not yet coalesced. While it is understood that multitasking is demanding on human resources such as attention, perception, and cognition, how these resources are coordinated during multitasking is not clear. One attempt at a comprehensive model is the theory of threaded cognition (Salvucci & Taatgen, 2008, 2010), which integrates perceptual, cognitive, and motor resources under a unified framework with both parallel and serial processing assumptions.

Threaded cognition, proposed as a computational model to simulate multitasking behaviors such as distracted driving, is best suited for concrete tasks with clear goals. The objective of this chapter is to extend threaded cognition to POPC multitasking, which is comprised of vague and emergent goals.

I begin by reviewing bottleneck (Broadbent, 1958), limited capacity (Kahneman, 1973; Lang, 2000), and multiple resource (Basil, 1994a; Wickens, 2002) theories, which are central to multitasking, and rely on Pashler's (1994) synthesis to connect these theories. This is followed by a review of threaded cognition (Salvucci & Taatgen, 2008, 2010) and the extension of threaded cognition to POPC multitasking, which is explained with a storyboard illustration. Finally, to expand threaded cognition to allow for multitasking activities with vague and emergent goals, a more prominent role for goals and motivation is proposed.

Multitasking and Boundary Conditions

Multitasking takes on different meanings based on context and disciplinary particularities. Research on multitasking can be found in areas such as human factors, computational theory, cognitive science, education, and communication. Though different explications of multitasking have been advanced by researchers from different disciplines, there are some common themes. Meyer and Kieras (1997) conceptualized multitasking as performing concurrent tasks, each with its own stimulus, response, and stimulus-response association. Salvucci and Taatgen (2010) explicated multitasking as performing multiple tasks within a timeframe by interleaving management and performance through multiple threads. Other researchers from education (Rosen et al., 2013) and communication (David, Xu, Srivastava, & Kim, 2013) characterize multitasking simply as the process of integrating multiple media-related activities at the same time.

Given the widespread prevalence of multitasking, it is not surprising that the topic has engendered interest in different disciplines. The breadth of interest also underscores the need for boundary conditions, which was addressed by Salvucci and Taatgen (2010), who described four groups of activities organized by time scale. Multitasking can be examined in the biological band, involving basic perceptual and cognitive processes that occur in milliseconds, such as the orienting response to an alert announcing a new message. The next level up is the cognitive band, which involves activities that take a few seconds, such as the cognitive process involved in encoding a text message or deciding whether to attend to or ignore the message. Then comes the rational band, which involves information processing and problem solving that may take many seconds or minutes, such as in exchanging text messages with a friend while responding to emails. The highest level is the social band, in which interactions evolve slowly, taking minutes, days, or even months, such as pursuing a relationship through ongoing messages, emails, phone conversations, and social media posts.

As activities move from the biological to the social band, responses become less automatic and more amenable to volitional control. For example, the orienting response to a sound or visual alert signaling a new text message may be automatic. But the cognitive task of ignoring the message is under volitional control, as are the subsequent responses to the message. The proposed model focuses on activities that are under volitional control, which limits the scope to activities that take a second or longer and are above the biological band.

Task Switching, Not Multitasking

Before proceeding, it is important to point out that the term multitasking is used loosely here, as it is elsewhere in the academic literature and in everyday parlance. The conflation of multitasking and task switching is common among laypersons and researchers alike, and the difference deserves attention (David et al., 2015). Multitasking occurs when two tasks co-occur simultaneously, in parallel, such as breathing and walking, driving and listening, playing the guitar and singing, or talking on the phone and emptying the dishwasher. Although rapid and very fine activity switching might occur in the biological band during concurrent activities, such as driving and conversing, to the observer it appears that both activities are being carried out simultaneously without a noticeable break. Likewise, listening to music when doing homework can be categorized as multitasking because the two activities occur concurrently, even though music may serve primarily as background noise.

In other situations, it is clear that activity switching is a more apt description for activities commonly referred to as multitasking. Take activities such as texting while doing homework, texting and driving, or social media and email. For such combinations, clean breaks and observable shifts occur between activities. One activity is temporarily placed on hold while attending to another, and such instances of multitasking are better categorized as activity switching. However, in popular culture and even among media researchers, multitasking is used interchangeably with activity switching. Despite the lack of clear differentiation in the literature between multitasking and activity switching, the distinction between the two is important to advance understanding of POPC multitasking.

Attention

In a POPC world, various activities compete for our attention. Attention is a finite resource, and its importance has been recognized by media scholars interested in the dual-processing of the audio and visual channels of television (Basil, 1994a, 1994b; Bergen, Grimes, & Potter, 2005; Lang, 2000, 2006). Attention, which is critical for multitasking, can be evaluated from two key perspectives—as a selection process and as a resource or capacity (Pashler, 1994).

Selective and Focused Attention

In a seminal study that sparked research on selective attention (Cherry, 1953), participants performed a dichotic listening task in which different messages were fed simultaneously to the right and left ears. When asked to attend to the message in one ear, participants were able to describe only the message that was attended to, but not the message in the unattended ear, thus demonstrating our ability to select from multiple inputs and also exposing our inability to process more than one input. The ability to select only one message was likened to a filtering mechanism.

Two categories of filter theories emerged to explain this effect—early and late selection theories—that differed in the stage of cognitive processing at which filtering occurred (Pashler, 1994). Proponents of early selection (Broadbent, 1958) believed that multiple inputs that reached the sensory system were processed quickly for certain key attributes, resulting in selective attention for one input that was submitted to semantic analysis and the filtering out of other inputs. Theorists who advocated late selection (e.g., Deutsch & Deutsch, 1963) proposed that all inputs are processed without filtering and that selective processing occurred only after some preliminary top-down analysis. They reasoned that stimulus filtering cannot be based solely on lower-level physical characteristics, but required some semantic processing.

Both early and late selection theorists allowed for the processing of only one input at a time, and their theories were challenged by findings from divided attention studies in which participants were able to perform more than one task simultaneously. To account for performance in divided attention tasks, Treisman (1960, 1964) proposed that filters may not completely block out unattended stimuli, but attenuate or reduce the probability of detailed processing of unattended stimuli. Though attenuation theory accounted for some of the limitations of filter theory, it was displaced by the divided attention paradigm.

Divided Attention Theories

In divided attention studies, researchers noticed that erosion in performance in dual-task situations varied by the nature of the tasks and the criteria used to assess performance. Two theoretical accounts emerged to explain performance deterioration in multitasking environments—central bottleneck and capacity limitation.

Central Bottleneck

Early research on multitasking was based on the PRP (psychological refractory period) paradigm (Pashler, 1999), which involves presentation of two stimuli in rapid succession (100–1,000 ms apart) and the analysis of response latencies or reaction time to each stimulus. As the duration between the two stimuli decreases (< 330 ms), respondents are slower to react to the second stimulus. Further, reaction time to the second stimulus is not affected by the match or mismatch in modalities between stimulus and response. One explanation for the slower response to the second stimulus is a processing bottleneck, or a serial processing mechanism that cannot perform two concurrent tasks. When the duration between the tasks increases to a half-second or more, the processor is not burdened by the previous task and the effect of the bottleneck disappears.

The central bottleneck theory supposes an insurmountable "hardware" limitation in human information processing, thus limiting attention to one task at a time. For decades, researchers found bottleneck theory to be compelling, because it offered a parsimonious account for a vast array of findings in the dual-task paradigm (Pashler, 1994). Unfortunately, bottleneck theory was unable to account for the human ability to attend to more than one task in some instances, which led to resource theory.

Resource Theory

While bottleneck theory limits cognition to serial processing, capacity or resource theory allows for parallel processing of concurrent tasks and offers an explanation for deterioration in performance during multitasking. Resource theory is founded on the reasoning that human capacity for processing is a limited resource that can be distributed to various tasks simultaneously (Kahneman, 1973). When multiple activities are attempted, they compete for the limited resources available in a common pool, and performance suffers when task demands exceed available resources. When task demands do not exceed resource capacity, the common pool of resources can be tapped by different activities at the same time, allowing for parallel processing.

Resource theory also invokes an executive function or cognitive control mechanism. When watching TV, for example, the executive function may automatically dispatch more resources to the audio or the video channel, sometimes giving preferential treatment to a channel to facilitate semantic processing (Basil, 1994a; Lang, 2000). In short, the executive function acts as a manager, allocating resources required to accomplish an activity, then retrieving control of these resources before dispatching them to another activity. When competing activities demand resources, it is the role of the executive function to decide which activity should receive priority.

A variant of resource theory is the multiple resource theory (Wickens, 2002), whose proponents have posited separate pools of specialized resources that operate in tandem. For example, perceptual and motor resources may reside in different pools. Further, within perceptual resources, the visual and auditory pools may be differentiated. By positing such distinct and specialized resource pools, we can explain multitasking such as listening to music (auditory resource) while operating a vehicle (primarily visual and motor resources).

In summary, both bottleneck and resource theories explain degradation in performance when multiple tasks are pursued, though each offers a different mechanism. While bottleneck posits a strict serial processor, resource theories offer a parallel processor with constraints. For a sufficient extension of resource theory to multitasking via mobile technologies, the role of goals and the longitudinal nature of multitasking interactions should be accounted for, which can be found in threaded cognition.

Threaded Cognition

By integrating bottleneck and resource theories and adding a number of original extensions, threaded cognition (Salvucci & Taatgen, 2008, 2010) offers a robust framework suitable for the longitudinal and perpetual use of multitasking in a POPC ecosystem. The central idea of threaded cognition is that activities can be translated into goals that can be maintained in cognition as autonomous threads. Although threads may be represented autonomously, they are interdependent because they compete for cognitive, perceptual, and motor resources that are shared among all threads. Perceptual resources are further divided into visual, aural, olfactory, and tactile, as developed in multiple resource theory. Likewise, motor resources may be further divided into resource pools that control various parts of the body, though for the purpose of communication and media multitasking, we focus only on hand motor function. Key resource pools used in threaded cognition are shown in Figure 9.1.

An important division of labor resides in the cognitive resource, which is divided into two distinct pools, declarative and procedural. While the chunks of knowledge are stored in the declarative resource, the procedural resource serves as the manager of the threaded cognition operation. When threads compete for resources, they have to go through the procedural resource, which acts as the coordinator or manager by evaluating needs and distributing resources.

The procedural resource has interesting attributes. The authors (Salvucci & Taatgen, 2008) characterize this resource as having a "liberal" management style, with a "tolerant and laissez-faire" approach in allowing threads to use resources. To prevent abuse or monopolizing of a resource by a rogue thread, threads are imbued with process etiquette values that make them greedy during consumption and polite after consumption. For example, consider the dangerous POPC activity of texting while driving. When the texting thread taps the visual resource to read a message, it grabs all the visual resources,

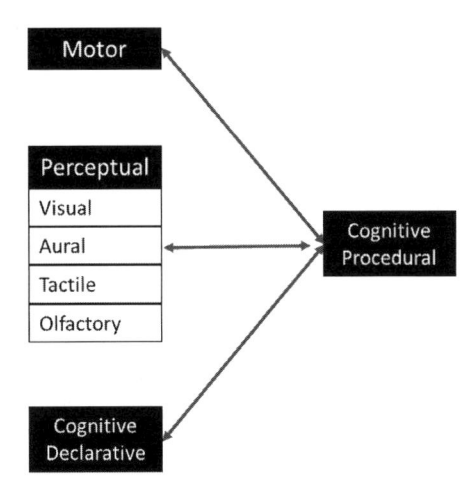

FIGURE 9.1 Key Resource Pools in Threaded Cognition.

Source: Salvucci & Taatgen (2008).

albeit briefly, from the driving thread. At the same time, the polite aspect of the process etiquette forces a quick release of the visual resource from the texting thread, which the driving thread quickly recaptures to avoid an accident.

Though multiple threads are held simultaneously, offering an illusion of parallel processing, autonomous threads alternate resources serially. This serial processing assumption of threaded cognition may run counter to our belief in the parallel processing capacity of neural networks. Yet, for multitasking activities in the cognitive, rational, and social bands, rapid serial processing is a more realistic description of the activity switching behaviors in the POPC ecosystem.

Despite the serial processing flavor in threaded cognition, the model uses parallel processing when allocating multiple perceptual resources. For example, while the visual resource may be fully utilized by the thread representing the driving goal, the aural resource may be simultaneously engaged by a conversation thread, in keeping with parallel processing findings from multiple resource theory.

To relate threaded cognition to real life, the authors of the theory (Salvucci & Taatgen, 2008) analogize it to a cook (procedural resource) who manages the various resources (oven, stove, and mixer) in a kitchen. The cook can use the oven, stove, and mixer simultaneously, which is akin to parallel processing. But once the cook places the fish in the oven, the cake has to wait its turn until the oven is free, which is akin to serial processing.

The kitchen analogy can be extended to POPC multitasking activities that are a mix of efficient parallel processes and some serial roadblocks that are immutable bottlenecks in the cognitive machinery. For example, when a homework thread is using the perceptual (visual) resource, the social media thread has to wait its turn to acquire the visual resources to read the latest on Snapchat, which in essence is a serial bottleneck. In contrast, the multitasking activity of listening to music and doing homework does not require a clean break from one to attend to the other because the auditory resource and visual resource can operate in parallel. Similarly, the motor resource needed for typing and the aural resource needed for listening to music can be processed in parallel.

To summarize, threaded cognition is a robust framework for examining POPC multitasking, with a number of appealing features. It is founded on the central idea that multiple goals can be maintained in cognition and each of these goals can be operationalized as an autonomous thread with its own resource needs. Each goal thread is divided into subgoals with a specific need for cognitive, perceptual, or motor resources. When a subgoal within a thread has access to a resource, that resource is temporarily unavailable to subgoals in other threads. Only when a thread releases a resource does it become available for subgoals in other threads, which causes bottlenecks. At the same time, threaded cognition allows for parallel processing of different resources. For example, when one thread is using the aural resource, the other thread can use the visual or motor resource. Thus, through a combination of serial and parallel processing, threaded cognition approximates both task switching and multitasking, two distinct behaviors that are commonly referred to as multitasking. Threaded cognition also allows for the role of practice, which makes multitasking easier over time by using less cognitive resources to accomplish perceptual and motor tasks. A storyboard illustration of threaded cognition in a typical homework scenario is presented in Figure 9.2.

The procedural resource manager plays the important role of coordinator in threaded cognition. It addresses conflict resolution and contention scheduling when multiple threads vie for scarce resources. Though functionally the procedural resource is similar to the executive function used in other models (Meyer & Kieras, 1997), the authors point out that the procedural resource is not a central or supervisory executive process. In their words, "multitasking emerges from the interaction of autonomous process threads" (Salvucci & Taatgen, 2008, p. 102) in accordance with the principles of the theory.

Homework	Music	Snapchat	Skype
Begins HW (V,M,D)			
	Decides on music: Yes (P)		
	Chooses playlist on mobile (V,M,D)		
Resumes HW (V,M,D)	Listens to music (A)		
		Snap alert: ignores (P)	
Resumes HW (V,M,D)	Resumes music (A)		
		Snap alert: attends (P)	
		Responds to Snap (V,M,D)	
Resumes HW (V,M,D)	Resumes music (A)		
			Skype alert: accepts (P)
			Video chat on Skype (A,V,D)
Resumes HW (V,M,D)	Resumes music (A)		

FIGURE 9.2 Storyboard Illustration of a POPC Scenario.

Note: Homework and music represent multitasking, whereas homework and Snapchat, or homework and Skype, represent task switching. V = visual resource, M = motor resource, A = aural resource, D = declarative, and P = procedural. D and P are components of the cognitive resource.

The idea that multitasking is simply an interaction among goal threads is appealing, because it represents a data-driven process that is representative of POPC behaviors. Yet, threaded cognition, which is driven by concrete goals, has to be loosened further to be useful for POPC multitasking. The computational model of threaded cognition has been validated in domains such as distracted driving, in which success is defined by right or wrong decisions signaled by pushing a button or applying the brake. Next, threaded cognition is extended to POPC multitasking in which various activities interact without clear, a priori goals.

Goals and Motivation

To extend threaded cognition to real-life situations, it should be robust enough to accommodate loose and emergent goals. Much of POPC multitasking is a combination of habit and spur-of-the-moment situated cognition that eventually becomes a goal with varying levels of clarity. To model such interactions in a threaded cognition framework, the goal module in the procedural resource needs to accommodate flexible goals.

Consider a typical combination of activities among POPC youth when doing homework, which includes listening to music via earphones and attending to bursts of interactions via messaging and social media. This cluster of activities would fall in the rational band, which was defined earlier. Despite the label, not all activities in this band are driven by clearly formed, rational goals. In multitasking scenarios, goals are typically amorphous and without clear criteria for success. In fact, work habits and habitual use of the media are made up of a mixture of goals that may seem to be in conflict with one another. For example, a student who wears earphones at a coffee shop to drown out background noise might appear to be pursuing conflicting goals—going to a noisy coffee shop in the first place and then trying to block out background noise by listening to music as background noise. But studying at a coffee shop may serve a social integration function and the student might find inspiration to study in the midst of other industrious students, which is in keeping with a POPC lifestyle.

In short, actions in the rational band are not necessarily rational, but they are under volitional control and amenable to rational evaluation, though rational self-evaluation is not a necessary condition. In general, multitasking interactions within the rational and social band follow a pattern of *loose, ill-formed*, and *emergent* goals with unclear criteria for *goal success*. Further, the goal module of threaded cognition should make room for activities whose utilities are not easily quantifiable, such as habitual use of music, browsing, or checking social media. For example, while writing this chapter, I am also browsing the Internet from time to time, checking Twitter, reading research articles by other researchers, and listening to music on Pandora. Perhaps that's the reason why it has taken me so long to finish this chapter.

But I find it difficult to articulate "why" I have chosen this cluttered, obviously inefficient, multitasking approach to writing rather than pursuing a single task with focused concentration. In part, I have been enticed by the offerings of a POPC lifestyle. As I ponder various motivations, different possibilities come to mind. Am I switching among these activities to make the writing task more enjoyable, am I using these activities as a procrastination strategy, or am I switching to other activities when I need inspiration or fresh ideas? I don't think I can point to one reason. It is likely a combination of all of the above and more. But I do know that despite my compulsive switching among activities, these activities are under my volitional control. And yet, despite knowledge of my suboptimal productivity, I persist with my POPC work habits. As I get closer to the deadline, however, my goals become more concrete and focused and multitasking is minimal and strategic.

To explicate the role of goals in POPC multitasking, each multitasking session can be conceptualized as a set of threaded interactions within a timeframe and each interaction as a cycle with a beginning, middle, and end. Such cycles, which were explicated and examined as hypermedia interaction cycles (David, Song, Hayes, & Fredin, 2007; Fredin & David, 1998) can be extended to POPC multitasking. Goals, however vague or ill formed, occur during the preparation phase, which is followed by an experiential phase, finally culminating in consolidation when the goals are evaluated. The outcomes of the evaluation of goals from a cycle influence goal setting for the next cycle, thus creating linked interaction cycles over time that constitute a session.

Motivation for Multitasking

The negative effects of multitasking on task performance are well documented in the literature (Srivastava, 2013; Wang et al., 2012; Xu, Wang, & David, 2016). In spite of these findings, POPC multitasking has become the norm, and it is hard to imagine that one is unaware of the potential erosion in task performance. After examining motivations for multitasking behaviors, Wang and Tchernev (2012) found that multitasking behaviors are not associated with task performance, efficiency, or gratification of cognitive needs, but strongly tied to emotional gratifications, including entertainment and avoidance of boredom. For example, listening to a talk show on the radio while driving may not enhance the quality of driving or the processing of the message on the radio, but it provides entertainment and alleviates boredom. In some cases, fulfillment of entertainment gratification in a multitasking situation may also contribute positively to cognitive performance. For example, in our example of listening to the radio while driving, a tired or bored driver may be able to better focus on driving because of the entertainment from the radio. Mildly distracted driving, in this instance, may improve rather than impair driving.

Motivations for communication and media use has a long history in media research under the umbrella of uses and gratifications (Katz, Blumler, & Gurevitch, 1973). One important distinction in this domain is between habitual use and instrumental use of media. Further, motivations such as alleviating boredom, relieving loneliness, seeking information, seeking entertainment, and simply using media as background noise have been identified. A recent study revealed that connection, control, entertainment, and addiction are the primary motivations for technology use (Kononova & Chiang, 2015). Increasingly, findings in the literature also point to addictive POPC behaviors facilitated by mobile technologies (Kim, Seo, & David, 2015).

In sum, findings suggest that motivation is an important part of POPC multitasking. During everyday activities such as driving, studying, watching television, talking with friends, or using mobile devices, the attention allocated to these activities is under volitional control. The resources allocated to a certain task at a certain time is a function of the motivation for a given task, and a function of other tasks pursued and the motivation for these tasks. Essentially, motivation serves as a weighting factor that can explain effort allocation and task persistence.

Extending Threaded Cognition to POPC Multitasking

Conceptualizing POPC multitasking activities as the interaction among autonomous threads is appealing, and the parallel and serial processing features of the theory approximate multitasking and activity switching behaviors that form the basis of a POPC life (see Figure 9.2). The extensions proposed in this section are intended to facilitate the application of threaded cognition to POPC activities.

If multitasking is under volitional control, Bandura's (2001) agentic perspective that humans have the innate capacity to actively shape behaviors suggests that self-efficacy can modulate multitasking in a POPC environment. Given the centrality of goals in threaded cognition, a more expansive conceptualization of goals is necessary to extend the theory to POPC multitasking. The number of threads active at a time, resources assigned to threads, interaction within and between threads, and persistence or decay of a thread are important descriptive metrics that should be informed by behavioral data. And goal-setting theory (Locke & Latham, 1984) offers numerous insights on goal properties, including goal clarity, that can be helpful.

Further, threaded cognition should accommodate emergent goals that change over time and include provisions for prioritizing goals. In the same vein, the model should allow for inclusion of habitual activities, such as listening to Internet radio, checking a favorite site or social media platform periodically, or having the television on for background noise. A more detailed handling of persistence and decay of goals is necessary to simulate the varying levels of goal persistence in POPC multitasking.

Threads also should come with affordances to adapt to different motivations, such as relational, emotional, or entertainment and to shifts in motivations over time. Similarly, threads should offer gateways for real-time data inputs for psychological variables such as affect, arousal, and flow.

With practice, we become more fluent with multitasking, and some tasks can be completed with fewer resources. Threads should account for practice effects and the social norms associated with real-world POPC multitasking. Also, threaded cognition should allow for individual differences, such as monochronicity and polychronicity (Poposki & Oswald, 2010).

Concluding Remarks

Threaded cognition was introduced as a theoretical vehicle to study and model POPC multitasking behaviors. Key components of theory were introduced and applied to various POPC examples. Using motivation and goals, various possibilities were presented to extend threaded cognition from computer simulations and laboratory studies to POPC multitasking. A deeper understanding of POPC multitasking can influence the design of affordances to make multitasking and activity switching more efficient, more enjoyable, less cumbersome, and less dangerous.

References

Bandura, A. (2001). Social cognitive theory: An agentic perspective. *Annual Review of Psychology*, *52*(1), 1–26. doi:10.1146/annurev.psych.52.1.1

Basil, M. D. (1994a). Multiple resource theory I: Application to television viewing. *Communication Research*, *21*(2), 177–207.

Basil, M. D. (1994b). Multiple resource theory II: Empirical examination of modality-specific attention to television scenes. *Communication Research*, *21*(2), 208–231.

Bergen, L., Grimes, T., & Potter, D. (2005). How attention partitions itself during simultaneous message presentations. *Human Communication Research*, *31*(3), 311–336.

Broadbent, D. E. (1958). The selective nature of learning. In *Perception and communication* (pp. 244–267). Elmsford, NY: Pergamon Press.

Carrier, L. M., Cheever, N. A., Rosen, L. D., Benitez, S., & Chang, J. (2009). Multitasking across generations: Multitasking choices and difficulty ratings in three generations of Americans. *Computers in Human Behavior*, *25*(2), 483–489. doi:10.1016/j.chb.2008.10.012

Cherry, E. C. (1953). Some experiments on the recognition of speech, with one and with two ears. *The Journal of the Acoustical Society of America*, *25*(5), 975–979.

David, P., Kim, J.-H., Brickman, J. S., Ran, W., & Curtis, C. M. (2015). Mobile phone distraction while studying. *New Media & Society*, *17*(10), 1661–1679. doi:10.1177/1461444814531692

David, P., Song, M., Hayes, A., & Fredin, E. S. (2007). A cyclic model of information seeking in hyperlinked environments: The role of goals, self-efficacy, and intrinsic motivation. *International Journal of Human—Computer Studies*, *65*(2), 170–182.

David, P., Xu, L., Srivastava, J., & Kim, J.-H. (2013). Media multitasking between two conversational tasks. *Computers in Human Behavior*, *29*(4), 1657–1663.

Deutsch, J. A., & Deutsch, D. (1963). Attention: Some theoretical considerations. *Psychological Review*, *70*(1), 80–90. doi:10.1037/h0039515

Fredin, E. S., & David, P. (1998). Browsing and the hypermedia interaction cycle: A model of self-efficacy and goal dynamics. *Journalism & Mass Communication Quarterly*, *75*(1), 35–54.

Garrett, R. K., & Danziger, J. N. (2007). IM= Interruption management? Instant messaging and disruption in the workplace. *Journal of Computer-Mediated Communication*, *13*(1), 23–42.

Jeong, S.-H., & Hwang, Y. (2016). Media multitasking effects on cognitive vs. attitudinal outcomes: A meta-analysis. *Human Communication Research*. doi:10.1111/hcre.12089

Katz, E., Blumler, J. G., & Gurevitch, M. (1973, May). *Utilization of mass communication by the individual*. Paper presented at the Conference on Directions in Mass Communication Research, Arden House, New York.

Kahneman, D. (1973). *Attention and effort*. Upper Saddle River, NJ: Prentice-Hall.

Kim, J.-H., Seo, M., & David, P. (2015). Alleviating depression only to become problematic mobile phone users: Can face-to-face communication be the antidote? *Computers in Human Behavior*, *51*, Part A, 440–447. http://dx.doi.org/10.1016/j.chb.2015.05.030

Kononova, A., & Chiang, Y.-H. (2015). Why do we multitask with media? Predictors of media multitasking among Internet users in the United States and Taiwan. *Computers in Human Behavior*, *50*, 31–41.

Lang, A. (2000). The limited capacity model of mediated message processing. *Journal of Communication, 50*(1), 46–70.

Lang, A. (2006). Using the limited capacity model of motivated mediated message processing to design effective cancer communication messages. *Journal of Communication, 56*(s1), S57–S80.

Locke, E. A., & Latham, G. P. (1984). *Goal setting for individuals, groups, and organizations.* Chicago, IL: Science Research Associates.

Meyer, D. E., & Kieras, D. E. (1997). A computational theory of executive cognitive processes and multiple-task performance. *Psychological Review, 104*(1), 3–65.

Ophir, E., Nass, C., & Wagner, A. D. (2009). Cognitive control in media multitaskers. *Proceedings of the National Academy of Sciences, 106*(37), 15583–15587. doi:10.1073/pnas.0903620106

Pashler, H. E. (1994). Dual-task interference in simple tasks. *Psychological Bulletin, 116*(2), 220–244.

Pashler, H. E. (1999). *The psychology of attention.* Cambridge, MA: MIT Press.

Poposki, E. M., & Oswald, F. L. (2010). The multitasking preference inventory: Toward an improved measure of individual differences in polychronicity. *Human Performance, 23*(3), 247–264. doi:10.1080/08959285.2010.487843

Rosen, L. D., Carrier, L. M., & Cheever, N. A. (2013). Facebook and texting made me do it: Media-induced task-switching while studying. *Computers in Human Behavior, 29*(3), 948–958.

Salvucci, D. D., & Taatgen, N. A. (2008). Threaded cognition: An integrated theory of concurrent multitasking. *Psychological Review, 115*(1), 101–130.

Salvucci, D. D., & Taatgen, N. A. (2010). *The multitasking mind.* New York; Oxford: Oxford University Press.

Srivastava, J. (2013). Media multitasking performance: Role of message relevance and formatting cues in online environments. *Computers in Human Behavior, 29*(3), 888–895. http://dx.doi.org/10.1016/j.chb.2012.12.023

Treisman, A. M. (1960). Contextual cues in selective listening. *Quarterly Journal of Experimental Psychology, 12*(4), 242–248. doi:10.1080/17470216008416732

Treisman, A. M. (1964). Monitoring and storage of irrelevant messages in selective attention. *Journal of Verbal Learning and Verbal Behavior, 3*(6), 449–459. http://dx.doi.org/10.1016/S0022-5371(64)80015-3

Wang, Z., David, P., Srivastava, J., Powers, S., Brady, C., D'Angelo, J., & Moreland, J. (2012). Behavioral performance and visual attention in communication multitasking: A comparison between instant messaging and online voice chat. *Computers in Human Behavior, 28*(3), 968–975. doi:10.1016/j.chb.2011.12.018

Wang, Z., & Tchernev, J. M. (2012). The "myth" of media multitasking: Reciprocal dynamics of media multitasking, personal needs, and gratifications. *Journal of Communication, 62*(3), 493–513.

Wickens, C. D. (2002). Multiple resources and performance prediction. *Theoretical Issues in Ergonomics Science, 3*(2), 159–177. doi:10.1080/14639220210123806

Xu, S., Wang, Z., & David, P. (2016). Media multitasking and well-being of university students. *Computers in Human Behavior, 55, Part A*, 242–250. http://dx.doi.org/10.1016/j.chb.2015.08.040

PART III
Social Dynamics of POPC
Self, Groups, and Relationships

10
Living in the Moment
Self-Narratives of Permanently Connected Media Users

Thilo von Pape

Scroll back through your Facebook timeline and compare the information that you and your Facebook friends have posted over the years for recurring events, such as Christmas or summer holidays. You may notice the following evolution: If your account reaches far enough back in time, then the first posts probably include numerous photographs with some text that provides a context for the depicted moments. In that distant past, pictures were sideloaded from a digital camera to a PC and then selected and edited using photograph management software in a cumbersome process for which you probably had no time until the event was over. Scrolling forward toward the present, status updates will appear which you managed to share during the course of the events, because you could share them directly from your smartphone during short breaks. In the more recent past, these momentary posts have increased because photograph and social media apps have made the selection, enhancement, and sharing of events increasingly simple, even proactively suggesting readily prepared pictures. As an ultimate point in the evolution, the "live video" feature allows an individual to continuously stream experiences in real time. The granularity and rhythm of narrating one's life, I maintain, has changed from a succession of discrete, sporadically exposed, and elaborate segments of different experiences to a more fluid series of snapshots emerging from situations in a seamless process. Through this evolution, the numerous tasks that were originally demanded from users to structure snapshots of their life into larger narratives have been made obsolete or have been taken over by technology.

Of course, this process extends beyond Facebook. In the past, people presented holiday memories through slideshows or lengthy accounts on the telephone rather than through the occasional pressing of a "share" button. What has propelled this process forward was not solely the evolution of one social networking service but a combination of more profound technological and social shifts. The most evident of these shifts is mobility in digital communication. As Campbell (2013, p. 10) emphasizes, "the affordance of mobility . . . allows for flows of information and communication to be more seamlessly weaved into the rhythms of everyday life." Exemplary mobile technologies that afford a flow of information without any disturbance in an ongoing activity are the Apple watch's feature that allows an individual to continually share his or her heartbeat, and self-tracking apps for athletes that automatically share their statistics after their workout is concluded.

The broader premise of this chapter is thus that, currently, permanently connected (PC) media users have the ability to immediately record and share events in real time, foregoing the effort to elaborate upon these bits into narratives and instead leave these tasks to their online social network's "timeline" or other forms of storytelling afforded by technology. The ensuing questions I want to ask are, provocatively put, the following: Are we not missing out on something? How can we observe the larger pictures of our lives and connect the proverbial dots of our experiences to overarching lines if we account for them solely through isolated snapshots? To put it in more differentiated and open terms: How does being permanently connected change the ways in which we narrate the events of our lives, experience their meaning and, more generally, experience meaningfulness in our lives?

These questions are ultimately empirical, yet they involve a number of premises and principles that should be first considered in view of existing literature. This chapter collects and structures these concepts and insights and will begin with the concept of meaningfulness, its preconditions with respect to the experience of events over time, and the different types of meaning that one may sense and need. We will then address how PC accounts may differ from default personal narratives in the ways in which they can provide meaningfulness. This involves both the question of how narrators express and experience meaningfulness during ongoing situations and how they are supported by technology in this work. The chapter concludes with analyzing the reflections in a broader context and by exploring possibilities to empirically study them.

Instant Meaningfulness

Happiness and a meaningful life overlap and often positively influence each other; however, they are distinct goals and depend on distinct conditions. In their proposition to theoretically and empirically distinguish between happiness and meaningfulness, Baumeister, Vohs, Aaker, and Garbinski (2013, p. 505) described happiness as "subjective well-being" and applied this concept both narrowly to a positive affect balance and more broadly to satisfaction in life. To distinguish happiness from meaningfulness, these authors relied on the Aristotelian distinction between hedonic well-being as feeling happy and the eudaimonic well-being as living a good life. They conceived of meaningfulness as being more central to living a good life. Meaningfulness is largely independent of happiness, because it both constitutes an altogether different goal and depends on different preconditions. Of particular interest for our questions is that Baumeister et al. (2013, p. 506) determined that the cause of the independence in the disposition of meaningfulness is time:

> One crucial advantage of meaning [over happiness] is that it is not limited to the immediately present stimulus environment. Meaningful thought allows people to think about past, future, and spatially distant realities . . . meaning can integrate events across time.

This allows individuals to perceive even moments of hardship in a positive light by anticipating a future for which they have labored, as Aeneas does in his famous address to a shipwrecked crew: "Forsan et haec olim meminisse iuvabit"—"An hour will come, with pleasure to relate/Your sorrows past, as benefits of Fate" in Dryden's (Virgil, 1997, p. 10) translation.

The construction of meaning, or "meaning-making" (Baumeister & Vohs, 2002, p. 613), is "an active process through which people revise or reappraise an event or series of events." Taylor (1989, p. 48) specified the precondition for this, "making sense of my present action . . . requires a narrative understanding of my life, a sense of what I have begun which can only be given in a story." Empirical studies have linked the cognitive process of creating self-narratives to experiencing meaningfulness, albeit primarily in the context of coping with negative events (Park, 2010).

This concept has substantiated the initial question of whether living in the instance of permanently connected accounts of life events may impede our ability to experience the greater picture that provides meaning to our lives. The concept of meaningfulness also provides guidance for further reflection. Baumeister (1991) proposed that there are four components of the need for meaningfulness in life. For a more differentiated perspective on how communication in a state of permanent connectedness ("PC communication") may influence our meaning-making, we rely on the following framework: *Purpose* endows meaning to present events because individuals are "able to interpret present events in relation to future events" (Baumeister, 1991, p. 56). *Value* can "serve as an independent source of justification and legitimacy" (Baumeister, 1991, p. 107). *Efficacy* is individuals' belief "that they have some control over events" (Baumeister, 1991, p. 41). Individuals' need for *self-worth* is "the need to make sense of their lives in a way that enables them to feel they have a positive value" (Baumeister, 1991, p. 44).

Narrators Entangled in the Moment

To provide a comprehensive understanding of how PC self-narratives may influence the process of meaning-making across the evoked needs for meaning, we will consider the various dimensions of personal narratives. In regards to literary linguistics, Ochs and Capps (2001) developed a widely used five-dimensional framework. Each dimension consists of a continuum between two poles as follows: (1) *tellership* (one vs. multiple tellers), (2) *tellability* (high vs. low noteworthiness of the narrative), (3) *embeddedness* (high vs. low detachment from the surrounding activity), (4) *linearity* (closed vs. open temporal and causal order), and (5) *moral stance* (certain and constant vs. uncertain and fluid). The origin of the resulting multidimensional space, uniting all of the poles that were evoked first in the above enumeration (one active teller, high noteworthiness, etc.), is defined by Ochs and Capps (2001, p. 20) as the "default narrative of personal experience"; what deviates from this origin, hence, distinguishes a specific type of narrative.

If we consider the seamlessness in which content is shared in PC communication as its essential characteristic, then the primary dimension for PC narratives may be their temporal *embeddedness* in the surrounding activity. This embeddedness refers to the crucial condition for the experience of meaningfulness, i.e., to consider an event detached from its current context and in relation to other points in time that may endow it with meaning.

To illustrate, we use the example of a live video recorded at a birthday party during the moment that the cake is brought into the room. For most PC accounts, the video is deeply embedded in the situation, because it is produced and perceived in synchronicity with the event it depicts. It is seamless because the parent filming the event is able to pursue various activities within the recorded situation, e.g., sing a birthday song or admonish the children regarding the danger of candles. Therefore, the narrative deviates from the default of high detachment from the ongoing situation posited by Ochs and Capps (2001). The narrator is involved in the ongoing situation, which does not allow for reflections that extend beyond the situation to be integrated into the film, and the parent probably does not consider them. Retelling the situation instead from a different and temporarily more detached context, the parent may have integrated the event into a larger narrative and possibly experienced meaningfulness through this integrated perspective. This meaningfulness could be achieved through a phone conversation during the same evening when the parent may sense the meaningfulness of the effort of baking the particular cake or during the compilation of a photograph album at the end of the year when the parent notes how all the children have grown up over time.

Linguists who observed self-narratives in social media have suggested a tendency toward shorter narrative units. Specifically, Page (2010, p. 440) noted, "Given the trend toward using mobile devices ... for connecting to Internet services, the importance of small narrative units in online text capable of episodic distribution looks set to continue." Empirical studies regarding self-narratives in social media that emerge out of permanent connectedness also confirm the high temporal embeddedness of numerous shared stories in the ongoing events. The type of account this applies to is described as being "characterized by the present tense of 'Breaking News'" (Page, 2010, p. 423, cf. Dayter, 2015) or as "developing news stor[ies]" (Papacharissi, 2015, p. 28). As this analogy with journalistic genres implies, these formats do not lend themselves easily to the creation of stories, because they continuously evolve and may continue to take unexpected turns while the narrator struggles to grasp them. Papacharissi (2015, p. 36) noted "temporal and other incompatibilities between live blogging the news and reporting" and stated that journalists who wanted to transmit live events lacked the time to process information into a more narrative report. If these difficulties apply to professional narrators, we expect them to apply just as well to untrained media users who share their personal content.

To consider how sharing this type of account may impact the experience of meaning in life, we will focus on the two components that are most directly linked to the experience of time. Both the sense of purpose and the sense of efficacy are experienced through linking the present with other moments in time. In the case of purpose, these are goals for the future; in the case of efficacy, these are past efforts that have had an impact. These links with other points in time are unlikely to be established in narratives that are limited to the present moment. Kaun and Stiernstedt (2014, p. 1161) observed such limitations in using Facebook during the age of smartphones: "Facebook users' temporal experience is one of immediacy, ephemerality, 'liveness,' and flow: to be immersed in an atmosphere and an interface of rapid change and forgetfulness, rather than of remembrance and preservation." Indeed, a comparatively low degree of meaningfulness from Facebook use was detected by Sagioglou and Greitemeyer (2014, p. 361) experimentally. "Namely, it appears that, compared to browsing the Internet, Facebook is judged as less meaningful, less useful, and more of a waste of time, which then leads to a decrease in mood." These authors' study focused on browsing Facebook rather than on posting messages to it, but it seems plausible that the temporal focus on the present has a similar effect on sharing as it does on receiving Facebook posts. However, research regarding the meaningfulness of social media's ephemeral communication is far from conclusive. In their mostly qualitative study of Snapchat users' experiences, Bayer and colleagues (Bayer, Ellison, Schoenebeck, & Falk, 2016, p. 26) identified ephemerality as key to the experience of meaningfulness in otherwise meaningless events: "the meaningfulness of Snapchat communication stems in part from the sharing of insignificant slices of personal life 'in the now.'" The context from which the meaning emerges is, in these cases, not a larger narrative but the plain "here and now" of the moment. Still, the question remains whether such instantaneous experiences of meaningfulness sustain over time or are ephemeral in themselves, such as instantaneous experiences of happiness.

In summary, we expect that accounts of personal events shared through PC communication lack a detachment from the ongoing situation, which is a default criterion of narratives of personal experience, and we expect this to impede users from obtaining a larger sense of how these particular events integrate into larger contexts that may provide a sense of meaningfulness. However, it is important to note that we are not referring to PC narratives in general but only to certain specific narratives in combination with other characteristics. In addition, it is unclear whether PC narratives displace the traditional, more elaborate narratives that would be related after an event or instead complement traditional narratives. One may argue in favor of the displacement hypothesis that any ex-post narrative would be spoiled by PC communication giving away its highlights and possible dramaturgical turns. However, PC communication can also serve as a teaser for the more elaborate ensuing narrative. Both spoiling and teasing should not only be considered in the quantitative terms of competition but also with respect to the content and functions fulfilled by the narratives; ex-post narratives may not become less frequent but less linear in their structure because any attempt to create suspense is made futile by spoilers provided to the audience through PC communication. If an ex-post narrative follows up on PC communication, the narrative may also become more dialogic, because the narrator first needs to take stock of what the listeners have already learned about the narrated event through the PC communication. Narrators may also diminish cues they provide by PC communication deliberately to build up suspense for the ex-post narrative. Therefore, before drawing any alarmist conclusions, we must consider other characteristics of these and other types of posts.

Meaning Provided by Artificial Tellers

A second dimension relevant to narratives of personal experience is *tellership*. According to the default for narratives of personal experiences (Ochs & Capps, 2001), self-narratives have only one teller, the self. However, as previously demonstrated, a teller involved in PC communication may be limited in the capacity to create a narrative that goes beyond a snapshot because he or she is involved in other ongoing activities. Furthermore, this may be compensated for in another manner, because the PC narratives we are dealing with here deviate from the norm; they are often provided with the assistance of two co-tellers.

The first type of co-teller includes individuals in the forms of the "friends" and followers with whom posts are shared. This type of co-tellership has been extensively addressed in previous studies regarding "networked narratives" (Page, Harper, & Frobenius, 2013). Co-tellers may ask the principle teller to provide additional context to the post to make it more meaningful. For instance, questions may include the following: How long did you prepare this activity? Why do you do it? Other individuals may enhance the meaning of shared events through their comments. Therefore, an account of an experienced episode may be complemented with suggestions of possible subsequent episodes, carrying the overall narrative in a particular direction. These comments may provide additional meaning to an episode (e.g., by providing someone who shares a difficult situation with an outlook on a possible positive future outcome). However, it may also conflict with the desired meaning; e.g., when information is added that questions the meaning expressed through the post. Page et al. (2013) provided an example of a teller who sought comfort because of the necessity to leave his hometown by observing that it was raining; he was contradicted by a friend who stated that the sun was coming out again.

Another type of co-teller is even more directly involved in PC communication. This type of co-teller does not contribute ex-post and through a clearly demarked comment but interferes in the very process of creating and sharing. Users increasingly delegate the construction of a narrative to a technological co-teller. Similar to human co-tellers, technology can compensate for the narrative shortcomings caused by the distractions of the primary teller and reintegrate elements that fulfill different needs for meaningfulness.

One very basic and widely used form of such technological co-tellership is the application of photograph filters. The most prevalent filters include a type of "faux vintage" effect, resembling the appearance of Polaroid photographs or antique 8-mm movies. This effect compensates for the embeddedness of snapshots used in PC accounts in their context of creation by detaching the photographs from that context. By enhancing the photograph with attributes of antiquity, they create what Jurgenson (2011) referred to as "nostalgia for the present." In his analysis of photographs with a faux-vintage effect, Bartoleyns (2014, p. 67) stressed that this detachment from the ongoing flow allows the snapshots to become meaningful. While we experience the present as a "series of isolated activities . . . not connected to one another in any significant way [,] the backward-looking aesthetic appears to be a way of cordoning off the time we find so hard to inhabit." This may be further explained with respect to the need for purpose. By presenting the present as the past, the viewer of the photographs is projected into a future moment for which the tasks at hand may be considered as achieved; that "hour" of the previously mentioned Virgil (1997) quote that one may relate with the pleasure of labors that one has endured in the past; for example, raising children.

More elaborate examples of technological tellers include videos and albums automatically generated by Facebook ("A year in review") and Google ("Auto-Awesome Movie," "Google+ Stories") that utilize past status updates or photographs and videos. These features constitute a complex endeavor involving such tasks as the selection of images and films, the cropping, cutting, and arranging of scenes, the application of special effects such as nostalgic or punk filters and transitions, the addition of background music, and the integration of metadata through contextualizing titles or maps. Google (2014, para. 3) advertises its "Stories" as a tool that provides meaningfulness without the cognitive burden demanded of storytelling:

> No more sifting through photos for your best shots, racking your brain for the sights you saw, or letting your videos collect virtual dust. We'll just gift you a story after you get home. This way you can relive your favorite moments, share them with others, and remember why you traveled in the first place.

Indeed, an experience of self-worth emerges from seeing oneself as the protagonist of a well-designed, professionally made "movie." A sense of efficacy may also be experienced from the pure scope and chronology of the video, because it summarizes a year or a vacation as something that was accomplished. By generating "Auto-Awesome Movies" along the aesthetic lines of certain genres both visually and acoustically, Google also endows personal footage with references to different values. The genre "punk" alludes to energy and raw individualism, the genre "glamour" alludes to consumerist values, and the genre "8 mm" arguably alludes to family values. However, this remains very limited when compared to the references a human teller or co-teller may make to values.

Various examples demonstrate that technological co-tellers may dramatically alter the stories against the users' understanding and will. In regard to self-worth, "The Verge" (2015) reported an example of the "On this day now" Facebook feature that brings users' posts from one year ago to their attention. In one case, a user was presented with a post in which he had expressed regret about rejecting a friend who died shortly after. The user was thus confronted with a shameful memory. Tiso (2014) reported an incident regarding a Google+ Story where the purpose of a voyage was incorrectly calculated by the algorithm. What had been a painful travel to the funeral of an individual's mother was presented as a banal holiday trip, "Reduced to a set of twenty-four pictures, that trip as it was presented to me by Google meant something else, something less. . . . it became the trite account of a holiday like any other."

A technological co-teller retroactively allows single shared photographs of life posts to include additional narrative and integrates them into a larger narrative structure. One example is the timeline feature of social networking sites. According to van Dijck (2013), the introduction of Facebook's

Timeline in 2011 emphasized the concept of presenting oneself through a linear narrative. Van Dijck (2013, p. 206) emphasized the unwanted consequences of this for users, who "were also expected to switch their presentation strategies from 'sending messages' to 'telling stories.'" However, it is unclear to what extent this has resulted in a greater awareness of the embeddedness of particular posts into larger narratives on Facebook. The previously quoted study regarding a great sense of immediacy in Facebook by Kaun and Stiernstedt (2014) was conducted after the timeline was introduced and suggested that its effect in raising awareness of larger narratives would be limited.

In sum, both human and technological co-tellers compensate for the shortcomings of PC human tellers who are engrossed in ongoing situations and solely provide snapshot accounts of their experiences. By integrating user comments and technological means, these accounts can evolve into extensive narratives and provide additional opportunities to perceive meaningfulness. However, this is accompanied with a loss of control over the narrative and the meaning that may emerge.

Perspectives

This essay began with a somewhat alarming question whether the ways in which we narrate our experiences when permanently connected may deprive us from experiencing meaningfulness in our lives. The ability to share every event in real time allows us to avoid the labor of compiling our experiences into larger stories but may also deprive us of the benefits of that exercise in experiencing meaningfulness. Thus exposed, this problem is similar to the alarmist scenarios described by Carr (2010) in his admonition regarding the Internet's threat to make us "shallow"; indeed, one might parallel the starting point with a quotation from Carr (2010, p. 108): "A personal letter written in, say, the nineteenth century bears little resemblance to a personal e-mail or text message written today. Our indulgence in the pleasures of informality and immediacy has led to a narrowing of expressiveness." However, we pose the problem as an open question and provide a theoretical conceptualization of possible causes, effects, and mechanisms linking them. The more closely we analyzed the question on this basis, the more nuanced it presented itself. Numerous other differentiations should be noted and premises should be tested that have not been discussed in this chapter. Therefore, the conclusion will address remaining questions regarding the levels of phenomena, theory, and method.

One phenomenon that needs closer analysis is technological tellership. On a general level, it is plausible that when the labor of constructing the narrative shifts entirely from a human to an algorithm, then no meaning-making occurs by the human during this production process. Therefore, technology may compensate for human shortcomings in the making of narratives but not in the making of meaning. However, it is possible that technology would not control the entire narrative task of meaning-making but support the human teller. An example is Google's Auto-Awesome Movies that are presented as finished movies but allow users to change essential aspects. Users can select from a variety of genres ("punk," "glamour," "8 mm," etc.), change the title and background music, and delete or modify images or sequences. Perhaps this leaves the most efficient component of meaning-making to the user, empowering him or her to eventually make more meaning in less time than would have been possible without such tools. For this assumption, it would still be important to understand the subtle influence that the algorithm has on meaning-making. How may these algorithms bias our perception of purpose, value, self-worth, and efficacy? As the previously quoted Tiso (2014, para. 12) stated regarding the individual who felt misunderstood by the Google+ Story album of his trip to the funeral of his mother, this may alienate the user from his own story, "I could go on allowing Google to document every future trip of mine in this way and find myself, years from now, with a perfect record of the life of a perfect stranger."

One fundamental theoretical issue that may help the analysis of the phenomenon of technological tellership regards the cognitive processes that take place during meaning-making. Thus far, we have treated these cognitive processes as an unknown, considering both the narrative particularities of the media and the needs of meaningfulness but not the processes that lead from one to the other. One approach used to analyze meaning-making and identify boundary conditions is the "Meaning Making Model" proposed by Park and Folkman (1997) and further developed by Park (2010). This model suggests important distinctions, such as "global meaning" as "individuals' general orienting system" (Park, 2010, p. 258) and "situational meaning" as the meaning experienced in a particular situational context. While meaning-making processes on the basis of the appraisal of specific events contribute to the experience of "global meaning," this is perceived as an indirect and very conditional process. This model may allow the investigation of the sustainability of meaningfulness that is experienced in instantaneous and ephemeral communications such as Snapchat (Bayer et al., 2016). This model has been applied for this purpose in research regarding the experience of meaningfulness by dementia patients (Menne, Kinney, & Morhardt, 2002).

Finally, empirical questions should be addressed. On a most basic level, these empirical questions concern the premise that individuals tend to share smaller, more momentary experiences when our media use evolves toward a state of being permanently connected. This premise is plausible on the basis that certain prior studies regarding communication through social media (Page, 2010; Sagioglou & Greitemeyer, 2014), and ephemeral technologies such as Snapchat underscore it further (see Bayer et al., 2016). However, it remains a hypothesis until empirically tested, and it is challenging to identify the right sample and indicators for such a test. One content analytical approach may utilize the self-experiment in Facebook with which this essay began. A proxy for increasing connectedness may be the adoption of mobile technologies, such as smartphones and specific apps. Indicators for a change in the narrative form of shared content include the frequency of posting in personal accounts, the length of the posts, and the scope of the temporal references to the present, past, and future. However, in the analysis of such a single-platform sample, other underlying trends would need to be controlled for. These trends include the following: individuals generally share less content on Facebook (The Information, 2016), the type of content individuals share on Facebook has changed from personal to general interest, and sharing in general and sharing of personal content, in particular, has shifted from Facebook to other platforms such as WhatsApp or Snapchat. Any general assertions regarding users' self-narratives, such as the hypothesis of PC narratives displacing traditional narratives, may depend on measures of the frequency and/or length of traditional self-narratives. Studies should include the indicators for all elements of the narrativity (embeddedness, which is only partially included in the question of timing, tellership, tellability, linearity, and moral stance), because it is plausible to expect that these elements manifest themselves differently in PC narratives than in traditional narratives and have different influences on the meaning-making. Finally, the experience of meaningfulness along with its components should be studied both in the immediate context of the creation and reception of self-narratives (e.g., in experimental settings) and over longer periods of time.

The theoretical and empirical efforts outlined in this chapter are immense and could not be undertaken in a solitary effort. However, the question of meaningfulness is also the focus of other studies regarding the consequences of being permanently connected, such as well-being (see Reinecke, this volume) and privacy (see Trepte and Oliver, this volume). Furthermore, the question regarding how permanently connected users experience meaningfulness when narrating their experiences is not simply a question regarding media effects. Such an analysis may advance the quest to understand "why we all seem to be online more and more even though it apparently doesn't work to our full advantage" (Vorderer & Kohring, 2013, p. 190). For example, the distinction between "global meaningfulness" and "situational meaningfulness" proposed by Park and Folkman (1997) may explain why users in search of meaningfulness use Snapchat despite the limitations that such an ephemeral form of communication apparently has for the traditional practice of making meaning of one's life through self-narratives. Perhaps the meaning these users seek when using Snapchat is of a very limited and situational nature. What would this imply in regards to the experience of meaningfulness in life? This chapter does not respond to this question but hopefully provides a proper vantage point for pursuing it.

References

Bartoleyns, G. (2014). The instant past: Nostalgia and digital retro photography. In K. Niemeyer (Ed.), *Media and nostalgia* (pp. 51–69). London: Palgrave Macmillan.
Baumeister, R. F. (1991). *Meanings of life*. New York: Guilford Press.
Baumeister, R. F., & Vohs, K. D. (2002). The pursuit of meaningfulness in life. In C. R. Snyder & S. H. Lopez (Eds.), *Handbook of positive psychology* (pp. 608–618). Oxford: Oxford University Press.
Baumeister, R. F., Vohs, K. D., Aaker, J. L., & Garbinski, E. N. (2013). Some key differences between a happy life and a meaningful life. *The Journal of Positive Psychology, 8*, 505–516.
Bayer, J. B., Ellison, N. B., Schoenebeck, S. Y., & Falk, E. B. (2016). Sharing the small moments: Ephemeral social interaction on Snapchat. *Information, Communication & Society, 19*(7), 956–977.
Campbell, S. W. (2013). Mobile media and communication: A new field, or just a new journal? *Mobile Media & Communication, 1*(1), 8–13.
Carr, N. (2010). *The shallows: How the Internet is changing the way we think, read and remember*. London: Atlantic Books.
Dayter, D. (2015). Small stories and extended narratives on Twitter. *Discourse, Context & Media, 10*, 19–26.
Google (2014). *Google+ stories and movies: Memories made easier*. Retrieved August 4, 2016, from http://googleindia.blogspot.de/2014/05/google-stories-and-movies-memories-made.html
The Information. (2016). *Facebook struggles to stop decline in 'original' sharing*. Retrieved August 4, 2016, from www.theinformation.com/facebook-struggles-to-stop-decline-in-original-sharing
Jurgenson, N. (2011, May 14). The faux-vintage photo: Full essay (parts I, II, and III). *The Society Pages*. Retrieved August 4, 2016, from http://thesocietypages.org/cyborgology/2011/05/14/the-faux-vintage-photo-full-essay-parts-i-ii-and-iii/
Kaun, A., & Stiernstedt, F. (2014). Facebook time: Technological and institutional affordances for media memories. *New Media & Society, 16*(7), 1154–1168.
Menne, H. L., Kinney, J. M., & Morhardt, D. J. (2002). 'Trying to continue to do as much as they can do' theoretical insights regarding continuity and meaning making in the face of dementia. *Dementia, 1*(3), 367–382.
Ochs, E., & Capps, L. (2001). *Living narrative: Creating lives in everyday storytelling*. Boston, MA: Harvard University Press.
Page, R. (2010). Re-examining narrativity: Small stories in status updates. *Text & Talk, 30*(4), 423–444.
Page, R., Harper, R., & Frobenius, M. (2013). From small stories to networked narrative: The evolution of personal narratives in Facebook status updates. *Narrative Inquiry, 23*(1), 192–213.
Papacharissi, Z. (2015). Toward new journalism (s) affective news, hybridity, and liminal spaces. *Journalism Studies, 16*(1), 27–40.
Park, C. L. (2010). Making sense of the meaning literature: An integrative review of meaning making and its effects on adjustment to stressful life events. *Psychological Bulletin, 136*(2), 257–301.
Park, C. L., & Folkman, S. (1997). Meaning in the context of stress and coping. *Review of General Psychology, 1*(2), 115–144.
Reinecke, L. (2017). POPC and well-being: A risk-benefit analysis. In P. Vorderer, D. Hefner, L. Reinecke & C. Klimmt (Eds.), *Permanently online, permanently connected: Living and communicating in a POPC world* (pp. 233-243). London: Routledge.
Sagioglou, C., & Greitemeyer, T. (2014). Facebook's emotional consequences: Why Facebook causes a decrease in mood and why people still use it. *Computers in Human Behavior, 35*, 359–363.

Taylor, C. (1989). *Sources of the self: The making of the modern identity*. Cambridge, MA: Harvard University Press.

Tiso, G. (2014). *We can remember it for you wholesale*. Retrieved from https://overland.org.au/2014/10/we-can-remember-it-for-you-wholesale/.

Trepte, S., & Oliver, M. B. (2017). Getting the best out of POPC while keeping the risks in mind: The calculus of meaningfulness and privacy. In P. Vorderer, D. Hefner, L. Reinecke & C. Klimmt (Eds.), *Permanently online, permanently connected: Living and communicating in a POPC world* (pp. 107–115). London: Routledge.

van Dijck, J. (2013). 'You have one identity': Performing the self on Facebook and LinkedIn. *Media, Culture & Society, 35*(2), 199–215.

The Verge (2015). *Facebook on this day nostalgia app bringing back painful memories*. Retrieved August 4, 2016, form www.theverge.com/2015/4/2/8315897/Facebook-on-this-day-nostalgia-app-bringing-back-painful-memories

Virgil. (1997). *Virgil's aeneid* (J. Dryden, Trans.). London: Penguin.

Vorderer, P., & Kohring, M. (2013, Feature). Permanently online: A challenge for media and communication research. *International Journal of Communication, 7*, 188–196.

11
Getting the Best Out of POPC While Keeping the Risks in Mind

The Calculus of Meaningfulness and Privacy

Sabine Trepte and Mary Beth Oliver

POPC is a phenomenon of communication that has recently been defined "1) As an overt behavior in the form of protracted use of electronic media and 2) as a psychological state of permanent communicative vigilance" (cf. for a similar distinction: Walsh, White, & Young, 2010), where one dimension may exist without the other (Vorderer, Krömer, & Schneider, 2016, p. 695; also see Klimmt, Hefner, Reinecke, Rieger, & Vorderer, this volume). Vorderer and Kohring (2013) earlier described the phenomenon as "constantly changing between reception and communication, thereby focusing on connection per se rather than on content" (p. 3). Vorderer (2015) added that the ubiquity of being connected with other people is one of the core characteristics of being POPC.

Being permanently online and permanently connected (POPC) provides users with broad opportunities for meaningfulness, in other words, for the opportunity to tackle meaning-in-life questions. In a state of POPC, users permanently and vigilantly produce and read content that supports them in their need for interconnectedness; they learn from other peoples' lives and stories with the aim of living a fulfilling life; they stay in touch with others to find answers for questions of virtue and wisdom. However, in online environments, not all that is meaningful for others can be shared. Content often not only discloses information about the person sharing it, but also information about third parties. Further, content being shared can easily be forwarded, archived, or falsely interpreted. Consequently, in addition to providing opportunities for meaningfulness, being POPC raises questions of privacy.

Although being POPC may allow individuals to more fully realize the benefits of meaningful communication, it also demands that users manage their privacy in these contexts. We will argue that POPC crucially intensifies meaningfulness and offers users enormous gratifications, but also puts more stress on individuals to deal with the challenges around their privacy. We conclude that POPC can be understood as having an intensifying effect on positive as well as risky online behaviors and as such can be a challenge to its users.

How and Why Social Media Use Affords POPC

Being POPC is mostly experienced within social media and thus with media that are designed to produce and exchange content and verbal messages. The most prominent examples of social media are social network sites such as Facebook; services that allow the exchange of pictures and videos such as Instagram or YouTube; and instant messaging services that are either stand-alone services or embedded into other services named above. Additionally, social media enable a great variety of uses, including chatting, messaging, posting, commenting, and publicizing, among others. In other words, there is no single way to use Facebook or Instagram. These services may be adjusted, modified, and interpreted by users. The various uses of social media have previously been defined as "affordances" (Chemero, 2003). Social media might set limits on what is possible but also allow for a broad array of different uses (Hutchby, 2001).

Social media particularly afford and facilitate POPC. This can be demonstrated along the lines of the two defining criteria of POPC: protracted use of electronic media and permanent communicative vigilance. First, social media—along with smartphones and mobile Internet connection—allow constant availability of online content and communication. In Ellison and Vitak's (2015) review of social network site (SNS) affordances, they particularly emphasized the visibility of content and its persistence as SNS affordances. Further, they emphasized that users can be connected with others and can maintain large networks of friends at very low cost. As such, the social media infrastructure clearly affords its protracted use.

Second, the technical infrastructure affords a psychological state of permanent communicative vigilance. For example, WhatsApp messages come in every other minute, and news is pushed to the user several times a day. The variety of services is wide, seems to proliferate its features by the second, and gets more advantageous for users when answered and monitored around the clock and across the world. The technical infrastructure is particularly designed to suit the users' needs and interests, and it demands a high amount of vigilance—in other words, it serves to heighten motivation to share content and to monitor the online social context and communication.

In sum, being POPC can take many forms, but we believe that social media affordances represent a confluence of factors that situate social media use as particularly important in encouraging constant connection and monitoring of online communication. In the next section, we consider how social media, in addition to being a form of communication, can also be considered a form of entertainment and can thus be experienced as both enjoyable and meaningful.

Social Media Communication as Entertainment

A rich body of research has dealt with how social media and POPC behaviors are driven by and affect social gratifications (Ellison & Vitak, 2015). However, we can also consider social media as entertaining media. For example, Kim, Sohn, and Choi (2011) showed that "seeking entertainment" was the most important motive of social network site use in the United States and Korea. Likewise, Quinn (2016) showed in a US sample that users find "entertainment" (use of social media for enjoyment, pleasure, and relaxation) to be as important as information sharing. Only using SNSs as a habit or for communication was rated to be more important than entertainment in this study. Similarly, Masur and Scharkow (2016) showed that among the different types of information that users post on SNS status updates or share in private messages, the category of "What I like or enjoy" is the one that is most frequently disclosed.

Whereas communication is the *purpose* of use, enjoyment seems to be the most important *user experience* accompanying it. In keeping with a growing body of scholarship suggesting at least two types of gratifications associated with media entertainment, social media, too, are likely to be associated with two forms of processing and user enjoyment: one being perhaps the most overt and observable type:

hedonic enjoyment (see Bartsch & Schneider, 2014; Oliver & Raney, 2014; Tamborini, 2012; Vorderer & Reinecke, 2015). On their Facebook walls, on Instagram, or in SoundCloud, users share funny pictures and stories that are likely to induce such forms of hedonically pleasant enjoyment. The second type of enjoyment elicited during social media use may be eudaimonic entertainment experience. In other words, users seek meaningfulness while sharing content online—an argument that we elaborate upon below.

Foundational Theories of Media Enjoyment

Popular conceptualizations and foundational theories of media use have tended to characterize it largely in hedonic terms (Zillmann & Bryant, 1994), with individuals described as using media (and particularly entertainment) as a means of maximizing pleasure and minimizing pain (Zillmann, 1988). In many respects, evolving forms of entertainment technologies including social media may be understood to be an extension and further illustration of hedonic media use. On Facebook, people view and share photos of their vacations, beautiful children, and exciting lifestyles; on YouTube, users post silly and sometimes hilarious videos of talking cats, "epic fails," and cute babies cooing for the camera; Tinder users browse through pictures to see their potential partners or sexual exploits; and on Snapchat, individuals share silly, trivial, or even incriminating photos that fade into oblivion after only a few seconds. In short, social media may be the ultimate in hedonic entertainment, as it appears to focus on the banal, the trivial, and the ephemeral (see Turkle, 2011).

With this background in mind, the last several decades have seen a shift among entertainment scholars who are taking notice of the nonhedonic or the *eudaimonic* and *meaningful* functions of media entertainment (Oliver & Bartsch, 2010; Oliver & Raney, 2014). Although a specific conceptual definition of what constitutes meaningful entertainment experiences has yet to be fully articulated, typical types of content and typical audience motivations and responses have been noted. In terms of content, scholars have argued that meaningful media content tends to be more somber or serious than typical hedonic fare, and hence dramas, tragedies, and sometimes inspiring or otherwise emotionally challenging content is frequently seen among examples of meaningful fare (Bartsch & Hartmann, 2015). Other scholars have suggested that meaningful entertainment tends to focus on human virtue, consistent with what the word "eudaimonic" implies. Here, content featuring characters displaying uncommon acts of courage, resilience, kindness, or wisdom are thought to be characteristic of meaningful content, as are portrayals of the suffering that individuals may experience when virtues are abandoned (Bartsch & Mares, 2014; Oliver & Bartsch, 2011; see also Lewis, Tamborini, & Weber, 2014; Tamborini, 2012). Still yet, other scholars have suggested that meaningful entertainment tends to focus on content that grapples with weighty concerns regarding meaning-in-life questions, including the human condition, the finitude of existence, or what gives us purpose (Hofer, 2013; Oliver & Hartmann, 2010).

With all of this background in mind, it is important to note that what constitutes *meaningful* media has been examined (largely) in the context of narrative content. That is, the experience of meaningful content has been studied in the context of traditional media such as film or literature, and it has therefore been implicitly conceptualized as something that individuals consume rather than something that individuals create, interact with, or share. Yet it is obvious that in today's landscape, media experiences are not simply passively consumed: People dance around their living rooms to Wii games, they photograph their environments (and particularly themselves) with their ever-present phones, and they create videos to be shared by (potentially) millions of people on YouTube. As a consequence, it is important that media scholars broaden the scope of their research regarding meaningful media to include considerations of newer technologies, and particularly those that are ever-present and have thus become part of our everyday lives—POPC.

POPC Behaviors and Meaningful Communication

Just as scholars have suggested that individuals' consumption of traditional media may be driven by both hedonic concerns (pleasure) and eudaimonic concerns (meaningfulness), we, too, believe that experiences of being POPC may be predicted by similar needs. We recognize that many scholars and essayists have expressed concerns that newer technologies are not only trivial in and of themselves, but that they also serve to trivialize real-life interactions that are now photographed or recorded as Facebook fodder, or that serve as the ever-present backdrop to face-to-face interactions that are constantly interrupted by text messages and social media alerts (Misra, Cheng, Genevie, & Yuan, 2016; Oliver & Woolley, 2015; "Phone stack," 2014; Przybylski & Weinstein, 2013; Sweet, 2012; Turkle, 2011). Despite the general scholarly and popular characterization of newer technologies and social media in particular as hedonistic or trivial, we believe that meaningfulness can be considered one of the most important POPC experiences.

We suggest that there are two aspects of being POPC that particularly address meaningfulness. First, meaningfulness is generated by the opportunity that POPC provides for individuals to connect with one another on a disclosive, personal level that can be deeply gratifying and very meaningful. POPC experiences constantly increase and intensify contact among a host of individuals who may not only share common interests, but also share a common history (e.g., elementary-school classmates) (Ellison & Vitak, 2015). As such, it holds promise of strengthening ties that may have faded otherwise and of also potentially triggering nostalgic, bittersweet thoughts of pleasant or meaningful histories (Chung, 2016).

Second, as POPC experiences are permanent, ubiquitous, and highly salient, they increase not only the quantity of what is shared (cf. protracted use of electronic media), but also the quality of how it is shared (cf. permanent communicative vigilance). Further, the popularity of inspiring media outlets (e.g., *Upworthy*, good news on *Huffington Post*, etc.) points to the idea that *meaningful* or *inspiring* content has an important place in newer forms of technologies. As such, when the motivations around meaningful communication are high and salient, meaningful content will move up in the individual's hierarchy of emotions to be aware of and information to process. Consistent with this reasoning, recent research suggests that individuals are particularly likely to share media content when it is perceived as meaningful, moving, or awe-inspiring (Berger & Milkman, 2012; Myrick & Oliver, 2015).

Although the sharing and self-disclosure that accompanies meaningful experiences in social media contexts may result in higher levels of social support and, hence, enhancements to self-esteem (Oh, Ozkaya, & LaRose, 2014), social media differ in many ways from face-to-face communication and are typically very far from confidential or discreet. Personal statements or photos about one's personal desires, sorrows, or even adolescent exploits that may be meaningful when shared with close others may also be overly disclosive or even incriminating when posted on social networking sites (Xie & Kang, 2015). As a result, one of the most potentially *meaningful* uses of being POPC may also make users more *vulnerable*. Therefore, the balance between meaningfulness and privacy in a POPC environment is a new consideration not readily applicable to more traditional media and therefore deserves our more careful consideration.

Privacy Needs in POPC Communication

Privacy is one of the major drivers of our behaviors, emotions, and cognitions. It can be understood as a process of optimizing and balancing the wish to exchange information with other people and the need to withhold (Altman, 1974). In addition, privacy describes an individual's balancing the needs of either being with others or being alone (Altman, 1975). Both needs can be considered basic human needs and have been shown to be crucial for well-being, both mentally and physically (Margulis, 2003; Vinsel, Brown, Altman, & Foss, 1980). This perspective has been shown to apply to both offline and online communication.

Again, we suggest that there are three aspects of being POPC that crucially pertain to privacy. First, POPC is defined as protracted electronic media use. Previous research has demonstrated how much privacy has become an issue of electronic media use (Trepte & Reinecke, 2011). We will not review the last 10 years of privacy research in detail here, but will mention that the individual management and negotiation of what information to share with others and what to withhold has become one of the most crucial questions of online communication. It goes without saying that because of the quantity of electronic media use, POPC is particularly apt for the importance of these kinds of privacy issues.

Second, POPC experiences are mostly communicative experiences in differing contexts. For privacy, this means that the users have to negotiate privacy between online and offline worlds, as POPC is rooted in both offline and online behaviors. Thus, POPC asks for routines of privacy management that fit into both worlds. However, there are vast differences between how privacy is understood and regulated in online versus offline contexts. Offline, privacy behaviors are usually based on what we would describe as an "assumption of control" (Margulis, 1974). Burgoon (1982) defines privacy as the control over physical, emotional, informational, and social boundaries. Individuals can close a door if they do not want somebody to come in. They can set physical boundaries to lock others out. Also, social privacy can be controlled by avoiding someone, not attending a meeting, not inviting somebody to an event, or not exposing oneself to another person. Likewise, emotional and informational privacy are given if we control which emotions, cognitions, or factual information we share.

In contrast, users' privacy routines work differently in online contexts. Online content can be forwarded, copied, archived, and edited (boyd, 2010). Very often users cannot control or foresee what others do with the content they post. Consequently, the important process of balancing disclosure and withdrawal does not always lie in their hands. First, some researchers doubt that the assumption of control may be transferred to online privacy (Trepte, 2015). They argue that balancing privacy asks for a fundamental amount of communication. As messages can be copied, edited, archived, and forwarded, control cannot be executed, anticipated, or expected when considering privacy in an online context. Second, privacy regulation may not lie in the hands of the users, as third parties may share and use individual data without users' knowledge or consent.

Hence, users now need to regulate their privacy by means of controlling and regulating access, but they also have to live with the fact that not all of their communication is controllable. In other words, users can control what they share face to face, but they have to negotiate what to share online and very often will have to accept that both control and negotiations do not work.

A third reason that issues of privacy are particularly relevant to POPC is that POPC usage behavior comes with more intense motivations and higher levels of online vigilance than previous social media uses. The privacy regulations outlined above become more important as they are more permanent and are executed under states of higher vigilance than other social media behaviors. The enormous intensity that accompanies permanent communicative vigilance can mean that users have to process more privacy-related information and that they spend more time and effort to negotiate privacy. This situation may result in stressful experiences for users on the one hand, but also trigger resignation regarding their own privacy on the other.

A Calculus of Needs for Meaningfulness and Privacy

As discussed previously, both hedonic as well as eudaimonic motives can be thought to be important gratifications of POPC behaviors. We also pointed out that people pursue certain privacy needs while being POPC. Bearing both needs in mind, the question, then, is how do people handle hedonic and eudaimonic needs on the one hand and the need for privacy on the other? We suggest that they weigh the risks and benefits while "calculating" their priorities and needs. Analogously, a "behavioral calculus" was first suggested by Laufer and Wolfe (1977) and implies that individuals take into account benefits of sharing information with others and of risking their privacy. They particularly referred to the risk of "being recorded" by others. The behavioral calculus was later transferred to online behaviors and termed the "privacy calculus" (Dinev & Hart, 2006; Dienlin & Metzger, 2016).

We assume also that the weighing of meaningful experiences on the one hand and protecting privacy on the other might follow such a calculus. In terms of meaningful experiences, being POPC may offer more gratifications. When listening to music, users do this for their own hedonic as well as meaningful experiences, *and* intensify this experience of meaningfulness by sharing it with friends. In terms of privacy, users have to calculate the risks of sharing information permanently and in a state of vigilance.

This POPC calculus implies that users are exposed to electronic media permanently, literally around the clock; also, they use these media vigilantly and intensely. POPC changes the ways of how meaningfulness is experienced and how privacy is calculated, because POPC is ubiquitous and comes along with high amounts of monitoring and often intense, emotional motivations. As more is shared, positive, meaningful experiences increase, but users are also more often confronted with questions around privacy. The more electronic media are used, the more privacy challenges occur. The more these experiences are reflected as psychological vigilance, the more important they become for the individual user. On the one hand, POPC can mean that privacy decisions have to be considered more often, and that they become more complex and effortful. On the other hand, individuals can use their experiences from both online and offline contexts to inform their privacy decisions.

In sum, the POPC calculus of meaningfulness and privacy is novel in terms of its intensity. When referring to the POPC definition, we learned that protracted media use and permanent communicative vigilance belong to the key defining criteria. The protracted use of electronic media and the participation with social media around the clock gives these communications an important meaning in the lives of users and intensifies their experiences around it. In addition, the state of vigilance that is characterized by high degrees of motivation and the wish to permanently monitor online communication increases the importance that both meaningfulness derived from online communication and privacy might have in users' lives. From this perspective, the intensity of POPC experiences might also impose enormous stress on an individual (Vorderer, 2015, 2016). All kinds of processes we can identify—social connections, identity processes, time management, performance, and efficacy experiences, to name but few—are affected by POPC experiences (Vorderer, 2015).

If we take into account what users gain from being POPC in terms of meaningful experiences and privacy, we can conclude that being POPC intensifies meaningful gratification, but also risks and the effort to negotiate privacy with others. Of course, the weighing of meaningfulness and privacy happens constantly using social media; however, POPC makes this process faster, more intense, and more frequent. Today, we are not yet in the position to evaluate both the positive and the negative consequences of POPC in terms of experience of meaningfulness and privacy management. More research will be needed to fully understand the perspective that users take while weighing meaningfulness and privacy.

Consequently, in the concluding section of our chapter, we will further outline open questions and areas of future research.

Concluding Thoughts

In this chapter, we have attempted to explore the implications of POPC media environments for the interplay between meaningful media and privacy needs. POPC serves hedonic functions, but it can also be used for deeply meaningful communication and reception as well. POPC experiences require new ways to deal with privacy, because they not only include protracted use of electronic media, but also permanent vigilance. The implications of balancing meaningfulness and privacy are widespread as individuals attempt to use POPC experiences for eudaimonic ends while not sacrificing their private lives. Being in an increased state of online vigilance, POPC intensifies the experiences of meaningfulness and allows individuals to deal with privacy more deliberately. However, this also implies that these intense experiences impose a higher amount of stress on us (Vorderer, 2015, 2016). Further, any gains in deliberateness ask for more decisions, negotiation, and communication. Both kinds of effects will have to be taken into account in future research.

The ideas presented in this chapter are exploratory and tentative and raise more questions than they answer. The implications of this new "calculus" that individuals now must compute suggest numerous additional variables and contexts that deserve our scholarly attention. For example, what might this balancing act mean for overall feelings of well-being and social support? Might people avoid seeking POPC experiences for meaningful communication because they are concerned about privacy concerns? Likewise, might some individual differences, such as public self-consciousness, predict lesser frequency of meaningful media use in an era of being POPC?

The flip side of this question regards the likelihood that individuals may disregard issues of privacy when they are in particular need of meaningful communication. That is, might individuals risk being too disclosive to too broad of an audience when they are in need of social support? Are there certain stages in life (e.g., new baby, loss of a job, death of a loved one) or even transient periods (e.g., sad or melancholy moods) when privacy concerns are downplayed for the sake of meaningful communication?

Although we cannot answer most of these questions at present, we are confident that we have come to a new and important field of research. Stand-alone online communication or stand-alone reception almost seem to belong to the past. While being POPC, both processes are now meshed and intertwined. Also, online and offline contexts in isolation seem obsolete. The POPC paradigm will allow us to overcome the strict boundaries between online vs. offline and reception vs. communication. It will open a new look on communication uses and effects as being messily connected (Vorderer, 2016). How to live with media in meaningful ways in our hyperconnected environments is a fruitful direction of future scholarship, as meaningfulness is both a deeply personal and profoundly social consideration.

References

Altman, I. (1974). Privacy: A conceptual analysis In D. H. Carson (Series Ed.) & S. T. Margulis (Vol. Ed.), *Man-environment interactions: Evaluations and applications* (pp. 3–28). Stroudsburg, PA: Dowden, Hutchinson & Ross.
Altman, I. (1975). *The environment and social behavior: Privacy, personal space, territory, crowding*. Monterey, CA: Brooks/Cole Publishing Company.
Bartsch, A., & Hartmann, T. (2015). The role of cognitive and affective challenge in entertainment experience. *Communication Research, 44*(1), 29–53. doi:10.1177/0093650214565921

Bartsch, A., & Mares, M. L. (2014). Making sense of violence: Perceived meaningfulness as a predictor of audience interest in violent media content. *Journal of Communication*, *64*(5), 956–976. doi:10.1111/jcom.12112

Bartsch, A., & Schneider, F. M. (2014). Entertainment and politics revisited: How non-escapist forms of entertainment can stimulate political interest and information seeking. *Journal of Communication*, *64*(3), 369–396. doi:10.1111/jcom.12095

Berger, J., & Milkman, K. L. (2012). What makes online content viral? *Journal of Marketing Research*, *49*, 192–205. doi:10.1509/jmr.10.0353

boyd, d. (2010). Social network sites as networked publics: Affordances, dynamics, and implications. In Z. Papacharissi (Ed.), *A networked self* (pp. 39–58). New York: Taylor & Francis.

Burgoon, J. K. (1982). Privacy and communication. In M. Burgoon (Ed.), *Communication yearbook 6* (pp. 206–249). Beverly Hills, CA: Sage.

Chemero, A. (2003). An outline of a theory of affordances. *Ecological Psychology*, *15*(2), 181–195. doi.org/10.1207/S15326969ECO1502_5

Chung, M.-Y. (2016). *Development and validation of a media nostalgia scale*. Ph.D., Pennsylvania State University.

Dienlin, T., & Metzger, M. (2016). An extended privacy calculus model for SNSs—Analyzing self-disclosure and self-withdrawal in a U.S. representative sample. *Journal of Computer Mediated Communication*. doi: 10.1111/jcc4.12163.

Dinev, T., & Hart, P. (2006). An extended privacy calculus model for e-commerce transactions. *Information Systems Research*, *17*(1), 61–80. doi:10.1287/isre.1060.0080

Ellison, N. B., & Vitak, J. (2015). Social network site affordances and their relationship to social capital processes. In S. S. Sundar (Ed.), *The handbook of the psychology of communication technology* (pp. 203–227). Chichester: John Wiley & Sons, Ltd.

Hofer, M. (2013). Appreciation and enjoyment of meaningful entertainment: The role of mortality salience and search for meaning in life. *Journal of Media Psychology*, *25*(4), 201–201. doi:10.1027/1864-1105/a000089

Hutchby, I. (2001). Technologies, texts and affordances. *Sociology*, *35*(2), 441–456. doi:10.1177/S0038038501000219

Kim, Y., Sohn, D., & Choi, S. M. (2011). Cultural difference in motivations for using social network sites: A comparative study of American and Korean college students. *Computers in Human Behavior*, *27*(1), 365–372. doi:10.1016/j.chb.2010.08.015

Laufer, R. S., & Wolfe, M. (1977). Privacy as a concept and a social issues: A multidimensional developmental theory. *Journal of Social Issues*, *33*(3), 22–42. doi:10.1111/j.1540-4560.1977.tb01880.x

Lewis, R. J., Tamborini, R., & Weber, R. (2014). Testing a dual-process model of media enjoyment and appreciation. *Journal of Communication*, *64*(3), 397–416. doi:10.1111/jcom.12101.

Margulis, S. T. (1974). Privacy as a behavioral phenomenon: Coming of age. In S. T. Margulis (Ed.), *Privacy* (pp. 101–123). Stroudsburg, PA: Dowden, Hutchinson & Ross.

Margulis, S. T. (2003). Privacy as a social issue and behavioral concept. *Journal of Social Issues*, *59*(2), 243–261. doi:10.1111/1540-4560.00063

Masur, P. K., & Scharkow, M. (2016, January–March). Disclosure management on social network sites: Individual privacy perceptions and user-directed privacy strategies. *Social Media + Society*, 1–13. doi:10.1177/2056305116634368

Misra, S., Cheng, L., Genevie, J., & Yuan, M. (2016). The iPhone effect: The quality of in-person social interactions in the presence of mobile devices. *Environment and Behavior*, *48*, 275–298. doi:10.1177/0013916514539755

Myrick, J. G., & Oliver, M. B. (2015). Laughing and crying: Mixed emotions, compassion, and the effectiveness of a YouTube PSA about skin cancer. *Health Communication*, *30*(8), 820–829. doi:10.1080/10410236.2013.845729

Oh, H. J., Ozkaya, E., & LaRose, R. (2014). How does online social networking enhance life satisfaction? The relationships among online supportive interaction, affect, perceived social support, sense of community, and life satisfaction. *Computers in Human Behavior*, *30*, 69–78. doi:10.1016/j.chb.2013.07.053

Oliver, M. B., & Bartsch, A. (2010). Appreciation as audience response: Exploring entertainment gratifications beyond hedonism. *Human Communication Research*, *36*(1), 53–81. doi:10.1111/j.1468-2958.1993.tb00304.x

Oliver, M. B., & Bartsch, A. (2011). Appreciation of entertainment: The importance of meaningfulness via virtue and wisdom. *Journal of Media Psychology: Theories, Methods, and Applications*, *23*(1), 29–33. doi:10.1027/1864-1105/a000029

Oliver, M. B., & Hartmann, T. (2010). Exploring the role of meaningful experiences in users' appreciation of "good movies." *Projections: The Journal of Movies and Mind, 4*(2), 128–150. doi:10.3167/proj.2010.040208

Oliver, M. B., & Raney, A. (2014). Broadening the boundaries of entertainment research [Special issue]. *Journal of Communication, 64*, 361–568. http://dx.doi.org/10.1111/jcom.12092

Oliver, M. B., & Woolley, J. K. (2015). Meaningfulness and entertainment: Fiction and reality in the land of evolving technologies. In H. Wang (Ed.), *Communication and the "good life."* New York: Peter Lang.

Phone stack. (2014). *Urban dictionary*. Retrieved from www.urbandictionary.com/define.php?term=Phone+Stack

Przybylski, A. K., & Weinstein, N. (2013). Can you connect with me now? How the presence of mobile communication technology influences face-to-face conversation quality. *Journal of Social and Personal Relationships, 30*(3), 237–246. doi:10.1177/0265407512453827

Quinn, K. (2016). Why we share: A uses and gratifications approach to privacy regulation in social media use. *Journal of Broadcasting & Electronic Media, 60*(1), 61–86. doi:10.1080/08838151.2015.1127245.

Sweet, N. G. (2012, September 30). *Put that away! Phone stacking and other solutions to your phone addiction*. Retrieved from http://blogs.kqed.org/pop/2013/09/30/put-that-away-phone-stacking-and-other-solutions-to-your-phone-addiction/

Tamborini, R. (2012). A model of intuitive morality and exemplars. In R. Tamborini (Ed.), *Media and the moral mind* (pp. 43–74). London: Routledge.

Trepte, S. (2015). Social media, privacy, and self-disclosure: The turbulence caused by social media's affordances. *Social Media and Society, 1*(1), 1–2. doi:10.1177/2056305115578681

Trepte, S., & Reinecke, L. (2011). *Privacy online. Perspectives on privacy and self-disclosure in the social web*. Berlin, Germany: Springer.

Turkle, S. (2011). *Alone together: Why we expect more from technology and less from each other*. New York: Basic Books.

Vinsel, A., Brown, B. B., Altman, I., & Foss, C. (1980). Privacy regulation, territorial displays, and effectiveness of individual functioning. *Journal of Personality and Social Psychology, 39*(6), 1104–1115. doi:10.1037/h0077718

Vorderer, P. (2015). Der mediatisierte Lebenswandel: Permanently online, permanently connected. *Publizistik, 60*, 259–276.

Vorderer, P. (2016). Communication and the good life: Why and how our discipline should make a difference. *Journal of Communication, 66*, 1–12. doi:10.1111/jcom.12194

Vorderer, P., & Kohring, M. (2013). Permanently online: A challenge for media and communication research. *International Journal of Communication, 7*, 188–196.

Vorderer, P., Krömer, N., & Schneider, F.M. (2016). Permanently online – permanently connected: Explorations into university students' use of social media and mobile smart devices. *Computers in Human Behavior, 63*, 694–703. doi:10.1016/j.chb.2016.05.085

Vorderer, P., & Reinecke, L. (2015). From mood to meaning: The changing model of the user in entertainment research. *Communication Theory, 25*(4), 447–453. doi:10.1111/comt.12082

Walsh, S. P., White, K. M., & Young, R. McD. (2010). Needing to connect: The effect of self and others on young people's involvement with their mobile phones. *Australian Journal of Psychology, 62*(4), 194–203. doi:10.1080/00049530903567229.

Xie, W. J., & Kang, C. Y. (2015). See you, see me: Teenagers' self-disclosure and regret of posting on social network site. *Computers in Human Behavior, 52*, 398–407. doi:10.1016/j.chb.2015.05.059

Zillmann, D. (1988). Mood management: Using entertainment to full advantage. In L. Donohew, H. E. Sypher, & E. T. Higgins (Eds.), *Communication, social cognition, and affect* (pp. 147–171). Hillsdale, NJ: Lawrence Erlbaum Associates.

Zillmann, D., & Bryant, J. (1994). Entertainment as media effect. In J. Bryant & D. Zillmann (Eds.), *Media effects: Advances in theory and research* (pp. 437–461). Hillsdale, NJ: Lawrence Erlbaum Associates.

12

The Experience of Narrative in the Permanently Online, Permanently Connected Environment

Multitasking, Self-Expansion, and Entertainment Effects

Kelsey Woods, Michael D. Slater, Jonathan Cohen, Benjamin K. Johnson, and David R. Ewoldsen

Stories are a major form of entertainment that can be experienced in many forms of media, from books and television to videogames, from large movie screens to mobile phones and tablets. Thus, we are never far from the possibility of experiencing a narrative (Vorderer, 2016), especially today in the permanently online, permanently connected (POPC) era. The online experience itself in some measure may meet fundamental human needs for competence, autonomy, and relatedness (Ryan & Deci, 2000). The temporarily expanded boundaries of the self model (Slater, Johnson, Cohen, Comello, & Ewoldsen, 2014) proposes that narrative can provide a subjective experience of nearly unlimited agency, freedom to move through time, space, and person, and vicariously experienced relationship to at least momentarily meet such needs in ways impossible through typical social experience. The online experience also provides expanded capacity for interpersonal connection, an experience of nearly unlimited choice of points of connection to the online world, and the capacity to make such choices easily, at the click of a mouse button. Being online, then, very likely also provides the sense (or perhaps the illusion) of having addressed these fundamental human needs. At the same time, the affordances of the online world have the potential to both facilitate and undermine the experience of the story world, of narratives, which are increasingly consumed online or in tandem with online media use.

Experiencing narrative in online environments, with opportunities for multiscreen use to access information about the story world, characters, and actors and to interact with friends and strangers via social media, blogs, and fan fiction, may transform what it means to be engaged with a narrative. For example, if while watching the US-produced fantasy television series *Game of Thrones*, a viewer posts to Twitter and Facebook about the episode, instant messages a friend, looks up gossip on an actor's sex life, retweets a humorous meme about a character, and checks a backstory line to clarify a plot twist—what happens to the ways people become engaged in a story? Such engagement has traditionally been conceptualized as combining the extent to which audiences feel as if they are inside the story world rather than simply experiencing it as readers or viewers (i.e., they are transported by a story; Gerrig, 1993) and the degree to which they are psychologically merged with, and feel connected to, characters (i.e., identify with characters; J. Cohen, 2001). The viewer is clearly not lost in the story world—but is *actively* immersed in the experience of the story, is engaged in social interaction centered around the story, and the story world and the life world of the individual have been brought closer together. What does this mean for our thinking about narrative processing and narrative persuasion?

In this chapter, we explore the interplay between the affordances of the online media, POPC society, and narrative experience. Our primary focus will be to outline a model for understanding media multitasking (see also Xu and Wang, this volume; David, this volume) and narrative engagement and to examine implications for various forms of involvement with narrative.

Media Multitasking and Narrative Engagement

The rapid proliferation of mobile devices has fundamentally altered the ways in which audiences experience and engage with mediated content. Media content and opportunities to engage such content are more available than ever, literally at our fingertips anytime and anywhere (Vorderer, 2016). Communication scholars, however, have not yet fully reconceptualized and reoperationalized traditional constructs to account for this new normal, in which people are nearly constantly connected to the Internet (Vorderer & Kohring, 2013). A model is needed to describe how using mobile devices while being exposed to other screen-based content may impact engagement with and processing of media content in a narrative context. We need to examine the questions: How does multiscreening affect our processing of screen-based content? And how does multitasking affect narrative engagement?

At its simplest, media multitasking occurs when two or more tasks are engaged in simultaneously and at least one of those tasks involves some form of media (Wang, Irwin, Cooper, & Srivastava, 2015). Thus, examples of media multitasking include behaviors in which a media task is combined with a non-media task (such as watching TV while eating, listening to music while completing homework, or texting while driving), as well as behaviors in which multiple media are used concurrently (such as watching TV while surfing the Internet, listening to music while playing a video game, or texting while watching a movie). As these examples show, media multitasking encompasses a wide range of behaviors that employ cognitive resources in different ways (see Xu and Wang, this volume; David, this volume, for more in depth discussion of multitasking behaviors).

One type of media multitasking, known as multiscreening, occurs when a person uses two or more screen-based media concurrently. With the proliferation of mobile devices, multiscreening has become a more and more prevalent practice. Research has found that 52% of cell phone owners use their phones while watching TV and 84% of smartphone/tablet owners use their devices while watching TV (Smith & Boyles, 2012; The Nielsen Company, 2014). Furthermore, behavioral data show that task switching during media multitasking is very fast-paced while also poorly recalled and underreported, both when viewing television in conjunction with a second screen (Brasel & Gips, 2011) and when switching between video and other content on the same device (Yeykelis, Cummings, & Reeves, 2014). Because television is a common medium for narratives, and research shows that multiscreening often occurs during television viewing (Giglietto & Selva, 2014; Gil de Zúñiga, Garcia-Perdomo, & McGregor, 2015; Voorveld & Viswanathan, 2015), multiscreening is an important concept to investigate in this context.

Though popular, multitasking has been found to have negative effects on comprehension, task accuracy, and task efficiency (Wang et al., 2015). Multitasking includes a wide range of behaviors (see Xu and Wang, this volume; David, this volume), yet most previous studies have operated under the assumption that any type of multitasking would have the same effects. In challenging this assumption, Wang, Irwin, Cooper, and Srivastava (2015) provide a useful framework for studying different types of media multitasking by using cognitive resource theories to describe 11 dimensions of media multitasking behaviors. All of these dimensions are relevant to any investigation of media multitasking, but the one that is most important when considering how multiscreening might moderate narrative processing is "task relevance." According to Wang et al. (2015, p. 109), during relevant media multitasking, the concurrent tasks "serve related goals (or a single overarching goal)." Salvucci and Taatgen's (2008) theory of threaded cognition proposes that people organize information around their goals via cognitive "threads." So tasks that have similar goals would be organized along the same thread and would, therefore, require fewer cognitive resources to complete simultaneously than tasks that have disparate goals and would, therefore, involve multiple threads competing for cognitive resources (see Xu and Wang, this volume; David, this volume, for a more in-depth discussion of the dimensions of media multitasking and the application of threaded cognition to multitasking).

Most media multitasking research in an experimental environment has involved the use of irrelevant tasks, though surveys and experiential sampling studies have suggested that relevant media multitasking is a more frequent practice. Wang et al. (2015), for example, used experiential sampling methods and found that participants were significantly more likely to report multitasking with relevant tasks (such as e-mailing and using Facebook, which are both social tasks) than irrelevant tasks (such as e-mailing and web browsing). In keeping with threaded cognition theory, relevant media multitasking may have fewer deleterious effects than irrelevant multitasking. Van Cauwenberge, Schaap, and van Roy (2014) experimentally tested irrelevant versus relevant multitasking with a small sample viewing television news, and found the expected difference for cognitive load yet not for comprehension. Participants who engaged in relevant multitasking (i.e., were instructed to look up online information about newscast stories while watching the newscast) reported that they found it easier to follow the storylines of the newscast items than did participants who engaged in irrelevant multitasking (i.e., instructed to look up information about different stories from those in the newscast). However, despite their perceived ease of processing, relevant multitaskers did not significantly outperform irrelevant multitaskers in their factual recall or comprehension of the storylines.

Traditional investigations of narrative engagement have examined various ways that people become involved with stories during exposure (e.g., J. Cohen, 2001; M. Green & Brock, 2000). Not all types of narrative engagement end as soon as the story ends, however. People continue to engage with a narrative even while not synchronously watching it. A common asynchronous construct studied in narrative is parasocial relationships (Horton & Wohl, 1956; Klimmt, Hartmann, & Schramm, 2006; Rubin & McHugh, 1987). There are, however, many other ways in which people may engage with the "universe" of a narrative, including reading or contributing to show or film wikis and blogs, participating in cosplay, producing videos, images, and memes, writing fan fiction, and so on. Fan fiction, for example, has proliferated in today's networked environment that facilitates creation of communities of shared passions. For example, in a recent survey with over 700 participants on Amazon MTurk (an online platform through which researchers can post online studies and "workers" can choose to participate for a small amount of compensation), 9% of the sample reported they had written fan fiction and about 40% of the sample reported seeking out fan fiction to read (Ewoldsen & Bogert, 2014). Granted, MTurk likely overrepresents a sample that is younger, is Internet-savvy, and has time on their hands. Nonetheless, these results represent a nontrivial percentage, even if of a younger, networked sample. Fanfiction.net is the most popular online repository of fan fiction. In 2010, there were over 2.6 million users of FanFiction.net (Lennard, 2012). Currently, there are over 735,000 pieces of fan fiction about the Harry Potter series alone! And, in addition to these creative media users who are engaged in remixing narratives via user-generated content, additional media users actively consume and recirculate that same user-generated content through online networks (J. Green & Jenkins, 2011; Hillman, Procyk, & Neustaedter, 2014; Petersen, 2014). In sum, engaging in fan fiction or other narrative-related tasks both during and after exposure are a new type of multitasking that challenge the expectation that multitasking can only distract us from our main task. Further, while multitasking typically focuses on tasks that take audiences away from the original narrative, readers of fan fiction in the POPC world may multitask by going back to the original narrative to engage in any number of activities, such as ascertaining the fidelity of the fan fiction to the original narrative or simply enjoying favored episodes of the original.

Multitasking may interfere with synchronous engagement by distracting audiences, but it may enhance engagement with the narrative universe by providing opportunities for audiences to interact with narrative content in a variety of ways. Therefore, explicating a wider range of engagement is important for accurately capturing how audiences engage with narratives in the highly connected online environment and how multitasking influences this engagement. This is likely to necessitate a more nuanced look at both the types of tasks engaged in by POPC individuals and the forms of narrative engagement that may be impacted by multitasking.

The proposed model (see Figure 12.1) hopes to contribute to theory by differentiating various dimensions of multitasking and suggesting that different types of multitasking may result in different outcomes. The model also distinguishes between engaging with the narrative itself and engaging with the narrative universe, so that the multitude of ways in which audiences can interact with narrative content both synchronously and asynchronously are highlighted. Updating these constructs will allow for the more accurate study of how narrative engagement occurs in a perpetually connected world of mobile devices.

Figure 12.1 illustrates the proposed model for the effects of multitasking on screen-based narrative engagement and outcomes. The main type of multitasking in this model is *relevant multitasking*. Relevant multitasking refers, for instance, to using the Internet to look up information about the characters, the actors, or elements of the plot. The opposite of relevant multitasking is *irrelevant multitasking*, in which the concurrent task is irrelevant to the screen-based narrative. For instance, irrelevant multitasking might involve using the Internet to read news, flip through a friend's online pictures, or look up sports scores. These activities represent competing sources of media content, which vary in the extent

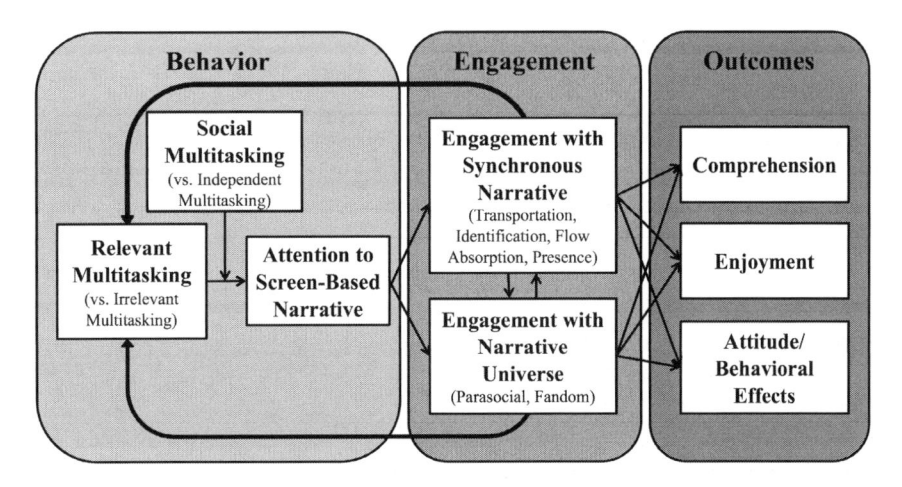

FIGURE 12.1 Model for the Effect of Multitasking on Screen-Based Narrative Engagement and Outcomes.

to which they present other forms of "narrative"—yet they all can represent rival means of satisfying intrinsic needs for agency, relatedness, and autonomy (Slater et al., 2014). Irrelevant multitasking during exposure to media entertainment should decrease attention to the narrative and, therefore, should decrease all types of narrative engagement and outcomes. As the model illustrates, however, relevant multitasking may have different effects that instead enhance attention, engagement, and outcomes.

Before explaining the model's processes further, it would be helpful to first define the different types of narrative engagement involved. The first type of engagement, *engagement with the synchronous narrative*, refers to narrative engagement as it is traditionally thought of and includes key variables such as transportation, identification, absorption, and flow. This is the type of engagement that occurs as a viewer is watching a narrative. The other type of engagement proposed by this model is that of *engagement with the narrative universe*. This refers to engagement that occurs even when the person is not currently watching the narrative. Key variables in the literature that would fit this type of engagement include parasocial relationships and fandom. Both of these variables focus mainly on relationships with characters, though engagement with the narrative universe could go beyond characters. For instance, fans of the books and films centered on boy wizard *Harry Potter* know many of the details of the world that J.K. Rowling created and may go to Universal Studios in Orlando to experience a recreation of that world. Similarly, fans of the *Star Wars* space opera saga may get into online arguments over the complex details of fictional spacecraft, creatures, and galactic laws. Devoted fans of the Marvel Cinematic Universe, eagerly awaiting the next installment of that comic book superhero movie series, may edit their own fan-made trailers and publish them on YouTube months or years before the first genuine trailer appears. Thus, there are many other ways that people may engage with these fictional universes beyond developing parasocial relationships with the characters.

Multitasking may interfere with synchronous narrative engagement, as limited cognitive resources make it difficult to fully attend to a narrative and complete a different task. Indeed, experiments have illustrated that irrelevant multitasking diminishes narrative transportation (Zwarun & Hall, 2012) and message comprehension (Jeong & Hwang, 2012, 2015). There is, however, some evidence that children can multitask while watching TV without sacrificing comprehension (Anderson & Field, 1983; Anderson & Lorch, 1983; Crawley et al., 2002) because they use the formal features of the program (e.g., cuts, edits, voice-overs) to direct their orienting of attention to the program (Calvert, Huston, Watkins, & Wright, 1982; Krull & Husson, 1979; Rice, Huston, & Wright, 1983). Future research on dual tasking needs to consider the role of formal features in viewers' orienting of attention to the program to come to a more complete understanding of how dual tasking is strategically managed (Roskos-Ewoldsen & Roskos-Ewoldsen, 2010).

Whereas viewers may be able to use formal features to reorient to the screen-based narrative enough to maintain transportation and engagement despite distractions, relevant multitasking has the potential to actually enhance these processes. Relevant multitasking may create a sort of attention cycle in which multitasking actually increases subsequent attention to the narrative, and thereby subsequent synchronous narrative engagement, and this synchronous narrative engagement may lead, in turn, to more relevant multitasking. Content analysis of tweets about television programming has found that viewers used the second screen to express opinions and emotions and to engage in interpretation (Giglietto & Selva, 2014), and survey data suggest that second screening heightens discussion and elaborative processing about television content (Gil de Zúñiga et al., 2015).

For instance, someone engaged in a storyline about an undocumented immigrant who may be deported while in a coma may decide to use the Internet to look up information about medical repatriation. What they learn about medical repatriation online may cause them to be even more engaged in the story, once their attention returns to the narrative. A stronger effect of relevant multitasking is likely its impact on engagement with the narrative universe. Deeper, more elaborative engagement (both during and outside of the actual viewing experience) may heighten the ability of the narrative experience to satisfy needs for competence, choice, and connectedness. For example, someone watching *Game of Thrones* may use the Internet to look up information about the book series or to read fan theories about the "death" of leading protagonist Jon Snow. This type of relevant multitasking, with what Gray (2010) calls *paratexts* (as they exist outside the primary text), may distract from engagement with the synchronous narrative but is likely to increase interest in and engagement with the narrative universe of *Game of Thrones*.

Indeed, a recent experiment placed television content in a multitasking situation with a second screen that featured a webpage with relevant program information as well as program-relevant tweets. While the presence of the second screen content diminished concentration and immersion, neither the presence of the webpage nor the tweets affected perceptions of the program, such as interest, trustworthiness, likeability, value, and relatedness (Kusumoto, Kinnunen, Kätsyri, Lindroos, & Oittinen, 2014). So, while relevant multitasking may strain attention, it does not necessarily harm, and in many cases may augment and enhance, the comprehension, enjoyment, and effects of the narrative.

In contrast, irrelevant multitasking presents both distractions that do not benefit narrative processing and also competing sources of intrinsic need satisfaction. The mere presence of a mobile device diminishes attention and cognitive engagement (Przybylski & Weinstein, 2012; Thornton, Faires, Robbins, & Rollins, 2014), likely because the connected device presents a link to competing social opportunities: other available real or ersatz social connections and experiences that have the potential to satisfy intrinsic needs through self-expansion. Przybylski and Weinstein (2012) found that the effect was strongest and most disruptive when the primary task involved more meaningful forms of communication. The allure of other possible social connections, if irrelevant and in competition with the primary task, can degrade the ability to engage with and glean gratifications.

For example, a recent study on the temporarily expanded boundaries of the self model (TEBOTS) illustrated that the presence of a self-affirmation buffer obviated the need for self-expansive viewing responses during narrative exposure (Johnson, Slater, Silver, & Ewoldsen, 2016). When individuals were prompted to reflect on their most valued attributes, the integrity of their self-concept was protected and they subsequently reported less enjoyment, appreciation, and transportation into narrative stories than did individuals who had not reflected on their own self-worth. This is evidence that engagement with narratives is more needed by, and useful to, people whose self-concept is threatened or under stress. Indeed, those who reported a high need for meaning in life but did not receive a self-affirmation reported the most expansion of their self-concept during reading a narrative (Johnson et al., 2016). Elsewhere, it has been convincingly demonstrated that Facebook use provides the same self-affirming boost to the self-concept as the reflection on positive personal values used in a self-affirmation induction (Toma & Hancock, 2013). So, taking these studies in tandem, we could hypothesize that feeling self-affirmed via social media use would lead to weaker needs for narrative engagement. The combination of mobile devices and social media place a large number of sources of self-expansion at our fingertips, which can either compete with (via irrelevant multitasking) or instead augment and improve (via relevant multitasking) more traditional staples of narrative entertainment, such as television drama and comedy.

Another type of multitasking may moderate the relationship between relevant multitasking and attention to the narrative: *social multitasking*. Social multitasking refers to multitasking that involves active interpersonal interactions (see also Rieger, this volume; Utz, this volume). For instance, watching a narrative while talking with other people who are physically present, texting or instant messaging with friends, or tweeting and receiving responses would all be examples of social multitasking. When others are physically present during entertainment television exposure, multiscreening is less prevalent (Voorveld & Viswanathan, 2015) and there is less distraction from the television as primary task (Christensen, Bickham, Ross, & Rich, 2015). This negative link between co-viewing and multiscreening is perhaps partly because social multitasking can occur face to face in these situations rather than through mediated channels. However, less is currently known about social multitasking via messaging or social media.

Social multitasking is in contrast to *independent multitasking*, in which the viewer is not interacting with anyone (e.g., simply looking up information online). Social multitasking may be relevant or irrelevant. Relevant social multitasking refers to social interactions that are germane to the narrative, such as discussing the plot twists with friends. Irrelevant social multitasking includes any social interactions that are not pertinent to the narrative. Relevant social multitasking may increase both types of narrative engagement, because active involvement with others may encourage viewers to attend to the narrative or the narrative universe so that they can fully participate in the social interaction. The social presence of others, either physically (Bowman, Weber, Tamborini, & Sherry, 2013) or through their mediated presence (Thornton et al., 2014) can also produce arousal that influences the engagement with narrative. The impact of this arousal is thought to be contingent on the complexity and challenge of the media stimulus (Bowman et al., 2013; Przybylski & Weinstein, 2012). Effects of co-viewing, attributed to modeling or emotional contagion, are also evident for happiness, enjoyment (E. Cohen, Bowman, & Lancaster, 2016), transportation, identification, and attitude change (Tal-Or, 2016; Tal-Or & Tsfati, 2015). Finally, social multitasking, whether mediated or unmediated, may involve synchronous or asynchronous co-viewing (Pittman & Tefertiller, 2015). Media users may consume narratives at different times, yet still be able to meaningfully interact with each other regarding the content.

Thus, the theoretical model broadly predicts that different types of multitasking (relevant vs. irrelevant; social vs. independent) will impact different types of narrative engagement (engagement with the synchronous narrative as well as engagement with the narrative universe), which will, in turn, impact the commonly studied narrative outcomes involving comprehension, enjoyment, and attitude/behavioral effects.

Narrative Engagement in the Era of POPC

The various forms of online multitasking behaviors that have been described in the above model should affect the ways readers and viewers engage with the content. It is likely that the practice of being POPC has an impact not only on the behaviors associated with narrative exposure (the left side of the model) but also on the psychological processes that accompany such exposure. For example, because transportation is based on attentive absorption and flow (M. Green and Brock, 2000), every time we turn our attention from the text to another task (relevant or irrelevant), this is likely to decrease our attention and transportation. It may be, as stated above, that relevant multitasking adds to our emotional connection and knowledge of the story world and hence increases the intensity of our overall experience and sense of transportation, but the duration of our attentive exposure will necessarily decrease the more we multitask. This is likely to be especially true if the multitasking is irrelevant (e.g., checking e-mails) or, most likely, mixed in nature. Indeed, when our mobile device beeps or vibrates indicating a message or a Facebook or Twitter post, we do not know whether it is relevant to what we are doing.

It is only after we are distracted that we may find out that this distraction is relevant to the narrative universe and thus likely to enhance our engagement.

Being POPC is also likely to change the nature of our mediated relationships and impact the ways we engage with fictional characters and the actors who play them. Identification, very much like transportation, may be negatively affected by decreases in flow, but much more interesting are the effects of online engagement with the narrative universe on parasocial relationships and fandom. J. Cohen (2009) has argued that whereas parasocial relationships are characterized by intimacy and resemble friendships, fandom is a more distant form of relationship. We may adore, and be fans of, those we admire, those who we perceive are better than we are and serve as our aspirational models. Superheroes, star athletes, talented actors, or musicians are all heroes adored by fans because they exist at a pinnacle of achievement (and may be unreachable). Thus, traditional fandom is characterized by distant adoration in contrast to parasocial relationships with more common personae (e.g., newscasters or talk show hosts) that are characterized by intimacy. In accordance with this difference, parasocial relationships also have a bidirectional component in which viewers imagine not only a one-sided liking (as in fandom) but also an imagined two-way relationship based on familiarity. But perhaps this distinction is no longer valid.

Being POPC is likely to blur the distinction between fandom and parasocial relationships. Being Facebook friends with a hero, or receiving daily tweets from them, is likely to diminish the imagined distance between hero and fan. As opposed to standing in a mass of adoring screaming fans in a concert, fans may now get a photo on Instagram of what our favorite musician ate for lunch or receive a tweet they sent out to a friend for a birthday (Marwick & boyd, 2011). Such celebrity performances, however, may be acts of impression management, as Marwick and boyd (2011, p. 144) argue: "Determining whether readers are watching an 'authentic' individual or a performed 'celebrity' persona is not entirely the point; it is the uncertainty that creates pleasure for the celebrity-watcher." It is hard to imagine that such increasingly frequent and less-formal contact would not increase intimacy.

And as for that local news anchor with whom audience members have had a parasocial relationship, these same daily interactions via social media channels allow them to feel as if the anchor is part of their lives in an ongoing way. This persistent interaction should increase the sense of intimacy in parasocial relationships even further. Permanent connection and frequent interaction are also likely to strengthen the illusion of reciprocity in that fans can now post and react to the frequent messages (seemingly) emanating from characters and celebrities. Fans can now also co-follow brands, music, and other celebrities along with a parasocial partner or hero (Rama, Garimella, & Weber, 2014). Some celebrities directly respond to fans (Marwick & boyd, 2011) and have even been known to follow some of their fans back, thus intensifying the illusion of a two-way relationship even further. Importantly and interestingly, the daily routine presence of mediated partners is not limited to actors and celebrities. Fictional characters also have Facebook pages and Twitter accounts that can strengthen the illusion that is at the basis of a parasocial relationship. Thus, it is possible to hypothesize that online involvement with celebrities should increase intimacy and decrease distance, thereby making fandom and parasocial relationships more similar.

Another significant way that the era of POPC has likely impacted mediated relationships is that it has increased, by orders of magnitude, their sociability and publicness. Social networks not only strengthen connections to media friends and heroes but also to other fans, so that ruminative performances about favorite media often become social. Johnson and Van Der Heide (2015) have argued that online, public display of media tastes will reinforce attitudinal liking of that same media content. Furthermore, they demonstrated that social feedback from others played a key role in this process of public commitment to media. If just a decade ago a fan of the sci-fi franchise *Star Trek* had to travel to fan conventions or wait until those came to their towns (Jenkins, 1992), now communities of fans are constantly around us, potentially interacting with us and alongside us in an "always on" fashion (Hillman et al., 2014). Technological affordances allow fans to interact in a multitude of modalities, by consuming, sharing, and discussing not only the original narrative texts but also user-generated content that reworks and appropriates the texts to take engagement with narratives even further.

This has another side effect. Even if fandom or parasocial relationship with a specific persona or hero may be viewed as odd by family and peers and perhaps even frowned upon (because of either our choices of mediated relationship partners or the intensity of this relationship), social networks provide constant access to others that share and support these feelings. Indeed, social network sites can be seen as sanctioning fandom and parasocial relationships, which is why celebrities expend great resources to develop their social media following. Though displaying extreme personal sadness following the death of a celebrity or a fictional character may be seen as overdramatic and inappropriate, social network sites provide communities that allow for sanctioned and very convenient outlets for such expressions (Forman, Kern, & Gil-Egui, 2012). In their analysis of memorial or R.I.P pages on Facebook, Forman et al. (2012) report that over 25% of the pages they found were set up for deceased celebrities and that 16% were for "deceased" fictional characters, places, or things. These figures suggest that social media are commonly used to perform mourning of people with whom one does not have a real-world social connection.

In sum, there are many ways in which being POPC and multitasking should impact how we engage with stories. Whether with the narrative itself or the narrative universe, synchronously or through subsequent ruminative performance, alone or together, media stories are often experienced in a much more complex way than they were before the diffusion of mobile computing devices. Such devices now offer multiple ways to integrate additional content as well as other people into the experience of narratives. Such integration can and should impact engagement with narratives in multiple and complex ways and should also affect the outcomes of narrative exposure. We have just begun thinking and theorizing about such processes.

Conclusion

In this chapter, we have outlined a model for the impact of online affordances and multiscreening on engagement with narrative. We have used this as a framework to explore in some detail the impact of online multitasking on narrative effects, given the interplay between multitasking and active engagement with both the synchronous narrative and the larger narrative world. Both forms of engagement allow audiences to meet the same core human needs of an expanded sense of agency, autonomy, and affiliation.

Previous work has illustrated how a need to expand the boundaries of the self-concept, to satisfy inherently frustrated self-determination needs, motivates human engagement with narratives (Johnson, Ewoldsen, & Slater, 2015; Johnson et al., 2016). Likewise, this TEBOTS perspective also describes how narrative effects are enhanced by storylines and portrayals that allow the individual to step beyond their own experiences and boundaries (e.g., by empathizing with an out-group member; Chung & Slater, 2013). In the present chapter, we have turned our attention to how self-expansion through narrative is both impeded and enhanced by the POPC environment. The relevance of multitasking to the narrative and the sociality of that multitasking have major implications for narrative engagement and the capacity of narrative media to expand boundaries and satisfy intrinsic needs.

Of course, laying out these ideas is just the beginning. Considerable work remains to be done in testing and refining the proposed model and in better understanding how the new world of multiscreen use will impact narrative experience. In addition, the phenomenon of asynchronous engagement with narratives, both off-screen and on other screens, may require some reconceptualization of what involvement with a narrative and story characters means outside of the immediate experience of the story world itself. Notably, the concepts of fandom, parasocial interaction, and involvement with the narrative universe may all require reconceptualization as well as new operationalizations.

New media have brought audiences not only new channels of delivery, but also new forms and new quantities of content choices. In addition to voluminous professional storytelling, the individual is now invited to produce and share their own life as a mediated narrative, and to consume the mediated lives of others as narratives, too (Stefanone, Lackaff, & Rosen, 2010). This explosive growth of narratives provides new opportunities for highly meaningful, satisfying engagement with all kinds of stories, by serving both interactivity and niches. Yet this growth also produces a staggering amount of competition among narratives and more potential for distributed, degraded attention.

Other issues may be broader and have additional social implications. As stories and entertainment meet social media, fan fiction, and audience/fan communities, what happens when these stories are closely associated with political, social, religious, and ideological identities? There is ample reason to believe that self-selection of media content and of online communities is a means for developing and maintaining distinctive social identities (Slater, 2015). Stories and narratives are means of expressing values and perspectives that characterize social identity. Communities centered on such stories are also likely to be communities of shared identity. It may be that the world of story, of narrative, may increasingly become, at least in some cases, a tribal one, in which cybercommunities can gather about their virtual fire and invest themselves that much more deeply in the values, the hopes, and the social roles implicit in the stories they have come to love.

These processes, in which managing multiple media, together and alone, shapes the engagement with narrative media, have important implications for media effects. By accounting for the nature of the permanently online, permanently connected media environment, we can better understand when, why, and how media narratives allow the individual to transcend the limits of their self-concept and satisfy their needs for competence, choice, and connectedness.

References

Anderson, D. R., & Field, D. E. (1983). Children's attention to television: Implications for production. In M. Meyer (Ed.), *Children and the formal features of television: Approaches and findings of experimental and formative research* (pp. 56–96). Munich, Germany: K. G. Saur.

Anderson, D. R., & Lorch, E. P. (1983). Looking at television: Action or reaction? In J. Bryant & D. R. Anderson (Eds.), *Children's understanding of television: Research on attention and comprehension* (pp. 1–33). New York: Academic Press.

Bowman, N. D., Weber, R., Tamborini, R., & Sherry, J. (2013). Facilitating game play: How others affect performance at and enjoyment of video games. *Media Psychology, 16*, 39–64. doi:10.1080/15213269.2012.742360

Brasel, S. A., & Gips, J. (2011). Media multitasking behavior: Concurrent television and computer usage. *Cyberpsychology, Behavior, and Social Networking, 14*, 527–534. doi:10.1089/cyber.2010.0350

Calvert, S. L., Huston, A., C., Watkins, B. A., & Wright, J. C. (1982). The relation between selective attention to television forms and children's comprehension of content. *Child Development, 53*, 601–610. doi:10.2307/1129371

Chung, A. H., & Slater, M. D. (2013). Reducing stigma and out-group distinctions through perspective-taking in narratives. *Journal of Communication, 63*, 894–911. doi:10.1111/jcom.12050

Cohen, E. L., Bowman, N. D., & Alexander, L. L. (2016). R u with some1? Using text message experience sampling to examine television coviewing as a moderator of emotional contagion effects on enjoyment. *Mass Communication and Society, 19*, 149–172. doi:10.1080/15205436.2015.1071400

Cohen, J. (2001). Defining identification: A theoretical look at the identification of audiences with media characters. *Mass Communication and Society, 4*, 245–264. doi:10.1207/S15327825MCS0403_01

Crawley, A. M., Anderson, D. R., Santomero, A., Wilder, A., Williams, M., Evans, M. K., & Bryant, J. (2002). Do children learn how to watch television? The impact of extensive experience with *Blue's Clues* on preschool children's television viewing behavior. *Journal of Communication, 52*, 264–280. doi:10.1111/j.1460-2466.2002.tb02544.x

Ewoldsen, D. R., & Bogert, A. (2014). *Prevalence of fan fiction*. Unpublished data.

Forman, A. E., Kern, R., & Gil-Egui, G. (2012). Death and mourning as sources of community participation in online social networks: R.I.P. pages in Facebook. *First Monday, 17*. doi:10.5210/fm.v0i0.3935

Gerrig, R. J. (1993). *Experiencing narrative worlds*. New Haven, CT: Yale University Press.

Giglietto, F., & Selva, D. (2014). Second screen and participation: A content analysis of a full season dataset of tweets. *Journal of Communication, 64*, 260–277. doi:10.1111/jcom.12085

Gil de Zúñiga, H., Garcia-Perdomo, V., & McGregor, S. C. (2015). What is second screening? Exploring motivations of second screen use and its effect on online political participation. *Journal of Communication, 65*(5), 793–815. doi:10.1111/jcom.12174

Gray, J. (2010). *Show sold separately: Promos, spoilers, and other media paratexts*. New York: New York University Press.

Green, J., & Jenkins, H. (2011). Spreadable media: How audiences create value and meaning in a networked economy. In V. Nightingale (Ed.), *The handbook of media audiences* (pp. 109–127). New York: Wiley-Blackwell.

Green, M. C., & Brock, T. C. (2000). The role of transportation in the persuasiveness of public narratives. *Journal of Personality and Social Psychology, 79*, 701–721. doi:10.1037//0022-3514.79.5.701

Hillman, S., Procyk, J., & Neustaedter, C. (2014). Tumblr fandoms, community, and culture. In S. Fussell & W. Lutters (Eds.), *CSCW Companion '14: Proceedings of the Companion Publication of the 17th ACM Conference on Computer Supported Cooperative Work and Social Computing*. New York: ACM. doi:10.1145/2556420.2557634

Horton, D., & Wohl, R. R. (1956). Mass communication and para-social interaction: Observations on intimacy at a distance. *Psychiatry: Interpersonal and Biological Processes, 19*(3), 215–229. doi:10.1521/00332747.1956.11023049

Jeong, S.-H., & Hwang, Y. (2012). Does multitasking increase or decrease persuasion? Effects of multitasking on comprehension and counterarguing. *Journal of Communication, 62*, 571–587. doi:10.1111/j.1460-2466.2012.01659.x

Jeong, S.-H., & Hwang, Y. (2015). Multitasking and persuasion: The role of structural interference. *Media Psychology, 18*, 451–474. doi:10.1080/15213269.2014.933114

Johnson, B. K., Ewoldsen, D. R., & Slater, M. D. (2015). Self-control depletion and narrative: Testing a prediction of the TEBOTS model. *Media Psychology, 18*, 196–220. doi:10.1080/15213269.2014.978872

Johnson, B. K., Slater, M. D., Silver, N. A, & Ewoldsen, D. R. (2016). Entertainment and expanding boundaries of the self: Relief from the constraints of the everyday. *Journal of Communication, 66*. doi:10.1111/jcom.12228

Johnson, B. K., & Van Der Heide, B. (2015). Can sharing affect liking? Online taste performances, feedback, and subsequent media preferences. *Computers in Human Behavior, 46*, 181–190. doi:10.1016/j.chb.2015.01.018

Klimmt, C., Hartmann, T., & Schramm, H. (2006). Parasocial interactions and relationships. In J. Bryant & P. Vorderer (Eds.), *Psychology of entertainment* (pp. 291–313). Mahwah, NJ: Lawrence Erlbaum Associates Publishers.

Krull, R., & Husson, W. (1979). Children's attention: The case of TV viewing. In E. Wartella (Ed.), *Children communicating: Media and development of thought, speech, understanding* (pp. 83–114). Beverly Hills, CA: Sage.

Kusumoto, K., Kinnunen, T., Kätsyri, J., Lindroos, H., & Oittinen, P. (2014). Media experience of complementary information and tweets on a second screen. In K. A. Hua, Y. Rui, & R. Steinmetz (Eds.), *MM '14: Proceedings of the 22nd ACM International Conference on Multimedia* (pp. 437–446). New York: ACM. doi:10.1145/2647868.2654925

Lennard, J. (2012). *Talking sense about "Fifty Shades of Grey", or, fanfiction, feminism, and BDSM* (Kindle ed.). Retrieved from Amazon.

Marwick, A., & boyd, D. (2011). To see and be seen: Celebrity practice on Twitter. *Convergence: The International Journal of Research into New Media Technologies, 17*(2), 139–158. doi:10.1177/1354856510394539

The Nielsen Company. (2014). *The digital consumer*. New York. Retrieved from www.nielsen.com/content/dam/corporate/us/en/reports-downloads/2014%20Reports/the-digital-consumer-report-feb-2014.pdf

Petersen, L. N. (2014). *Sherlock* fans talk: Mediatized talk on Tumblr. *Northern Lights*, *12*, 87–104. doi:10.1386/nl.12.87_1

Pittman, M., & Tefertiller, A. C. (2015). With or without you: Connected viewing and co-viewing Twitter activity for traditional appointment and asynchronous broadcast television models. *First Monday*, *20*(7), article 3. doi:10.5210/fm.v20i7.5935

Przybylski, A. K., & Weinstein, N. (2012). Can you connect with me now? How the presence of mobile communication technology influences face-to-face conversation quality. *Journal of Social and Personal Relationships*, *30*, 237–246. doi:10.1177/0265407512453827

Rama, V., Garimella, K., & Weber, I. (2014). Co-following on Twitter. In *Proceedings of the 25th ACM Conference on Hypertext and Social Media* (pp. 249–254). ACM. doi:10.1145/2631775.2631820

Rice, M. L., Huston, C. A., & Wright, J. C. (1983). The forms of television: Effects on children's attention, comprehension, and social behavior. In M. Meyer (Ed.), *Children and the formal features of television: Approaches and findings of experimental and formative research* (pp. 21–55). Munich, Germany: K. G. Saur.

Roskos-Ewoldsen, D. R., & Roskos-Ewoldsen, B. (2010). Message processing. In C. R. Berger, M. E. Roloff, & D. R. Roskos-Ewoldsen (Eds.), *Handbook of communication science* (2nd ed., pp. 129–144). Los Angeles, CA: Sage.

Rubin, R. B., & McHugh, M. P. (1987). Development of parasocial interaction relationships. *Journal of Broadcasting & Electronic Media*, *31*(3), 279–292. doi:10.1080/08838158709386664

Ryan, R. M., & Deci, E. L. (2000). Self-determination theory and the facilitation of intrinsic motivation, social development, and well-being. *American Psychologist*, *55*, 68–78. doi:10.1037/0003-066X.55.1.68

Salvucci, D. D., & Taatgen, N. A. (2008). Threaded cognition: An integrated theory of concurrent multitasking. *Psychological Review*, *115*, 101–130. doi:10.1037/0033-295X.115.1.101

Slater, M. D. (2015). Reinforcing spirals model: Conceptualizing the relationship between media content exposure and the development and maintenance of attitudes. *Media Psychology*, *18*, 370–395. doi:10.1080/15213269.2014.897236

Slater, M. D., Johnson, B. K., Cohen, J., Comello, M. L. G., & Ewoldsen, D. R. (2014). Temporarily expanding the boundaries of the self: Motivations for entering the story world and implications for narrative effects. *Journal of Communication*, *64*, 439–455. doi:10.1111/jcom.12100

Smith, A., & Boyles, J. L. (2012). *The rise of the "connected viewer."* Washington, DC. Retrieved from http://pewInternet.org/Reports/2012/Connected-viewers.aspx

Stefanone, M. A., Lackaff, D., & Rosen, D. (2010). The relationship between traditional mass media and "social media": Reality television as a model for social network site behavior. *Journal of Broadcasting & Electronic Media*, *54*, 508–525. doi:10.1080/08838151.2010.498851

Tal-Or, N. (2016). How co-viewing affects attitudes: The mediating roles of transportation and identification. *Media Psychology*, *19*, 381–405. doi:10.1080/15213269.2015.1082918

Tal-Or, N., & Tsfati, Y. (2015). Does the co-viewing of sexual material affect rape myth acceptance? The role of the co-viewer's reactions and gender. *Communication Research*, *42*, 1–26. doi:10.1177/0093650215595073

Thornton, B., Faires, A., Robbins, M., & Rollins, E. (2014). The mere presence of a cell phone may be distracting: Implications for attention and task performance. *Social Psychology*, *45*, 479–488. doi:10.1027/1864-9335/a000216

Toma, C. L., & Hancock, J. T. (2013). Self-affirmation underlies Facebook use. *Personality and Social Psychology Bulletin*, *39*, 31–331. doi:10.1177/0146167212474694

Van Cauwenberge, A., Schaap, G., & van Roy, R. (2014). "TV no longer commands our full attention": Effects of second-screen viewing and task relevance on cognitive load and learning from news. *Computers in Human Behavior*, *38*, 100–109. doi:10.1016/j.chb.2014.05.021

Voorveld, H. A. M., & Viswanathan, V. (2015). An observational study on how situational factors influence media multitasking with TV: The role of genres, dayparts, and social viewing. *Media Psychology*, *18*, 499–526. doi:10.1080/15213269.2013.872038

Vorderer, P. (2016). Communication and the good life: Why and how our discipline should make a difference. *Journal of Communication*, *66*, 1–12. doi:10.1111/jcom.12194

Vorderer, P., & Kohring, M. (2013). Permanently online: A challenge for media and communication research. *International Journal of Communication*, *7*, 188–196. Retrieved from http://ijoc.org/index.php/ijoc/article/view/1963

Wang, Z., Irwin, M., Cooper, C., & Srivastava, J. (2015). Multidimensions of media multitasking and adaptive media selection. *Human Communication Research, 41*, 102–127. doi:10.1111/hcre.12042

Yeykelis, L., Cummings, J. J., & Reeves, B. (2014). Multitasking on a single device: Arousal and the frequency, anticipation, and prediction of switching between media content on a computer. *Journal of Communication, 64*, 167–192. doi:10.1111/jcom.12070

Zwarun, L., & Hall, A. (2012). Narrative persuasion, transportation, and the role of need for cognition in online viewing of fantastical films. *Media Psychology, 15*, 327–355. doi:10.1080/15213269.2012.700592

13
Being POPC Together

Permanent Connectedness and Group Dynamics

Katharina Knop-Huelss, Julia R. Winkler, and Jana Penzel

Human beings are inherently social. From an evolutionary perspective, participation in groups was the only way to survive and satisfy basic needs. Individuals, therefore, have a need to belong (Baumeister & Leary, 1995), which they satisfy with dyadic interpersonal relationships and as members of social groups. Before the rise of telecommunication (Short, Williams, & Christie, 1976) and nowadays' ubiquitous online tools, interaction of a social group as a whole was dependent on the physical presence of its group members (Licoppe, 2004). Computer-mediated communication (e.g., e-mailing, online forums, and social networking sites) then allowed group members to interact and exchange messages without being physically present as a group (boyd & Ellison, 2007). However, with mobile communication technologies now allowing people to be POPC, group members can be permanently connected to their groups, most easily through mobile instant messaging applications (MIMAs). MIMAs enable private, near-synchronous interaction not only for dyads (Rieger, this volume; Utz, this volume), but also for larger social groups. People appreciate group functionality as one of the most important features of these applications (Church & Oliveira, 2013) and frequently use them (Ling & Lai, 2016; Qiu et al., 2016; Seufert, Schwind, Hoßfeld, & Tran-Gia, 2016): They organize and coordinate face-to-face meetings, discuss various topics, spread group-relevant information, inform each other about news in their lives, send funny pictures, or in short: stay in touch. They are *POPC as a group*.

How does the adoption of MIMAs and being POPC together affect the dynamics of a social group? What does permanent connectedness do to social bonds within groups? The present chapter examines the POPC phenomenon from a group perspective and thus builds on past research in social psychology and other fields on small-group processes. This research, and work on computer-mediated group communication in particular, has historically focused on groups in "organizational and applied settings" (Putnam & Stohl, 1990, p. 248). The majority of these studies have addressed issues such as the influence of the peer group on either prosocial (e.g., Hoorn, Dijk, Meuwese, Rieffe, & Crone, 2016) or antisocial behavior (e.g., Ellis & Zarbatany, 2007), online collaboration (e.g., how groups can increase their performance; e.g., Oliveira, Tinoca, & Pereira, 2011), and online social support (e.g., in self-help online forums for cancer patients; e.g., Shim, Cappella, & Han, 2011). The latter two examples in particular focused on groups that are primarily tied to a specific task or can be situated in a formal setting, such as a work environment. With the use of mobile online-based group communication, the dynamics of such groups are changed. However, this relatively new way of group communication is also—or maybe even more so—relevant for informal, more socially oriented groups, such as friends and families. A lot of mobile online-based group communication revolves around the organization of an event or a specific task and thus is of ephemeral and purposive nature. As this chapter is concerned with the relevance of MIMAs for group relationships and dynamics rather than MIMAs as an organization tool, we are particularly interested in more permanent groups that outlast the organization of single events. However, we will argue that groups with an organizational purpose can also be influenced by and develop into something more sustainable because of being POPC together. Being POPC as a social group (be it formal or informal) thus presents a new object of investigation. The goal of the chapter is to outline the implications this phenomenon may have, which should guide future research on POPC and call for more investigative efforts on the group perspective of mobile online interaction.

Being POPC as a Group

Being POPC does not fundamentally change the way in which a number of people come to constitute themselves as a social group and act within the context of their group. However, by creating an additional, permanently and ubiquitously available online communication space, the dynamics of these group processes are likely to change fundamentally. We define a social group as a constellation of three or more people who repeatedly interact with each other (Howard, 2014), "share a common social identification of themselves" (Turner, 1982, p. 15), and collectively perceive themselves as a social unity. In addition, we focus primarily on groups whose members either regularly meet or have met physically at some point during their group history and now use MIMAs as an *additional* communication channel. We thus exclude groups that are formed via online communication first and are mainly or solely in contact via the Internet, such as fan groups on social network sites.

Via MIMAs, group members can exchange text and audio messages, images, videos, and location information, addressing all group members at the same time. MIMAs thus open up "an imagined shared social space" (Panek, Bayer, Dal Cin, & Campbell, 2015, p. 385) for both formal and informal social groups (e.g., colleagues at work/a school class vs. families/friends). Because of affordable data plans and extensive network coverage, this communication environment is permanently available and can be accessed at any time in any given situation (Jensen, 2013). Group members can always tap into the latent streams of the group's conversation regardless of time and location (Klimmt, Hefner, Reinecke, Rieger, and Vorderer, this volume). Thus, we argue that these individuals are POPC as a group.

Attachment to a Group and Group Boundaries

It does not take much for a number of individuals to feel attached to each other and eventually perceive of themselves as a group (Baumeister & Leary, 1995). According to the minimal group paradigm (cf. Smith, 2010), individuals that have been sorted into groups based on arbitrary characteristics (e.g., preference of particular artists) quickly demonstrate in-group over out-group favoritism. Likewise, feeling as a member of a social group should be enhanced by the use of MIMAs. In most MIMAs, users form a new group conversation by actively and consciously adding group-members-to-be to the newly formed group. Individuals know that they are part of the group because they see on their mobile device that they have been added to the group conversation. Group boundaries are thus clearly visible to in-group members. We argue that the explicitness and unambiguity of group boundaries that are defined through MIMAs may be an important factor for the perception of a group's unity and attachment of members to the group: The existence of a group within a MIMA environment creates perceived facticity of the social connection among its members.

Social groups can be distinguished by the type of attachment of their members to the group as a whole (Prentice, Miller, & Lightdale, 1994): There are groups of *common bond* and groups of *common identity*. In groups based on *common bond*, members are part of the group because of the personal attraction between group members. Knowledge, liking, feelings of similarity, and the perceived homogeneity influence the strength of their common bond (Sassenberg, 2002). A group of best friends is an example of a common-bond group. In groups based on a *common identity*, members are part of the group because of a shared interest that results in "identification with the group as a whole, its goal and its purpose" (Sassenberg, 2002, p. 28). This type of attachment depends on "one's commitment to the identity of the group" (Prentice et al., 1994, p. 485) and is independent from interpersonal attraction to members (Prentice et al., 1994). Sport teams or amateur theater groups, but also school classes or project teams at work or university, are examples for this type of group. Sassenberg (2002) emphasizes that these two types of attachment (common bond and common identity) do not represent poles of a single continuum, but rather "mark a pole of different dimensions" (p. 35). Therefore, groups can vary on both dimensions, with the more pronounced dimension determining their type. For example, a group of students can be formed to work on a class assignment. Here, group attachment should be strong due to the shared interest of submitting the assignment in a satisfactory way, thus marking a pole of the common-identity dimension. However, in the course of working together, the students could grow to like each other and develop member attachment. Therefore, increasing levels on the other dimension, that is, common bond, are to be expected.

These group types have been shown to exist in both the physical and the online realms (Prentice et al., 1994; Sassenberg, 2002). We expect both common-bond and common-identity groups to use MIMAs. It is plausible to assume, however, that being POPC fulfills different functions for the two types of groups, and the use of MIMAs should thus hold different significance for them. We therefore believe that this distinction is beneficial when looking at and differentiating the functions of being POPC for social groups that rely on both face-to-face interactions and mobile online communication.

Type of Attachment Predicts Function of Group Communication via MIMA

Past research has identified several motivations and gratifications for the use of stationary instant messaging (e.g., with the messaging service ICQ). Relationship maintenance appears to be the most important gratification (Ku, Chu, & Tseng, 2013), but passing time, entertainment, relaxation, and information seeking are also relevant (Hwang & Lombard, 2006; Ku et al., 2013; Leung, 2001; Quan-Haase & Young, 2010). Little is known about how and why social groups use MIMAs, however. Seufert and colleagues (2016) categorized group conversations in MIMAs with regards to whether they were created for a "unique event" (e.g., organizing a birthday present), a "repetitive event" (e.g., soccer training), or "no event" (e.g., a group of family members; p. 233). It seems MIMAs are used to organize and coordinate short-term events, but also to maintain relationships. These findings can be mapped onto the distinction between groups of common bond and of common identity.

Bond-based groups are built on interpersonal attachment. It is likely that group members primarily use MIMAs to stay in touch with each other and to maintain this interpersonal attachment. Group members can share personal information, thus increasing knowledge about each other and liking (because self-disclosure is positively related to liking; Collins & Miller, 1994). The importance of the online communication space should increase with the strength of the group's bond and the spatial disparity of group members. Being POPC as a group should be especially important to groups whose members have strong interpersonal attachment and are not able to meet physically (e.g., a group of very good friends who all moved to different cities). With the help of MIMAs, these groups can nurture their bond of attachment and increase the group's longevity even after its members' situations in life have changed, thus ensuring their group's continuity. Early studies on the effect of Internet-based communication among friends showed that using instant messaging services was positively related to quality and closeness of friendships (Blais, Craig, Pepler, & Connolly, 2008; Valkenburg & Peter, 2007).

In contrast, identity-based groups are formed around a shared interest. The online communication space can be used to share information related to the group's identity. Members can organize face-to-face encounters and discuss issues regarding their group's goals and purpose. For example, MIMAs may serve the rapid solution of problems within a work team through circulation of knowledge among group members. There is a higher likelihood to conform to group norms in identity-based groups (Postmes, Spears, & Lea, 2000; Sassenberg & Boos, 2003). Off-topic conversations should be less likely than in bond-based groups, because divergence from the topic leads to less group attachment (Sassenberg, 2002).

POPC and the Blending of Group Attachment Types

Repeated interaction via MIMAs and being POPC together should thus strengthen the bonds within the group, enhance members' awareness of the group (Hogg & Reid, 2006; Petersen, Dietz, & Frey, 2004), and add to its stability and longevity. But being POPC might also serve as a catalyst to change the type of attachment to a group. We argue that especially groups based on common identity are affected by the characteristics of communication via MIMAs. Whereas it is not as easy to chat about idle topics during soccer practice or choir rehearsal, the online communication space created in MIMAs can be used to exchange information on just about anything, thus softening clear-cut boundaries between aspects usually ascribed to a certain type of group. One could, for example, imagine that a sports team will use the mobile communication not only to organize how to travel to the next away match, but also to send images from last night's party, either when the group was celebrating together or when group members were out individually and want to share their experiences. In addition, MIMAs allow for *interstitial* communication (Utz, this volume), where communication partners exchange mostly short messages as a "frequent reminder of their presence." Communication in the context of POPC is close to everyday life, and MIMAs pose a low threshold for participation, thus encouraging to share personal information or funny cat pictures. This might be especially beneficial for common-identity groups to strengthen liking and interpersonal attraction. As a consequence, POPC behavior would render common-identity groups more similar in their communication dynamics to common-bond groups, with possible benign (or problematic) effects on individual members and group performance. Under certain circumstances, for example, when faced with an external challenge or a threat to the group, members of bond-based groups can also develop a common identity (Gaffney & Mahajan, 2010; Sassenberg, 2002). However, the role of being POPC together remains unclear. For example, how does the fact that group boundaries are explicitly and unambiguously defined by MIMA groups affect attachment, feelings of the group's unity, sense of belonging, and the longevity of a group? How does nicknaming the group, sending photos, videos, experiences of daily life, and other content help to build and nourish a group's identity and/or a common bond among members? Future research should work to identify and investigate the effects of the features that are unique to communication via MIMAs and that may play an important role in this respect.

Being POPC as a group does not only affect ongoing communication dynamics. MIMAs and other applications also create a "digital archive" of a group's memories and its digital presence. These archives are not only made up of plain text messages, but also of shared pictures, memes, and videos, thus adding richness to the group's collective memories. This opens up interesting questions for communication research. Do these digital archives enhance awareness of the group, thus fostering its stability and the group's sense of belonging? How do groups use cross-references to and interplay with other social media such as Facebook?

To sum up, this section described how the attachment between group members can be conceptualized in terms of a group's common bond and identity. Research suggests that this distinction will have implications for the way and the reasons groups use MIMAs and thus the functions that being POPC holds for the group. Over time, the quality and intensity of group attachment may alter. We propose that certain aspects of POPC behavior and MIMAs may play an important role in that process.

Group Norms in the Context of POPC

A second perspective on how POPC is intertwined with group dynamics are possible shifts in communication norms. Every social group has their set of appropriate and inappropriate behaviors and attitudes (Rimal & Lapinski, 2008). Once a social group starts being POPC, group members have to negotiate norms on the usage of their additional communication space. What exactly and how much is shared via MIMAs within a group's mobile communication environment is guided by group-specific norms. Group norms do not exist per se but "are socially constructed over time" (McLaughlin & Vitak, 2012, p. 301) through social interaction (Martey & Stromer-Galley, 2007). These norms then serve as a "framework through which people determine what behaviors are acceptable and unacceptable" (McLaughlin & Vitak, 2012, p. 300).

Group Norms to Be Established: Quantity and Content of Messaging

In general, group norms have to be established regarding the amount and frequency of communication and the appropriate time passing between replies (response latency). Due to its technical characteristics, MIMAs encourage highly frequent, mostly informal, and conversational interaction among users (Church & Oliveira, 2013). This is reflected in reports by adolescents among whom it is not uncommon to receive hundreds of messages within a few hours (Lenhart, 2012). The extent to which group members use their online communication space, that is, how much and how often members exchange messages, and how much time is acceptable to pass between replies, may be a result of the purpose and significance of the online communication space for the group. Little is known about this so far, however.

In order to communicate via MIMAs, the group also has to (at least implicitly) agree on the topics discussed concerning variety and the level of intimacy. Regarding variety, identity-based and bond-based groups differ in the extent to which they engage in and tolerate off-topic conversations (Sassenberg, 2002). However, it is unclear how the respective type of group uses the online communication space and whether the variety of acceptable topics offline is transferred to the mobile group conversation. In common-identity groups, the extent of interpersonal attachment between group members should play a role with regards as to whether off-topic discussions are deemed acceptable. Common-bond groups may discuss a broad variety of topics; however, the more group members share a common goal or purpose, the more often topics related to this common interest should occur.

Regarding the level of intimacy of the topics discussed online, one could argue that due to the limited cues available in computer-mediated communication, some group members might feel encouraged to share private information. However, self-disclosure in a social group is reported to occur more often in offline settings than in MIMAs (Knop et al., 2016); the distinction between the types of group attachment may help to put this finding into perspective.

Activation of Group Norms

Members can either learn about group norms directly, when people explicitly talk about or nonverbally indicate the appropriate behavior within the group, or infer norms indirectly from behavior and communication content of group members (Hogg & Reid, 2006). However, in order for group members to act in accordance with group norms, group membership has to be made salient (Hogg & Reid, 2006). With groups being POPC, opportunities for members to communicate with the whole group increase, which consequently creates new opportunities for the group membership to become salient.

In MIMAs, the respective group comes into focus with every message activity. This occurs independently from whether the individual group member decides to send a message to the group or whether a new message is posted by another group member (unless users deactivate automatic notifications). The more a group is POPC, the more salience opportunities there are. However, whether this motivates group members to act accordingly to group norms will depend on the members' situational context. In the context of Facebook, Lampinen, Tamminen, and Oulasvirta (2009) state that oftentimes "many groups important to an individual are simultaneously present in one context and their presence is salient for the individual" (p. 1), a phenomenon they refer to as *group co-presence* and which can be transferred to MIMAs. Do group members receive the message while alone at home or are they among another group of friends? Are group members active in simultaneous MIMA conversations and have to continuously switch back and forth (i.e., multitasking, see David, this volume, and Wang, this volume)? In that case, with every message that is received, a group member has to quickly switch between group conversations, to activate the appropriate group identity, and to adhere to the respective group norms. The topics discussed should also influence whether a group identity is made salient. A topic close to the original purpose of the group might render the group identity more salient than a discussion that is not concerned with central topics.

Communication norms mainly originate from the "offline reality" of a social group. For example, a group will have established a level of intimacy and implicitly agreed to not talk about certain topics. These norms will probably be used as guideline for the online communication space. However, we argue that communicating via MIMAs will produce new group norms that apply specifically to the online communication environment (e.g., how many messages are sent a day, how many emoticons are appropriate to use). These "online norms" can eventually change the originally negotiated group norms in the offline domain. Hence, the online communication space does not exist separately from the offline sphere, but is an extension thereof. For instance, if someone is posting memes and jokes to the group, members learn something about the kind of humor that is acceptable within the group, which may change the way members interact face-to-face.

In this section, we outlined how groups have to develop a set of rules for communication in terms of the quantity, quality, and frequency of their message exchange. Again, the distinction between common-bond and common-identity groups is considered to be a crucial factor in this respect. We argue that being POPC activates cognitions of group membership and consequently, group norms, with every message that members receive. However, these activated norms may coincide and possibly concur with other norms relevant in a particular situation, online or offline. Most importantly, it should be noted that even though the terms "offline" and "online" refer to different modes of communication for a group, these spheres should not be understood as separate but as deeply intertwined and mutually reactive.

Effects of Being POPC as a Group on Individual Members

So far, we have reviewed an attachment and a norm perspective on the implications of POPC behavior for group dynamics. A third important view on what to expect and to investigate is the consequence of being POPC as a group for individual members. In general, group membership has numerous relevant effects on individuals. Specific effects of POPC behavior of the group on members that can be expected may include the social and emotional support received through group belonging, but also negative consequences such as digital stress or social exclusion.

Gaining social and emotional support from interactions with the group and the feeling of belonging may be one effect for individuals from being POPC together (Vorderer et al., 2015). Research has shown that online self-disclosure among close friends and relationships can yield such positive outcomes, for example, in the context of social networking sites (Ellison & Vitak, 2015; Trepte & Reinecke, 2013) or instant messaging (Valkenburg & Peter, 2009). Being POPC means that through MIMAs, social and emotional support by the group is available in almost any situation if needed. Quick help can be expected and issues can be discussed with multiple groups simultaneously, directly catering to one's needs. For example, a young academic may have received different job offers and may ask for opinions and advice from family as well as a group of fellow students.

On the other hand, a flood of incoming messages as described above (Lenhart, 2012) can lead to high levels of perceived pressure to answer and thus impose stress on the individual group members (Hefner & Vorderer, 2016). Members might want to leave the group conversation under such circumstances; however, explicit messages that proclaim the member's withdrawal may hinder them to actually quit the conversation. This adds to another aspect where people report having been added to a group conversation without wanting to talk to the respective members (Karapanos, Teixeira, & Gouveia, 2016), and others having been added for the sole purpose of being ridiculed and bullied (Knop et al., 2015).

Being POPC as a group can also change the social position of group members. On the one hand, those who are not POPC are excluded from a certain amount of (online) communication and might thus be pushed to the periphery of the group. As a consequence, these members might feel ostracized (e.g., Sacco, Bernstein, Young, & Hugenberg, 2014). On the other hand, socially inhibited members can take advantage of the perks of computer-mediated communication. Studies have shown that for people who are shy but sociable, the reduced-cues environment of online communication allows them to overcome social inhibition (e.g., Sheeks & Birchmeier, 2007; Stritzke, Nguyen, & Durkin, 2004). They can therefore become more important members of the group.

Thus, group membership holds a number of both positive and negative possible consequences for individuals. Group members can take advantage of the permanent availability of social and emotional support through MIMAs. The online communication space may also be beneficial for those with social inhibitions to develop meaningful relationships to their group. However, the multitude of messages that many users of MIMAs are confronted with may cause stress under certain circumstances, which may partly result from the pressure to reply in order to prevent social exclusion.

Conclusions and Outlook

This chapter's aim was to provide an overview of how POPC behavior may affect group dynamics. The POPC phenomenon has changed the reality of many groups. We provided three perspectives on the phenomenon, namely attachment type, group norms, and effects on individual group members. Each of these perspectives brings about new challenges for research on POPC.

As we have argued above, social groups can be distinguished based on the substance that keeps them together: their common bond or their common identity. However, these qualities are neither mutually exclusive nor static. Group attachment may change over time, both in quality and intensity, and the ways that being POPC and the use of MIMAs can aid this process is a question that future communication research should look into. How does the use of MIMAs encourage or hinder specific ways of communication that may lead to a change in the way a group's members feel about their group? Two challenges arise from this demand: On the one hand, longitudinal perspectives and methods are required to account for the development of group *dynamics* over time. On the other hand, being POPC as a group also requires careful consideration of the levels of analysis. One has to clearly distinguish—both theoretically, as well as methodologically—between those effects and processes that occur at the group level (e.g., cohesion as a group property), those that occur at the individual level (e.g., increased/decreased attachment to the group), and cross-level phenomena (e.g., the interplay of individual members' attachment and group cohesion).

In order to appropriately investigate the phenomenon of POPC, research is in need of theoretical models that are able to integrate the interplay of offline and online communication situations. This becomes apparent in the context of the social construction of group norms. A group requires specific norms that apply for communication via MIMAs (e.g., how many messages can be posted before the other members feel annoyed). But what happens online is also part of the group's social reality, independent from the communication context (online/offline). Theoretical models are needed that integrate these different realms while still taking into account the specific characteristics of the respective communication context (e.g., reduced cues in online communication).

We also described possible effects of group membership in the context of POPC for individual members. Most importantly, we ask whether being POPC together is beneficial or detrimental for an individual's (social) well-being. How does an individual (who is not only part of one group) manage the increased volume of group communication to maximize her or his benefits of group membership(s)?

By no means do we claim to have covered all group processes that are possibly affected by being POPC. Research on communication in small groups has traditionally covered topics of social influence, such as conformity, intra- and intergroup conflict, information sharing, and group decision-making (e.g., Fisher & Ellis, 1980; Hirokawa, Cathcart, Samovar, & Henman, 2003). Clearly, these types of group dynamics deserve examinations concerning the consequences of being POPC just as those perspectives elaborated in the present chapter. Likewise, future research challenges emerge from the fact that neither people's media diets nor interactions within a social group are restricted to face-to-face meetings and communication via MIMAs, but are rather characterized by media multiplexity (Haythornthwaite, 2005). Although it might seem obvious, it is important to note that being POPC via MIMAs should not be regarded as a communication channel that is isolated from any offline context. It is rather an extension and a new influencer of the group's offline reality.

References

Baumeister, R. F., & Leary, M. R. (1995). The need to belong: Desire for interpersonal attachments as a fundamental human motivation. *Psychological Bulletin, 117*, 497–529. doi:10.1037/0033-2909.117.3.497

Blais, J., Craig, W. M., Pepler, D. J., & Connolly, J. (2008). Adolescents online: The importance of Internet activity choices to salient relationship. *Journal of Youth and Adolescence, 37*(5), 49–58. doi:10.1007/s10964-007-9262-7

boyd, d., & Ellison, N. B. (2007). Social network sites: Definition, history, and scholarship. *Journal of Computer-Mediated Communication, 13*, 210–230.

Church, K., & Oliveira, R. D. (2013). What's up with WhatsApp? Comparing mobile instant messaging behaviors with traditional SMS. In *Proceedings of the 15th International Conference on Human-Computer Interaction With Mobile Devices and Services* (pp. 352–361). New York: ACM Press.

Collins, N. L., & Miller, L. C. (1994). Self-disclosure and liking: A meta-analytic review. *Psychological Bulletin, 116*, 457–475. http://dx.doi.org/10.1037/0033-2909.116.3.457

Ellis, W. E., & Zarbatany, L. (2007). Peer group status as a moderator of group influence on children's deviant, aggressive, and prosocial behavior. *Child Development, 78*(4), 1240–1254. doi:10.1111/j.1467-8624.2007.01063.x

Ellison, N. B., & Vitak, J. (2015). Social network site affordances and their relationship to social capital processes. In S. Sundar (Ed.), *The handbook of the psychology of communication technology* (pp. 203–227). Chichester: John Wiley & Sons Ltd.

Fisher, B. A., & Ellis, D. G. (1980). *Small group decision making: Communication and the group process*. New York: McGraw-Hill.

Gaffney, A. M., & Mahajan, N. (2010). Common-identity/Common-bond groups. In J. M. Levine & M. A. Hogg (Eds.), *Encyclopedia of group processes & intergroup relations* (pp. 117–119). Thousand Oaks, CA: Sage Publications Ltd. doi:10.4135/9781412972017.n22

Haythornthwaite, C. (2005). Social networks and Internet connectivity effects. *Information, Communication & Society, 8*, 125–147. doi:10.1080/13691180500146185

Hefner, D., & Vorderer, P. (2016). *Digital stress*. In L. Reinecke & M. B. Oliver (Eds.), *The Routledge handbook of media use and well-being: International perspectives on theory and research on positive media effects* (pp. 237–249). New York: Routledge.

Hirokawa, R., Cathcart, R., Samovar, L., & Henman, L. (Eds.). (2003). *Small group communication: Theory and practice*. Los Angeles, CA: Roxbury Publishing Company.

Hogg, M. A., & Reid, S. A. (2006). Social identity, self-categorization, and the communication of group norms. *Communication Theory, 16*, 7–30. doi:10.1111/j.1468-2885.2006.00003.x

Hoorn, J., Dijk, E., Meuwese, R., Rieffe, C., & Crone, E. A. (2016). Peer influence on prosocial behavior in adolescence. *Journal of Research on Adolescence, 26*, 90–100. doi:10.1111/jora.12173

Howard, M. C. (2014). An epidemiological assessment of online groups and a test of a typology: What are the (dis)similarities of the online group types? *Computers in Human Behavior, 31*, 123–133. doi:10.1016/j.chb.2013.10.021

Hwang, H. S., & Lombard, M. (2006). Understanding instant messaging: Gratifications and social presence. Paper presented at the *9th Annual PRESENCE Conference*, Cleveland, OH. Retrieved from http://www.temple.edu/ispr/prev_conferences/proceedings/2006/Hwang%20and%20Lombard.pdf

Jensen, K. B. (2013). What's mobile in mobile communication? *Mobile Media & Communication, 1*, 26–31. doi:10.1177/2050157912459493

Karapanos, E., Teixeira, P., & Gouveia, R. (2016). Need fulfillment and experiences on social media: A case on Facebook and WhatsApp. *Computers in Human Behavior, 55*, 888–897. doi:10.1016/j.chb.2015.10.015

Knop, K. [Katharina], Öncü, J. S., Penzel, J., Abele, T. S., Brunner, T., Vorderer, P., & Wessler, H. (2016). Offline time is quality time: Comparing within-group self-disclosure in mobile messaging applications and face-to-face interactions. *Computers in Human Behavior, 55*, 1076–1084. doi:10.1016/j.chb.2015.11.004

Knop, K. [Karin], Hefner, D., Schmitt, S., & Vorderer, P. (2015). *Mediatisierung mobil: Handy- und mobile Internetnutzung von Kindern und Jugendlichen*. Schriftenreihe Medienforschung der Landesanstalt für Medien NRW, Vol. 77. Leipzig: Vistas.

Ku, Y. C., Chu, T. H., & Tseng, C. H. (2013). Gratifications for using CMC technologies: A comparison among SNS, IM, and e-mail. *Computers in Human Behavior, 29*, 226–234.

Lampinen, A., Tamminen, S., & Oulasvirta, A. (2009). All my people right here, right now: Management of group co-presence on a social networking site. In *Proceedings of the International Conference on Supporting Group-Work* (pp. 281–290). New York: ACM Press.

Lenhart, A. (2012, March 19). *Teens, smartphones & texting*. Retrieved from www.pewInternet.org/files/old-media/Files/Reports/2012/PIP_Teens_Smartphones_and_Texting.pdf

Leung, L. (2001). College student motives for chatting on ICQ. *New Media & Society, 3*, 483–500. doi:10.1177/14614440122226209

Licoppe, C. (2004). 'Connected' presence: The emergence of a new repertoire for managing social relationships in a changing communication technoscape. *Environment and Planning D: Society and Space, 22*, 135–156.

Ling, R., & Lai, C. H. (2016). Microcoordination 2.0: Social coordination in the age of smartphones and messaging apps. *Journal of Communication*, 66(5), 834–856. doi:10.1111/jcom.12251

Martey, R. M., & Stromer-Galley, J. (2007). The digital dollhouse context and social norms in the sims online. *Games and Culture*, 2, 314–334. doi:10.1177/1555412007309583

McLaughlin, C., & Vitak, J. (2012). Norm evolution and violation on Facebook. *New Media & Society*, 14, 299–315. doi:10.1177/1368430204041397

Oliveira, I., Tinoca, L., & Pereira, A. (2011). Online group work patterns: How to promote a successful collaboration. *Computers & Education*, 57, 1348–1357. doi:10.1016/j.compedu.2011.01.017

Panek, E. T., Bayer, J. B., Dal Cin, S., & Campbell, S. W. (2015). Automaticity, mindfulness, and self-control as predictors of dangerous texting behavior. *Mobile Media & Communication*, 3, 380–400. doi:10.1177/2050157915571591

Petersen, L.-E., Dietz, J., & Frey, D. (2004). The effects of intragroup interaction and cohesion on intergroup bias. *Group Processes and Intergroup Relations*, 7, 107–118. doi:10.1177/1368430204041397

Postmes, T., Spears, R., & Lea, M. (2000). The formation of group norms in computer-mediated communication. *Human Communication Research*, 26, 341–371. doi:10.1111/j.1468-2958.2000.tb00761.x

Prentice, D. A., Miller, D. T., & Lightdale, J. R. (1994). Asymmetries in attachments to groups and to their members: Distinguishing between common-identity and common-bond groups. *Personality and Social Psychology Bulletin*, 20, 484–493. doi:10.1177/0146167294205005

Putnam, L. L., & Stohl, C. (1990). Bona fide groups: A reconceptualization of groups in context. *Communication Studies*, 41, 248–265. doi:10.1080/10510979009368307

Qiu, J., Li, Y., Tang, J., Lu, Z., Ye, H., Chen, B., Yang, Q., & Hopcroft, J. E. (2016). The lifecycle and cascade of WeChat social messaging groups. In *Proceedings of the 25th International Conference on World Wide Web* (pp. 311–320). International World Wide Web Conferences Steering Committee.

Quan-Haase, A., & Young, A. (2010). Uses and gratifications of social media: A comparison of Facebook and instant messaging. *Bulletin of Science Technology and Society*, 30, 350–361. doi:10.1177/0270467610380009

Rimal, R. N., & Lapinski, M. K. (2008). Social norms. In W. Donsbach (Ed.), *The international encyclopedia of communication*. Malden, MA: Blackwell Publishing. Retrieved from www.communicationencyclopedia.com/subscriber/tocnode.html?id=g9781405131995_chunk_g978140513199524_ss71-1

Sacco, D. F., Bernstein, M. J., Young, S. G., & Hugenberg, K. (2014). Reactions to social inclusion and ostracism as a function of perceived in-group similarity. *Group Dynamics: Theory, Research, and Practice*, 18, 129–137. doi:10.1037/gdn0000002

Sassenberg, K. (2002). Common bond and common identity groups on the Internet: Attachment and normative behavior in on-topic and off-topic chats. *Group Dynamics: Theory, Research, and Practice*, 6, 27–37. doi:10.1037/1089-2699.6.1.27

Sassenberg, K., & Boos, M. (2003). Attitude change in computer-mediated communication: Effects of anonymity and category norms. *Group Processes & Intergroup Relations*, 6, 405–422. doi:10.1177/13684302030064006

Seufert, M., Schwind, A., Hoßfeld, T., & Tran-Gia, P. (2016). Analysis of group-based communication in WhatsApp. In R. Agüero, T. Zinner, M. García-Lozano, B. L. Wenning, & A. Timm-Giel (Eds.), *Mobile networks and management: 7th international conference, MONAMI 2015* (pp. 225–238). Cham: Springer. doi:10.1007/978-3-319-26925-2_17

Sheeks, M. S., & Birchmeier, Z. P. (2007). Shyness, sociability, and the use of computer-mediated communication in relationship development. *CyberPsychology & Behavior*, 10, 64–70. doi:10.1089/cpb.2006.9991

Shim, M., Cappella, J. N., & Han, J. Y. (2011). How does insightful and emotional disclosure bring potential health benefits? Study based on online support groups for women with breast cancer. *Journal of Communication*, 61, 432–454. doi:10.1111/j.1460-2466.2011.01555.x

Short, J., Williams, E., & Christie, B. (1976). *The social psychology of telecommunications*. London: Wiley.

Smith, J. (2010). Minimal group effect. In J. M. Levine & M. A. Hogg (Eds.), *Encyclopedia of group processes & intergroup relations* (pp. 555–557). Thousand Oaks, CA: Sage. doi:10.4135/9781412972017.n169

Stritzke, W. G. K., Nguyen, A., & Durkin, K. (2004). Shyness and computer-mediated communication: A self-presentational theory perspective. *Media Psychology*, 6, 1–22. doi:10.1207/s1532785xmep0601_1

Trepte, S., & Reinecke, L. (2013). The reciprocal effects of social network site use and the disposition for self-disclosure: A longitudinal study. *Computers in Human Behavior*, 29, 1102–1112. doi:10.1016/j.chb.2012.10.002

Turner, J. C. (1982). Towards a cognitive redefinition of the social group. In H. Tajfel (Ed.), *Social identity and intergroup relations* (pp. 15–40). Cambridge: Cambridge University Press.

Valkenburg, P. M., & Peter, J. (2007). Preadolescents' and adolescents' online communication and their closeness to friends. *Developmental Psychology, 43*, 267–277. doi:10.1037/0012-1649.43.2.267

Valkenburg, P. M., & Peter, J. (2009). The effect of instant messaging on the quality of adolescents' existing friendships: A longitudinal study. *Journal of Communication, 59*, 79–97. doi:10.1111/j.1460-2466.2008.01405.x

Vorderer, P. (2015). Der mediatisierte Lebenswandel: Permanently online, permanently connected [The mediatized lifestyle: Permanently online, permanently connected]. *Publizistik, 60*, 259–276. doi:10.1007/s11616-015-0239-3

14
POPC and Social Relationships

Sonja Utz

It's a common picture nowadays: Two people are sitting at a table in a café, but instead of talking with each other, they stare at their smartphones. They might check the updates on their Facebook timeline, share the location of the café at Swarm, post a picture of their food on Instagram, and exchange Whats-App messages with friends. What are the consequences of these changed communication patterns for social relationships? Some people worry that the ubiquity of smartphones has deteriorated social relationships since face-to-face conversations are replaced by superficial short messages on electronic devices (Turkle, 2012). Others—often younger people—value the possibility to be permanently connected with their network and the new ways of maintaining relationships (Pettegrew & Day, 2015; Rainie & Wellman, 2012). Vorderer et al. (2015) introduced the acronym POPC (permanently online and permanently connected) to describe the fact that thinking and acting is nowadays influenced by the possibility to be permanently in touch with one's network via smartphones and other technologies. The goal of this chapter is to explore the potential effects of POPC on social relationships.

There cannot be a simple answer to the question how POPC affects relationships. First, because close relationships are often characterized by media multiplexity (Haythornthwaite, 2005): People use various communication media and tend to use more media to communicate with closer friends. Being permanently in touch via the smartphone is just one part of this communication mix and does not exclude frequent face-to-face (FTF) communication. Second, the type of communication might matter. Smartphones allow for a huge range of communication modes—phone calls, text messages, public posts on Facebook, private messages via the Facebook messenger, WhatsApp groups, and so on. These communication modes can be characterized in public and private modes, one-to-one and one-to-many or many-to-many conversations, synchronous or asynchronous forms of communication, or according to their media richness (Daft & Lengel, 1986), that is, the availability of different channels (text only; voice, picture, video, . . .). Third, the effects of POPC depend also on the type of relationship—the effects will most likely differ between intimate relationships (Rieger, this volume), close relationships with friends (strong ties), and less close relationships with acquaintances or former classmates (weak ties); it also might matter whether the interaction partner lives in a different city or country, so that mediated communication is necessary (Wessler, Rieger, Cohen, and Vorderer, this volume).

It would be far beyond the scope of this chapter to review all studies that focus on the effects of specific communication technologies on specific types of relationships. Instead, I will focus on the question of how the changed overall communication pattern might affect personal relationships. To do so, I will build on conceptual papers on the potential effects of POPC on relationships and discuss studies that provide empirical evidence for some of the claims made in these papers. The main focus is on close friendships, because people are mainly "permanently" connected with closer ties, although the use of social network sites (SNS) via smartphones increases also the communication frequency with weaker ties.

Toward Connected Presence and Interstitial Communication

Although the phenomenon POPC only recently started to receive attention from communication scholars and media psychologists (Bayer, Campbell, & Ling, 2016; Pettegrew & Day, 2015; Vorderer et al., 2015), sociologists have been pondering about the question of how POPC changes social relationships for a while. Especially the work by Licoppe and Smoreda (2005) is relevant here, as these authors noted already in 2005—before Facebook conquered countries outside of the United States and before smartphones were widely available—that "the traditional communication model, where tele-communication is used to connect people who are physically separated from each other, is gradually being supplanted with a new pattern of 'connected presence.'" (p. 317). They also predicted a new pattern of sociability in which especially mobile phones play an important role and where phatic communication has a central role in strengthening relationships. It is thus helpful to place the discussion on the effects of POPC in this broader historical context.

An important point in the discussion of media effects on social relationships is the (normative) evaluation of mediated communication. For a long time, FTF communication has been considered the gold standard when judging the quality of communication; early research of computer-mediated communication (CMC), for example, considered CMC an impersonal and less rich communication medium, since it lacked nonverbal cues (Daft & Lengel, 1986; Kiesler, Siegel, & McGuire, 1984). This has been criticized earlier, and research concluded already in the 1990s that online relationships are not necessarily less deep or intimate than FTF relationships (Parks & Roberts, 1998). According to Licoppe and Smoreda (2005, p. 321), this devaluation of mediated context might however no longer be valid at all in a time where the "boundaries between absence and presence get blurred," since people can constantly be in touch with each other. More recently, Pettegrew and Day (2015) postulated that communication scientists should stop considering CMC and mobile communication just an addendum to FTF communication and "recognize that individuals use mobile communication to develop close relationships across a wide variety of interrelated and converging contexts" (p. 122).

POPC is thus not a completely new phenomenon but developed gradually with the introduction of mobile phones. The first signs of a change of relationship maintenance behavior had been already detected more than 10 years ago (Licoppe & Smoreda, 2005). In these studies, two communication patterns were distinguished: relational and interstitial communication. Relational communication is the communication that has occurred over centuries between close friends or family members: the exchange of long messages (in the past, letters) that overcame distance. This pattern has also been found in a study on the use of the phone in social relationships: The further away a communication partner moved, the less frequent but longer the phone calls became. In these long conversations, people used to tell each other what happened in their life to construct a shared world despite the distance.

In contrast, interstitial communication is characterized by many short calls and messages. People who engage in this form of communication are not necessarily geographically far apart; even if they see each other frequently FTF, they express commitment in the frequent reminders of their presence. According to Licoppe and Smoreda (2005), the boundary between co-existence and co-presence becomes blurred, and the combination of various short calls and messages with FTF meetings creates an "always connected presence" (p. 330). In a similar vein, Vorderer et al. (2015) claimed that availability might replace geographical proximity, and Pettegrew and Day (2015) concluded that digital natives use several communication modes at the same time to be continuously connected with their interaction partner.

POPC can thus be considered a further shift toward the interstitial communication pattern. Since smartphones have become ubiquitous, bandwidth has increased, and Internet flat rates have become affordable, people no longer mainly briefly call and text their friends, but they now include richer media and also share photos and videos. The latest trend is video-stream platforms, such as Periscope, that allow people to share their life in real time with their friends. Absent friends can thus always "be there" via shared updates, photos, and even video streams; this might replace retelling each other what has happened (Vorderer et al., 2015). A related implication of the interstitial and multiplex communication is that latent conversation threads replace or at least supplement classical conversations, because there is no clear beginning and end of conversations anymore (Vorderer et al., 2015); instead, conversations are picked up whenever needed by whatever medium. A similar observation has been made in organizational settings; Majchrzak, Faraj, Kane, and Azad (2013) reported a shift from online knowledge sharing in centralized knowledge management systems toward continuous online knowledge conversations. In general, skimming and reacting to streams/newsfeeds became a more dominant form of communication. Although the short updates in these streams are usually only skimmed, it has been shown that they can create ambient awareness, that is, knowledge about what network members are doing (Levordashka & Utz, 2016), and in some cases, even ambient intimacy (Lin, Levordashka, & Utz, 2016).

Theories on the Role of Communication in Relationship Building and Maintenance

Before turning to the question of how POPC changes social relationships, it is useful to briefly review classical theories on the role of communication on relationship development and maintenance. When it comes to relationship development, self-disclosure has been considered the driving variable (Altman & Taylor, 1973). Social penetration theory characterizes self-disclosure according to its breadth and depth and argues that more intimate self-disclosure results in closer friendships. Indeed, a meta-analysis showed that people disclose more to people they like and like the ones more who disclose to them (Collins & Miller, 1994).

There is also work on the role of capitalization, i.e., the sharing of positive events, on relationship building (Gable & Reis, 2010). People have shared the positive events that happened to them with their partner or close others already before they were permanently connected, and it has been shown that the act of sharing itself can trigger positive emotions and subjective well-being. Effects on relationship satisfaction are however larger when the interaction partner responds in an enthusiastic and constructive way (Gable, Reis, Impett, & Asher, 2004; Gable & Reis, 2010).

Relationship maintenance has mainly be studied in romantic relationships (see also Rieger, this volume), and the most famous typology of maintenance behaviors comes from Stafford and Canary

(1991). They identified positivity, openness (relating again to self-disclosure), assurances, shared tasks, and networks (common friends) as relationship maintenance behaviors. Not all of these behaviors relate equally to communication, however, or can be easily applied to CMC or POPC.

Tong and Walther (2011) have adapted this typology to the context of publicly viewable online spaces such as SNS and introduced presence, tie signs, and mundane communication as new relationship maintenance behaviors. With presence, they refer to the perceived social presence of the friend and argue that this can be triggered by short little messages on various media. Tie signs are related to the networks aspect by Stafford and Canary (1991) and refer to the associations between people that are displayed on many social networks (e.g., Facebook friend, relationship status). Additionally, the (semi-) public displays of affection expressed on these social media (Donath & boyd, 2004) fall under this maintenance strategy. Moreover, Tong and Walther (2011) also argue that the mundane communication that is so often found on social media platforms has a relationship-strengthening function. The idea that seemingly meaningless communication can fulfill a relationship-building function had already been stressed in 1923 when the anthropologist Malinowski (cited in Miller, 2008) coined the term "phatic communication" for describing the communication in primitive languages. Phatic communication signals sociability while having no or little information value. Small talk or polite phrases are traditional examples for phatic communication; in the context of POPC, the widely spread short little updates on social media platforms or the pressing of the "like" button on Facebook are well-known examples.

Empirical Support for the Relationship-Building Function of POPC

To my knowledge, no study has yet systematically tested the effects of POPC on relationships. There are studies, however, that focus on the role of SNS in relationship maintenance. These are relevant since the majority of SNS users nowadays checks Facebook several times a day, often via the smartphone. Several studies have shown that SNS use mainly strengthens the bond with weak ties (Burke & Kraut, 2014; Ellison, Steinfield, & Lampe, 2007). In a similar vein, Vitak (2014) found that the perceived benefits of Facebook maintenance strategies for relationship quality occur not among the closest friends, but among people who are geographically separated and rely mostly on Facebook.

Regarding the underlying processes, it has been shown that the classical assumption that mainly intimate self-disclosure drives relationship building no longer holds. One reason is that intimate self-disclosure is often perceived as inappropriate in (semi-)public status updates (Bazarova, 2012). Instead, a strong positivity norm has developed; people preferably present themselves in a favorable light. As a consequence, many status updates are cool and entertaining rather than intimate (Barash, Duchenaut, Isaacs, & Bellotti, 2010; Utz, 2015). However, reading positive and entertaining status updates on Facebook also results in a feeling of connection (Utz, 2015). These findings support the claim by Tong and Walther (2011) that mundane communication fulfills an important function in relationship maintenance.

Licoppe and Smoreda (2005, p. 321) predicted that "simply keeping in touch may be more important than what is said when one actually gets in touch." In a conceptual paper, Miller (2008) interpreted status updates on social media as communication that serves primarily the goal of saying something to maintain social connections rather than as having something to say. Even more subtle communication acts such as clicking the "like" button might have a relationship-building function. There is recent empirical evidence for this claim. Levordashka, Utz, and Ambros (2016) asked Facebook users to go through their list of recently given "likes" and indicate their motives for "liking" a post. Although positive evaluations of the posted content was the most frequent reason for giving a "like," in many cases, a post was also "liked" because of the person who posted it and with the goal to maintain or strengthen the relationship. Similar findings have been reported by Hayes, Carr, and Wohn (2016), who conducted focus group and semi-structured interviews. Social grooming was frequently named as a reason for using "like" or similar buttons. Carr, Wohn, and Hayes (2016) examined the receiver perspective and found that people perceived receiving "likes" as social support. This effect was stronger when the likes came from a strong tie and when the receivers believed that the "likes" have not been given habitually. Levordashka et al. (2016) found that about 25% of "likes" are given almost automatically without much deliberation according to the self-report of users; taking this automaticity into account makes therefore sense. Taken together, the results from these three papers indicate that interstitial instances of phatic communication serve a relationship-strengthening function, especially in the case of close relationships.

Seo, Kim, and Yang (2016) were among the first who studied not the content, but the temporal pattern of communication on Facebook and found that frequent and fast reactions on Facebook predicted perceived social support and reduced loneliness, thereby supporting the idea that people expect permanent presence and reactions from friends. Studies on SNS use capture only parts of the effects of POPC on relationships, but there is not much systematic research on mobile instant messaging (MIM) on relationship maintenance yet; papers in this domain mainly describe communication patterns (Cui, 2016). However, Valkenburg and Peter (2009) found that using instant messaging (also from a desktop computer) had a positive effect on existing relationships of adolescents.

Thus, there is first empirical evidence from studies on SNS and instant messaging that frequent short messages can foster relationships. These messages do not need to be very intimate; positive and entertaining status updates also strengthen the feeling of connection, and subtle "like" clicks can function as a short signals of attention. It is unclear yet whether these findings from (semi-)public communication on SNS hold also for dyadic exchanges via WhatsApp, SMS, or short voice messages. However, one can assume that being POPC further increases the relative share of interstitial (vs. relational) communication and that this decrease of intimate communication does not necessarily imply a decline in relationship strength.

Downsides of POPC

Just like every technology, POPC offers not only new possibilities, but has also some drawbacks, which should be briefly addressed. Many platforms display information about who is online and who has read which messages; this information can give a new sense of control, but might backfire and create (a) jealousy and feelings of exclusion and (b) a pressure to respond; both could negatively affect relationships. Additionally, being POPC with someone via one's smartphone might negatively affect the relationship with the person physically co-present at the moment.

People who regularly post on Facebook or Twitter or check in at places via location-sharing services can be tracked without much effort. Moreover, since many of these venues push the activities of the friends into a user's newsfeed, the boundary between monitoring and normal use of the platform has become blurry (Utz & Beukeboom, 2011). These new subtle forms of social control have been shown to trigger jealousy in romantic relationships (Muise, Christofides, & Desmarais, 2009; Utz, Muscanell, & Khalid, 2015; see also Rieger, this volume). Not receiving an answer (within a short timeframe) although one's message has obviously been read might also lead to negative emotions such as feeling exclusion. When WhatsApp introduced the two blue ticks that indicated that a message has been read, the expression "feeling blue" has been used on Twitter and in the popular press to describe that people feel blue when they see that a friend has read their message but not responded to them (Hughes,

2014). In a similar vein, it has been shown that people who do not receive feedback on their Facebook updates expressed lower levels of belonging (Tobin, Vanman, Verreynne, & Saeri, 2015).

The displayed information of whether an interaction partner is online right now raises expectations on availability and the pressure to respond to messages (Fox & Moreland, 2015); some people even experience connection overload (LaRose, Connolly, Lee, Li, & Hales, 2014). However, not logging into social media is for many users also not an option, as they experience a fear of missing out (FOMO) when they do not regularly check online what their friends are up to. FOMO in turn correlates negatively with the satisfaction of psychological needs such as relatedness (Przybylski, Murayama, DeHaan, & Gladwell, 2013), indicating that higher FOMO might negatively affect relationships.

FOMO also affects offline relationships as it predicts phubbing (Chotpitayasunondh & Douglas, 2016). The term phubbing—a combination of phone and snubbing—has been coined to describe the behavior of snubbing someone by paying more attention to one's smartphone than to the face-to-face interaction partner (see also Rieger, this volume). Turkle (2012) argues that people busy with their smartphones are simply "alone together" but not more connected to their friends. Vanden Abeele, Antheunis, and Schouten (2016) conducted an experiment on the effects of phubbing and found that conversation partners who are texting on their mobile phone are perceived as less polite and attentive; the perceived conversation quality was also lower, although there was no effect on social attraction. Hall, Baym, and Miltner (2014) found that the internalized norms of people matter more than general societal norms. When both partners considered mobile phone use during FTF interactions as adequate, it was even positively correlated with relationship satisfaction. If these findings also hold for friendships, one can assume that no or smaller phubbing effects occur when both friends find it acceptable to focus on the mobile phone in the presence of the other.

POPC as a Double-Edged Sword

The previous sections suggest that both positive and negative effects of POPC on social relationships are possible. Hall and Baym (2012) examined both of these processes simultaneously in a quantitative study on the positive and negative effects of mobile phone use on close relationships. In a survey among almost 250 students, they found that mobile maintenance expectations, i.e., the expectations that the friend calls or texts frequently, created both higher levels of dependence, but also overdependence. Dependence had a strong positive effect on friendship satisfaction, whereas overdependence created a feeling of entrapment (pressure to respond) that had a negative influence on friendship satisfaction.

George and Odgers (2015) reviewed common fears of parents, such that being online distracts their children from FTF or creates a barrier between them and their parents. However, a look at empirical studies often identified positive effects, such as a strengthened bond with parents. In general, the studies reviewed in their paper often found that offline and online communication and relationships were closely entangled and many online effects simply mirrored offline effects (George and Odgers, 2015). In general, one can assume that being POPC has simultaneously desirable and less desirable effects on relationships, and that there might be personal and relationship characteristics that moderate these complex effects (e.g., attachment styles, cf. Rieger, this volume).

Conclusion

This chapter has shown that the pattern and also the content of communication with friends have changed since people are POPC. Less frequent but long conversations on the phone have been replaced with frequent short conversations on various (social media) platforms. This shift toward interstitial communication has resulted in new relationship maintenance behaviors. The intimacy of self-disclosure matters less; instead, presence, tie signs, and mundane communication (Tong & Walther, 2011) gain in importance. People expect frequent and fast reactions (Seo et al., 2016), but experience the expectation of permanent availability at the same time as a burden (Fox & Moreland, 2015; Hall & Baym, 2012).

POPC is a relatively new phenomenon, and therefore there are still many desiderata in this young research field. Whereas there are many studies on SNS use and relationships, not many studies addressed the effects of MIM on social relationships. Although studies on the effects of specific communication modes are needed as a first step, to fully capture the effects of POPC, studies need to take into account the multiplexity of media use in close relationships and look at the entirety of mediated and FTF communication. Most studies look at either the temporal patterns (frequency, speed) or the content (e.g., intimacy, positivity) of the communication, but do not bring these aspects together. The downsides of being POPC have mainly been studied in the context of work–life balance, but not so much in friendships. Finally, positive and negative effects need to be integrated; Hall and Baym (2012) took a promising first step here. Future research could examine these processes over time to see whether and how people find a healthy balance between permanent connection and the pressure to be available permanently.

References

Altman, I., & Taylor, D. A. (1973). *Social penetration: The development of interpersonal relationships.* New York: Holt, Rinehart, & Winston.

Barash, V., Duchenaut, N., Isaacs, E., & Bellotti, V. (2010). Faceplant: Impression (Mis) management in facebook status updates. In *Proceedings of the Fourth International AAAI Conference on Weblogs and Social Media* (pp. 207–210). Palo Alto, CA.

Bayer, J. B., Campbell, S. W., & Ling, R. (2016). Connection cues: Activating the norms and habits of social connectedness. *Communication Theory, 26*(2), 128–149. doi:10.1111/comt.12090

Bazarova, N. N. (2012). Public intimacy: Disclosure interpretation and social judgments on facebook. *Journal of Communication, 62*(5), 815–832. doi:10.1111/j.1460-2466.2012.01664.x

Burke, M., & Kraut, R. E. (2014). Growing closer on facebook: changes in tie strength through social network site use. In *Proceedings of the 32nd Annual ACM Conference on Human Factors in Computing Systems* (pp. 4187–4196). ACM.

Carr, C. T., Wohn, D. Y., & Hayes, R. A. (2016). Like as social support: Relational closeness, automaticity, and interpreting social support from paralinguistic digital affordances in social media. *Computers in Human Behavior, 62*, 385–393. doi:10.1016/j.chb.2016.03.087

Chotpitayasunondh, V., & Douglas, K. M. (2016). How "phubbing" becomes the norm: The antecedents and consequences of snubbing via smartphone. *Computers in Human Behavior, 63*, 9–18. http://dx.doi.org/10.1016/j.chb.2016.05.018

Collins, N. L., & Miller, L. C. (1994). Self-disclosure and liking: A meta-analytic review. *Psychological Bulletin, 116*(3), 457–475. doi:10.1037/0033-2909.116.3.457

Cui, D. (2016). Beyond "connected presence": Multimedia mobile instant messaging in close relationship management. *Mobile Media & Communication, 4*(1), 19–36. doi:10.1177/2050157915583925

Daft, R. L., & Lengel, R. H. (1986). Organizational information requirements, media richness and structural design. *Management Science, 32*(5), 554–571.

Donath, J., & boyd, D. (2004). Public displays of connection. *Bt Technology Journal, 22*(4), 71–82.

Ellison, N. B., Steinfield, C., & Lampe, C. (2007). The benefits of Facebook "friends:" Social capital and college students' use of online social network sites. *Journal of Computer-Mediated Communication, 12*(4), 1143–1168. doi:10.1111/j.1083-6101.2007.00367.x

Fox, J., & Moreland, J. J. (2015). The dark side of social networking sites: An exploration of the relational and psychological stressors associated with Facebook use and affordances. *Computers in Human Behavior, 45*, 168–176. doi:10.1016/j.chb.2014.11.083

Gable, S. L., & Reis, H. T. (2010). Good news! Capitalizing on positive events in an interpersonal context. *Advances in Experimental Social Psychology, 42*, 195–257.

Gable, S. L., Reis, H. T., Impett, E. A., & Asher, E. R. (2004). What do you do when things go right? The intrapersonal and interpersonal benefits of sharing positive events. *Journal of Personality and Social Psychology, 87*(2), 228–245. doi:10.1037/0022-3514.87.2.228

George, M., & Odgers, C. (2015). Seven fears and the science of how mobile technologies may be influencing adolescents in the digital age. *Perspectives on Psychological Science, 10*(6), 832–851.

Hall, J. A., & Baym, N. K. (2012). Calling and texting (too much): Mobile maintenance expectations, (over)dependence, entrapment, and friendship satisfaction. *New Media & Society, 14*(2), 316–331. doi:10.1177/1461444811415047

Hall, J. A., Baym, N. K., & Miltner, K. M. (2014). Put down that phone and talk to me: Understanding the roles of mobile phone norm adherence and similarity in relationships. *Mobile Media & Communication, 2*(2), 134–153. doi:10.1177/2050157913517684

Hayes, R. A., Carr, C. T., & Wohn, D. Y. (2016). One click, many meanings: Interpreting paralinguistic digital affordances in social media. *Journal of Broadcasting & Electronic Media, 60*(1), 171–187. doi:10.1080/08838151.2015.1127248

Haythornthwaite, C. (2005). Social networks and Internet connectivity effects. *Information, Communication & Society, 8*(2), 125–147. doi:10.1080/13691180500146185

Hughes, N. (2014). *WhatsApp read receipts leave users feeling blue* (Online). Retrieved from www.linkedin.com/pulse/20141108141951-98377657-whatsapp-read-receipts-leaves-users-feeling-blue [retrieved November 19, 2016]

Kiesler, S., Siegel, J., & McGuire, T. W. (1984). Social psychological aspects of computer-mediated communication. *American Psychologist, 39*(10), 1123–1134.

LaRose, R., Connolly, R., Lee, H., Li, K., & Hales, K. D. (2014). Connection overload? A cross cultural study of the consequences of social media connection. *Information Systems Management, 31*(1), 59–73. doi:10.1080/10580530.2014.854097

Levordashka, A., & Utz, S. (2016). Ambient awareness: From random noise to digital closeness in online social networks. *Computers in Human Behavior, 60*, 147–154. doi:10.1016/j.chb.2016.02.037

Levordashka, A., Utz, S., & Ambros, R. (2016). What's in a like? Motivations for pressing the like button. In *Proceedings of the Tenth International AAAI Conference on Web and Social Media (ICWSM 2016)* (pp. 623–626). Cologne, Germany. Retrieved from www.aaai.org/ocs/index.php/ICWSM/ICWSM16/paper/view/13022

Licoppe, C., & Smoreda, Z. (2005). Are social networks technologically embedded? How networks are changing today with changes in communication technology. *Social Networks, 27*(4), 317–335. doi:10.1016/j.socnet.2004.11.001

Lin, R., Levordashka, A., & Utz, S. (2016). Ambient intimacy on Twitter. *Cyberpsychology: Journal of Psychosocial Research on Cyberspace, 10*(1), article 6. doi:10.5817/CP2016-1-6

Majchrzak, A., Faraj, S., Kane, G. C., & Azad, B. (2013). The contradictory influence of social media affordances on online communal knowledge sharing. *Journal of Computer-Mediated Communication, 19*(1), 38–55. doi:10.1111/jcc4.12030

Muise, A., Christofides, E., & Desmarais, S. (2009). More information than you ever wanted: Does Facebook bring out the green-eyed monster of jealousy? *Cyberpsychology & Behavior, 12*(4), 441–444.

Parks, M. R., & Roberts, L. D. (1998). 'Making MOOsic': The development of personal relationships on line and a comparison to their off-line counterparts. *Journal of Social and Personal Relationships, 15*(4), 517–537.

Pettegrew, L. S., & Day, C. (2015). Smart phones and mediated relationships: The changing face of relational communication. *The Review of Communication, 15*(2), 122–139.

Przybylski, A. K., Murayama, K., DeHaan, C. R., & Gladwell, V. (2013). Motivational, emotional, and behavioral correlates of fear of missing out. *Computers in Human Behavior, 29*(4), 1841–1848. doi:10.1016/j.chb.2013.02.014

Rainie, L., & Wellman, B. (2012). *Networked: The new social operating system.* Cambridge, MA: MIT Press.

Seo, M., Kim, J., & Yang, H. (2016). Frequent interaction and fast feedback predict perceived social support: Using crawled and self-reported data of Facebook users. *Journal of Computer-Mediated Communication*. doi:10.1111/jcc4.12160

Stafford, L., & Canary, D. J. (1991). Maintenance strategies and romantic relationship type, gender and relational characteristics. *Journal of Social and Personal Relationships*, 8(2), 217–242. doi:10.1177/0265407591082004

Tobin, S. J., Vanman, E. J., Verreynne, M., & Saeri, A. K. (2015). Threats to belonging on Facebook: Lurking and ostracism. *Social Influence*, 10(1), 31–42. doi:10.1080/15534510.2014.893924

Tokunaga, R. S. (2011). Social networking site or social surveillance site? Understanding the use of interpersonal electronic surveillance in romantic relationships. *Computers in Human Behavior*, 27(2), 705–713. doi:10.1016/j.chb.2010.08.014

Tong, S., & Walther, J. B. (2011). Relational maintenance and CMC. In K. B. Wright & L. M. Webb (Eds.), *Computer-mediated communication in personal relationships* (pp. 98–118). New York: Peter Lang.

Turkle, S. (2012). *Alone together: Why we expect more from technology and less from each other*. New York: Basic Books.

Utz, S. (2015). The function of self-disclosure on social network sites: Not only intimate, but also positive and entertaining self-disclosures increase the feeling of connection. *Computers in Human Behavior*, 45, 1–10. doi:10.1016/j.chb.2014.11.076

Utz, S., & Beukeboom, C. (2011). The role of social network sites in romantic relationships: Effects on jealousy and relationship happiness. *Journal of Computer-Mediated Communication*, 16, 511–527. doi:10.1111/j.1083-6101.2011.01552.x

Utz, S., Muscanell, N., & Khalid, C. (2015). Snapchat elicits more jealousy than Facebook: A comparison of Snapchat and Facebook use. *Cyberpsychology, Behavior, and Social Networking*, 18(3), 141–146. doi:10.1089/cyber.2014.0479

Valkenburg, P. M., & Peter, J. (2009). The effects of instant messaging on the quality of adolescents' existing friendships: A longitudinal study. *Journal of Communication*, 59(1), 79–97. doi:10.1111/j.1460-2466.2008.01405.x

Vanden Abeele, M. M. P., Antheunis, M. L., & Schouten, A. P. (2016). The effect of mobile messaging during a conversation on impression formation and interaction quality. *Computers in Human Behavior*, 62, 562–569. http://dx.doi.org/10.1016/j.chb.2016.04.005

Vitak, J. (2014). Facebook makes the heart grow fonder: Relationship maintenance strategies among geographically dispersed and communication-restricted connections. In *Proceedings of the 17th ACM Conference on Computer Supported Cooperative Work & Social Computing* (pp. 842–853). ACM.

Vorderer, P., Klimmt, C., Rieger, D., Baumann, E., Hefner, D., Knop, K., Krömer, N., Mata, J. Pape, T. von, Quandt, T., Reich, S., Reinecke, L., Trepte, S., Sonnentag, S., & Wessler, H. (2015). Der mediatisierte Lebenswandel: Permanently online, permanently connected [The mediatized way of life: Permanently online, permanently connected]. *Publizistik—Vierteljahreshefte für Kommunikationsforschung*, 60(3), 259–276.

15
Between Surveillance and Sexting
Permanent Connectedness and Intimate Relationships

Diana Rieger

> Once "non-moments" were moments of inevitable solitude (Augé, 1995, pp. 94–103) . . . in which we accumulated dreams and sentences to share with and say to our loved ones. With the new technologies of communication, they have gained a new dimension: they have become a tunnel from the here and now to a "somewhere else" of immediate communicability. They may still be non-moments of solitude, but within this solitude, we can send and receive messages, and engage in a (even very intense) relationship with another person who does not happen to share this "here and now" with us.
> (Cantó-Milà, Núnez-Mosteo, & Seebach, 2016, p. 2397)

Intimate relationships are a substantial element of subjective experiences of sense and meaning in life as well as overall life satisfaction, because they can satisfy the fundamental human need to belong (Baumeister & Leary, 1995). On a societal level, intimate relationships take an important position for social cohesion, continuity, and stability within families (Vangelisti & Perlman, 2006). Scholars in psychology and communication have therefore been interested in the dynamics of starting, ongoing, and ending intimate relationships. Substantial theoretical and empirical contributions have addressed the role of communication for such relationship dynamics. Mobile online and communication devices, smartphones in particular, have brought about new patterns of behavior, manifestations, and determinants of such dynamics and experiences in romantic relationships (Coyne, Stockdale, Busby, Iverson, & Grant, 2011; Lenhart, Anderson, & Smith, 2015): Many couples are nowadays "permanently online, permanently connected" (POPC, see Klimmt, Hefner, Reinecke, Rieger, and Vorderer, this volume), which has also been labeled "connected presence"(Licoppe, 2004, p. 135). Moreover, interesting technological innovations (e.g., dating apps) and behavioral phenomena (e.g., digital stalking of ex-partners) have emerged that relate to pre- and post-relationship stages.

Mobile technologies provide the user with a huge variety of possibilities for communication with (potential, current, and former) romantic partners, and satisfaction with communication has been found to be a key difference between happy and unhappy couples (Olson, Olson-Sigg, & Larson, 2008). Accordingly, happy couples also use the potential of permanent connectedness more beneficially than do unhappy couples (Coyne et al., 2011; Saslow, Muise, Impett, & Dubin, 2012; Stewart, Dainton, &

Goodboy, 2014). Hence, POPC may not simply change the surface manifestations of communication among romantic partners, but may have profound consequences for the perceived quality, stability, and functionality of romantic relationships.

On the one hand, connection via mobile technologies could be regarded as an opportunity to improve partner communication. In a recent survey, 21% of interrogated individuals reported to feel closer to their partner due to online communication or text messages (Lenhart & Duggan, 2014). More importantly, these technologies offer tools to generate relatedness when physical presence is not possible (Hassenzahl, Heidecker, Eckoldt, Diefenbach, & Hillmann, 2012). Through the possibility to be connected no matter of location and time, infusions of relatedness when being apart can amplify the shared experience, thereby creating greater psychological proximity (Boothby, Smith, Clark, & Bargh, 2016).

On the other hand, the penetration of mobile technologies into all spheres of everyday life has led to descriptions of partner phubbing, that is "the extent to which an individual uses or is distracted by his/her cell phone while in the company of his/her relationship partner" (Roberts & David, 2016, p. 134). As a consequence, the distractions caused by partner phubbing could undermine relationship satisfaction, commitment, intimacy, or closeness.

Turkle (2011) argues that young people nowadays grow up with the expectation of continuous connection and that media use is in fact separating people from one another. Partners may be physically together, but not fully present for each other because at least part of their attention is dedicated to a virtual communication partner. Couples may also be physically apart, and additionally feel new insecurities: Recent studies found partners to experience jealousy (sometimes even labeled "social media jealousy") due to the evaluation of their partner's online behavior (e.g., Elphinston & Noller, 2011) or tensions that arise through discussing POPC issues (Fox, Warber, & Makstaller, 2013).

Since new mobile technologies offer a huge variety of options, it is reasonable to assume that their use can have very different effects on intimate relationships, depending on personality traits of users and their partners, the phase of the relationship, and the content of communication practiced via the new technologies. In research on interpersonal relationships, three stages of importance for relationships can be distinguished: The initiation or formation of a relationship, its maintenance, and its dissolution (Vangelisti & Perlman, 2006). Each of these stages has specific characteristics and comes along with affordances and typical behaviors. Accordingly, the impact and the utility of permanent connectedness are mirrored differently within each stage. The present chapter will focus on the implications of POPC for these stages of intimate relationships and discuss the factors that may modulate the probability of positive versus negative outcomes of being POPC.

Permanent Connectedness at the Stage of Relationship Formation

During the phase of relationship formation, individuals meet for the first time, become acquainted, and eventually start dating. This phase is usually accompanied by gathering information about the other person, for example, by screening one another or talking to each other to determine whether the other person could become a romantic partner (Knapp, 1978). In this phase, it is decided whether a romantic relationship is formed, and whether it is serious or casual in nature (Bergdall et al., 2012). One important goal in this initial stage is uncertainty reduction (Knobloch & Solomon, 2002). Berger and Calabrese (1975) distinguish three strategies through which uncertainty can be reduced: Passive strategies (e.g., gathering information about the target by observation), active strategies (e.g., gathering information about the target by talking to third persons), and interactive strategies (e.g., gathering information by talking with the target him- or herself). In general, smartphones with their potential for permanent connectedness offer a lot of opportunities for individuals to get to know new people, to stay in touch at high frequency (which is crucial during the formation stage, cf. McCormack, 2015), and also to seek information about them (Antheunis, Valkenburg, & Peter, 2010; Gibbs, Ellison, & Lai, 2011). Permanent connectedness has amplified the potential for dating partners to engage in communication, be it through passive (observing the other one online), active (being in contact with related third parties) and interactive (conversation with the other person) strategies (Fox, 2016).

Less Effort, Lower Risk in Online Dating

Smartphones and the POPC lifestyle affect the culture, practices, and social conventions around dating. Engaging in the search for and contact with possible future partners has become an activity that is possible anywhere and anytime. For instance, survey findings indicate that 44% of men and 37% of women report that it has become easier to get to know someone and start flirting due to smartphones (Amplitude Research, 2013).

Permanent connectedness and mobile communication devices seem to ease the obstacles of first real contact (e.g., getting to know someone who lives close, is about the same age, has similar interests) and pave the way for ongoing contact with each other. This facilitation of matchmaking was perfected by new online dating platforms, such as Tinder or Lovoo: They are tailored to mobile use and take the wish for permanent connectedness into account.

Mobile app-based dating may have further implications for relationship initiation. Because rejection remains nearly invisible, the perceived risks or costs involved in examining possible partners may be much lower than in conventional offline dating. By the same token, online dating requires only low effort and engagement, so starting and maintaining contact with multiple potential partners in parallel seems to become a normal, common behavior. In addition, online daters may expect rather casual, "low investment" relationships to result from their low-effort initiation activities. Consequently, relationships that merely happen in a virtual sphere are perceived as less intimate than face-to-face relationships (Scott, Mottarella, & Lavooy, 2006).

More Control, Less Anxiety in POPC Dating

In particular for adolescents, being POPC opens ways to test strategies and experiment with ideas on how to get into contact and start a relationship and how to display affection and maintain high-frequency contact (McCormack, 2015). To satisfy the desire for intense exchange and information about the prospective partner, one-to-one mediated communication (e.g., FaceTime, Skype) is often perceived as very suitable during the initiation stage (Len-Ríos et al., 2016).

Users seem to value the options for greater control that electronic communication provides: Adolescents mention that they can better control how and when they answer to messages from a flirt partner, and how much of this conversation they want to share with other friends. Further, it is perceived as easier to manage face loss in case of rejection. Young users also feel more at ease to send emotionally laden messages without direct face-to-face contact (Christopher, McKenney, & Poulsen, 2015). Users can select from and combine passive strategies, that is, reading a partner's profile, as well as active strategies, e.g., "friending" a third party to acquire information, asking a friend to collect information (also referred to as "friend-sourcing"), and interactive strategies, such as commenting on the target person's wall, liking, or sending private messages (Fox & Anderegg, 2014). All these strategies can help to reduce uncertainties, contribute to perceived similarity and social attraction with the target person (Antheunis

New Conventions of Announcing Romantic Commitment

Finally, POPC also seems to change how young people plan and experience the act of agreeing to have a relationship with a partner and of informing relevant others about a newly begun relationship. Social media feature instruments to announce the beginning of a romantic relationship, and partners who engage in POPC behavior need to discuss on how to handle these instruments. In particular, in a beginning relationship it has become necessary to define the moment when it is legitimate to "go FBO" (Facebook Official) (Fox & Warber, 2012). Being FBO is perceived as a cue for increased commitment toward the partner and is associated with issues of uploading new pictures or exchanging wall posts online. Sharing the same attitude on becoming FBO and adjusting profiles on SNS can have a positive impact on relationship satisfaction (Papp, Danielewicz, & Cayemberg, 2012), which underlines the relevance of online announcements of new relationships.

POPC Couples: Mobile Communication and Maintenance of Intimate Relationships

Once an intimate relationship is initiated, partners aim at intensifying their relationship, integrating it into their self-concepts, and engaging in bonding with their partner (Knapp, 1978). The phase of maintenance is therefore characterized by strategic communication used to ensure the continued existence and desired level of closeness in the relationship (Canary & Stafford, 1994). The functions of relational maintenance can aim at keeping a relationship in existence, keeping it in a satisfactory condition, or repairing it (Dindia & Canary, 1993). Various strategies of relationship maintenance have been differentiated: Engaging in *positivity* aims at demonstrating to each other hopefulness and optimism in interactions. *Assurances* are defined as signals used by partners to convey their affection, commitment, and appreciation for each other. *Openness* points at directly discussing the nature of the relationship, also referred to as relational meta-communication (see Brody & Peña, 2015). All kinds of instrumental efforts, such as housework, childcare, and everyday errands are subsumed under the category of *sharing tasks*. The final strategy is called *social networks*, which refers to the reliance on common friends and family for maintenance purposes, such as joint activities (Stafford & Canary, 1991).

Much research has provided evidence that using maintenance strategies positively contribute to relational characteristics, such as perceived equity, satisfaction, and closeness (Stafford & Canary, 2006). It is important to note that these behaviors are evident not only in face-to-face interactions but also in computer-mediated communication (Ledbetter, 2010). While there is theoretical and empirical support for assumptions of positive effects of being POPC for the perceived quality of and satisfaction with intimate relationships, there are also concerns about various potential downsides.

Positive Aspects of Being POPC for Romantic Relationships

Increased Probability and Frequency of Close Contact

All strategies of relationship maintenance require repeated or frequent communication among partners. Therefore, being POPC may dramatically change the conditions for relationship maintenance in everyday life, because it implies an exponentially greater amount of opportunities for partners to (re)connect, in particular in long-distance relationships. Couples use text-based mobile online communication to engage in all five of the relational maintenance strategies (Brody & Peña, 2015). Specifically, permanent connectedness can be used to share experiences and information of interest, as well as to show caring for the partner, but also to discuss difficult topics, such as commitment, feelings, and conflict (Bergdall et al., 2012). Accordingly, common reasons for conversations over mobile devices among couples comprise the expression of affection, the discussion of serious issues, and apologies (Coyne et al., 2011). Various studies show that communication among partners that is intensified through permanent or frequent online exchange contributes to positive outcomes: Both the *quantity* and *quality* of phone calls and text messages have positive effects on relationship commitment, love, and relational certainty (Jin & Peña, 2010), partner idealization (Toma & Choi, 2016), as well as relationship satisfaction and intimacy (Morey, Gentzler, Creasy, Oberhauser, & Westerman, 2013; Slatcher, Vazire, & Pennebaker, 2008).

POPC Routines and Rituals Strengthen Couples' Social Identity

Being POPC enables couples to develop a particular communication pattern, represented, for example, by rituals of short and frequent calls, messages or posts on social media that reaffirm feelings of connectedness, commitment, and love (Ishii, 2006; Licoppe, 2004; McCormack, 2015; Utz & Beukeboom, 2011). The dyadic nature of text messaging between romantic partners can lead to the development of idiosyncratic text codes that only the couple will understand (Pettigrew, 2009). Such couple-specific codes and patterns of (online) communication can strengthen the shared social identity of being part of a romantic partnership and thus contribute to its stabilization and maintenance on a daily basis (Slatcher, Vazire, & Pennebaker, 2008). Through POPC, the amount of shared moments of couple idiosyncrasy can increase dramatically, because they can now also occur and be enjoyed during times when partners are not meeting face to face. Moreover, mobile online communication expands the repertoire of possible idiosyncrasies, for example, through new symbols such as "emojis" that are only available within specific applications and that partners can associate within individual or couple-specific contexts (see also Hassenzahl et al., 2012; Pettigrew, 2009).

POPC Can Enhance Couples' Sexuality

Satisfaction with sexual aspects is an important element of couple happiness and relationship satisfaction (Byers, 2005). Being POPC offers innovative means for partners to contribute to satisfying sexual interactions, which is once more of particular relevance in long-distance relationships (see Hassenzahl et al., 2012). In a qualitative interview study with people in long-term relationships, McCormack (2015) found that couples perceived the advantages of being POPC also regarding an enhancement in their sexual life. They describe the sexual part of a relationship to be amplified by sending and receiving flirtatious and sexual messages, pictures, or videos with sexual content (either of oneself or by filming "real" sex when being together and watching it later when apart).

Sexting has been defined as "sending and receiving sexually suggestive images, videos, or texts" via mobile devices (Weisskirch & Delevi, 2011, p. 1697). Among college samples, over half of people in intimate relationships reported having sent sexually explicit material to their partner (Drouin & Landgraff, 2012). It has often been associated with more risky health behavior, in particular for adolescents (Van Ouytsel, Walrave, Ponnet, & Heirman, 2015). Focusing on adults, however, there were no associations between sexting and health risks or sexually risky behavior (Gordon-Messer, Bauermeister, Grodzinski, & Zimmerman, 2013). Through sexting, POPC renders the sexual dimension of intimate relationship more accessible and relevant to both partners throughout the day and expands the space of opportunities to negotiate and enjoy sexual interaction beyond episodes of face-to-face contact. Similar to old-fashioned love letters, partners can use mobile phones to create new kinds of artifacts that symbolize the substance of the (sexual) relationship, such as images and videos. The mere existence and exchange of such artifacts may be considered a new, POPC-specific factor in relationship maintenance.

Negative Aspects of Being POPC for Romantic Relationships

Intoxication of Face-to-Face Encounters

Being POPC implies high levels of attention and considerable time investment in mobile online communication (Klimmt et al., this volume). When romantic partners spend time together, usage of mobile online devices may undermine positive interaction dynamics, which has been described as "technoference" (McDaniel & Coyne, 2016, p. 85). By looking at the smartphone when the partner is present, even if it happens unintentionally and for brief moments only, individuals send implicit messages about what they value more and pay greater attention to. One example for how being POPC in the presence of the romantic partner competes with positive face-to-face interaction is the risk of failure in initiating sexual contact. In the study by McCormack (2015), couples report having delayed sex due to one partner's smartphone use, for example, for finishing a video game or engaging in an online conversation with somebody else.

In particular, when being POPC becomes an excessive or compulsive behavior (Kerkhof, Finkenauer, & Muusses, 2011; van Koningsbruggen, Hartmann, and Du, this volume; Klimmt and Brand, this volume), the frequent interruptions during couple leisure time, conversations, or mealtimes are likely to put pressure on the quality of intimate relationships, such as increasing the amount of conflict and feelings of exclusion and decreasing intimacy, passion, and relationship satisfaction (Coyne et al., 2011; Karadağ et al., 2015; Kerkhof et al., 2011; McDaniel & Coyne, 2016; Roberts & David, 2016).

In sum, being POPC may have substantial advantages for romantic relationships if partners engage in mobile online communication when they are geographically separated (see above). But if they turn to their mobile devices during face-to-face encounters, phubbing experiences bear considerable risks that the partner suffers from feelings of jealousy, being neglected, unnoticed, less important, uninteresting, or isolated, which are likely to lead to a relationship crisis if the problems persist over time (Krasnova, Abramova, Notter, & Baumann, 2016).

Online Information Can Trigger Jealousy

Romantic partners who are POPC experience their relationship as part of a larger network of friends and important others who share multiple streams of online interaction. Being POPC thus means to receive much information about one's partner through the online social network, for instance, by observing one's partner's online exchange with others. This way, POPC users may receive ambiguous information about their partners that would have remained inaccessible without the new possibilities of mobile online communication and social media (Muise, Christofides, & Desmarais, 2009). This additional information may trigger emotions of jealousy that can put stress on the relationship. Many elements and opportunities on (mobile) social media provide a couple with points for discussion that can cause relational uncertainty and jealousy: (1) *Visual information* can create uncertainty, for instance by seeing one's partner with somebody else or witnessing him/her "liking" the picture of somebody else. (2) *Partner communication* can cause conflict, for example over how partners deal with each other's online messaging and profile (liking, commenting on, and sharing his/her posts). (3) *Third-party communication* can lead to conflicts, for instance by reading what others comment, send, and like about one's own relationship or interfere with it; flirtatious behavior by members of a couple's online social network is discussed as one special "interferer" (Fox & Moreland, 2015; Len-Ríos et al., 2016).

Various studies show that these characteristics of (mobile) social media can indeed cause negative feelings that would not have occurred if partners had remained completely offline (Fox, Osborn, & Warber, 2014; Muscanell & Guadagno, 2016; Utz & Beukeboom, 2011). For instance, the time a partner spends on Facebook was associated with an increased feeling of jealousy (Muise et al., 2009) and negative relationship outcomes such as lower satisfaction with the partner and seeing more defects in the other (Clayton, Nagurney, & Smith, 2013; Hammond & Chou, 2016). The amount of conflict due to technology use (e.g., activities on SNS that trigger confrontations, irritation, or arguments) mediated the relationship between time spent on social media and negative effects for the relationship (Clayton, 2014).

POPC Brings About New Modes of Dysfunctional Partner Behavior

While being POPC may cause the onset of jealousy that would not have occurred without permanent connectedness, heavy smartphone involvement may also have detrimental effects on intimate relationships, because partners who display dysfunctional behaviors can find new ways to expand or amplify their problematic activities. Exploiting the rich information resources of mobile social media, users may engage in excessive controlling and monitoring of their partner, which has been termed surveillance behavior (Muise, Christofides, & Desmarais, 2014; Tokunaga, 2011). Jealousy and monitoring have a hampering effect on relationship satisfaction (Elphinston & Noller, 2011). Moreover, abusive individuals may utilize social media to cause harm to their partners, for instance by breaking the privacy of their partner or leaking intimate images to large audiences ("revenge porn," cf. Bates, 2016).

Breaking Up but Staying Connected? POPC and the Dissolution of Intimate Relationships

The "final" stage of a relationship, namely its dissolution, is often a stressful and painful process that involves aversive emotions (anxiety, guilt, anger) and requires immense self-control to maintain everyday functioning (Chung et al., 2002). Breakups and divorces most often cause a high amount of undesired change in people's daily lives, come along with challenges, and require adaptions in order to cope with potential negative effects (Frost, Rubin, & Darcangelo, 2015).

For this third stage of intimate relationships, mobile communication is perceived as being helpful when a partner is pursuing an "evacuation" strategy: The frequency and intensity of contact can be controlled and slowly reduced, so partners willing to increase "distance" can fade out step by step. Abrupt breakups are also possible due to the low effort it takes to send a "breakup text" or a quick phone call without having to go through a stressful personal encounter (Bergdall et al., 2012). However, as this phase is characterized by the need and wish to create distance between partners and to begin the "mental disentangling," permanent connectedness can be assumed to have detrimental consequences.

This is because (mobile) social media and their heavy use make it extremely difficult to realize offline as well as online separation. The many online connections that have grown among and around partners over time cannot easily be removed and partially persist after a romantic breakup. These connections enable (and sometimes afford) continuing communication among separated partners. Research has identified three categories of dysfunctional communication with romantic ex-partners over social media, *covert provocation*, *public harassment*, and *venting* (Lyndon, Bonds-Raacke, & Cratty, 2011). Each of these categories was related to obsessively stalking the ex-partner online and enduring obsessive relational pursuit. That is, through monitoring and stalking the ex-partner—which is still possible after breakups via electronic devices and the information available on Instant Messenger and SNS—healing and mental separation take longer. These effects are particularly likely to appear for individuals with an anxious attachment style (Hazan & Shaver, 1987). They tend to invest longer in the (broken) relationship, and the more somebody still shows relational investment, the higher is his/her emotional distress and partner monitoring after the breakup. In sum, being POPC holds great danger to amplify the emotional distress associated with relationship dissolution and requires additional efforts to effectively implement and cope with separation.

POPC for Better or Worse? Attachment Styles Moderate the Effects of Mobile Online Communication on Romantic Relationships

The previous sections have reviewed possible benign and detrimental implications of being POPC for romantic relationships across the stages of initiation, maintenance, and dissolution. While it is unrealistic to assume that being POPC will either have positive or negative consequences for a given relationship, it is important for research and intervention to understand which factors render positive versus negative consequences of being POPC more likely.

From this perspective, it is especially plausible to assume interactive effects of being POPC with partners' *attachment styles* (Hazan & Shaver, 1987). The attachment style is defined along two continuous dimensions of insecure attachments, namely anxiety and avoidance. Someone low in anxious or avoidant attachment shows a secure attachment. Anxiously attached individuals perceive themselves as unlovable and fear abandonment. As a consequence, they engage in hyperactive maintenance strategies and practice extreme vigilance for threats to their relationship (Luo, 2014). Avoidant-attached individuals dislike too much closeness and intimacy and show high levels of distrust in others (Collins & Allard, 2001). It is very likely that these trait-like tendencies of perceiving oneself in a relationship in an insecure manner interact with POPC behavior and bring about problematic outcomes for relationship quality.

Avoidant individuals are less likely to make their relationships visible and to engage with their partner as far as absolute frequency and length, both via phone calls (Jin & Peña, 2010) and via text messages (Drouin & Landgraff, 2012) are concerned. The potential for being POPC seems to be an extra burden for those preferring self-reliance over interdependence, because their wish for less intimacy stands in contradiction to the manifold opportunities to stay in contact. This might cause additional stress and make them feel even more insecure about the relationship, as they have to cope with increased pressures to engage in intimacy and closeness (Emery, Muise, Dix, & Le, 2014). Accordingly, when choosing channels for communication with their partner, avoidant-attached individuals are less likely to prefer communication channels that come with greater closeness and immediacy, face-to-face communication in particular (Wardecker, Chopik, Boyer, & Edelstein, 2016).

Interpreted differently, this points to the benefits they could be able to draw from being POPC: For instance, avoidant-attached individuals preferred less close and immediate means of communication because they believed that the latter provide easier ways to resolve interpersonal conflicts (Wardecker et al., 2016). Consequently, they showed a higher relative proportion of text-based communication compared to other means of exchange (Luo, 2014) which could be associated with more positive relationship qualities for them (Morey et al., 2013).

In contrast, anxiously attached individuals act out their hyperactive vigilant style when being POPC. For instance, they are more likely to frequently text with their partner (Luo, 2014) and engage in sexting (Weisskirch & Delevi, 2011), but also stalk their partners electronically (Reed, Tolman, & Safyer, 2015) to find relief from their fear of loss, betrayal, and abandonment, partly due to their heightened feelings of jealousy (Marshall, Bejanyan, Di Castro, & Lee, 2013). Reed and colleagues (2016) state that POPC can create a "cycle of anxiety" (p. 261) for anxiously attached individuals because the new forms of permanent connectedness provide the technological opportunities to monitor the partner as well as to nurture relationship anxiety (e.g., through pictures with others, comments that can be interpreted as flirtatious, tags, etc.).

In sum, while additional research is needed to establish moderating relationships among POPC and attachment styles, it is plausible to assume that individuals with an avoidant or anxious attachment who engage in POPC behavior are more likely to encounter negative relationship dynamics than individuals who are securely attached. There may be constellations in which "smart" use of POPC behaviors may compensate for disadvantages of insecure attachment styles (e.g., greater control over levels of intimacy through text-based messaging for the avoidant-attached), but further theorizing and research will be required to identify the specific opportunities that may result from benign interactions of being POPC and attachment styles.

Conclusion

The present chapter has discussed the fact that POPC has entered the sphere of intimate relationships. Being POPC can have numerous implications for intimate relationships across the stages of initiation, maintenance, and dissolution, and the direction of these effects may be positive or negative in terms of relationship outcomes. During initiation and maintenance, the greater advantages seem to be possible when being POPC is practiced while partners are geographically apart, and the greater risks seem to emerge when people are POPC while their partner is present. In general, past research has put more emphasis on negative implications of smartphone use and online communication on intimate relationships than on positive consequences.

Some scholars draw the conclusion from the manifold possibilities to stay connected permanently through mobile technologies that modern communication technologies are powerful in ruining people's social encounters. However, each couple—at least to a certain extent—can form their own habits and rules about how to handle being POPC and adjust to meeting the goals of the relationship (see e.g, Baym, Zhang, Kunkel, Ledbetter, & Lin, 2007). Reflecting and negotiating POPC rituals and habits holds great potential for realizing the advantages of permanent connectedness for romantic relationships and intimacy.

If permanent connectedness is able to increase or establish feelings of intimacy, it is also capable to unfold a stabilizing effect for the relationship, since perceived intimacy has been discussed as one important buffer against negativity in relationships, including aversive experiences stemming from POPC-related behavior (Hand, Thomas, Buboltz, Deemer, & Buyanjargal, 2012). As perceived understanding during conflicts has been found to reduce the relationship-damaging effects of conflicts (Gordon & Chen, 2016), it might still be the best solution to clarify important, challenging, serious, or very emotional topics in face-to-face encounters. Against this background, the manifold and partially threatening implications of being POPC suggest that it is worthwhile for couples to consider reintegrating "non-moments" into the relationship (Cantó-Milà et al., 2016), in which partners can engage in connectedness without needing electronic media between them.

References

Amplitude Research (2013). *Mobile's impact on dating & relationships*. Retrieved November 14, 2016, from www.stateofdatingreport.com/docs/FINAL_Mobiles_Impact_on_Dating_and_Relationships_Study.pdf

Antheunis, M. L., Valkenburg, P. M., & Peter, J. (2010). Getting acquainted through social network sites: Testing a model of online uncertainty reduction and social attraction. *Computers in Human Behavior, 26*(1), 100–109. http://doi.org/10.1016/j.chb.2009.07.005

Augé, M. (1995). *Non-places: Introduction to an anthropology of supermodernity*. London: Verso.

Bates, S. (2016). Revenge porn and mental health: A qualitative analysis of the mental health effects of revenge porn on female survivors. *Feminist Criminology, 12*(1), 22–42. http://doi.org/1557085116654565

Baumeister, R. F., & Leary, M. R. (1995). The need to belong: Desire for interpersonal attachments as a fundamental human motivation. *Psychological Bulletin, 117*(3), 497–529.

Baym, N. K., Zhang, Y. B., Kunkel, A., Ledbetter, A., & Lin, M.-C. (2007). Relational quality and media use in interpersonal relationships. *New Media & Society, 9*(5), 735–752. http://doi.org/10.1177/1461444807080339

Bergdall, A. R., Kraft, J. M., Andes, K., Carter, M., Hatfield-Timajchy, K., & Hock-Long, L. (2012). Love and hooking up in the new millennium: Communication technology and relationships among urban African American and Puerto Rican young adults. *Journal of Sex Research, 49*(6), 570–582. http://doi.org/10.1080/00224499.2011.604748

Berger, C. R., & Calabrese, R. J. (1975). Some explorations in initial interaction and beyond: Toward a developmental theory of interpersonal communication. *Human Communication Research, 1*, 99–112.

Boothby, E. J., Smith, L. K., Clark, M. S., & Bargh, J. A. (2016). Psychological distance moderates the amplification of shared experience. *Personality and Social Psychology Bulletin, 42*(10), 1–14. http://doi.org/10.1177/0146167216662869

Brody, N., & Peña, J. (2015). Equity, relational maintenance, and linguistic features of text messaging. *Computers in Human Behavior, 49*, 499–506. http://doi.org/10.1016/j.chb.2015.03.037

Byers, E. S. (2005). Relationship satisfaction and sexual satisfaction: A longitudinal study of individuals in long-term relationships. *Journal of Sex Research, 42*(2), 113–118. http://doi.org/10.1080/00224490509552264

Canary, D. J., & Stafford, L. (1994). *Communication and relational maintenance*. San Diego, CA: Academic Press.

Cantó-Milà, N., Núnez-Mosteo, F., & Seebach, S. (2016). Between reality and imagination, between you and me: Emotions and daydreaming in times of electronic communication. *New Media & Society, 18*(10), 2395–2412. http://doi.org/10.1177/1461444815586985

Christopher, F. S., McKenney, S. J., & Poulsen, F. O. (2015). Early adolescents' "crushing": Pursuing romantic interest on a social stage. *Journal of Social and Personal Relationships, 33*(4), 1–19. http://doi.org/10.1177/0265407515583169

Chung, M. C., Farmer, S., Grant, K., Newton, R., Payne, S., Perry, M., . . . Stone. (2002). Self-esteem, personality and post traumatic stress symptoms following the dissolution of a dating relationship. *Stress and Health, 18*, 83–90.

Clayton, R. B. (2014). The third wheel: The impact of twitter use on relationship infidelity and divorce. *Cyberpsychology, Behavior, and Social Networking, 17*(7), 425–430. http://doi.org/10.1089/cyber.2013.0570

Clayton, R. B., Nagurney, A., & Smith, J. R. (2013). Cheating, breakup, and divorce: Is Facebook use to blame? *Cyberpsychology, Behavior, and Social Networking, 16*(10), 717–720. http://doi.org/10.1089/cyber.2012.0424

Collins, N. L., & Allard, L. M. (2001). Cognitive representations of attachment: The content and function of working models. In G. O. Fletcher & M. S. Clark (Eds.), *Blackwell handbook of social psychology: Interpersonal processes* (pp. 60–85). Malden, MA: Blackwell.

Coyne, S. M., Stockdale, L., Busby, D., Iverson, B., & Grant, D. M. (2011). "I luv u :)!": A descriptive study of the media use of individuals in romantic relationships. *Family Relations, 60*(2), 150–162. http://doi.org/10.1111/j.1741-3729.2010.00639.x

Dindia, K., & Canary, D. J. (1993). Definitions and theoretical perspectives on maintaining relationships. *Journal of Social and Personal Relationships, 10*, 163–173. doi:10.1177=026540759301000201

Drouin, M., & Landgraff, C. (2012). Texting, sexting, and attachment in college students' romantic relationships. *Computers in Human Behavior*, *28*(2), 444–449. http://doi.org/10.1016/j.chb.2011.10.015

Elphinston, R. a, & Noller, P. (2011). Time to face it! Facebook intrusion and the implications for romantic jealousy and relationship satisfaction. *Cyberpsychology, Behavior and Social Networking*, *14*(11), 631–635. http://doi.org/10.1089/cyber.2010.0318

Emery, L. F., Muise, A., Dix, E. L., & Le, B. (2014). Can you tell that I'm in a relationship? Attachment and relationship visibility on Facebook. *Personality and Social Psychology Bulletin*, *40*(11), 1466–1479. http://doi.org/10.1177/0146167214549944

Fox, J. (2016). The dark side of social networking sites in romantic relationships. In G. Riva, B. K. Wiederhold, & P. Cipresso (Eds.), *The psychology of social networking: Communication, presence, identity, and relationships in online communities* (pp. 78–89). Berlin, Germany: Versita.

Fox, J., & Anderegg, C. (2014). Romantic relationship stages and social networking sites: Uncertainty reduction strategies and perceived relational norms on facebook. *Cyberpsychology, Behavior, and Social Networking*, *17*(11), 685–691. http://doi.org/10.1089/cyber.2014.0232

Fox, J., & Moreland, J. J. (2015). The dark side of social networking sites: An exploration of the relational and psychological stressors associated with Facebook use and affordances. *Computers in Human Behavior*, *45*, 168–176. http://doi.org/10.1016/j.chb.2014.11.083

Fox, J., Osborn, J. L., & Warber, K. M. (2014). Relational dialectics and social networking sites: The role of Facebook in romantic relationship escalation, maintenance, conflict, and dissolution. *Computers in Human Behavior*, *35*, 527–534. http://doi.org/10.1016/j.chb.2014.02.031

Fox, J., & Warber, K. M. (2012). Romantic relationship development in the age of Facebook: An exploratory study of emerging adults' perceptions, motives, and behaviors. *Cyberpsychology, Behavior, and Social Networking*, *16*(1), 121025083321009. http://doi.org/10.1089/cyber.2012.0288

Fox, J., Warber, K. M., & Makstaller, D. C. (2013). The role of Facebook in romantic relationship development: An exploration of Knapp's relational stage model. *Journal of Social and Personal Relationships*, *30*(6), 771–794. http://doi.org/10.1177/0265407512468370

Frost, D. M., Rubin, J. D., & Darcangelo, N. (2015). Making meaning of significant events in past relationships: Implications for depression among newly single individuals. *Journal of Social and Personal Relationships*, *33*(7), 1–23. http://doi.org/10.1177/0265407515612241

Gibbs, J. L., Ellison, N. B., & Lai, C.-H. (2011, December). First comes love, then comes Google: An investigation of uncertainty reduction strategies and self-disclosure in online dating. *Communication Research*, *38*, 70–100. http://doi.org/10.1177/0093650210377091

Gordon, A. M., & Chen, S. (2016). Do you get where I'm coming from? Perceived understanding buffers against the negative impact of conflict on relationship satisfaction. *Journal of Personality and Social Psychology*, *110*(2), 239–260. http://doi.org/10.1037/pspi0000039

Gordon-Messer, D., Bauermeister, J. A., Grodzinski, A., & Zimmerman, M. (2013). Sexting among young adults. *Journal of Adolescent Health*, *52*(3), 301–306. http://doi.org/10.1016/j.jadohealth.2012.05.013

Hammond, R., & Chou, H. G. (2016). Using facebook: Good for friendship but not so good for intimate relationships. In G. Riva, B. K. Wiederhold, & P. Cipresso (Eds.), *The psychology of social networking: Communication, presence, identity, and relationships in online communities* (pp. 41–52). Berlin, Germany: Versita.

Hand, M. M., Thomas, D., Buboltz, W. C., Deemer, E. D., & Buyanjargal, M. (2012). Facebook and romantic relationships: Intimacy and couple satisfaction associated with online social network use. *Cyberpsychology, Behavior, and Social Networking*, *16*(1), 121026063615008. http://doi.org/10.1089/cyber.2012.0038

Hassenzahl, M., Heidecker, S., Eckoldt, K., Diefenbach, S., & Hillmann, U. (2012). All you need is love: Current strategies of mediating intimate relationships through technology. *ACM Transactions on Computer-Human Interaction*, *19*(4), 1–19. http://doi.org/10.1145/2395131.2395137

Hazan, C., & Shaver, P. (1987). Romantic love conceptualized as an attachment process. *Journal of Personality and Social Psychology*, *52*, 511–524.

Ishii, K. (2006). Implications of mobility: The uses of personal communication media in everyday life. *Journal of Communication*, *56*(2), 346–365. http://doi.org/10.1111/j.1460-2466.2006.00023.x

Jin, B., & Peña, J. F. (2010). Mobile communication in romantic relationships: Mobile phone use, relational uncertainty, love, commitment, and attachment styles. *Communication Reports*, 23(1), 39–51. http://doi.org/10.1080/08934211003598742

Karadağ, E., Tosuntaş, Ş. B., Erzen, E., Duru, P., Bostan, N., Şahin, B. M., . . . Babadağ, B. (2015). Determinants of phubbing, which is the sum of many virtual addictions: A structural equation model. *Journal of Behavioral Addictions*, 4(2), 1–15. http://doi.org/10.1556/2006.4.2015.005

Kerkhof, P., Finkenauer, C., & Muusses, L. D. (2011). Relational consequences of compulsive Internet use: A longitudinal study among newlyweds. *Human Communication Research*, 37(2), 147–173. http://doi.org/10.1111/j.1468-2958.2010.01397.x

Knapp, M. L. (1978). *Social intercourse: From greeting to goodbye*. Needham Heights, MA: Allyn & Bacon.

Knobloch, L. K., & Solomon, D. H. (2002). Information seeking beyond initial interaction—negotiating relational uncertainty within close relationships. *Human Communication Research*, 28(2), 243–257. http://doi.org/10.1111/j.1468-2958.2002.tb00806.x

Krasnova, H., Abramova, O., Notter, I., & Baumann, A. (2016). Why phubbing is toxic for your relationship : Understanding the role of smartphone jealousy among "Generation Y" users. In *24th European Conference on Information Systems (ECIS)*. Istanbul, Turkey.

Ledbetter, A. M. (2010). Assessing the measurement invariance of relational maintenance behavior when face-to-face and online. *Communication Research Reports*, 27, 30–37. http://doi.org/10.1080=08824090903526620

Lenhart, A., Anderson, M., & Smith, A. (2015). *Teens, technology and romantic relationships*. Retrieved November 14, 2016, from www.pewInternet.org/2015/10/01/teens-technology-and-romantic-relationships/

Lenhart, A., & Duggan, M. (2014). *Couples, the Internet, and social media*. Retrieved November 14, 2016, from www.pewInternet.org/2014/02/11/couples-the-Internet-and-social-media/

Len-Ríos, M. E., Streit, C., Killoren, S., Deutsch, A., Cooper, M. L., & Carlo, G. (2016, April). US Latino adolescents use of mass media and mediated communication in romantic relationships. *Journal of Children and Media*, 2798, 1–16. http://doi.org/10.1080/17482798.2016.1144214

Licoppe, C. (2004). "Connected" presence: The emergence of a new repertoire for managing social relationships in a changing communication technoscape. *Environment and Planning D: Society and Space*, 22(1), 135–156.

Luo, S. (2014). Effects of texting on satisfaction in romantic relationships: The role of attachment. *Computers in Human Behavior*, 33, 145–152. http://doi.org/10.1016/j.chb.2014.01.014

Lyndon, A., Bonds-Raacke, J., & Cratty, A. D. (2011). College students' Facebook stalking of ex-partners. *CyberPsychology, Behavior & Social Networking*, 14(12), 711–716. http://doi.org/10.1089/cyber.2010.0588

Marshall, T. C., Bejanyan, K., Di Castro, G., & Lee, R. A. (2013). Attachment styles as predictors of Facebook-related jealousy and surveillance in romantic relationships. *Personal Relationships*, 20(1), 1–22. http://doi.org/10.1111/j.1475-6811.2011.01393.x

McCormack, M. (2015). *The role of smartphones and technology in sexual and romantic lives*. Project Report. Durham University. Retrieved April 20, 2017, from http://dro.dur.ac.uk/14770/1/14770.pdf?DDD34+dvmq56

McDaniel, B. T., & Coyne, S. M. (2016). "Technoference": The interference of technology in couple relationships and implications for women's personal and relational well-being. *Psychology of Popular Media Culture*, 5(1), 85–98. http://doi.org/10.1037/ppm0000065

Morey, J. N., Gentzler, A. L., Creasy, B., Oberhauser, A. M., & Westerman, D. (2013). Young adults' use of communication technology within their romantic relationships and associations with attachment style. *Computers in Human Behavior*, 29, 1771–1778.

Muise, A., Christofides, E., & Desmarais, S. (2009). More information than you ever wanted: Does Facebook bring out the green-eyed monster of jealousy? *CyberPsychology & Behavior*, 12(4), 441–444. http://doi.org/10.1089/cpb.2008.0263

Muise, A., Christofides, E., & Desmarais, S. (2014). "Creeping" or just information seeking? Gender differences in partner monitoring in response to jealousy on Facebook. *Personal Relationships*, 21(1), 35–50. http://doi.org/10.1111/pere.12014

Muscanell, N., & Guadagno, R. (2016). 12 Social networking and romantic relationships: A review of jealousy and related emotions. In G. Riva, B. K. Wiederhold, & P. Cipresso (Eds.), *The psychology of social networking: Communication, presence, identity, and relationships in online communities* (pp. 143–158). Berlin, Germany: Versita.

Olson, D., Olson-Sigg, A., & Larson, P. (2008). *The couple checkup: Finding your relationship strengths*. Nashville, TN: Thomas Nelson.

Papp, L. M., Danielewicz, J., & Cayemberg, C. (2012). "Are we Facebook official?" Implications of dating partners' Facebook use and profiles for intimate relationship satisfaction. *Cyberpsychology, Behavior and Social Networking*, 15(2), 85–90. http://doi.org/10.1089/cyber.2011.0291

Pettigrew, J. (2009). Text messaging and connectedness within close interpersonal relationships. *Marriage & Family Review*, 45, 697–716. http://doi.org/10.1080/01494920903224269

Reed, L. A., Tolman, R. M., & Safyer, P. (2015). Too close for comfort: Attachment insecurity and electronic intrusion in college students' dating relationships. *Computers in Human Behavior*, 50, 431–438. http://doi.org/10.1016/j.chb.2015.03.050

Reed, L. A., Tolman, R. M., Ward, L. M., & Safyer, P. (2016). Keeping tabs: Attachment anxiety and electronic intrusion in high school dating relationships. *Computers in Human Behavior*, 58, 259–268. http://doi.org/10.1016/j.chb.2015.12.019

Roberts, J. A., & David, M. E. (2016). My life has become a major distraction from my cell phone: Partner phubbing and relationship satisfaction among romantic partners. *Computers in Human Behavior*, 54, 134–141. http://doi.org/10.1016/j.chb.2015.07.058

Saslow, L. R., Muise, A., Impett, E. a., & Dubin, M. (2012). Can you see how happy we are? Facebook images and relationship satisfaction. *Social Psychological and Personality Science*, 4(4), 411–418. http://doi.org/10.1177/1948550612460059

Scott, V. M., Mottarella, K. E., & Lavooy, M. J. (2006). Does virtual intimacy exist? A brief exploration into reported levels of intimacy in online relationships. *Cyberpsychology & Behavior*, 9(6), 759–761. http://doi.org/10.1089/cpb.2006.9.759

Slatcher, R. B., Vazire, S., & Pennebaker, J. W. (2008). Am "I" more important than "we"? Couples' word use in instant messages. *Personal Relationships*, 15(4), 407–424. http://doi.org/10.1111/j.1475-6811.2008.00207.x

Stafford, L., & Canary, D. J. (1991). Maintenance strategies and romantic relationship type, gender and relational characteristics. *Journal of Social and Personal Relationships*, 8, 217–242.

Stafford, L., & Canary, D. J. (2006). Equity and interdependence as predictors of relational maintenance strategies. *Journal of Family Communication*, 6, 227–254.

Stewart, M. C., Dainton, M., & Goodboy, A. K. (2014). Maintaining relationships on Facebook: Associations with uncertainty, jealousy, and satisfaction. *Communication Reports*, 27(1), 13–26. http://doi.org/10.1080/08934215.2013.845675

Tokunaga, R. S. (2011). Social networking site or social surveillance site? Understanding the use of interpersonal electronic surveillance in romantic relationships. *Computers in Human Behavior*, 27(2), 705–713. http://doi.org/10.1016/j.chb.2010.08.014

Toma, C. L., & Choi, M. (2016). Mobile media matters: Media use and relationship satisfaction among geographically close dating couples. In *Proceedings of the 19th ACM Conference on Computer-Supported Cooperative Work & Social Computing—CSCW '16*, February (pp. 394–404). http://doi.org/10.1145/2818048.2835204

Turkle, S. (2011). *Alone together: Why we expect more from technology and less from each other*. New York: Basic Books.

Utz, S., & Beukeboom, C. J. (2011). The role of social network sites in romantic relationships: Effects on jealousy and relationship happiness. *Journal of Computer-Mediated Communication*, 16(4), 511–527. http://doi.org/10.1111/j.1083-6101.2011.01552.x

Vangelisti, A., & Perlman, D. (2006). *Cambridge handbook of personal relationships* (A. Vangelisti & D. Perlman, Eds.). Cambridge: Cambridge University Press.

Van Ouytsel, J., Walrave, M., Ponnet, K., & Heirman, W. (2015). The association between adolescent sexting, psychosocial difficulties, and risk behavior: Integrative review. *The Journal of School Nursing*, 31(1), 54–69. http://doi.org/10.1177/1059840514541964

Wardecker, B. M., Chopik, W. J., Boyer, M. P., & Edelstein, R. S. (2016). Individual differences in attachment are associated with usage and perceived intimacy of different communication media. *Computers in Human Behavior*, 59, 18–27. http://doi.org/10.1016/j.chb.2016.01.029

Weisskirch, R. S., & Delevi, R. (2011). "Sexting" and adult romantic attachment. *Computers in Human Behavior*, 27(5), 1697–1701. http://doi.org/10.1016/j.chb.2011.02.008

PART IV

Socialization in a POPC Environment

Development, Skill Acquisition, and Cultural Influences

16

Growing Up Online

Media Use and Development in Early Adolescence

Amy B. Jordan

Introduction

The field of youth and media has historically been concerned about the effects of media on children's healthy development (Wartella & Jennings, 2000). For example, we ask how media shape the way children learn (Huston & Wright, 1998), play (Singer, Singer, & D'Agnostino, 2009), or socially interact (Cingel, Lauricella, Wartella, & Conway, 2014). More commonly, we ask about the negative effects of media use on children's development. Does violent video game play make children and adolescents more violent (Möller & Krahe, 2009), less compassionate (Funk, Buchman, Jenks, & Bechtoldt, 2003), or less trusting (Rothmund, Gollwitzer, Bender, & Klimmt, 2015)? Are girls who watch movies featuring Disney princesses more accepting of gender stereotypes (Coyne, Linder, Rasmussen, Nelson, & Birbeck, 2016)? Do digital media reduce young people's ability to sustain attention (Nikkelen, Valkenburg, Huizinga, & Bushman, 2014)? While it is important to examine the effects of media on children's development, it is, I would argue, equally important to ask what children's media choices can tell us about their developmental needs. Children clearly enjoy media, and have for decades been appropriating media technologies initially intended for adults because they gratify a need—real or perceived (Jones, 2002; Carroll, Howard, Vetere, Peck, & Murphy, 2002; Troseth, Russo, & Strouse, 2016). In this chapter, therefore, I consider the cognitive characteristics of children at a particular developmental stage—early adolescence—in order to more fully explore not only what media do to children but also what children's media preferences and habits might say about their developmental characteristics. Moreover, I consider the experience of early adolescence in an era in which youth have an opportunity to be online and connected 24 hours a day, 7 days a week. As Wartella and colleagues have observed, "In the age of digital media, teens are virtually tethered to technology and digital devices" (Wartella, Rideout, Montague, Beaudoin-Ryan, & Lauricella, 2016, p. 21).

The Importance of Early Adolescence in the Study of Media Use

This chapter is focused on early adolescence for several reasons. First, the preteen years—ages 9 to 12—are a critically important yet surprisingly overlooked stage of childhood in media research. Media preferences and patterns often develop in early adolescence, and these have been found to carry through later adolescence (Leung, 2014) and even into adulthood (Potts & Seger, 2013). Second, children in this stage are often becoming more autonomous in their media consumption as they are less frequently supervised by their parents (Bjelland et al., 2015). Third, as will be discussed below, this is the age at which many children first become involved with social media, despite policies like Facebook's which state that the site should not be used by children under the age of 13 (Blackwell, Lauricella, Conway, & Wartella, 2014).

Early adolescence is a time of intense cognitive, emotional, and physical change. There are, as Eccles points out,

> few developmental periods . . . characterized by so many changes at so many different levels as early adolescence, when children face the biological transformations of puberty, the educational transition from elementary to secondary school, and the psychological shifts that accompany the emergence of sexuality.
>
> *(1999, p. 37)*

Indeed, the "founder" of the field of adolescent psychology, G. Stanley Hall (1904), labeled this phase of life as one of *"sturm und drang"* (literally, storm and stress)—which he and many others since have characterized as "universal" and "inevitable" (Arnett, 2006; Petersen et al., 1993).

An important driver of adolescent behavior is the need to develop a sense of self that is autonomous and individualistic (Connell & Wellborn, 1991). This autonomy emerges from both shifts in social roles and expectations but also physiological and cognitive changes (Eccles, 1999). For some adolescents, the shifts can be particularly dramatic, and for many the decisions made at this crossroad can lead to negative outcomes, including addiction, sexual risk taking, and isolation (Eccles, 1999; Rutter, 1988). Additionally, "identity" and "autonomy" will carry quite different meanings, depending on psychosocial and cultural factors. It is well documented that girls and boys experience different pressures during early adolescence (Buhrmester & Prager, 1995; Valkenburg & Peter, 2007), as do ethnic and racial minorities (Umaña-Taylor et al., 2014), and LGBTQ youth (Poteat, 2015).

Despite these differences, however, there are common if not universal changes that occur in early adolescence, and recognizing these can help illuminate how and why media come to play such a prominent role in the lives of early adolescents. First, children this age are increasingly able to not only think abstractly, but also consider the hypothetical. Changes in cognition also allow them to more deeply understand the perspectives of others, including their internal psychological characteristics (Steinberg, 2017). Second, preteens begin the process of "distancing" themselves from their parents, a transition that can lead to conflict but can also help to foster independence and self-efficacy (Lerner & Steinberg, 2009). Third, during early adolescence, there emerges a greater focus on peer groups, social acceptance, and conformity. They spend more time with their peers, and develop closer relationships than they had in early childhood (Huston & Ripke, 2006).

A heightened peer orientation may bring adolescents into the modern phenomenon which Vorderer and colleagues have termed "permanently online/permanently connected," or POPC (Vorderer, Krömer, & Schneider, 2016). POPC consists of two dimensions: "An overt behavior in the form of protracted electronic media use and a psychological state of permanent communicative vigilance" (p. 695). Though there has yet to be systematic research on this phenomenon with youth, the hypothesized psychological origins of POPC reflect many of the developmental traits of adolescence; including a need to belong, a fear of ostracism, and a fear of missing out (Vorderer et al., 2016, p. 695).

This period of childhood has not always been recognized as unique or particularly important. In many arenas, 9- to 12-year-olds have been classified as "school age" children or "preteens." In the

United States, however, media makers (specifically television program producers) recognized that as an audience, this age group acted neither like their younger nor older counterparts. As content began to be created specifically for this age group, they received their own label—"tweens"—(a blend of "in between" and "teen"), and were treated as a separate target audience. The Centers for Disease Control and Prevention, for example, spent millions of dollars developing, disseminating, and evaluating a social marketing campaign (the VERB campaign) specifically designed for "tweens" to encourage them to be more physically active (Huhman, Bauman, & Bowles, 2008). Parenting books provided new guidelines for dealing with tweens (Goodstein, 2008), and researchers, for their part, began separating tweens from children and teenagers (Azzarone, 2003; Common Sense Media, 2015). Increasingly, this American neologism has been increasingly adopted outside the US context. Researchers in Denmark and Hong Kong, for example, examined "tween" consumers' perceptions of advertising on television and the Internet (Andersen, Tufle, Rasmussen, & Chan, 2007). Though the margins of their age range may change, they are now consistently recognized as having unique interests and characteristics, including media use patterns (Common Sense Media, 2015).

Media Use by Early Adolescents

The majority of published research on the current media use patterns by "tweens" is based on samples of youth from the United States, the United Kingdom, and Europe. This is an unfortunate limitation, but may offer a starting point for thinking more globally about youth and media in future research.

The EU Kids Online network of 33 mainly European countries conducts targeted analyses of cross-national surveys and interviews, and they have found that nearly two thirds (63%) of 11- to 16-year-olds in these countries "visit a social networking profile" daily (and only 18% of parents say they are not allowed to be on social media) (EU Kids Online, 2014). Though most social networking sites like Facebook, Instagram, Snapchat, WhatsApp, and Twitter have policies restricting children from accessing their websites, it is clear that tweens are both accessing them and participating in their communities. A 2016 survey conducted by the BBC found that three quarters of 10- to 12-year-olds in the UK use social media (Coughlan, 2016). In another survey of 8- to 12-year olds in the US, nearly one in five (18%) said that Facebook is a "favorite" site. Despite the age restrictions, parents don't seem terribly concerned. Research by danah boyd and colleagues (2011) found that many parents know that their underage children are using social media and that they are "often complicit in helping their children join" the site(s) (boyd, Hargittai, Schultz, & Palfrey, 2011).

Young people's media preferences will, of course, reflect their access to the technologies. In the US, virtually all higher income families own a laptop (92%) and/or a tablet (89%), but far fewer children in lower income families have these devices (54% and 71%, respectively). And while a Common Sense Media poll highlights the technology access gap (commonsensemedia.org), others have pointed to an even greater gap: the technology use divide. As Dolan argues, the definition of "access" must now include:

> the accessibility of the locations of the technology, the availability of complementary technologies (such as software), the explosion of mobile technology, and the personal skills students possess to understand and use the technology. In addition, students' access to technology at home and the ways they use technology outside of school appears to be disconnected to their access to, and use of, technology in school.

(2016, p. 19)

The Developmental Characteristics of Early Adolescents and the Role of Media in their Lives

As noted earlier, the space of childhood representing early adolescence can be understood through several important benchmarks: increasing cognitive capacities for understanding the abstract and hypothetical; developing an independent identity and self-concept; and strengthening connections to peers in the context of changing ties with family. Through these simultaneous lenses, one might view the concept of POPC within its developmental context.

Media and Cognition

During early adolescence, there is a steady increase in the sophistication of children's learning, as they begin to be able to consider multiple dimensions of a problem, as well as move into abstract and hypothetical reasoning (Eccles, 1999). What might the plethora and ubiquity of digital media technologies mean for adolescents, cognitive development, particularly within the context of a need to be POPC? One concern has to do with adolescents' tendency to multitask, which a majority of teens say they do "most" or "some" of the time (Rideout, Foehr, & Roberts, 2010). Multitasking has been shown to affect academic performance (Pool, Koolstra, & van der Voort, 2003) and cognitive functions (Ophir, Nass, & Wagner, 2009). Multitasking with mobile media, for example, is hypothesized to impair learning because learners have limited capacity to deal with competing incoming information (Chen & Yan, 2016; see also David, this volume, and Xu and Wang, this volume). For the POPC individual, media multitasking is more like serial tasking, with learners stopping and starting and interruptions requiring recovery and resume time (Firat, 2013; Ophir, Nass, & Wagner, 2009). Research conducted with college students finds that people multitask, despite the "high cognitive costs," because their emotional needs are met and also out of habit (Wang & Tchernev, 2012). For adolescents who are just developing learning routines and who may be less able to control their impulses, media multitasking may hinder effective learning. A Dutch study of early adolescents' executive functioning (i.e., working memory, shifting, and inhibition) found that 11- to 15-year-olds who media multitask more frequently reported having more problems staying focused and concentrating for long periods of time (Baumgartner, Weeda, van der Heijden, & Huizinga, 2014). The heavy multitasking adolescents in this study also reported more school and social problems.

Digital media technologies have great appeal for adolescents who are constantly seeking stimulation and who have little internal locus of control. A three-year longitudinal investigation of adolescents in the US found that the male and female cohorts diverged, with girls moving toward greater external locus of control and boys developing greater internal locus of control (Kulas, 1996). The impulse to be POPC may reflect adolescents' sense of the extent to which they feel they have influence over life's events and outcomes.

Social media may also allow adolescents to play out their new abilities to form hypotheses and their interest in understanding others' motivations and perceptions. And social media can play into these new cognitive capacities, particularly as they provide constant feedback for the adolescent who is POPC. Simmons (2014) writes, for example, that

> Instagram's simplicity is . . . deceiving: look more closely, and you find the Rosetta Stone of girl angst: a way for tweens and teens to find out what their peers really think of them (Was that comment about my dress a joke or did she mean it?), who likes you (Why wasn't I included in

that picture?), even how many people like them (if you post and get too few likes, you might feel "Instashame").

Other media, too, have captured adolescents' time and attention. The draw of digital game play among adolescents has been linked to their curiosity, agency, and immersion (Klimmt, 2009; Bryant & Fondren, 2009). Game players have been found to have enhanced inductive reasoning (Greenfield et al., 1994), metacognition (VanDeventer & White, 2002), and spatial distribution of attention (Boot, Kramer, Simons, Fabini, & Gratton, 2008). Even violent video gaming has been found to facilitate scientific reasoning (Dickey, 2011)—though observers are quick to point out that the benefits of violent video game play "need to be considered in light of perceived risks" (Blumberg, Blades, & Oats, 2013).

Media and Identity Development

One of the most important milestones of the early adolescent years is the development of an identity separate from one's parents and siblings, a sense of a self that has a personality, a set of beliefs, and a moral compass that guides future decisions (Moreno & Kolb, 2012). Media can play an important role in identity development, as it offers a window into other ways of thinking, behaving, and presenting oneself.

Early studies of online teen chat rooms found that the "virtual world" of teen chat may offer a safer environment for exploring emerging sexuality than the real world. A study conducted in 2001 by the Pew Center found that 55% of online teens had visited a chat room. Participants in chat rooms are typically anonymous and "disembodied," though a study by Subramanyam and colleagues (2004) of adolescents in chat rooms found that teens find ways to overcome the "facelessness" and "placelessness" of the platform in order to both present themselves and also figure out the key categories (gender, sexual orientation) of others. Thus, the authors argue, "the medium is not doing something to adolescents; they, instead, are doing something with the medium. Teen chat provides new affordances for old adolescent issues" (p. 664).

An online presence provides adolescents with opportunities to explore other aspects of their identity as well, and in doing so they receive feedback from their peers. Social media can provide pathways to civic engagement through the expression of political views (Weinstein, 2014). Social media can also offer safe spaces for adolescents who perceive themselves to be outside of the mainstream culture, for example, medically fragile youth (Wong et al., 2016), LGBTQ youth (DeHaan et al., 2013), or adolescents with disabilities (Soderstrom, 2009). Online peer groups may provide adolescents with support they need that cannot be found in "real-life" settings. As DeHaan writes:

> Youth who cannot disclose details about their personal life offline tend to engage in online relationships. . . . [which can] decrease feelings of loneliness and social rejection, increase social skills, and help youth create meaningful online relationships that occasionally move from online to offline.
>
> *(2013, p. 422)*

While there are many opportunities for youths' identity development as they move through the media landscape, there are also many challenges. The video game culture, for example, systematically overrepresents males, Whites, and adults, while systematically underrepresenting females, Hispanics, Native Americans, children, and the elderly (Williams, Martins, Consalvo, & Ivory, 2009). Females and ethnic minorities are invisible or marginalized in mainstream Hollywood films (Erigha, 2015). Social identity theory suggests that groups look for representations of themselves and then compare those representations with those of other groups (Tajfel, 1978). The presence of a group in mainstream media suggests that those group members "matter" in society, while absences suggest unimportance and powerlessness (Mastro & Behm-Morawitz, 2005).

There are also challenges for youth who are in developmental transition in terms of their bodies. Objectification theory posits that

> through the pervasiveness of objectification, women and girls are gradually socialized to adopt an observers' perspective of their physical self. As they go through puberty, they come to view themselves as primarily an object to be looked at and evaluated on the basis of appearance, in part because of how they are positioned by the media.
>
> *(Tiggeman & Slater, 2015)*

A study of Australian adolescents found that girls as young as 10 and 11 self-objectified, a belief associated in this sample with body shame, dieting, and depressive symptoms. Though the research was cross-sectional, it found a significant association between media consumption and appearance conversations, which were the strongest predictors of self-objectification (Tiggeman & Slater, 2015). Girls who self-objectify embrace the thin beauty ideal, and in the extreme may experience eating disorders that are exacerbated by content that is "pro-anorexic" (Rogers, Lowry, Halperin, & Franko, 2016). For the POPC adolescent, the ready availability of digital media to reinforce these tendencies may exacerbate body dysmorphia and disordered eating.

Media in the Peer Context

Two of the key tasks of adolescence are to simultaneously stand out and fit in (Shapiro & Margolin, 2014). These seemingly divergent goals, Crosnoe and Johnson (2011) write, reflect an interplay between the need for one's own personal identity and the need for strong group affiliation. Adolescents can connect to their peers in many ways, and indeed have used media long before social networking sites arrived on the scene to connect, relate, and affiliate. A 1977 study with students from a diverse suburban Chicago high school concluded that "rock [music] in particular may be embraced by the young, because its very sounds and words mirror the intensity and turbulence of adolescent experience" (Larson & Kubey, 1983). Using a method known as experience sampling method, they asked adolescents to report on their activities and moods at random intervals.

> Listening to music, in comparison [to television], appears more compatible with life in the adolescent-structured peer group ...The experience of charged participation in music appears to enrich particularly the part of their lives they share with friends.
>
> *(p. 27–28)*

Perhaps the most significant introduction of media into the peer cultures of early adolescents' lives has been social networking sites. As noted earlier, these are widely used by tweens and grudgingly accepted by the adults in their lives. Developmentally, it would seem natural that adolescents would gravitate to such environments, as social media allow them opportunities for self-presentation as well as peer comparison. A particularly salient characteristic of the "tween" years is what developmental psychologists have labeled the "imaginary audience" (Elkind & Bowen, 1979). Adolescents' newly sophisticated cognitive skills allow them to take the perspective of others as well as be more introspective about themselves and their place in the world. This leads to the sense that others are as critical of them as they are of themselves, a form of adolescent egocentrism that diminishes by the later teen years (Enright, Shukla, & Lapsley, 1980).

Some have argued that the tendency toward the imaginary audience leads to engagement in social comparison—be it upward or downward—which may affect adolescents' self-esteem (Krayer, Ingledew, & Iphofen, 2008). Carefully curated self-presentations on social media may make it seem that others' lives are happier, more interesting, or more popular (boyd & Ellison, 2007), which some observers have worried might lead to negative outcomes, including more negative body image or less perceived success in school or social life (Haferkamp & Krämer, 2011; Appel, Gerlach, & Crusius, 2016). A Dutch study of friend networking sites revealed that the effect of participation in social media reflected the type of feedback adolescents received on their profiles. As might be expected, positive feedback on the profiles enhanced adolescents' social self-esteem and well-being, whereas negative feedback decreased their self-esteem and well-being (Valkenburg, Peter, & Schouten, 2006).

Scholars have recently proposed that a relatively modern concept links adolescent's social needs with their engagement on social networking sites: fear of missing out. FOMO is "a pervasive apprehension that others might be having rewarding experiences from which one is absent" (Przybylski, Murayama, DeHaan, & Gladwell, 2013) and is viewed as one of the psychological origins of POPC (Vorderer et al., 2016). A cross-sectional survey of Belgian adolescents assessed social media participation, the need to belong, need for popularity, and fear of missing out, as well as perceived stress related to Facebook use (Beyens, Frison, & Eggermont, 2016). The researchers found that adolescents' need to belong and need for popularity were related to increased FOMO, which, in turn, was associated with increased Facebook use. The authors argue that "A vicious circle may develop in which FoMO may drive people toward social media, which, in turn, may increase adolescents' FoMO" (p. 6), potential leading to reinforcing spirals. Moreover, they found, one in four adolescents indicated that not being popular on Facebook was stressful to extremely stressful.

Conclusion

This chapter has considered the ways in which "tween" media both influence and reflect the developmental characteristics of early adolescence. The convergence of adolescent vulnerability with the pervasive access adolescents have to media—in which they are permanently online and permanently connected—deserves closer study. Although the evidence base is beginning to grow, it is limited by the particularly "WEIRD" profile of the research participants—Heinrich, Heine, & Norenzayan's (2010) acronym for Western, educated, industrialized, rich, and democratic. The context of childhood is not monolithic, nor is the experience of media within the lives of adolescents who grow up in non-Western, nondeveloped settings. An additional limitation of the research to date is its cross-sectional nature. Though valuable to observe the covariance of factors, such as friendship and social media participation, the directionality is not always clear (e.g., are friendly people more likely to use social media, or does social media use develop friendship skills?). More likely, media use interacts with psychosocial characteristics, reflecting nonrecursive relationships. Longitudinal surveys beginning in early adolescence and tracking youth through early adulthood can shed light on whether and how media use plays a factor in development. Understood through the lens of the concept of permanently online and permanently connected, one can better understand the ways in which the characteristics of the developing child interact with the pull of the technological environment.

References

Andersen, L. P., Tufle, B., Rasmussen, J., & Chan, K. (2007). Tweens and new media in Denmark and Hong Kong, *Journal of Consumer Marketing, 24*(6), 340–350.

Appel, H., Gerlach, A. L., & Crusius, J. (2016). The interplay between Facebook use, social comparison, envy, and depression. *Current Opinion in Psychology, 9,* 44–49. doi:10.1016/j.copsyc.2015.10.006

Arnett, J. J. (2006). G. Stanley Hall's adolescence: Brilliance and nonsense. *History of Psychology, 9*(3), 186–197.

Azzarone, S. (2003). Tweens, teens and technology: What's important now? *Young Consumers, 5*(1), 57–61.

Baumgartner, S. E., Weeda, W. D., van der Heijden, L. L., & Huizinga, M. (2014). The relationship between media multitasking and executive function in early adolescents. *The Journal of Early Adolescence, 34*(8), 1120–1144.

Beyens, I., Frison, E., & Eggermont, S. (2016). "I don't want to miss a thing": Adolescents' fear of missing out and its relationship to adolescents' social needs, Facebook use, and Facebook related stress. *Computers in Human Behavior, 64,* 1–8.

Bjelland, M., Soenens, B., Bere, El., Kovacs, E., Lien, N., Maes, L., Manios, Y., Moschonis, G., & Velde, S. (2015). Associations between parental rules, style of communication and children's screen time. *BMC Public Health, 15*(1002), 1–13.

Blackwell, C., Lauricella, A., Conway, A., & Wartella, E. (2014). Children and the Internet: Developmental implications of web site preferences among 8- to 12-year-old children. *Journal of Broadcasting and Electronic Media, 58*(1), 1–20.

Blumberg, F.C., Blades, M., & Oates, C. (2013). Youth and new media: The appeal and educational ramifications of digital game play for children and adolescents. *Zeitschrift fur Psychologie, 221*(2), 67–71.

Boot, W. R., Kramer, A. F., Simons, D. J., Fabiani, M., & Gratton, G. (2008). The effects of video game playing on attention, memory, and executive control. *Acta Psychologica, 129,* 387–398.

boyd, d., & Ellison, N. B. (2007). Social network sites: Definition, history, and scholarship. *Journal of Computer-Mediated Communication, 13,* 210–230.

boyd, d., Hargittai, E., Schultz, J., & Palfrey, J. (2011, November). Why parents help their children lie to Facebook about age: Unintended consequences of the "Children's Online Privacy Protection Act." *First Monday, 16*(11). http://journals.uic.edu/ojs/index.php/fm/article/view/3850/3075.

Bryant, J., & Fondren, W. (2009). Psychological and communicological theories of learning and emotion underlying serious games. In U. Ritterfeld, M. Cody, & P. Vorderer (Eds.), *Serious games: Mechanisms and effects* (pp. 103–116). New York: Routledge/Taylor & Francis.

Buhrmester, D., & Prager, K. (1995). Patterns and functions of self-disclosure during childhood and adolescence. In K. J. Rotenberg (Ed.), *Disclosure processes in children and adolescents: Cambridge studies in social and emotional development* (pp. 10–56). New York: Cambridge University Press.

Carroll, J., Howard, S., Vetere, F., Peck, J., & Murphy, J. (2002, January). Just what do the youth of today want? Technology appropriation by young people. *Proceedings of the 35th Hawaii International Conference on System Sciences.*

Chen, Q., & Yan, Z. (2016). Does multitasking with mobile phones affect learning? A review. *Computers in Human Behavior, 54,* 34–42.

Cingel, D. P., Lauricella, A. R., Wartella, E., & Conway, A. (2014). Predicting social networking site use and online communication practices among adolescents: The role of access and device ownership. *Media and Communication, 2*(2), 1–30.

Common Sense Media. (2015). *The common sense census: Media use by tweens and teens.* San Francisco, CA: Common Sense Media.

Connell, J. P., & Wellborn, J. G. (1991). Competence, autonomy, and relatedness: A motivational analysis of self-system processes. In R. Gunnar & L. A. Srofe (Eds.), *Minnesota symposia on child psychology* (Vol. 23, pp. 43–77). Hillsdale, NJ: Lawrence Erlbaum Associates.

Coughlan, S. (February 9, 2016). Safer Internet day: Young ignore 'social media age limit.' *BBC News.* Retrieved April 7, 2016, from www.bbc.com/news/education-35524429.

Coyne, S. M., Linder, J. R., Rasmussen, E. E., Nelson, D. A., & Birbeck, V. (2016). Pretty as a princess: Longitudinal effects of engagement with Disney princesses on gender stereotypes, body esteem, and prosocial behavior in children. *Child Development.* Retrieved from http://onlinelibrary.wiley.com/doi/10.1111/cdev.12569/full. doi:10.1111/cdev.12569

Crosnoe, R., & Johnson, M. K. (2011). Research on adolescence in the 21st century. *Annual Review of Sociology*, *37*, 439–460.

DeHaan, S., Kuper, L. E., Magee, J. C., Bigelow, L., & Mustanski, B. S. (2013). The interplay between online and offline explorations of identity, relationships, and sex: A mixed-methods study with LGBT youth. *The Journal of Sex Research*, *50*(5), 421–434.

Dickey, M. D. (2011). World of Warcraft and the impact of game culture and play in an undergraduate game design course. *Computers and Education*, *56*, 200–209.

Dolan, J. E. (2016). Splicing the divide: A review of research on the evolving digital divide among K–12 students. *Journal of Research on Technology in Education*, *48*(1), 16–37.

Eccles, J. S. (1999). The development of children ages 6 to 13. When school is out. *The Future of Children*, *9*(2), 30–44.

Elkind, D., & Bowen, R. (1979). Imaginary audience behavior in children and adolescents. *Developmental Psychology*, *15*(1), 38–44.

Enright, R. D., Shukla, D. G., & Lapsley, D. K. (1980). Adolescent egocentrism-sociocentrism and self-consciousness. *Journal of Youth and Adolescence*, *9*(2), 101–116.

Erigha, M. (2015). Race, gender, Hollywood: Representation in cultural production and digital media's potential for change. *Sociology Compass*, *9*(1), 78–89.

EU Kids Online (2014). *EU Kids Online: findings, methods, recommendations*. EU Kids Online, LSE. Retrieved from https://lsedesignunit.com/EUKidsOnline/index.html?r=64

Firat, M. (2013). Multitasking or continuous partial attention: A critical bottleneck for digital natives. *Turkish Online Journal of Distance Education*, *14*(1), 266–272.

Funk, J. B., Buchman, D. D., Jenks, J., & Bechtoldt, H. (2003). Playing violent video games, desensitization, and moral evaluation in children. *Journal of Applied Developmental Psychology*, *24*, 413–436.

Goodstein, A. (2008). *Totally wired: What teens and tweens are really doing online*. New York: St. Martins Press.

Greenfield, P., Camaioni, L., Ercolani, P., Weiss, L., Lauber, B. A., and Perucchini, P. (1994). Cognitive socialization by computer games in two cultures: Inductive discovery or mastery of an iconic code? Journal of *Applied Developmental Psychology*, *15*, 59–85.

Haferkamp, N., & Krämer, N. C. (2011). Social comparison 2.0: Examining the effects of online profiles on social-networking sites. *Cyberpsychology, Behavior and Social Networking*, *14*(5), 309–314. doi:10.1089/cyber.2010.0120

Hall, G. S. (1904). *Adolescence: Its psychology and its relations to physiology, anthropology, sociology, sex, crime, religion, and education* (Vols. I & II). New York: D. Appleton & Co.

Heinrich, J., Heine, S., & Norenzayan, A. (2010). The weirdest people in the world? *Behavioral and Brain Sciences*, *33*, 61–135.

Huhman, M., Bauman, A., & Bowles, H. R. (2008). Initial outcomes of the VERB Campaign: Tweens' awareness and understanding of campaign messages. *American Journal of Preventive Medicine*, *34*(6S), S2441–S248.

Huston, A. C., & Ripke, M. N. (2006). Middle childhood: Contexts of development. In A. C. Huston & M. N. Ripke (Eds.), *Developmental contexts in middle childhood: Bridges to adolescence and adulthood*. New York: Cambridge University Press.

Huston, A. C., & Wright, J. C. (1998). Television and the informational and educational needs of children. *Annals of the American Academy of Political & Social Science*, *557*, 24.

Jones, G. (2002). *Killing monsters: Why children need fantasy, super heroes, and make-believe violence*. New York: Basic Books.

Klimmt, C. (2009). Serious games and social change. Why they (should) work. In U. Ritterfeld, M. Cody, & P. Vorderer (Eds.), *Serious games: Mechanisms and effects* (pp. 248–270). New York: Routledge/Taylor & Francis.

Krayer, A., Ingledew, D.K., & Iphofen, R. (2008). Social comparison and body image in adolescence: A grounded theory approach. *Health Education Research*, *23*(5), 892–903.

Kulas, H. (1996). Locus of control in adolescence: A longitudinal study. *Adolescence*, *31*(123), 721–730.

Larson, R., & Kubey, R. (1983). Television and music: Contrasting media in adolescent life. *Youth & Society*, *15*(1), 13–31.

Lerner, R., & Steinberg, L. (Eds.). (2009). *The handbook of adolescent psychology* (3rd ed.). New York: Wiley.

Leung, L. (2014). Predicting Internet risks: A longitudinal panel study of gratifications-sought, Internet addiction symptoms, and social media use among children and adolescents. *Health Psychology and Behavioral Medicine*, *2*(1), 424–439.

Mastro, D., & Behm-Morawitz, E. (2005). Latino representation on primetime television. *Journalism and Mass Communication Quarterly, 82*(1), 110–130.

Möller, I., & Krahe, B. (2009). Exposure to violent video games and aggression in German adolescents: A longitudinal analysis. *Aggressive Behavior, 35*, 75–89.

Moreno, M. A., & Kolb, J. (2012). Social networking sites and adolescent health. *Pediatric Clinics of North America, 59*(3), 601–612.

Nikkelen, S. W. C., Valkenburg, P. M., Huizinga, M., & Bushman, B. J. (2014, September). Media use and ADHD-related behaviors in children and adolescents: A meta-analysis. *Developmental Psychology, 50*(9), 2228–2241.

Ophir, E., Nass, C., & Wagner, A. D. (2009). Cognitive control in media multitaskers. *Proceedings of the National Academy of Sciences, 106*, 15583–15587.

Petersen, A. C., Compas, B. E., Brooks-Gunn, J., Stemmler, M., Ey, S., & Grant, K. E. (1993). Depression in adolescence. *American Psychologist, 48*, 155–168.

Pew Internet and American Life Project. (2001). *Teenage life online: The rise of the instant-message generation and the Internet's impact on friendships and family relationships*. Retrieved from www.pewinternetInternet.org/2001/06/21/teenage-life-online/.

Pool, M. M., Koolstra, C. M., & Voort, T. H. A. van der (2003). The impact of background radio and television on high school students' homework performance. *Journal of Communication, 53*, 74–87.

Poteat, V. P. (2015). Individual psychological factors and complex interpersonal conditions that predict LGBT-affirming behavior. *Journal of Youth and Adolescence, 44*(8), 1494–1507.

Potts, R., & Seger, J. (2013). Validity of adults' retrospective memory for early television viewing. *Communication Methods and Measures, 7*, 1–25.

Przybylski, A. K., Murayama, K., DeHaan, C. R., & Gladwell, V. (2013). Motivational, emotional, and behavioral correlates of fear of missing out. *Computers in Human Behavior, 29*, 1841–1848.

Rideout, V. J., Foehr, U. G., & Roberts, D. F. (2010). *Generation M2: Media in the lives of 8- to 18-year-olds*. Menlo Park, CA: Henry J. Kaiser Family Foundation.

Rogers, R. F., Lowry, A. S., Halperin, D. M., & Franko, D. L. (2016). A meta-analysis examining the influence of pro-eating disorder websites on body image and eating pathology. *European Eating Disorders Review, 24*(1), 3–8.

Rothmund, T., Gollwitzer, M., Bender, J., & Klimmt, C. (2015). Short- and long-term effects of video game violence on interpersonal trust. *Media Psychology, 18*, 106–133.

Rutter, M. (1988). *Studies of psychosocial risk: The power of longitudinal data*. New York: Cambridge University Press.

Shapiro, L. A., & Margolin, G. (2014). Growing up wired: Social networking sites and adolescent psychosocial development. *Clinical Child and Family Psychological Review, 17*(1), 1–18.

Simmons, R. (2014, November 10). The secret language of girls on Instagram. *Time Magazine*. Retrieved from http://time.com/3559340/instagram-tween-girls/.

Singer, D. G., Singer, J. L., & D'Agnostino, H. (2009). Children's pastimes and play in sixteen nations: Is free-play declining? *American Journal of Play, 1*(3), 283–312.

Soderstrom, S. (2009). Offline social ties and online use of computers: A study of disabled youth and their use of ICT advances. *New Media & Society, 11*(5), 709–727.

Steinberg, L. (2017). *Adolescence* (11th ed.). New York: McGraw-Hill.

Subrahmanyam, K., Greenfield, P. M., & Tynes, B. (2004). Constructing sexuality and identity in an online teen chat room. *Journal of Applied Developmental Psychology, 25*(6), 651–666.

Tajfel, H. (1978). *Differentiation between social groups: Studies in the social psychology of intergroup relations*. London: Academic Press.

Tiggeman, M., & Slater, A. (2015). The role of self-objectification in the mental health of early adolescent girls: Predictors and consequences. *Journal of Pediatric Psychology, 40*(7), 704–711.

Troseth, G. L., Russo, C., & Strouse, G. A. (2016). What's next for research on young children's interactive media? *Journal of Children and Media, 10*(1), 54–62.

Umaña-Taylor, A. J., Quintana, S. M., Lee, R. M., Cross, W. E., Rivas-Drake, D., Schwartz, S. J., & Seaton, E. (2014). Ethnic and racial identity during adolescence and into young adulthood: An integrated conceptualization. *Child Development, 85*(1), 21–39.

Valkenburg, P. M., & Peter, J. (2007). Preadolescents' and adolescents' online communication and their closeness to friends. *Developmental Psychology*, *43*(2), 267–277.

Valkenburg, P. M., Peter, J., & Schouten, A. P. (2006). Friend networking sites and their relationship to adolescents' well-being and social self-esteem. *CyberPsychology & Behavior*, *9*(5), 584–590.

VanDeventer, S. S., & White, J. A. (2002). Expert behavior in children's video game play. *Simulation & Gaming*, *33*, 28–48.

Vorderer, P., Krömer, N., & Schneider, F. M. (2016). Permanently online—permanently connected: Explorations into university students' use of social media and mobile smart devices. *Computers in Human Behavior*, *63*, 694–703. doi:10.1016/j.chb.2016.05.085

Wang, Z., & Tchernev, J. M. (2012). The "myth" of media multitasking: Reciprocal dynamics of media multitasking, personal needs, and gratifications. *Journal of Communication*, *62*, 493–513.

Wartella, E. A., & Jennings, N. (2000). Children and computers: New technology—old concerns. *Future of Children*, *10*(2), 31–34.

Wartella, E. A., Rideout, V., Montague, H., Beaudoin-Ryan, L., & Lauricella, A. (2016). Teens, health and technology: A national survey. *Media and Communication*, *4*(3), 13–23.

Weinstein, E. C. (2014). The personal is political on social media: Online civic expression patterns and pathways among civically engaged youth. *International Journal of Communication*, *8*, 210–233.

Williams, D., Martins, N., Consalvo, M., & Ivory, J. (2009). The virtual census: Representations of gender, race and age in video games. *New Media and Society*, *11*(5), 815–834.

Wong, C. A., Ostapovich, G., Kramer-Golinkoff, E., Griffis, H., Asch, D. A., & Merchant, R. M. (2016). How U.S. children's hospitals use social media: A mixed methods study. *Healthcare*, *4*(1), 15–21.

17

Being Mindfully Connected

Responding to the Challenges of Adolescents Living in a POPC World

Dorothée Hefner, Karin Knop, and Christoph Klimmt

The ubiquitous availability of online services implies new possibilities for individuals' (digital) social lives: Users can get in touch with others almost permanently, exchange information, share thoughts and feelings, tap social support, post pictures, and thus present themselves and observe the lives of others. These opportunities are particularly attractive for adolescents in a developmental stage characterized by the important role that peers have for them and the development of an individual and social identity (Arnett, 2004; Grusec & Hastings, 2015). Social interactions, both offline and mediated, are thus particularly important for adolescents. This is also the reason why they often experience incoming messages or the possibility to share thoughts or just to be in touch with somebody as highly welcomed distractions from other, less captivating activities. Even though human needs, such as the need to belong (Baumeister & Leary, 1995) or the fear of missing out (Przybylski, Murayama, DeHaan, & Gladwell, 2013) may—especially in adolescence—explain the attractiveness of being "permanently connected," an overuse or overinvolvement with the mobile phone can have negative side effects. Users may feel overwhelmed by the quantity of communication incidences and obliged to be permanently accessible and to instantly respond or even generate their own messages (LaRose, Connolly, Lee, Li, & Hales, 2014; Mai, Freudenthaler, Schneider, & Vorderer, 2015). As a result, digital stress can emerge (Hefner & Vorderer, 2016; Kushlev & Dunn, 2015; Misra & Stokols, 2012). Moreover, the temptations of the mobile phone—especially if it is signaling an incoming message—can stimulate multitasking (see also David, this volume, and Xu and Wang, this volume) and thus impair necessary attention on the fulfillment of other important tasks, such as driving (Bayer & Campbell, 2012) or doing (home)work (David, Kim, Brickman, Ran, & Curtis, 2015). Next to these downsides regarding the quantity of digital communication, adolescent users also face challenges regarding the content of communication. Permanent, fast, and therefore often automatic and mindless creating of messages and posts and processing communication content is related to often-discussed Internet risks, such as privacy issues, cyberbullying, or negative emotions stemming from upward social comparison (Appel, Gerlach, & Crusius, 2016; Livingstone, Haddon, Gorzig, & Olafsson, 2011).

In order to benefit from the gratifications of mobile phone communication and to avoid the negative side effects of permanent distractions at the same time, users have to develop and adopt useful strategies on how to manage their online availability, how to respond to incoming messages, and deciding when and how to circulate their own messages, posts, and pictures. These strategies obviously involve an active, reflective steering of mobile phone use. However, mobile phone communication often happens so fast and is highly habitual and automatic (Bayer, Campbell, & Ling, 2016). Therefore, we need to address adolescents' competences of mastering manifold challenges, while simultaneously appreciating the attraction mobile phones have to them. This aims at supporting these adolescents in developing or reacquiring a beneficial mode of living in a POPC world.

It is the goal of this chapter to propose ideas on how to successfully engage in this endeavor. First, we will review the communication-related aspects of adolescence as a stage of human development. Second, we will describe the challenges that adolescents face in a world that is characterized by a myriad of opportunities (and also perceived obligations) to digitally communicate with others throughout the day. Third, we will define several competencies that we believe are important to (re)gain a healthy use of todays' affordances of the mobile Internet. Finally, we will suggest promising ways to support adolescents in acquiring important facets of POPC-related media literacy.

Adolescents as Connection Seekers

Mobile media scholars have come to refer to contemporary youth culture as a "mobile youth culture" (e.g., Campbell & Park, 2008; Vanden Abeele, 2016). Particularly among adolescents, mobile phone use is on the rise (Knop, Hefner, Schmitt & Vorderer, 2015; Lenhart, 2015; Mascheroni & Ólafsson, 2014; Sambira, 2013). Most relevant to this age group are social apps and functions of the mobile phone such as Facebook, Instagram, or Instant Messaging apps (Lenhart, 2015).

How can the strong appeal—if not even fascination—that mobile communication has for this particular age group be explained? Answers may be found by considering the developmental process and the various tasks of adolescence (see also Jordan, this volume). The life stage of adolescence is characterized by several important developments. Particularly relevant in respect to mobile phone use seem to be the growing importance of peers and the need to be connected to them, the development of autonomy and identity (Eccles, Early, Fraser, Belansky, & McCarthy, 1997; Steinberg & Morris, 2001), and the susceptibility to risky or reckless behavior due to the brain's complex maturation processes (Dahl, 2001; Steinberg, 2008).

Mobile phones and their affordances seem to tap right into the needs that accompany the described developments: The possibilities of being POPC enable teens to maintain their social networks, to manage their relationships, and to feel belongingness, receive social support, and reduce loneliness (e.g., Liu & Wei, 2014; Valkenburg & Peter, 2009; Vanden Abeele, 2016). Moreover, digital communication and self-disclosure via the mobile phone and the Internet offer plenty of opportunities for identity work (Valkenburg & Peter, 2009). Adolescents can also act out newly gained autonomy with their mobile phones, even within their homes (Blair & Fletcher, 2011). It is thus not surprising that texting has become the preferred channel of communication among teenagers (Lenhart, Ling, Campbell, & Purcell, 2010).

Simultaneously, the intensive need for group affiliation can lead to a "fear of missing out" (FOMO), which is defined as "the fears, worries, and anxieties people may have in relation to being out of touch with the events, experiences, and conversations happening across their extended social circles" (Przybylski, Murayama, DeHaan, & Gladwell, 2013, p. 1482). FOMO is especially pronounced in late childhood and early adolescence and has been found to explain a great deal of variance in dysfunctional mobile phone use within this age group (Hefner, Knop, & Vorderer, in press). Similarly, an intensive need for social assurance promotes an "always-on-and-connected" mode and explains multicommunicating, meaning upholding (at least) two parallel synchronous conversations (Seo, Kim, & David, 2015). Furthermore, the central importance of peers makes adolescents highly susceptible to following (risky) peer norms (Berndt & Ladd, 1989; Furman & Gavin, 1989). If these norms support a POPC mentality, adolescents are more likely to adjust to them (Bayer, Campbell, & Ling, 2016). Both FOMO and adherence to communication norms imply that heavy smartphone use in adolescence is not only goal-oriented behavior driven by social gratifications, but partially also an involuntary response to powerful external social forces.

Of course, there are personality characteristics such as self-esteem or the tendency to act impulsively that moderate the susceptibility to peer norms and social obligations (Stautz & Cooper, 2014). Particularly important is the extent of adolescents' self-control in respect to their mobile phone behavior—a trait related to impulsivity. Due to maturation processes of the brain, adolescence in general is a phase of low self-control (Dahl, 2001; Steinberg, 2008), thus promoting unregulated and compulsive use of the Internet and the mobile phone especially among vulnerable individuals (e.g., Billieux & Van der Linden, 2012, Khang, Woo, & Kim, 2012; van Deursen, Bolle, Hegner, & Kommers, 2015).

Therefore, the wish to be POPC appears as an almost necessary consequence of adolescents' needs and developmental tasks, and some of them may even display specific developmental conditions that can easily facilitate an overuse of given communication opportunities. But how do these young individuals find a beneficial mode of using POPC opportunities and how can they develop the necessary competencies to cope with them?

Challenges of Living Permanently Connected

Obviously, the POPC world in which we live today provides plenty of opportunities to satisfy basic human needs (such as the need to belong) and to help individuals organize and optimize their lives (Vincent, 2015; Liu & Wei, 2014). But there are also downsides of this new world, such as an excessive and uncontrolled use of smartphones that prevents adolescents from pursuing other important goals (such as getting schoolwork done) or from appreciating face-to-face interactions, and there are also risks in respect to creating or reading messages and postings (Appel et al., 2016; Livingstone et al., 2011). Thus, the overall challenge of using the mobile phone in a beneficial way is to take advantage of the opportunities while refraining from uncontrolled and risky use. In this regard, we will discuss the challenges of (1) integrating the online and the offline worlds in a beneficial way, (2) creating one's own content under POPC conditions, and (3) processing content created by other users under POPC conditions.

Challenge 1: Integrating the Online and the Offline Worlds

Using and enjoying the opportunity to get in touch with friends over the mobile phone, to digitally exchange jokes and social support, and to organize leisure time are much appreciated possibilities of today's POPC environment. However, getting important tasks such as homework done, enjoying and appreciating face-to-face interactions, or having a good night's sleep equally contribute to adolescents' well-being. These young individuals therefore face the challenge of constantly deciding whether they should reach out to others or digitally connect to specific websites, games, and other opportunities or stay offline. Most of the time, this decision is likely not made in a conscious and deliberate way, but rather happens habitually and thus automatically (Bayer et al., 2016, see also van Koningsbruggen, Hartmann, and Du, this volume).

In their sociocognitive model of (digital social) connectedness, Bayer and colleagues (2016) describe how connection habits conjointly with social norms shape a more or less habitual and heavy use of social functions of the mobile phone. Habitual behavior is one form of automatic behavior that is triggered by a cue (Orbell & Verplanken, 2010). In Bayer et al.'s (2016) definition, connection habits thus represent an automaticity regarding connecting behavior, such as checking the mobile for updates. These automatically performed actions are triggered by connection cues that can be technical (e.g., a signal tone), spatial (e.g., being on the train around people staring at their mobile phones), or mental (e.g., a specific emotional or cognitive state such as boredom) in nature.

In contemporary society, social norms of more or less permanent digital availability and connectedness have evolved (Ling, 2012; Vorderer & Kohring, 2013; Vorderer, Krömer, & Schneider, 2016). The more pronounced this social norm of being connected and available, the more vigilant individuals are toward internal and external connection cues and, as a result, the more often connection behavior is executed (Bayer et al., 2016). As the extent of "internalized connectedness" (Bayer et al., 2016, p. 8) is particularly strong among adolescents, they should be prone to continuous communication vigilance and frequent, automatic use of the mobile phone and its social functions.

This, however, may evoke digital stress (LaRose et al., 2014; Misra & Stokols, 2012; Reinecke et al., 2017; Thomée, Härenstam, & Hagberg, 2011; for an overview see Hefner & Vorderer, 2016) and diminish the quality of sleep (e.g., Munezawa et al., 2011; Thomée et al., 2011). Moreover, if strongly connected adolescents automatically instead of consciously react to connection cues, the likelihood of (automatic) mobile phone multitasking—i.e., using the phone while simultaneously performing other activities—increases (see David, this volume; Xu and Wang, this volume). Research demonstrates, for example, that habitual texting predicts sending and reading texts while driving (Bayer & Campbell, 2012). The same should apply to the use of a mobile phone while doing homework (David et al., 2015) or having a face-to-face conversation. But why is mobile phone multitasking considered problematic? Because it consumes cognitive capacity and produces task-switching costs and thus impedes the performance of the parallel (offline) task—be it learning (Chen & Yan, 2016; Junco & Cotten, 2012; Wood et al., 2012), contributing to face-to-face conversations (Misra, Cheng, Genevie, & Yuan, 2016; Przybylski & Weinstein, 2013), or driving a car (Bayer & Campbell, 2012). On the other hand, media multitasking is emotionally gratifying, as an experience sampling study demonstrates (Wang & Tchernev, 2012). This might explain why individuals engage in multitasking to such a high extent despite the fact that it impairs cognitive performance. It also underlines the importance of creating or maintaining a balance of both offline and online activities, as obviously both contribute to an individual's well-being. However, a tendency toward automatic behavior and a strong manifestation of internalized connectedness seem to disturb this balance as they conjointly promote permanent connection and distraction, thus provoking an imbalance toward online activities. It is thus a key challenge for adolescents to counteract the constant and often unconscious temptations provided by mobile phones.

Challenge 2: Creating One's Own Content Under POPC Conditions

Today, young individuals spend a lot of time and energy on distributing self-generated content: Sending messages via WhatsApp, posting pictures on Instagram or Snapchat, or sharing experiences, activities, and emotions on Tumblr are just a few prominent examples (Knop et al., 2015; Lenhart, 2015). And they are particularly at risk "since the young are still developing the social and emotional competencies to manage self-expression, intimacy, and relationships" (Livingstone, Ólafsson, & Staksrud, 2013, pp. 303–304; also see Coleman & Hagell, 2007). The production of harmful content may be a consequence of this, for example, disclosure of (too much) private information on SNS (see also Trepte and Oliver, this volume) or bullying others via digital channels (e.g., Livingstone et al., 2013). Both can cause harm to the person creating the content as well as to others involved. The POPC environment facilitates an "anytime anyplace" communication (Quinn & Oldmeadow, 2013) without much time and incentive for reflecting on the content that is sent and posted. Therefore, senders are more susceptible to overlook possible risks that go along with the production of these posts and messages. Developing a conscious and mindful handling of POPC opportunities, one that considers the integrity of self and others, seems to be one of the most important challenges adolescents face in today's world.

Challenge 3: Processing Content of Others Created Under POPC Conditions

Similar challenges occur for adolescents with regard to *processing* and *interpreting* content generated by others under POPC conditions. Many posts, pictures, videos, and messages are processed in situations where the cognitive capacity is limited—for instance, while sitting in class, talking to another person, riding a bike, watching a movie, following numerous chats and SNS at the same time, or immediately before going to sleep (e.g., Seo, Kim, & David, 2015). Limited attention and awareness while reading or listening to messages facilitate information processing in a fast and mindless mode and may induce equally fast and potentially thoughtless responses. It furthermore promotes misunderstanding and misinterpretations. Depending on habits, on strategies learned in early childhood, on sociocultural norms, and on implicit goals (Mauss, Bunge, & Gross, 2007), automatic information processing can also stimulate cognitions and emotions that are detrimental to individuals' well-being. For example, Beck's cognitive theory of depression (Beck, 1964) rests on the notion that automatic negative thoughts about the self, the world, and the future are often the cause of depressive symptoms. Similarly, anxiety disorders go along with specific automatic negative self-related thoughts (e.g., Calvete, Orue, & Hankin, 2013). Applying this to fast and automatic processing of digital communication content in "POPC mode," there are indeed many incidents that bear the risk of triggering automatic negative thoughts. One example is the opportunity to compare oneself to others in social media apps. If the comparison is unfavorable for oneself and envy is involved, detrimental effects on well-being can evolve and depressive symptoms may be reinforced (e.g., Feinstein et al., 2013; Nesi & Prinstein, 2015; Appel, Gerlach, & Crusius, 2016). Negative outcomes of social comparisons are likely to affect adolescents in particular, as their "newly sophisticated cognitive skills allow them to take the perspective of others as well as be more introspective about themselves and their place in the world" (Jordan, this volume, p. 170–171, Enright, Shukla, & Lapsley, 1980). This facilitates one's own and even anticipated others' social comparison that often involves critical thoughts. Living in POPC mode can thus have negative side effects, particularly for vulnerable individuals. This, once more, underlines the importance of supporting adolescents to practice a more conscious, reflected, and mindful and less reactive handling of the mobile Internet and its plethora of opportunities.

Encountering the Challenges

We have discussed three major challenges that go along with growing up in a POPC environment. All of them have their source in the importance of adolescents' needs and gratifications sought with mobile communication (e.g., to belong to, to be informed what others are up to, to compare oneself to others) and in risks that come along with this almost permanent, fast, automatic, and "by-the-way" communication. How can these challenges be encountered in a way that takes into account the needs and motives for (permanent) digital communication and protects adolescents against a fully habitualized and thoughtless use of smartphones, which often impedes other important, long-term goals? We propose four pathways through which adolescents can improve their abilities to practice smartphone use as a benign, positive force in their life and development while avoiding problematic and risky side effects.

(1) Knowledge and Awareness Regarding Characteristics of Mobile Phone Use and of CMC

In order to regulate one's mobile phone use, it is necessary to be aware of the specific characteristics and processes of this usage. If individuals know, for example, that a big part of mobile phone use is rather automatic and cue dependent, they are better prepared to monitor and reflect on their own use (see below). Also, the knowledge about certain features and trends of computer-mediated communication (CMC), such as the tendency for selective self-presentation that is favorable for oneself (Walther, 2007) can prevent misinterpretations or detect detrimental automatic cognitions that involve negative social comparisons. Moreover, knowing that social connection norms fuel permanent connectedness can sensitize a young users in respect to his or her own behavior that might otherwise strengthen these norms.

(2) Observing and Reflecting One's Own Digital Communication

Equally important as knowledge about general communication mechanisms is to observe and reflect one's own personal cognitions, emotions, and behaviors. Following LaRose and colleagues, deficient self-observation is an important component of habits (LaRose, Lin, & Eastin, 2003; LaRose, Kim, & Peng, 2011). Therefore, monitoring one's activities can also disrupt habits "when individuals note the degradation of important life activities" (LaRose et al., 2014, p. 70).

(3) Defining Goals and Setting Intentions for Living With POPC Opportunities

Developing and defining goals and setting behavioral intentions in order to reach these goals have proved to be effective in behavioral change (Webb & Sheeran, 2006). Goals not only influence deliberate action, but also unconscious and automatic processes, such as automatic emotion regulation (Bargh, Gollwitzer, Lee-Chai, Barndollar, & Trötschel, 2001; Mauss, Bunge, & Gross, 2007). This suggests that adolescents should be encouraged not only to observe their actual mobile phone behavior, but also to develop goals and intentions regarding their use and their responses to connection cues and other-generated content. Young people should be encouraged to compare and evaluate short-term needs and long-term goals and to develop intentions of how they want to live their digital connectedness. One possibility might be to set personal offline zones that can be time based, location based, or activity based.

(4) Self-Regulating Digital Connection

In order to implement goals, sufficient self-regulation is always needed. Self-regulation or self-control "refers to the capacity for altering one's own responses, especially to bring them into line with standards such as ideals, values, morals, and social expectations, and to support the pursuit of long-term goals" (Baumeister, Vohs, & Tice, 2007, p. 351). Research has shown that deficient self-regulation facilitates problematic compulsive use of the Internet (e.g., Bianchi & Phillips, 2005; Billieux & Van der Linden, 2012), of mobile phones (Khang, Woo, & Kim, 2012; van Deursen, Bolle, Hegner, & Kommers, 2015), or of texting (Igarashi, Motoyoshi, Takai, & Yoshida, 2008). Moreover, it facilitates cyberbullying, both as a perpetrator and as a victim (Vazsonyi, Machackova, Sevcikova, Smahel, & Cerna, 2012).

How can parents, educators, and institutions support adolescents to build up skills and abilities for such mindful, reflective, goal-oriented, self-directed POPC behavior? For adolescents' use of "old" media, the concept of parental mediation has been developed to address the question of effective and benign media education quite some time ago (e.g., Nathanson, 1999). Clearly, strategies for promoting the skills needed today point to the cultivation of what has been labeled mindfulness. Mindfulness is described as a mindset where the individual focuses on the present moment and is nonreactive and nonjudgmental (e.g., Brown & Ryan, 2003; Kabat-Zinn, 1990). Vago and Silbersweig (2012) describe mindfulness as "meta-awareness (self-awareness), an ability to effectively modulate one's behavior (self-regulation), and a positive relationship between self and other that transcends self-focused needs and increases prosocial characteristics (self-transcendence)" (p. 1). Applying this concept to life in a POPC environment would accordingly mean that individuals are aware of their behavior or responses in a nonjudgmental way (e.g., noticing the urge to check the phone, but not condemning oneself for feeling this urge), being present both in offline and in online activities, and thus spending all attention on one task at a time, not automatically reacting to every potential opportunity to communicate online but rather acting and reacting in a self-regulated manner and to take the needs of others into account.

In fact, there are initial findings demonstrating a protective function of mindfulness concerning automatic and detrimental mobile phone use. Loy, Bauer, Masur, and Schneider found that mindfulness is negatively correlated to perceived stress while being involved in instant messaging and is positively correlated to positive affect. In addition to this direct relationship, mindfulness also indirectly led to autonomous motivation for being engaged in instant messaging that, in turn, heightened positive affect and reduced stress (Loy, Bauer, Masur, & Schneider, 2016). Bayer and colleagues found negative relationships between texting automaticity and dimensions of mindfulness (Bayer, Dal Cin, Campbell, & Panek, 2016). A study on texting while driving also found that mindfulness and texting while driving correlated negatively (Feldman, Greeson, Renna, & Robbins-Monteith, 2011). On a more general level, a growing body of research demonstrates that mindfulness-based trainings can be effective in the treatment of compulsive-addictive behaviors of several kinds (Baer, 2003; Brewer, Elwafi, & Davis, 2013; Witkiewitz, Lustyk, & Bowen, 2013). Theoretically, the success of these trainings is explained by their potential to strengthen the ability of an individual and to accept negative states that usually trigger craving and performing compulsive behavior (Baer, 2003; Feldman et al., 2011; Witkiewitz et al., 2013). This way, habitual processes may be "deautomatized" (Brewer et al., 2013). This should not only help adolescents to deal with permanently incoming messages, it should also prevent their fast and thoughtless responses and help them to deal with negative cognitions and emotions that are triggered by the communication's content.

The question remains how adolescents can be encouraged and empowered to increase their mindfulness at a stage of life that is not only characterized by the growing importance of peers and by constant communication with them (Brown & Larson, 2009; Vanden Abeele, 2016), but also by a complex maturation process of the brain that challenges self-control (Steinberg, 2008). First, this stage of life should also be considered a "window of opportunity," namely a phase that is particularly suitable for the cultivation of positive identities, values, skills, and mindsets (Lerner, Dowling, & Anderson, 2003; Roeser & Pinela, 2014). To encourage the development of mindfulness on a general level, mindfulness group trainings have been developed specifically for adolescents. These trainings have already shown to yield positive results for various dimensions of adolescents' well-being (e.g., Broderick & Metz, 2009; Raes, Griffith, Van der Gucht, & Williams, 2014). Those trainings should also positively influence how young people deal with the affordances of the mobile phone and the (mobile) Internet in a beneficial way. We thus suggest a combination of parental mediation adapted to the POPC context and of cultivating general mindfulness as strategic educational response to the challenges of adolescent POPC behavior.

Conclusion

In this chapter, we have described the challenges young people face while growing up POPC. Because being online and connected almost permanently appears to be a "perfect match" with the developmental dynamics during adolescence, and because young people both feel positive motivations and social pressures to be online as much as possible, it is particularly important to balance benefits and risks, however difficult it may be at this stage of life. Many risks root in habitualized, nonreflected modes of permanent online behavior; finding effective strategies to promote competences (knowledge, reflection, goal-setting, and self-regulation) in handling POPC habits and behaviors in a benign way is thus imperative for parents, educators, the school systems, and society at large. The present contribution offers conceptual access points for developing such strategies from existing approaches in media literacy, parental mediation, and as an innovative element, in mindfulness trainings. Because the many episodes of POPC behavior that occur over the course of a day of many adolescents are deeply rooted in automatic cognitions and habits, and because the smartphone is such a powerful affordance, building up mindfulness and the ability to resist urges and temptations of engaging in permanent communication is key to maintaining autonomy and self-directedness in today's media ecology.

References

Appel, H., Gerlach, A. L., & Crusius, J. (2016). The interplay between Facebook use, social comparison, envy, and depression. *Current Opinion in Psychology, 9*, 44–49. doi:10.1016/j.copsyc.2015.10.006

Arnett, J. J. (2004). *Emerging adulthood: The winding road from the late teens through the twenties.* New York: Oxford University Press.

Baer, R. A. (2003). Mindfulness training as a clinical intervention: A conceptual and empirical review. *Clinical Psychology: Science and Practice, 10*(2), 125–143.

Bargh, J. A., Gollwitzer, P. M., Lee-Chai, A., Barndollar, K., & Trötschel, R. (2001). The automated will: Nonconscious activation and pursuit of behavioral goals. *Journal of Personality and Social Psychology, 81*, 1014–1027.

Baumeister, R. F., & Leary, M. R. (1995). The need to belong: Desire for interpersonal attachments as a fundamental human motivation. *Psychological Bulletin, 117*(3), 497–529. doi:10.1037/0033-2909.117.3.497

Baumeister, R. F., Vohs, K. D., & Tice, D. M. (2007). The strength model of self-control. *Current Directions in Psychological Science, 16*(6), 351–355. doi:10.1111/j.1467-8721.2007.00534.x

Bayer, J. B., & Campbell, S. W. (2012). Texting while driving on automatic: Considering the frequency-independent side of habit. *Computers in Human Behavior, 28*(6), 2083–2090. doi:10.1016/j.chb.2012.06.012

Bayer, J. B., Campbell, S. W., & Ling, R. (2016). Connection cues: Activating the norms and habits of social connectedness. *Communication Theory, 26*(2), 128–149. doi:10.1111/comt.12090.

Bayer, J. B., Dal Cin, S., Campbell, S. W., & Panek, E. (2016). Consciousness and self-regulation in mobile communication. *Human Communication Research, 42*, 71–97. doi:10.1111/hcre.12067.

Beck, A. T. (1964). Thinking and depression: Theory and therapy. *Archives of General Psychiatry, 10*, 561–571.

Berndt, T. J., & Ladd, G. W. (Eds.). (1989). *Peer relationships in child development.* New York: Wiley.

Bianchi, A., & Phillips, J. G. (2005). Psychological predictors of problem mobile phone use. *Cyberpsychology & Behavior, 8*(1), 39–51. doi:10.1089/cpb.2005.8.39.

Billieux, J., & van der Linden, M. (2012). Problematic use of the Internet and self-regulation: A review of the initial studies. *The Open Addiction Journal, 5*(1), 24–29. doi:10.2174/1874941001205010024

Blair, B. L., & Fletcher, A. C. (2011). "The only 13-year-old on planet earth without a cell phone": Meanings of cell phones in early adolescents' everyday lives. *Journal of Adolescent Research, 26*(2), 155–177.

Brewer, J. A., Elwafi, H. M., & Davis, J. H. (2013). Craving to quit: Psychological models and neurobiological mechanisms of mindfulness training as treatment for addictions. *Psychology of Addictive Behaviors, 27*(2), 366.

Broderick, P. C., & Metz, S. (2009). Learning to breathe: Pilot trial of a mindfulness curriculum for adolescents. *Advances in School Mental Health Promotion, 2,* 35–46.

Brown, B. B., & Larson, J. (2009). Peer relationships in adolescence. In R. M. Lerner & L. Steinberg (Eds.), *Handbook of adolescent psychology* (3rd ed., pp. 74–103). New York: Wiley. doi:10.1002/9780470479193.adlpsy002004.

Brown, K. W., & Ryan, R. M. (2003). The benefits of being present: Mindfulness and its role in psychological well-being. *Journal of Personality and Social Psychology, 84*(4), 822–848. doi:10.1037/0022-3514.84.4.822

Calvete, E., Orue, I., & Hankin, B. L. (2013). Early maladaptive schemas and social anxiety in adolescents: The mediating role of anxious automatic thoughts. *Journal of Anxiety Disorders, 27,* 278–288.

Campbell, S. W., & Park, Y. J. (2008). Social implications of mobile telephony: The rise of personal communication society. *Sociology Compass, 2*(2), 371–381.

Chen, Q., & Yan, Z. (2016). Does multitasking with mobile phones affect learning? A review. *Computers in Human Behavior, 54,* 34–42. doi:10.1016/j.chb.2015.07.047

Coleman, J., & Hagell, A. (2007). *Adolescence, risk and resilience: Against the odds.* Chichester, West Sussex: John Wiley & Sons.

Dahl, R. E. (2001). Affect regulation, brain development, and behavioral/emotional health in adolescence. *CNS Spectrums, 6,* 60–72. doi:10.1017/S1092852900022884

David, P., Kim, J.-H., Brickman, J. S., Ran, W., & Curtis, C. M. (2015). Mobile phone distraction while studying. *New Media & Society, 17*(10), 1661–1679. doi:10.1177/1461444814531692

Eccles, J. S., Early, D., Fraser, K., Belansky, E., & McCarthy, K. (1997). The relation of connection, regulation, and support for autonomy to adolescents' functioning. *Journal of Adolescent Research, 12,* 263–286.

Enright, R. D., Shukla, D. G., & Lapsley, D. K. (1980). Adolescent egocentrism-sociocentrism and self-consciousness. *Journal of Youth and Adolescence, 9*(2), 101–116.

Feinstein, B. A., Hershenberg, R., Bhatia, V., Latack, J. A., Meuwly, N., & Davila, J. (2013). Negative social comparison on Facebook and depressive symptoms: Rumination as a mechanism. *Psychology of Popular Media Culture, 2*(3), 161–170. doi:10.1037/a0033111

Feldman, G., Greeson, J., Renna, M., & Robbins-Monteith, K. (2011). Mindfulness predicts less texting while driving among young adults: Examining attention- and emotion-regulation motives as potential mediators. *Personality and Individual Differences, 51*(7), 856–861. doi:10.1016/j.paid.2011.07.020

Furman, W., & Gavin, L. A. (1989). Age differences in adolescents' perception of their peer groups. *Developmental Psychology, 25*(5), 827–834. doi:10.1037/0012-1649.25.5.827

Grusec, J. E., & Hastings, P. D. (Eds.). (2015). *Handbook of socialization* (2nd ed.). New York: Guilford.

Hefner, D., Knop, K., & Vorderer, P. (in press). "I wanna be in the loop!"–The role of fear of missing out (FoMO) for the quantity and quality of young adolescents' mobile phone use. In S. Baumgartner, R. Kühne, T. Koch & M. Hofer (Eds.), *Youth and media.* Baden-Baden: Nomos.

Hefner, D., & Vorderer, P. (2016). Digital stress: Permanent connectedness and multitasking. In L. Reinecke & M.-B. Oliver (Eds.), *Handbook of media use and well-being* (pp. 237–249). New York: Routledge.

Igarashi, T., Motoyoshi, T., Takai, J., & Yoshida, T. (2008). No mobile, no life: Self-perception and text-message dependency among Japanese high school students. *Computers in Human Behavior, 24*(5), 2311–2324. doi:10.1016/j.chb.2007.12.001

Junco, R., & Cotten, S. R. (2012). No A 4 U: The relationship between multitasking and academic performance. *Computers & Education, 59*(2), 505–514.

Kabat-Zinn, J. (1990). *Full catastrophe living: Using the wisdom of your body and mind to face stress, pain, and illness.* New York: Delacourt.

Khang, H., Woo, H.-J., & Kim, J. K. (2012). Self as an antecedent of mobile phone addiction. *International Journal of Mobile Communication, 10*(1), 65–84. doi:10.1504/IJMC.2012.044523

Knop, K., Hefner, D., Schmitt, S., & Vorderer, P. (2015). *Mediatisierung mobil—Handy- und mobile Internetnutzung von Kindern und Jugendlichen.* Band der Schriftenreihe Medienforschung der Landesanstalt für Medien

Nordrhein-Westfalen (LfM) [Mobile mediatization. Cellphone and mobile Internet use of children and adolescents. Monograph Series Media Research of the Federal Institute for the Media Northrhine Westfalia, Vol. 77]. Düsseldorf; Leipzig: Vistas.

Kushlev, K., & Dunn, E. W. (2015). Checking email less frequently reduces stress. *Computers in Human Behavior, 43*, 220–228. doi:10.1016/j.chb.2014.11.005.

LaRose, R., Connolly, R., Lee, H., Li, K., & Hales, K. D. (2014). Connection overload? A cross cultural study of the consequences of social media connection. *Information Systems Management, 31*(1), 59–73.

LaRose, R., Kim, J., & Peng, W. (2011). Social networking: Addictive, compulsive, problematic, or just another media habit? In Z. Papacharissi (Ed.), *A networked self: Identity, community, and culture on social network sites*. New York: Routledge.

LaRose, R., Lin, C. A., & Eastin, M. S. (2003). Unregulated Internet usage: Addiction, habit, or deficient self-regulation? *Media Psychology, 5*(3), 224–253. doi:10.1207/S1532785XMEP0503_01

Lenhart, A. (2015). *Teens, social media & technology overview 2015*. Retrieved from www.pewInternet.org/2015/04/09/teens-social-media-technology-2015/

Lenhart, A., Ling, R., Campbell, S., & Purcell, K. (2010). *Teens and mobile phones*. Retrieved from www.pewinternet.org/2010/04/20/teens-and-mobile-phones/

Lerner, R. M., Dowling, E. M., & Anderson, P. M. (2003). Positive youth development: Thriving as the basis of personhood and civil society. *Applied Developmental Science, 7*, 172–180.

Ling, R. S. (2012). *Taken for grantedness: The embedding of mobile communication into society*. Cambridge, MA: MIT Press.

Liu, X., & Wei, R. (2014). Maintaining social connectedness in a fast-changing world: Examining the effects of mobile phone uses on loneliness among teens in Tibet. *Mobile Media & Communication, 2*(3), 318–334. doi:10.1177/2050157914535390

Livingstone, S., Haddon, L., Gorzig, A., & Olafsson, K. (2011). *Risks and safety on the Internet: The perspective of European children. Full findings*. LSE, London: EU Kids Online.

Livingstone, S., Ólafsson, K., & Staksrud, E. (2013). Risky social networking practices among 'underage' users: Lessons for evidence-based policy. *Journal of Computer-Mediated Communication, 18*(3), 303–320.

Loy, L. S., Bauer, A., Masur, P. K., & Schnieder, F. M. (2016). Stressed by smartphone use? The interplay of motivation and mindfulness during instant messaging. Presentation at the 66th annual conference of the International Communication Association (ICA), June 9–13, Fukuoka, Japan.

Mai, L. M., Freudenthaler, R., Schneider, F. M., & Vorderer, P. (2015). "I know you've seen it!" Individual and social factors for users' chatting behavior on Facebook. *Computers in Human Behavior, 49*, 296–302. http://dx.doi.org/10.1016/j.chb.2015.01.074

Mascheroni, G., & Ólafsson, K. (2014). *Net children go mobile: Risks and opportunities* (2nd ed.). Milan, Italy: Educatt.

Mauss, I. B., Bunge, S. A., & Gross, J. J. (2007). Automatic emotion regulation. *Social and Personality Psychology Compass, 1*, 146–167.

Misra, S., Cheng, L., Genevie, J., & Yuan, M. (2016). The iPhone effect: The quality of in-person social interactions in the presence of mobile devices. *Environment and Behavior. 48*(2), 275–298. doi:10.1177/0013916514539755

Misra, S., & Stokols, D. (2012). Psychological and health outcomes of perceived information overload. *Environment and Behavior, 44*(6), 737–759. doi:10.1177/0013916511404408

Munezawa, T., Kaneita, Y., Osaki, Y., Kanda, H., Minowa, M., Suzuki, K., . . . Ohida, T. (2011). The association between use of mobile phones after lights out and sleep disturbances among Japanese adolescents: A nationwide cross-sectional survey. *Sleep, 34*(8), 1013–1020. doi:10.5665/SLEEP.1152

Nathanson, A. I. (1999). Identifying and explaining the relationship between parental mediation and children's aggression. *Communication Research, 26*(2), 124–143.

Nesi, J., & Prinstein, M. J. (2015). Using social media for social comparison and feedback-seeking: Gender and popularity moderate associations with depressive symptoms. *Journal of Abnormal Child Psychology, 43*(8), 1427–1438. doi:10.1007/s10802-015-0020-0

Orbell, S., & Verplanken, B. (2010). The automatic component of habit in health behavior: Habit as cue-contingent automaticity. *Health Psychology, 29*(4), 374–383.

Przybylski, A. K., Murayama, K., DeHaan, C. R., & Gladwell, V. (2013). Motivational, emotional, and behavioral correlates of fear of missing out. *Computers in Human Behavior, 29*(4), 1841–1848.

Przybylski, A. K., & Weinstein, N. (2013). Can you connect with me now? How the presence of mobile communication technology influences face-to-face conversation quality. *Journal of Social & Personal Relationships, 30*(3), 237–246.

Quinn, S., & Oldmeadow, J. A. (2013). The Martini effect and social networking sites: Early adolescents, mobile social networking and connectedness to friends. *Mobile Media & Communication, 1*(2), 237–247. doi:10.1177/2050157912474812

Raes, F., Griffith, J. W., Van der Gucht, K., & Williams, J. M. G. (2014). School-based prevention and reduction of depression in adolescents: A cluster-randomized controlled trial of a mindfulness group program. *Mindfulness, 5*, 477–486. doi:10.1007/s12671-013-0202-1.

Reinecke, L., Aufenanger, S., Beutel, M. E., Dreier, M., Quiring, O., Stark, B., Wölfling, K., & Müller, K. W. (2017). Digital stress over the life span: The effects of communication load and Internet multitasking on perceived stress and psychological health impairments in a German probability sample. *Media Psychology, 20*(1), 90–115. doi:10.1080/15213269.2015.1121832

Roeser, R. W., & Pinela, C. (2014). Mindfulness and compassion training in adolescence: A developmental contemplative science perspective. *New Directions for Youth Development, 2014*(142), 9–30.

Sambira, J. (2013, May). Africa's mobile youth drive change. Cell phones reshape youth cultures. *AfricaRenewal*, p. 19. Retrieved from www.un.org/africarenewal/magazine/may-2013/africa%E2%80%99s-mobile-youth-drive-change

Seo, M., Kim, J.-H., & David, P. (2015). Always connected or always distracted? ADHD symptoms and social assurance explain problematic use of mobile phone and multicommunicating. *Journal of Computer-Mediated Communication, 20*(6), 667–681. doi:10.1111/jcc4.12140

Stautz, K., & Cooper, A. (2014). Brief report: Personality correlates of susceptibility to peer influence in adolescence. *Journal of Adolescence, 37*(4), 401–405. doi:10.1016/j.adolescence.2014.03.006

Steinberg, L. (2008). A social neuroscience perspective on adolescent risk-taking. *Developmental Review, 28*(1), 78–106.

Steinberg, L., & Morris, A. S. (2001). Adolescent development. *Annual Review of Psychology, 52*, 83–110.

Thomée, S., Härenstam, A., & Hagberg, M. (2011). Mobile phone use and stress, sleep disturbances, and symptoms of depression among young adults—a prospective cohort study. *BMC Public Health*. doi:10.1186/1471-2458-11-66

Vago, D. R., & Silbersweig, D. A. (2012). Self-awareness, self-regulation, and self-transcendence (S-ART): A framework for understanding the neurobiological mechanisms of mindfulness. *Frontiers in Human Neuroscience, 6*, 296. doi:10.3389/fnhum.2012.00296

Valkenburg, P. M., & Peter, J. (2009). The effects of instant messaging on the quality of adolescents' existing friendships: A longitudinal study. *Journal of Communication, 59*(1), 79–97.

Vanden Abeele, M. M. P. (2016). Mobile youth culture: A conceptual development. *Mobile Media & Communication, 4*(1), 85–101. doi:10.1177/2050157915601455

van Deursen, A. J., Bolle, C. L., Hegner, S. M., & Kommers, P. A. (2015). Modeling habitual and addictive smartphone behavior. *Computers in Human Behavior, 45*, 411–420. doi:10.1016/j.chb.2014.12.039

Vazsonyi, A. T., Machackova, H., Sevcikova, A., Smahel, D., & Cerna, A. (2012). Cyberbullying in context: Direct and indirect effects by low self-control across 25 European countries. *European Journal of Developmental Psychology, 9*(2), 210–227. doi:10.1080/17405629.2011.644919

Vincent, J. (2015). *Mobile opportunities: exploring positive mobile opportunities for European children*. POLIS, The London School of Economics and Political Science, London, UK.

Vorderer, P., & Kohring, M. (2013). Permanently online: A challenge for media and communication research. *International Journal of Communication, 7*, 188–196.

Vorderer, P., Krömer, N., & Schneider, F. M. (2016). Permanently online—permanently connected: Explorations into university students' use of social media and mobile smart devices. *Computers in Human Behavior, 63*, 694–703. doi:10.1016/j.chb.2016.05.085

Walther, J. B. (2007). Selective self-presentation in computer-mediated communication: Hyperpersonal dimensions of technology, language, and cognition. *Computers in Human Behavior, 23*(5), 2538–2557.

Wang, Z., & Tchernev, J. M. (2012). The "myth" of media multitasking: Reciprocal dynamics of media multitasking, personal needs, and gratifications. *Journal of Communication, 62*(3), 493–513. doi:10.1111/j.1460-2466.2012.01641.x

Webb, T. L., & Sheeran, P. (2006). Does changing behavioral intentions engender behavior change? A meta-analysis of the experimental evidence. *Psychological bulletin, 132*(2), 249–268. doi:10.1037/0033-2909.132.2.249

Witkiewitz, K., Lustyk, M. K. B., & Bowen, S. (2013). Retraining the addicted brain: A review of hypothesized neurobiological mechanisms of mindfulness-based relapse prevention. *Psychology of Addictive Behaviors, 27*(2), 351.

Wood, E., Zivcakova, L., Gentile, P., Archer, K., De Pasquale, D., & Nosko, A. (2012). Examining the impact of off-task multi-tasking with technology on real-time classroom learning. *Computers & Education, 58*(1), 365–374.

18

Permanent Connections Around the Globe

Cross-Cultural Differences and Intercultural Linkages in POPC

Hartmut Wessler, Diana Rieger, Jonathan Cohen, and Peter Vorderer

Introduction

As mobile communication has come to take a central role in our daily lives, people spend more and more time with their gaze directed at their communication devices. This has made it easy to believe that everyone is really permanently connected to everyone else and permanently online. We tend to forget that the world outside of our smartphones and tablets still asserts its power on whom we can communicate with and how we do so. It is often said that we can communicate and collaborate with anyone, anytime, regardless of physical and social distance and that technology has "flattened" the world and made communication possible where it was once impossible. And while it is true that the collaboration across borders, space, and time is easier and more frequent, the world is not a global village. This chapter will examine some factors that restrict communication across borders and cultures and that therefore serve as boundary conditions for POPC. The long lines of business travelers in airports throughout the world attest that such obstacles to online communication continue to be significant enough to justify the expense and hardship of traveling around the world for face-to-face meetings.

As an example of the difficulties that remain in collaborating across borders, one can imagine a committee for an international organization with members residing in the United States, Europe, and China. Given the time differences between the US and China, there is no single time to set up a video conference that would fall in normal business hours for all members of the committee. Thankfully, technology has allowed such meetings to occur when some of the participants may be in their homes, cars, or anywhere else, even if that means that they are distracted, tired, or otherwise restricted. And yet, some of the participants will need to agree to forfeit what they may consider work/life boundaries and join meetings at rather unusual hours.

Furthermore, as anyone who uses videoconferencing technologies (e.g., Skype, Google Hangouts) on a regular basis knows, the quality of such meetings depends greatly on all participants having good equipment (computer or mobile devices, microphones, and cameras) as well as sufficient bandwidth. In addition, speech patterns must be very structured so that only one person may speak at a time and must accommodate certain delays in speech that make turn-taking a hassle, whereas in face-to-face meetings conversations flow more naturally (Sellen, 1992). It should also be noted that the cross-cultural communication made available by the new communication technologies supporting the POPC culture are available mostly to individuals who either share the same language or possess a level of comfort in English that allows them to communicate. But even among global English speakers, different understandings of nuance, irony, sarcasm, and humor may create obstacles to communication that technology cannot eliminate.

Anecdotal evidence like this hints to the more general insight that, apart from technical issues, *cultural identities* play a crucial role when we study POPC in today's globalized communication setting. In this chapter, we wish to explore the role of cultural identities in two distinct ways. On the one hand, we can think of cultural identities as *generalized dispositions* that structure POPC behaviors and perceptions. Cultural values, habits, and rules influence the extent and the forms of POPC around the globe. We call these dispositions generalized because (a) they are not idiosyncratic characteristics but collectively shared among members of a particular cultural group, and (b) on the level of each individual they exert their influence across situations and are thus more or less durable.

Yet cultures and cultural identities are not stable entities. Values, habits, and rules do change over time, and in an age of globalized interactions, few cultural groups remain isolated from such exchanges. In fact, one important conduit for such changes in values, habits, and rules can be found in the kind of cross-cultural communication we have described above. Partners in cross-cultural POPC communication influence and adapt to each other and develop new competencies and sometimes a unique blend of formerly diverging cultural orientations. In this second perspective, therefore, cultural identities must be conceptualized as *shifting and negotiated qualities* of POPC behaviors and perceptions. From this angle, culture is not an external factor influencing POPC, but an integral quality of POPC processes.

An investigation of cultural identities as generalized dispositions lends itself to cross-cultural comparison in POPC behavior and perceptions, a route that we explore in the first section of this chapter. Conversely, studying cultural identities as negotiated qualities of POPC processes calls for in-depth relational analysis of communication in concrete pairs or groups of people from different cultural backgrounds—a theme we pursue in the second section. Based on the (limited) knowledge that exists on both perspectives, we point to some fruitful avenues for future POPC research in the concluding section of this chapter.

Cross-Cultural Differences in POPC Communication

In each culture, media users operate according to different values, habits, rules, requirements, and expectations that constitute important elements of modern cultural identities (Baron & Segerstad, 2010; LaRose, Connolly, Lee, Li, & Hales, 2014; Campbell, 2007a, 2007b). Several studies provide evidence for the cross-cultural differences with regard to the appropriateness of engaging with a mobile phone in distinct situations (Campbell, 2007a, 2007b). In a cross-cultural survey, the perceptions of mobile phones were found to differ along five dimensions: (a) perception of the mobile phone as fashion, (b) attitudes about mobile phone use in public settings, (c) the use of mobile phones for safety and security concerns, (d) their use for instrumental purposes, e.g., for logistical coordination, and (e) their use for expressive purposes, e.g., to stay in contact with friends (Campbell, 2007a). Comparing five different cultural groups (from Hawaii, Japan, Sweden, Taiwan, and the US mainland), the results point toward differences between dimensions: Whereas Asian students were more tolerant regarding mobile usage in public communication settings, North American students reported significantly more often that they used mobiles for security/safety reasons (Campbell, 2007b). As far as the appropriateness of mobile phone usage in the work context is concerned, Caporael and Xie (2003) found that Chinese participants regarded mobile phone calls from employers as acceptable during non-work hours, but Americans found work-related calls during these times to be largely unacceptable.

Although some of these findings already date back more than 10 years and mobile phone behavior has changed notably in the last decade, they elucidate the cross-cultural component in a global phenomenon (Gudykunst et al., 1996; Hofstede, 2001; Schwartz & Sagiv, 1995). Hall (1976) explained such intercultural differences by distinguishing between high- and low-context communication. In countries that are considered to be low-context cultures (such as the United States and Germany, most Western countries), a message is explicitly stated in its wording. In high-context cultures (such as Korea or Japan, most Asian, Arab, and Mediterranean cultures), the message is typically coded more implicitly (Hall & Hall, 1990). In high-context cultures, interpersonal contact is considered more important than everything else is (Hall, 1976). Due to the implicit or explicit ways of message encodings, there are differences in how the mobile phone is used: For example, the Chinese habit to develop personal networks (*guanxiwang*) in order to secure goods and to feel protected has been related to their usage patterns with mobile technologies (Yu & Tng, 2003). Specifically, as *guanxiwang* usually would require face-to-face contact, mobile phones at least provide opportunity for immediate and private voice or even video communication. In Chinese *guanxiwang* manners, this form of communication enables giving and accepting of favors as well as creation and fulfillment of indebtedness. It was concluded that in the Chinese market, the mobile phone entered as a tool to augment and foster *guanxiwang*, because it provides a contact list and enables private conversations, a highly personalized relationship even when face-to-face contact is not possible or when personal meetings and appointments cannot be coordinated. This is further in accordance with research pointing toward a connection between some of the cultural dimensions described by Hofstede (2001). Cardon et al. (2009) demonstrated that a high degree of collectivism was significantly associated with having more online ties to people not personally known. In line with this idea, Abbas and Mesch (2015) investigated the role of cultural dimensions on the motivation to use Facebook in an Israeli sample. They found that respondents with a higher degree of collectivism and a higher degree of uncertainty avoidance (see Hofstede, 2001) were also more motivated to use Facebook in order to maintain existing relationships.

Another difference concerns politeness issues when in public spaces (cafés, public transport, etc.). In a survey comparing five different cultures (US, Sweden, Japan, Korea, and Italy), Japanese participants in general showed more concern about politeness issues than did respondents from other countries (Baron & Campbell, 2012). One reason for this difference could lie in Japanese education; Japanese children are trained to avoid *meiwaku* (bothersome) behavior. For instance, Swedish and American participants were found to be more approving with regard to mobile phone use in cafés than were Japanese participants (Baron & Segerstad, 2010). In accordance with these findings, Americans showed a higher frequency in voice calls during an average day than did Japanese, whereas Japanese reported using text messages significantly more frequently than did Americans. At the same time, Japanese judged loudness when talking on the phone as more disturbing than Americans did (Baron & Segerstad, 2010).

Taking these studies together, one could conclude that high-context cultures emphasize contact situations in which they are able to maintain and comfort their interpersonal contacts but at the same time conform to norms (no *meiwaku* behavior, *guanxiwang* manners). Low-context cultures, in contrast, put more emphasis on issues of self-expression while eventually neglecting politeness issues. This is further mirrored in research on customization practices: In a recent study on mobile phone customization patterns, South Koreans showed a stronger other-directedness than Americans and in consequence reported more aesthetic-concerned customization of their mobile phone. This aesthetic customization, in turn, was associated with the idea that the phone is a means to reflect the self—which is a more implicit, modest way of self-expression (Lee & Sundar, 2015). The US sample, in contrast, valued self-expression more than Koreans did and scored higher on self-promotion as part of impression management. This tendency, however, was not associated with customization patterns of people's mobile phones.

Further explanation lies in the type of self-construal: People differ with regard to the extent by which they perceive themselves as dependent or independent from their social environment. This differentiation has been termed independent vs. interdependent self-construal (Markus & Kitayama, 1991). Independence is more strongly associated with the Western industrial nations (e.g., United States). In such industrial countries, people's overall goal is to achieve uniqueness, to show superiority, and to pursue their own goals (Uchida & Kitayama, 2009). In contrast, interdependence is associated with Asian nations (e.g., Japan) and relates to values such as striving for assimilation toward others, conservation, relationships, and harmony with one's social context. Likewise, values have been categorized along the line of individualist (e.g., power and achievement), collectivist (e.g., tradition, conformity) and universal values (e.g., benevolence) (Schwartz & Bilsky, 1990; Schwartz & Sagiv, 1995). Thus, the culture of a person shapes his/her attitudes and values that, in turn, influence the way people use communication technologies to meet their needs (Erumban & de Jong, 2006; Silverstone & Haddon, 1996). For instance, Lee, Choi, Kim, and Hong (2007) reported a positive relationship between independence and post-adoption perception of mobile Internet services. The more independent the self-construal of a person, the more positive the perception of mobile services.

In the context of using social network sites (SNS), these cultural dimensions can be related to different motivations of maintaining and expanding social ties through the use of SNS. Kim, Sohn, and Choi (2011) found US students on average to have more social connections on Facebook than Korean students had. Their interpretation of this finding implies that cultural dimensions (such as collectivism) are tied to distinct perspectives toward social relationships: One perspective may value expanding social relationships (e.g., in order to enhance a sense of positive self-worth) by seeking new friends online; another perspective values maintaining existing social relationships, e.g., through showing commitment to families and close friends. Jackson and Wang (2013) also found Americans to spend more time on SNS, to consider them more important, and to have more online friends than Chinese participants. They argue that the stronger emphasis on close friends and family in collectivistic cultures may in part explain the lesser extent of SNS use. The tendency of individualist cultures to focus on a greater number of, but less intimate and enduring, friendships might then explain the higher usage of SNS in the US sample.

Additionally, research points to some influencing factors with regard to using new technologies that may differ between cultures. First, diffusion rates (i.e., owning technologically advanced devices such as mobile phones) were higher in cultures that were becoming "technologically smart" (Beckers, Mante, & Schmidt, 2003). The term "technologically smart" refers to individuals or societies becoming more involved with modern advanced technologies such as mobile phones (or the Internet two decades ago) and developing an anxiety-free attitude toward those new technologies (Beckers et al., 2003). Therefore, technological affinity is one key dimension that could differentiate between usage patterns and behaviors. Second, in 2002 Schejter and Cohen reported mobile phone use in Israel to be among the highest in the world, which was close to double the average in Europe and almost four times the US average during that time. They attributed the growth of the mobile phone in Israel to the Israelis' need "to be connected, their need to chatter and their basic audacious (chutzpadic) temperament" (p. 38). Inherent in this explanation is the idea that cultures might differ in the extent to which their members want to be in constant contact, communication, or discourse with their social network (online and offline). A need to communicate or maybe even a fundamental need to belong (Baumeister & Leary, 1995) might therefore serve as explanatory motivation.

Besides the extent of intercultural differences in usage pattern of media and technology, Katz and Aakhus (2002) discuss the idea of cultural similarities through the lens of apparatgeist. According to the concept of apparatgeist, there is an underlying human spirit that guides the adoption and use of personal communication technologies. This spirit is suggested to be universal, that is, it tends to be consistent across different cultures. Katz and Aakhus (2002) argue that people have a universal drive for perpetual contact (although this may vary on the interindividual level; see comments on need to be connected, Schejter & Cohen, 2002) which shapes how people judge, invent, and use communication technology. For instance, apart from some differences found between cultural groups, Campbell (2007a, 2007b) argues his results to be in line with the general assumption of an apparatgeist, a global idea or instinct on how to use communication technologies and to handle their affordances. Comparing Korean and American students, Kang and Jung (2014) also found that both countries show similar associations between smartphone usage and the fulfillment of human needs.

Intercultural Linkages in POPC Communication

In today's globalized world, people from different cultural backgrounds do not only *differ* with respect to their cultural identities and associated POPC behaviors, they also increasingly communicate with each other across countries and cultures in professional and personal contexts. Such intercultural communication between colleagues, family members, and friends as well as partners in intimate relationships can of course happen locally, connecting people of different backgrounds who work or live in more or less the same place. But increasingly, such intercultural exchanges are translocal and strongly mediated. This is due to the proliferation of workplaces in a globalized economy and to migration, student exchange, tourism, and other such dislocating practices that create opportunities and needs to connect with people from different cultural backgrounds. These intercultural connections are facilitated and shaped by the mobile and online technologies and platforms available today, particularly SNS such as Facebook, mobile messaging applications such as WhatsApp, and videoconferencing platforms such as Skype, and they are also embedded in cross-border flows of mass media content (Brüggemann & Wessler, 2014).

Two qualifications are important here, however. First, the services mentioned are not available in all countries to the same degree. Individual governments may opt to block a service (such as Facebook in China) or monitor and censor it so heavily that users are hesitant to use it freely. As POPC behavior presupposes the availability of *the same* platform or service to those engaging in it at the same time, such constraints clearly curtail the global reach and personal engagement in POPC. Second, countries differ in the degree to which they are integrated into the global economy, participate in international exchange programs, enable international travel, and provide access to media technologies. Thus, the opportunities to actually come into contact with people from other cultural backgrounds varies widely between countries with higher or lower levels of prosperity and economic development. Of course, even within one country, individuals differ greatly with respect to the opportunities for intercultural encounters, with educated, affluent, urban elites having the best chances. Both factors—the degree of government control as well as the level of integration into global flows of exchange and communication—have been combined into a "cosmopolitanism" index by Norris and Inglehart (2009). Cosmopolitan societies are those that combine media freedom with strong global integration, whereas parochial societies are characterized by restricted media and weak global connections. Western countries are usually high on the cosmopolitanism scale, while emerging countries such as South Africa, Brazil, Mexico, India, and Russia are located around the middle of the field, and China as well as many developing countries populate the lower half. Such macro-level differences in opportunities for intercultural POPC communication should not be neglected in studies addressing permanent cross-border linkages.

In addition, it is important to remember that "different cultural backgrounds" are not absolute, but are gradual categories. Cultural differences can be bigger and smaller, they can pertain more to some values and habits than to others, and in particular, they can be experienced in a naïve or reflexive mode. Consider the example of a German exchange student in China who, after her return to her home country, stays in permanent contact with a former Chinese fellow student over Facebook and WhatsApp, as well as has an occasional conversation over Skype. The cross-cultural encounter she has experienced while being in China has in all likelihood given her a new perspective on what it means to be German and Chinese that somebody without her experience would not have. While she enters into the POPC relationship with an already partly reflexive perspective on the cultural differences relevant to her experience, the POPC process itself will contribute to the gradual shrinking or expansion, as well as a further level of reflection, on such differences.

A differentiated and dynamic understanding of cultural identity as an integral part of the POPC process offers new opportunities to explore how cultural identities are negotiated and shifting in intercultural POPC communication. This interplay has mostly been studied with respect to migrant and diaspora communities, albeit without a special focus on the permanency of communicative connections. In their ethnographic study on three migrant communities in Germany, Hepp, Bozdag, and Suna (2012) identified three prototypical cultural orientations that are instructive for POPC research as well. Origin-oriented migrants self-identify as members of their community of origin (i.e., as Turks, Moroccans, and Russians) even though second- or third-generation members may only know that "origin" from hearsay and occasional vacation visits. They are connected locally to other members of their own diaspora community and translocally to family and friends in the country of origin. Although they maintain cross-border linkages, for origin-oriented migrants intercultural communication plays a relatively minor role. By contrast, ethno-oriented migrants develop an identification marked by the tension between the country of origin and the country in which they presently live. They think of themselves as "German-Turks" etc., and such ethnic positioning is a central part of their identity (Hepp et al., 2012). This identification is connected to a diversified communication network that comprises both local and translocal connections to members of both communities, but the center of belonging lies in their diasporic community in Germany, with some connections to other migrants in the same place and to some indigenous Germans. The third type, finally, consists of world-oriented migrants who self-identify as "European" or "cosmopolitan." This relatively young and well-educated group shares with the ethno-oriented an expanded communication network that extends, however, to more people of different origins living in more than just the country of origin and the country of residence. World-oriented migrants most clearly resemble our example of the German exchange student returning from China. And it is therefore no wonder that in this group of migrants, the use of mobile devices and the engagement in permanent connections across cultural boundaries is most strongly developed (Hepp et al., 2012).

POPC researchers are usually not interested in migrant communities per se. But through the lens of migrant communication networks, it becomes possible to appreciate the differentiated and dynamic interplay between cultural identities and POPC behavior more clearly than in other contexts. It is not necessary to establish a fixed causal order between cultural identification on the one hand and POPC behavior and perceptions on the other. At the current stage of knowledge, it seems more promising to study permanent connections across cultural boundaries in concrete pairs and groups of people as a process in which cultural identities are becoming somewhat fluid and are renegotiated precisely through the permanent exchange.

Research Perspectives

Both the comparative and the intercultural perspectives on POPC communication, which we have sketched above, have their own strengths. The comparative perspective can help to disentangle just how low-context and high-context cultures, and how a more independent versus a more interdependent self-construal, impinge on POPC behavior and perceptions. For example, it stands to reason that low-context cultures, which privilege explicit, straightforward messaging, would take absence or presence cues in POPC communication literally, so that an indication that somebody is present or online would open the door for direct initiation of communication. By contrast, in high-context cultures it might be deemed more appropriate to first ask whether my communication partner is really available or whether a different point in time would be more suitable. Once communication has been initiated, a culture of self-asserting independence might give communicators more leeway in whether and how they respond, whereas in a culture of interdependence, communicative behavior would possibly be more adapted to maintaining a harmonious relationship with the communication partner. Many other such hypotheses and research questions can be addressed in a cross-cultural comparative framework. For example, cultures seem to differ strongly on how long I need to wait for an answer to arrive before I am culturally allowed to check back with my communication partner in POPC communication.

Conversely, the intercultural perspective on cross-border POPC linkages helps clarify how I can negotiate a common practice with a communication partner from a different cultural background so that my needs will be satisfied and my partner is not offended. The sustained or permanent nature of such intercultural exchanges is highly likely to lead to mutual adaptation processes in what both partners deem appropriate POPC behavior and to a heightened level of awareness and reflection about cultural differences surfacing in such behavior. In this way, permanent intercultural encounters are set to increase the willingness to tolerate or even the ability to appreciate such differences as enriching rather than only a necessary nuisance. More generally, the spatial and temporal separation might affect my sense of what exactly permanency is supposed to mean in my connection with my communication partner. Separation might also affect my perception of the value of nonmediated face-to-face interaction.

Finally, the real strength of both perspectives is realized, we contend, when they are combined in empirical POPC research. For example, the likelihood to even engage in permanent intercultural connections will in part be driven by the generalized dispositions produced by cultural identities. Also, the potential adaptation processes experienced during intercultural POPC communication will in part depend on what the cultural values of the communicators actually are. Conversely, these values might be partly changed in the course of sustained connections, e.g., whether they adhere to a more independent or interdependent self-construal. We are well aware that the investigation of questions and claims like these necessitates a research design that captures both the dispositions (i.e., values, habits, and rules) of POPC communication partners separately as well as the qualities of their mutual interaction (i.e., perceptions of closeness, cultural differences, need satisfaction, etc.). This is no small task, especially if the investigation is supposed to also contain a temporal dimension that captures change over time. But as communicative entanglements across cultural borders are becoming more and more dense, sustained, and complex in today's globalized world, our strategies of investigation should also be able to grasp that complexity.

References

Abbas, R., & Mesch, G. S. (2015). Cultural values and Facebook use among Palestinian youth in Israel. *Computers in Human Behavior, 48*, 644–653. doi:10.1016/j.chb.2015.02.031

Baron, N. S., & Campbell, E. M. (2012). Gender and mobile phones in cross-national context. *Language Sciences, 34*(1), 13–27. doi:10.1016/j.langsci.2011.06.018.

Baron, N. S., & Segerstad, Y. (2010). Cross-cultural patterns in mobile-phone use: Public space and reachability in Sweden, the USA, and Japan. *New Media & Society, 12*(1), 13–34.

Baumeister, R. F., & Leary, M. R. (1995). The need to belong: Desire for interpersonal attachments as a fundamental human motivation. *Psychological Bulletin, 117*(3), 497–529.

Beckers, J., Mante, E., & Schmidt, H. G. (2003). Communication anxiety among "smart" Dutch computer users. In J. Katz (Ed.), *Machines that become us: The social context of communication technology* (pp. 147–160). New Brunswick, NJ: Transaction Publishers.

Brüggemann, M., & Wessler, H. (2014). Transnational communication as deliberation, ritual and strategy. *Communication Theory, 24*(4), 394–414.

Campbell, S. W. (2007a). A cross-cultural comparison of perceptions and uses of mobile telephony. *New Media & Society, 9*(2), 343–363. doi:10.1177/1461444807075016

Campbell, S. W. (2007b). Perceptions of mobile phone use in public settings: A cross-cultural comparison. *International Journal of Communication, 1*, 738–757. Retrieved from http://ijoc.org/ojs/index.php/ijoc/article/view/169

Caporael, L. R., & Xie, B. (2003). Breaking time and place: Mobile technologies and reconstituted identities. In J. Katz (Ed.), *Machines that become us: The social context of communication technology* (pp. 219–232). New Brunswick, NJ: Transaction Publishers.

Cardon, P. W., Marshall, B., Choi, J., El-Shinnaway, M. M., North, M., Svensson, L., . . . Valenzuala, J. P. (2009). Online and offline social ties of social network website users: An exploratory study in eleven societies. *Journal of Computer Information Systems, 50*(1), 54–64. doi:10.1177/1080569908330376

Erumban, A. A., & Jong, S. B. de (2006). Cross-country differences in ICT adoption: A consequence of culture? *Journal of World Business, 41*(4), 302–314. doi:10.1016/j.jwb.2006.08.005

Gudykunst, W. B., Matsumoto, Y., Ting-Toomey, S., Nishida, T., Kim, K., & Heyman, S. (1996). The influence of cultural and individual values on communication styles across cultures. *Human Communication Research, 22*(4), 510–543. doi:10.1111/j.1468-2958.1996.tb00377.x

Hall, E. T. (1976). *Beyond culture*. Garden City, NY: Anchor Press, Doubleday.

Hall, E. T., & Hall, M. R. (1990). *Hidden differences*. New York: Anchor Books.

Hepp, A., Bozdag, C., & Suna, L. (2012). Mediatized migrants. Media cultures and communicative networking in the diaspora. In L. Fortunati, R. Pertierra, & J. Vincent (Eds.), *Migrations, diaspora, and information technology in global societies* (pp. 172–188). London: Palgrave.

Hofstede, G. (2001). *Culture's consequences: Comparing values, behaviors, institutions and organizations across nations* (2nd ed.). Thousand Oaks, CA: Sage Publications.

Jackson, L. A., & Wang, J.-L. (2013). Cultural differences in social networking site use: A comparative study of China and the United States. *Computers in Human Behavior, 29*(3), 910–921. http://dx.doi.org/10.1016/j.chb.2012.11.024

Kang, S., & Jung, J. (2014). Mobile communication for human needs: A comparison of smartphone use between the US and Korea. *Computers in Human Behavior, 35*, 376–387. doi:10.1016/j.chb.2014.03.024

Katz, J. E., & Aakhus, M. A. (Eds.) (2002). *Perpetual contact: Mobile communication, private talk, public performance*. Cambridge, UK: Cambridge University Press.

Kim, Y., Sohn, D., & Choi, S. M. (2011). Cultural difference in motivations for using social network sites: A comparative study of American and Korean college students. *Computers in Human Behavior, 27*(1), 365–372. http://dx.doi.org/10.1016/j.chb.2010.08.015

LaRose, R., Connolly, R., Lee, H., Li, K., & Hales, K. D. (2014). Connection overload? A cross cultural study of the consequences of social media connection. *Information System Management, 31*(1), 59–73.

Lee, I., Choi, B., Kim, J., & Hong, S.-J. (2007). Culture-technology fit: Effects of cultural characteristics on the post-adoption beliefs of mobile Internet users. *International Journal of Electronic Commerce, 11*(4), 11–51.

Lee, S., & Sundar, S. (2015). Cosmetic customization of mobile phones: Cultural antecedents, psychological correlates. *Media Psychology, 18*(1), 1–23. doi:10.1080/15213269.2013.853618

Markus, H., & Kitayama, S. (1991). Culture and the self: Implications for cognition, emotion, and motivation. *Psychological Review, 98*(2), 224–253. Retrieved from http://psycnet.apa.org/journals/rev/98/2/224/

Norris, P., & Inglehart, R. (2009). *Cosmopolitan communications. Cultural diversity in a globalized world*. Cambridge: Cambridge University Press.

Schejter, A., & Cohen, A. (2002). Israel: Chutzpah and chatter in the holy land. In J. Katz & M. Aakhus (Eds.), *Perpetual contact: Mobile communication, private talk, public performance* (pp. 30–41). Cambridge: Cambridge University Press.

Schwartz, S. H., & Bilsky, W. (1990). Toward a theory of the universal content and structure of values: Extensions and cross-cultural replications. *Journal of Personality and Social Psychology, 58*(5), 878–891. doi:10.1037//0022-3514.58.5.878

Schwartz, S. H., & Sagiv, L. (1995). Identifying culture-specifics in the content and structure of values. *Journal of Cross-Cultural Psychology, 26*(1), 92–116. doi:10.1177/0022022195261007

Sellen, A. J. (1992). Speech patterns in video mediated conversations. Proceedings of the Conference on Computer Human Interaction '92, Monterey, CA, May 4–7.

Silverstone, R., & Haddon, L. (1996). Design and the domestication of ICTs: Technical change and everyday life. In R. Mansell & R. Silverstone (Eds.), *Communicating by design: The politics of information and communication technologies* (pp. 44–74). Oxford: Oxford University Press.

Uchida, Y., & Kitayama, S. (2009). Happiness and unhappiness in East and West: Themes and variations. *Emotion, 9*(4), 441–456. doi:10.1037/a0015634

Yu, L., & Tng, T. H. (2003). Culture and design for mobile phones in China. In J. Katz (Ed.), *Machines that become us: The social context of communication technology* (pp. 187–198). New Brunswick, NJ: Transaction Publishers.

PART V
The POPC Citizen
Politics and Participation

19
The POPC Citizen
Political Information in the Fourth Age of Political Communication

Dorothée Hefner, Eike Mark Rinke, and Frank M. Schneider

Introduction

A woman checking messages on her phone while standing next to a newspaper rack. A girl waiting in line scrolling down the Facebook timeline, stumbling upon a video clip about the outcome of the recent US presidential elections. A young man playing a game on his tablet, with TV news running in another window. These are just three everyday scenarios that illustrate how today's "permanently online, permanently connected" (POPC) communication environment has created new conditions for the access to and consumption of political information. A myriad of options to choose from regarding the form and content of communication make it easy to acquire political information continuously, but also to avoid political content given the many other interesting things to do online. At the same time, social networking sites (SNS) have made it more difficult to abstain completely from political information, as they often push news to unsuspecting users. With the permanent potential to activate social ties through SNS and instant messaging services, the political information of citizens has become embedded into their mediated social networks whose members like, share, and comment on it. The implications of widespread digitization and mediatization for the political domain are so profound and far-reaching that they have recently led Jay Blumler (2016) to announce a new "fourth age of political communication." Political communication in the fourth age is characterized by "yet more communication abundance" (p. 24) compared to the preceding ages, particularly due to new, mobile-access devices that have led to an ever more intense competition for audience attention. The fact that the Internet has gone mobile reinforces developments it initiated much earlier: Mobility increases the frequency of communication and thus the frequency of situations in which more or less conscious choices regarding the modes and content of communication are necessary. Because people often initiate and process digital communication in parallel with an ongoing "offline life," communication acts may also become more impulsive and automatic (van Koningsbruggen, Hartmann, & Du, this volume), and attention paid to content more superficial than in the past.

However, the affordances of a POPC media environment affect more than just the way people select, are exposed to, and process political communication. In this chapter, we propose that the POPC environment interacts with the individual characteristics of citizens, with profound implications for some of the most important communication outcomes for a well-functioning democracy such as citizens' political knowledge, involvement, and participation. Prior (2007) demonstrated a growing importance of people's preference for entertainment relative to their appetite for serious news in high-choice media environments. We build on his insights and argue that well-known predictors of news use, like citizens' preference for "hard" news over entertainment and their political interest, will become even more important under POPC conditions and in a high-choice and high-stimulation environment. Put simply, a person not interested in anything political does not only lack the motivation, but also—more than ever—the necessity to follow and elaborate on the news, because there will always be more appealing messages to enjoy online and on the go. In addition, personal characteristics such as a general disposition to be distracted (Reinecke & Hofmann, 2016) may become more influential in the political information process in a POPC world. The seemingly unlimited number of options to communicate and receive information as well as greater technology-enabled stimulation through push messages are likely to cause new variation among citizens concerning their routine contact with political news.

The goal of this chapter is to describe how the POPC environment operates in tandem with personal characteristics to influence people's exposure to and processing of political information. In describing the political consequences of the POPC phenomenon, we take a social-psychological perspective and focus on the individual level (for a more sociological perspective see the chapter by Vromen, Xenos, and Loader, this volume). We sketch the psychological contours of the contemporary "POPC citizen" and outline recent developments in citizens' use of mobile information and communication technologies (ICTs) for political informationas well as their consequences for individual civic competencies, and democracy at large.

Characteristics of the POPC Environment

In the last decades, our media environment has changed drastically. Mobile devices have been a catalyst for this development, as they enabled us to be permanently online and permanently connected (Klimmt, Hefner, Reinecke, Rieger, & Vorderer, this volume). The central component of this new environment is the modern smartphone, a device that bundles new and traditional mass media (e.g., digital TV and radio, newspaper content, music, and video) together with interpersonal communication channels (e.g., SNS, email, and texting). These various media, services, and functions can be used at virtually any time, in any place, and even simultaneously. And because the smartphone is a steady companion, this flow of mediated cues seems to neither have an end nor a start. More than anything else, this high-choice, high-stimulation POPC media environment produces a high load of information and continuous affordances for the user. Unread instant messages, newsletters in the mailbox, the online game to be continued, or the never-ending updates, tweets, retweets, or link shares of online news pages and social network sites—they all are opportunities and obligations for information, communication, and entertainment at the same time. Recent data show that today digital mobile media are one of the most important and most frequently accessed sources of news, second only to television (e.g., Hölig & Hasebrink, 2013; Pew Research Center, 2016). The POPC environment has created a completely new context in which political information is produced, disseminated, and received. Accordingly, the mechanisms through which the information environment is politically important may be changing dramatically as well. The ubiquity of mobile phones, their perpetual contact and instant information features, as well as location-based and personalized services (for examples, see Martin, 2014) play an important role—not only with regard to political content but also with regard to entertainment and interpersonal communication. It is the permanence and ubiquity aspects of this new environment that increase opportunities for individuals to get in touch with political information both intentionally and incidentally.

Exposure to Political Information in a POPC Environment

For POPC citizens, a multiplicity of information flows intersect, compete, and feed into one another, leading to a dizzying array of channels and opportunities through which they may be exposed to political information. The contemporary political information ecology is increasingly complex and contingent (Thorson & Wells, 2016), and the affordances of smartphones and other mobile ICTs as well as the POPC mindset of many citizens today contribute significantly to that complexity and contingency in the reception of political news.

Recent assessments of audiences for political news reveal that the consumption of political information is becoming increasingly integrated into the POPC media routines of citizens, at least in countries with high Internet penetration rates. In 2015, in most countries of Western Europe as well as in the United States, around 40% of citizens used their mobiles for consuming news and almost as many indicated they were using social media as a gateway to political information (Hölig, Nielsen, & Schrøder, 2016). Indeed, Swedish data show that 2015 was the first year in which citizens accessed online news more frequently via mobile devices than via stationary computers (Westlund, 2016).

These changes towards the use of mobiles—the technological bedrock of the POPC condition—for political information are significant in several ways. Mobile devices are often, and increasingly (Westlund & Färdigh, 2015), used for cross-media news consumption and as a complement to traditional sources of news (Damme, Courtois, Verbrugge, & Marez, 2015). While much of the content consumed on the go on mobile devices is content produced by legacy news media (Wolf & Schnauber, 2015), the technological affordances of mobile ICTs introduce important inequalities in media activities, decreasing potential benefits for those accessing the web primarily on handheld devices (Pearce & Rice, 2013). Indeed, research shows that citizens accessing the news through mobile devices do so more expansively, but also more superficially (Westlund, 2016).

The increasing exposure to news anywhere, at any time through mobile online media brings about several problems related to their technological makeup: Mobiles come with smaller screens, which limits choice, reading ease, and consequently, the average time spent reading an article as well as the amount of learning from the news. Their connections to the Internet are often slower than those of stationary computers, which may lead to higher defection rates during news consumption and a lower probability of users returning to news sites, especially if they rarely use news. Moreover, mobile Internet connections are more costly and are likely to remain that in the foreseeable future (Dunaway, 2016). While mobile ICTs open up new times and spaces for news consumption (Struckmann & Karnowski, 2016), these opportunities are seized particularly by those who are better educated and receive higher incomes, at least when it comes to high-quality journalistic news content (Thorson, Shoenberger, Karaliova, Kim, & Fidler, 2015).

Given this reproduction of well-known inequalities in political information with regard to education and income, some have concluded that the proliferation of mobile online communication has led to the emergence of a mobile Internet underclass that is characterized by diminished levels of political engagement (Napoli & Obar, 2014). This assessment seems to be more broadly valid than the occasionally expressed optimism regarding citizen engagement through news exposure on mobile media (Martin, 2015, 2016).

A specific POPC-related phenomenon that recently has garnered particular attention by political communication researchers may aggravate this trend: The increasing proclivity, especially among younger citizens, to rely on purely incidental news exposure for their political information. The "news finds me" (NFM) expectation underlying such behavior may be seen as a product of the permanent salience and vigilance associated with a POPC mindset that is enabled by mobile ICTs. But while vigilant NFM use of mobiles may lead to the occasional unanticipated engagement with political information, its primary effect appears to be a more passive, even apathetic stance toward the political world. Adopting an NFM posture in reaction to POPC conditions leads to gradual decreases in political interest and knowledge, which, in turn, makes people engage less in political participation (Gil de Zúñiga & Diehl, 2016). Even worse, incidental news exposure—such as that anticipated by high-NFM individuals— tends to benefit the political participation of particularly those citizens that are already interested in politics (Kim, Chen, & Gil de Zúñiga, 2013; see also Tewksbury, Weaver, & Maddex, 2001), which may deepen political divides. Importantly, this conclusion may not to the same extent apply to incidental news exposure via SNS (Valeriani & Vaccari, 2016). One possible explanation is that SNS users do not have many choices once they have decided to "enter" a particular SNS (Bode, 2016). On Facebook, for example, posts of friends are listed in a single message stream so that users are virtually forced to at least take note of every post—be it one with political content or without. However, as a result of "learning" algorithms of the SNS, politically uninterested users will find progressively fewer political messages on their SNS, because the less interest in and engagement with political posts they have demonstrated in the past, the less content of this kind will be displayed to them (Thorson & Wells, 2016). In addition, they may also create less political and/or politically diverse SNS settings over time themselves by "filtering" messages from or even unfriend contacts that have post political or politically uncomfortable content (John & Dvir-Gvirsman, 2015).

A second relevant phenomenon in media exposure patterns related to POPC is the tendency to use "second screens," consuming political news events via an additional web-connected device attended to in parallel to a primary media source. Such behaviors have been cast as a new form of online political engagement that may also translate into offline political participation and civic engagement (Gil de Zúñiga, Garcia-Perdomo, & McGregor, 2015; Vaccari, Chadwick, & O'Loughlin, 2015). However, if looked at more closely from an information-processing perspective, the multitasking nature of the reception situations produced by dual-screen use may well lead to diminished cognitive benefits of exposure to the news (Jeong & Hwang, 2016; see next section).

Processing Political Information in a POPC Environment

The POPC environment may influence not only citizens' exposure to political information but also how individuals process the news once it reaches them. Two characteristics of the POPC environment in particular impact the way individuals process political information, both with likely consequences for relevant outcomes such as political knowledge and participation: (1) The abundance of variegated content on almost any conceivable topic made available to people through the mobile Internet anytime and anywhere, and (2) the social embeddedness of large portions of political content available to citizens through social media. With regard to the abundant availability of information and communication options in a POPC media ecology, we may expect that multitasking (or fast task switching) while processing political information becomes the norm rather than the exception. Multitasking, however, tends to reduce productivity in fulfilling the primary task (in this case, processing news) and affects learning (e.g., Chen & Yan, 2016; Junco & Cotten, 2012; Wood et al., 2012; see also the chapters by David and by Xu and Wang, this volume). A recent study demonstrated that the general frequency of media multitasking (i.e., engaging in additional media activities such as text messaging, watching TV, or using SNS) during exposure to political news is negatively associated with general political knowledge, but positively related to subjective political knowledge (Ran, Yamamoto, & Xu, 2016). Multitasking news users thus not only learn less while following the news, they also seem to overestimate their knowledge.

We may assume, however, that people will differ in the degree to which they translate the affordances of a POPC environment into multitasking behavior as a function of their personal characteristics. Individual polychronicity, for example, has been proposed as a personality trait that reflects the preference for multitasking (Poposki & Oswald, 2010). Individuals high in polychronicity prefer to perform multiple threads of tasks at a time rather than only one single task. A polychronic individual, hence, will more likely engage in parallel activities at the same screen or, e.g., activate an additional screen while watching the news. Another relevant and probably related individual characteristic is general distractibility (Forster & Lavie, 2016), which influences how easily individuals become sidetracked from pursuing their primary goal. The more distractible, one may assume, the higher the probability that individuals will get disturbed by the permanent opportunity to access multitudes of unrelated contents or engage in alternative communication activities. For example, easily distractible users should be more prone to react to messages coming in on their mobile phone while they read an online newspaper article (Reinecke & Hofmann, 2016; Klimmt et al., this volume).

There is also an argument for a more optimistic outlook regarding the news processing of politically uninterested citizens. It relates to the social embeddedness of political information in a POPC environment mentioned earlier. In SNS and mobile online applications, much news content diffuses through sharing: Friends forward media messages to their circles of relevant others and thus create a social context to news items. Consequently, as media users in a POPC environment learn about which political articles their friends and network members are reading, which videos they are watching, and which petition they are signing, they may adjust their selection of content to that of their friends. In other words, the POPC environment may magnify the social dimension of news consumption, with political information serving as preparation for anticipated (political) talk with friends, colleagues, and acquaintances. The amount of effort people expend on preparing for political interactions with others by seeking out news also increases their elaborative processing and political knowledge (Beaudoin & Thorson, 2004). This socially induced effect even outsizes learning effects due to a motivation to achieve surveillance of the social world and obtain guidance on political issues (Eveland, 2001). If the POPC environment in fact produces more frequent triggers of such anticipated interaction motivations in citizens through the presentation of information on the political interests of relevant others, users' motivation to elaborate socially relevant political news could increase. This effect would of course apply to all individuals independent of their political interest. Because of its general mechanism, it could, however, possibly contribute to alleviating gaps between the more and less politically involved. On the other hand, the likelihood for such an effect will depend on the political interest of one's social network and its members' willingness to communicate about the news (Thorson & Wells, 2016).

Another positive effect of today's media ecology and people's POPC mindset could be that they open up new opportunities for citizens to engage in political talk and deliberation online. Social media offer new low-effort opportunities to participate in political opinion expression and debate, because there are always opportunities to like, share, and comment on news, to talk about politics, and to deliberate (Stromer-Galley & Wichowski, 2011). The POPC environment may thus strengthen the degree to which citizens process the news collectively (e.g., Graham, 2015; Halpern & Gibbs, 2013). All this may stimulate at least situational political awareness (such as in the case of breaking high-profile news stories), but may also lead to greater, possibly sustained political interest, discussion, knowledge, and participation (Ahmed, 2011). However, here again, the degree to which these benign consequences of POPC environments transpire likely depends on individuals' predispositions (e.g., their political interest) more strongly than in the pre-POPC world.

Conclusion

The POPC phenomenon relates closely to the fourth age of political communication. It is an era that is characterized, for the first time in history, by a permanently available, ubiquitous, and borderless system of political information and discourse. In this chapter, we have outlined both well-established and more speculative consequences of the POPC environment on exposure to and the processing of political news. Under conditions of "abundant choice" (Webster & Nelson, 2016), individual characteristics such as informational preferences, motives, and personality traits, individual mediated social networks, and individuals' perceptions and interpretations of their media environment are becoming more important for people's everyday exposure to political news. The current plethora of opportunities for citizens to acquire information and to participate in political discussions and activism is unprecedented in human history. Citizens today can access political information from different sources and in different modes at almost any time and anywhere. Moreover, there are plenty of opportunities to discuss politics with others online and participate in the political process with little effort.

However, the reality of sociopolitical life often looks different: Citizens rarely exploit such new opportunities (Norris, 2001). The reasons can likely be found within the POPC environment: Not only does the mobile Internet offer permanent access to political information, it also offers entertainment, and lifeworld content that is not primarily political (such as weather forecasts or public transportation information) as well as new opportunities for digital interpersonal communication. Today's citizens are constantly confronted with a myriad of options for reading, watching, searching, or otherwise engaging with information and communication. Our brief overview of the literature reinforces concerns related to this abundance. Moreover, due to the growing importance of personal preferences and interests, gaps between the politically interested and uninterested segments of society regarding their exposure to and processing of news are likely to increase rather than decrease in the future. In addition, new individual differences such as citizens' distractibility come into play in a high-choice, high-stimulation environment characterized by a ceaseless stream of incoming messages.

However, this environment is also prone to promote incidental encounters with news bits, especially in SNS (Bode, 2016). Due to the fact that a lot of political information on the Internet is shared, liked, and commented on within social networks, social norms, such as a perceived civic duty to keep informed (Poindexter & McCombs, 2001) or social motives for being ready to discuss current events, can stimulate news consumption. This, once more, indicates the growing importance of curation processes on and by SNS, but also by the algorithms of web applications (Thorson & Wells, 2016).

The current POPC media environment is one that is no longer characterized only by citizens being faced with a great number of media channels to choose from. Instead, it is one in which an ever-increasing number of citizens self-selects into a media environment characterized by high stimulation through permanent information. Citizens in the fourth age are not only required to make more media choices at a faster pace but also to navigate the oversupply of information and communication opportunities under conditions of limited human capacities to process information.

We have good reason to believe that how rich in political information people's individual media environments will be and how productively they will engage with them will, more than in the past ages of political communication, depend on their individual characteristics—their personal qualities, both innate and obtained. While systematic empirical study of these tendencies is lacking and sorely needed, we may suggest, for the time being, that the current move into a POPC world will tend to aggravate inequalities in political knowledge and participation, rather than reduce them.

References

Ahmed, M. A. K. (2011). *Students' exposure to political news on the Internet and political awareness: A comparison between Germany and Egypt*. Doctoral dissertation, Technical University of Dresden, Germany. Retrieved from www.qucosa.de/fileadmin/data/qucosa/documents/8441/Mohamed_Ahmed_phD_Dissertation.pdf

Beaudoin, C. E., & Thorson, E. (2004). Testing the cognitive mediation model: The roles of news reliance and three gratifications sought. *Communication Research, 31*, 446–471. doi:10.1177/0093650204266098

Blumler, J. G. (2016). The fourth age of political communication. *Politiques de Communication, 6*, 19–30.

Bode, L. (2016). Political news in the news feed: Learning politics from social media. *Mass Communication and Society, 19*, 24–48. doi:10.1080/15205436.2015.1045149

Chen, Q., & Yan, Z. (2016). Does multitasking with mobile phones affect learning? A review. *Computers in Human Behavior, 54*, 34–42. doi:10.1016/j.chb.2015.07.047

Damme, K. V., Courtois, C., Verbrugge, K., & Marez, L. D. (2015). What's APPening to news? A mixed-method audience-centred study on mobile news consumption. *Mobile Media & Communication, 3*, 196–213. http://doi.org/10.1177/2050157914557691

Dunaway, J. (2016). *Mobile vs. computer: Implications for news audiences and outlets* (Discussion Paper Series No. D-103). Cambridge, MA: Shorenstein Center on Media, Politics and Public Policy. Retrieved from http://shorensteincenter.org/mobile-vs-computer-news-audiences-and-outlets/

Eveland, W. P. (2001). The cognitive mediation model of learning from the news: Evidence from nonelection, off-year election, and presidential election contexts. *Communication Research, 28*, 571–601. doi:10.1177/009365001028005001

Forster, S., & Lavie, N. (2016). Establishing the attention-distractibility trait. *Psychological Science, 27*, 203–212. doi:10.1177/0956797615617761

Gil de Zúñiga, H., & Diehl, T. H. (2016, June). *Detachment from surveillance needs: Effects of "news finds me" perception on political knowledge, interest, and voting*. Presented at the 66th Annual Conference of the International Communication Association, Fukuoka, Japan.

Gil de Zúñiga, H., Garcia-Perdomo, V., & McGregor, S. C. (2015). What is second screening? Exploring motivations of second screen use and its effect on online political participation. *Journal of Communication, 65*, 793–815. doi:10.1111/jcom.12174

Graham, T. S. (2015). Everyday political talk in the Internet-based public sphere. In S. Coleman & D. Freelon (Eds.), *Handbook of digital politics* (pp. 247–263). Cheltenham, UK: Edward Elgar Publishing.

Halpern, D., & Gibbs, J. (2013). Social media as a catalyst for online deliberation? Exploring the affordances of Facebook and YouTube for political expression. *Computers in Human Behavior, 29*, 1159–1168. doi:10.1016/j.chb.2012.10.008

Hölig, S., & Hasebrink, U. (2013). Nachrichtennutzung in konvergierenden Medienumgebungen: International vergleichende Befunde auf Basis des Reuters Institute digital news survey 2013. *Media Perspektiven, 44*, 522–536.

Hölig, S., Nielsen, R. K., & Schrøder, K. C. (2016). Changing forms of cross-media news use in Western Europe and beyond. In J. L. Jensen, M. Mortensen, & J. Ørmen (Eds.), *News across media: Production, distribution and consumption* (pp. 102–122). New York: Routledge.

Jeong, S.-H., & Hwang, Y. (2016). Media multitasking effects on cognitive vs. attitudinal outcomes: A meta-analysis. *Human Communication Research, 42*, 599–618. doi:10.1111/hcre.12089

John, N. A., & Dvir-Gvirsman, S. (2015). "I don't like you any more": Facebook unfriending by Israelis during the Israel-Gaza conflict of 2014. *Journal of Communication, 65*(6), 953–974. doi:10.1111/jcom.12188

Junco, R., & Cotten, S. R. (2012). No A 4 U. The relationship between multitasking and academic performance. *Computers & Education, 59*, 505–514. doi:10.1016/j.compedu.2011.12.023

Kim, Y., Chen, H.-T., & Gil de Zúñiga, H. (2013). Stumbling upon news on the Internet: Effects of incidental news exposure and relative entertainment use on political engagement. *Computers in Human Behavior, 29*, 2607–2614. doi:10.1016/j.chb.2013.06.005

Martin, J. A. (2014). Mobile media and political participation: Defining and developing an emerging field. *Mobile Media & Communication, 2*, 173–195. doi:10.1177/2050157914520847

Martin, J. A. (2015). Mobile news use and participation in elections: A bridge for the democratic divide? *Mobile Media & Communication, 3*, 230–249. doi:10.1177/2050157914550664

Martin, J. A. (2016). Mobile media activity breadth and political engagement: An online resource perspective. *International Journal of Mobile Communications, 14*, 26–42. doi:10.1504/IJMC.2016.073354

Napoli, P. M., & Obar, J. A. (2014). The emerging mobile Internet underclass: A critique of mobile Internet access. *The Information Society, 30*, 323–334. doi:10.1080/01972243.2014.944726

Norris, P. (2001). *Digital divide: Civic engagement, information poverty, and the Internet worldwide*. Cambridge: Cambridge University Press.

Pearce, K. E., & Rice, R. E. (2013). Digital divides from access to activities: Comparing mobile and personal computer Internet users. *Journal of Communication, 63*, 721–744. doi:10.1111/jcom.12045

Pew Research Center. (2016). *State of the news media 2016*. Retrieved from www.journalism.org/files/2016/06/State-of-the-News-Media-Report-2016-FINAL.pdf

Poindexter, P. M., & McCombs, M. E. (2001). Revisiting the civic duty to keep informed in the new media environment. *Journalism & Mass Communication Quarterly, 78*, 113–126. doi:10.1177/107769900107800108

Poposki, E. M., & Oswald, F. L. (2010). The multitasking preference inventory: Toward an improved measure of individual differences in polychronicity. *Human Performance, 23*, 247–264. doi:10.1080/08959285.2010.487843

Prior, M. (2007). *Post-broadcast democracy: How media choice increases inequality in political involvement and polarizes elections*. New York: Cambridge University Press.

Ran, W., Yamamoto, M., & Xu, S. (2016). Media multitasking during political news consumption: A relationship with factual and subjective political knowledge. *Computers in Human Behavior, 56*, 352–359. doi:10.1016/j.chb.2015.12.015

Reinecke, L., & Hofmann, W. (2016). Slacking off or winding down? An experience sampling study on the drivers and consequences of media use for recovery versus procrastination. *Human Communication Research, 42*, 441–461. doi:10.1111/hcre.12082

Stromer-Galley, J., & Wichowski, A. (2011). Political discussion online. In M. Consalvo, C. Ess, & R. Burnett (Eds.), *Blackwell handbook of Internet studies* (pp. 168–187). London: Blackwell.

Struckmann, S., & Karnowski, V. (2016). News consumption in a changing media ecology: An MESM-study on mobile news. *Telematics & Informatics, 33*, 309–319. doi:10.1016/j.tele.2015.08.012

Tewksbury, D., Weaver, A. J., & Maddex, B. D. (2001). Accidentally informed: Incidental news exposure on the World Wide Web. *Journalism & Mass Communication Quarterly, 78*, 533–554. doi:10.1177/107769900107800309

Thorson, E., Shoenberger, H., Karaliova, T., Kim, E., & Fidler, R. (2015). News use of mobile media: A contingency model. *Mobile Media & Communication, 3*, 160–178. doi:10.1177/2050157914557692

Thorson, K., & Wells, C. (2016). Curated flows: A framework for mapping media exposure in the digital age. *Communication Theory, 26*, 309–328. doi:10.1111/comt.12087

Vaccari, C., Chadwick, A., & O'Loughlin, B. (2015). Dual screening the political: Media events, social media, and citizen engagement. *Journal of Communication, 65*, 1041–1061. doi:10.1111/jcom.12187

Valeriani, A., & Vaccari, C. (2016). Accidental exposure to politics on social media as online participation equalizer in Germany, Italy, and the United Kingdom. *New Media & Society, 18*, 1857–1874. doi:10.1177/1461444815616223

Webster, J. G., & Nelson, J. L. (2016). The evolution of news consumption: A structurational interpretation. In J. L. Jensen, M. Mortensen, & J. Ørmen (Eds.), *News across media: Production, distribution and consumption* (pp. 84–101). New York: Routledge.

Westlund, O. (2016). News consumption across media: Tracing the revolutionary uptake of mobile news. In J. L. Jensen, M. Mortensen, & J. Ørmen (Eds.), *News across media: Production, distribution and consumption* (pp. 123–141). New York: Routledge.

Westlund, O., & Färdigh, M. A. (2015). Accessing the news in an age of mobile media: Tracing displacing and complementary effects of mobile news on newspapers and online news. *Mobile Media & Communication, 3*, 53–74. doi:10.1177/2050157914549039

Wolf, C., & Schnauber, A. (2015). News consumption in the mobile era: The role of mobile devices and traditional journalism's content within the user's information repertoire. *Digital Journalism, 3*, 759–776. doi:10.1080/21670811.2014.942497

Wood, E., Zivcakova, L., Gentile, P., Archer, K., Pasquale, D. de, & Nosko, A. (2012). Examining the impact of off-task multi-tasking with technology on real-time classroom learning. *Computers & Education, 58*, 365–374. doi:10.1016/j.compedu.2011.08.029

20
The Networked Young Citizen as POPC Citizen

Ariadne Vromen, Michael A. Xenos, and Brian D. Loader

Introduction

There can be little doubt that the institutions and practices of modern representative government have been subject to growing disillusionment from young citizens. A reluctance to vote at elections, join political parties, or have a high regard for their politicians all suggest that many young people are turning away from formal politics in many countries (Fieldhouse, Tranmer, & Russell, 2007; Van Biezen, Mair, & Poguntke, 2012). Instead, engagement in alternative or new forms of political participation all point to the possible displacement of traditional models of representative democracy as the dominant cultural form of engagement, by approaches increasingly characterized through networking practices. The political identity and attitudes of young citizens are increasingly shaped less by their social ties to family, neighborhood, school, or work, and more by the ways in which they participate and interact through the social networks which they themselves have had a significant part in constructing. Central to this model of networked individualism (Rainie & Wellman, 2012) is the role played by digital and networked communication technologies, and therefore how young people's lives are being irrevocably changed from being permanently online and permanently connected to their social networks (Vorderer, Krömer, & Schneider, 2016). In this chapter, we highlight how young people's political engagement has generally moved online and is less likely to occur in traditional offline formats, and we also analyze the emergence of new forms of political engagement based on social media platforms, such as Facebook, where young people are taking the lead from older generations. Rather than finding disaffection, we demonstrate that many young people are politically engaged, and the emergence of networked communication technologies has enhanced this engagement. However, we also caution against generalizing to all young people, as significant barriers to engagement remain that have more to do with the structure, openness, and appeal of broader political systems and processes. Being POPC does not lead to young people being comfortable with an ongoing presence of politics on social media platforms within their everyday lives.

The debates over young people's citizenship practices are filled with discourses that expect young people to adopt the dutiful practices of participation that correspond to the civic norms established by earlier generations. Thus, active citizens should vote at elections, respect their representatives, access traditional media, join political groups, and engage in voluntary activities in their civic communities. It is a model of the citizen as someone who should be *seen* to support the representative system through their dutiful actions but whose *voice* is seldom heard or recognized. Indeed, the future prospects for democracy are seen to depend upon the support of dutiful citizens, leading to concern in many democracies about the apparent disaffection of young people (Stoker, 2006; Amna & Ekman, 2013). However, academic analysis has also suggested that the political attitudes of many young people in many parts of the world can increasingly be characterized as less deferential and more individualized (Beck, 1992), with a critical disposition (Norris, 2002) that marks a departure from the dutiful norms of citizenship (Dalton, 2008). In the work of Bennett and colleagues, new civic engagement norms are underpinned by a fundamental shift toward participation as a project of self-actualization through expressive, individualized acts, often growing out of engagement with horizontal peer networks. This is purposefully contrasted with duty-bound obligations to participate via established, hierarchical institutional structures of media, government, and civil society (Bennett, Wells, & Rank, 2009). Such cultural changes to political participation are shaped by wider economic and social forces and do not occur universally or overnight. Moreover, the decline in formal political engagement has been ongoing for some time in many countries across all age groups (Norris, 2002). Instead of regarding the emergence of new citizenship norms as the death knell of advanced democracy, it may be more useful to see them as pointing to a recalibration of modern political institutions and practices in ways that are more responsive to the dissatisfaction felt by many young people. Young citizens may be finding new ways to take action, voice their opinions, and shape new spaces from which to envision their views.

It is helpful to take a number of key features to assemble what we call the *networked young citizen* (see Loader, Vromen, & Xenos, 2014). Networking young citizens are far less likely to become members of political or civic organizations, such as parties or trades unions, and are more likely to participate in horizontal or nonhierarchical networks (Cammaerts, Bruter, Banaji, Harrison, & Anstead, 2014; Kahne, Lee, & Feezell, 2013); they are more project orientated (Bang, 2005); they reflexively engage in lifestyle politics (Bennett, 1998); they are not dutiful but self-actualizing (Bennett, Wells, & Rank, 2009); their historical reference points are less likely to be those of modern welfare capitalism but rather global information networked capitalism; and their social relations are increasingly enacted in a social media environment (Collin, 2015; Ekstrom, 2016). This is, of course, an ideal type of construction and is not intended to represent all young citizens in every respect. Its value is as a framework against which we may assess the normative political dispositions of young people. Our objective is not to provide another generalization about all young people being characterized as a type, instead it is a useful analytical device to assess the evidence for cultural and political change. Some further clarifications need to be made to our assemblage. First, this does not represent an all-encompassing discontinuity with previous dutiful models. Networked young citizens may live conterminously with other dutiful citizens and indeed share some of each other's attributes on occasions. Second, networked citizenship can be seen as fluid and always under construction within regulatory norms and structuring processes. A model of citizenship that is fluid and based on young people's lived experience does not lead to political apathy, but instead means that identity is socially constructed through young people's everyday actions and interactions. These actions may include challenging dominant ideals of dutiful models of citizenship and are now more likely to occur within their everyday, interactive online social networks. Third, networking young citizens are shaped by different individual lived experiences that will not be the same for everyone. Consequently, issues of inequality and power come into play, and recent developments suggest a positive relationship between social media use and political engagement (e.g., Gil de Zuniga, Jung, & Valenzuela, 2012) that raises questions about the potential for social media to help stem or even reverse patterns of political inequality (see Schlozman, Verba, & Brady, 2010). The interactive, collaborative, and user-generated capacities of social media facilitate new modes of political communication that are more commensurate with contemporary youth cultures associated with the networked young citizen (Bakker & de Vreese, 2011). They point to an electoral affinity between what are perceived as the inherent democratic features of social media and their potential for enhancing the participative and deliberative skills of young citizens (Benkler, 2006; Jenkins, 2006). Overall, existing studies have often looked for, and found, engaged online users and inspiring participatory practices—especially among young people. Yet how do these social networking environments influence political participation and engagement among young citizens? Do they make it easier for young citizens to talk about the public issues that affect their lived experience? Are they more likely to share political opinions and views?

In advanced democracies, Internet access and use has become ubiquitous. In 2016, the Pew Research Center published analysis of Internet and smartphone use across 40 countries, and found that in half these countries, mostly advanced democracies, 90% or more young people aged 18–34 used the Internet; often, young people's Internet use was twice as much as that of those aged 35+, especially in emerging democracies (Poushter, 2016). Younger users everywhere were found to access the Internet at least daily and participate in social networking at higher rates than do their older counterparts. Internet access and use is steadily increasing in the developing world, and this is led by young people with access to smartphones. A majority of young people in two thirds of the countries surveyed now use a smartphone, in seven countries (South Korea, Australia, Canada, Germany, US, Spain, and the UK) over 90% of young people use a smartphone (Poushter, 2016). Pew began systematically collecting data on social media use by Americans in 2005. Since that time, they have charted the everyday mainstreaming of social media use, rising from use by 10% of the adult Internet population to 76% by 2015. Consistently over time citizens aged 18–29 have been the most likely social media users, with 90% using social media by 2015 (Perrin, 2015). Based on these studies, we can safely say that in the developed world young people are now networked young citizens, they are permanently online and permanently connected via social media (Vorderer, Krömer, & Schneider, 2016), as are the more educated and wealthier in the developing world.

We started The Civic Network project in 2012 to systematically compare young people's use of social media for civic and political engagement in Australia, the United States, and the United Kingdom. We were particularly interested in identifying first, whether young people's everyday use of social media had the potential to redress well-established patterns of inequality in political engagement based on educational and socioeconomic backgrounds; and second, whether there was evidence of the new citizenship norms, discussed above, shaping young people's use of social media for politics. Our project, funded by the philanthropic Spencer Foundation in the United States, used both multi-stage and multi-method primary research data collection. We conducted in-person focus groups with affinity groups of campus-based student activists across political and civic groups; we then surveyed over 3,600 young people aged 16–29 in the three countries using original measures of political participation and social media-based political engagement; followed by 12 online qualitative discussion forums with a total of 107 young people from selected survey subsamples based on their level of political engagement and socioeconomic background. Some of the key findings from this project are highlighted in this chapter, and have been expanded upon in our existing publications (see Xenos, Vromen, & Loader, 2014; Vromen, Loader, Xenos, & Bailo, 2016; Loader, Vromen, & Xenos, 2016).

Young People's Use of the Internet and Social Media Affects How Much They Engage in Individualized and Group-Based Forms of Political Engagement

To operationalize political engagement in the quantitative survey, we constructed two distinct measures. The first we called *individual political engagement*, and it was based on a series of questions about 12 distinct acts of civic or political engagement, modeled on items used by Zukin and colleagues (Zukin, Keeter, Andolina, Jenkins, & Delli Carpini, 2006). This inclusive list featured conventional political activities, such as contacting leaders and trying to influence how others might vote in an election, as well as more civic-oriented acts like raising money for charitable causes, and newer political activities such as buying (or not buying) goods or services based on political or ethical reasons and attending a demonstration or a political rally. Figure 20.1 shows the distribution across the three countries of what proportion of young people had participated in each act in the previous year. There is only one act that a majority had participated in: discussing politics with friends and family. An average of 19% of young people across the three countries had not participated in *any* of these 12 acts in the previous year; or 81% of young people had engaged in at least one form of individual political engagement, with a mean of 4.10 acts and a standard deviation of 3.88, demonstrating a broad spread of political engagement among most networked young citizens (see Xenos et al., 2014; also Zukin et al., 2006). There were relatively few differences across the three countries, with the 12 acts staying in more or less the same rank order of occurrence. The exceptions are the two acts of "persuade others to vote" and "wear a symbol," which young Americans were much more likely to have done. This can be attributed to the 2012 presidential election having occurred within the year timeframe that the survey asked about.

Participants were also asked if they engaged in these activities online, offline, or in some combination of online or offline forms. Figure 20.2 shows that in all three countries, most of these political acts are no longer predominantly engaged in offline by young people. In fact, participation happened online for

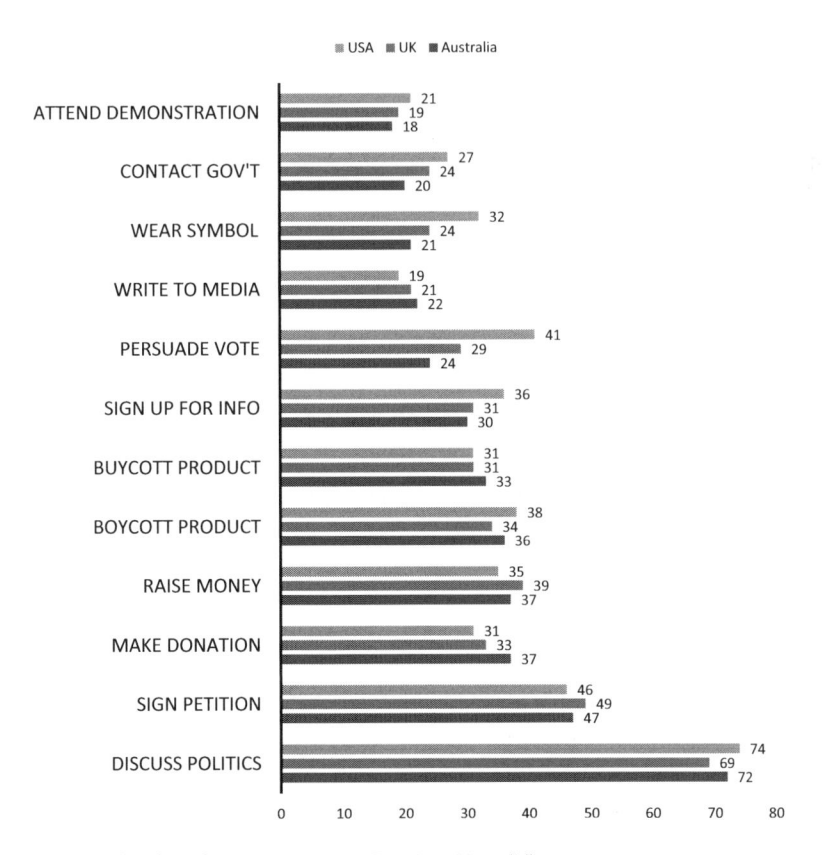

■ USA ■ UK ■ Australia

Act	USA	UK	Australia
ATTEND DEMONSTRATION	21	19	18
CONTACT GOV'T	27	24	20
WEAR SYMBOL	32	24	21
WRITE TO MEDIA	19	21	22
PERSUADE VOTE	41	29	24
SIGN UP FOR INFO	36	31	30
BUYCOTT PRODUCT	31	31	33
BOYCOTT PRODUCT	38	34	36
RAISE MONEY	35	39	37
MAKE DONATION	31	33	37
SIGN PETITION	46	49	47
DISCUSS POLITICS	74	69	72

FIGURE 20.1 Individual Political Engagement in Previous Year (%).

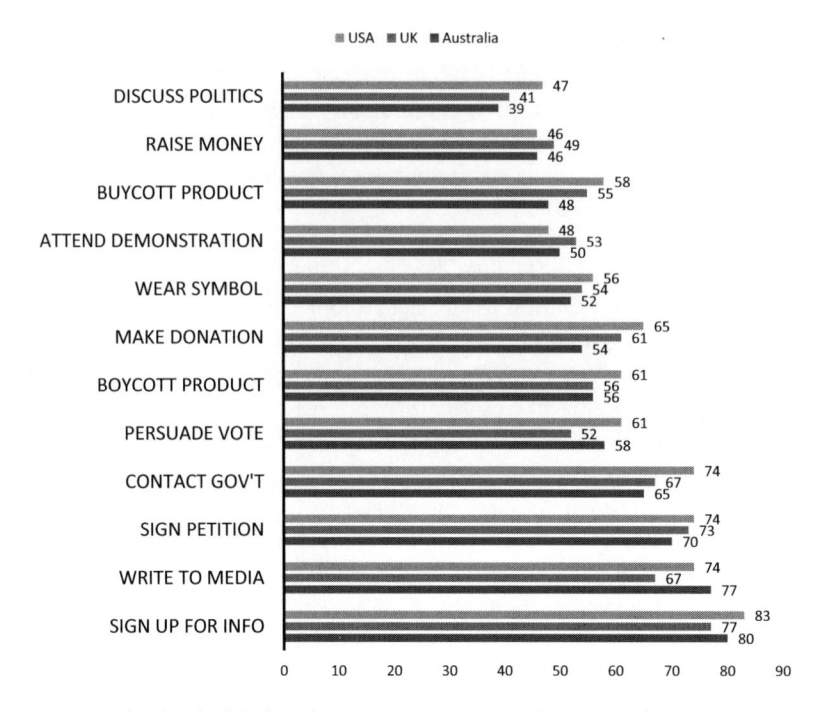

FIGURE 20.2 Percent of Individual Political Engagement Acts Performed Online.

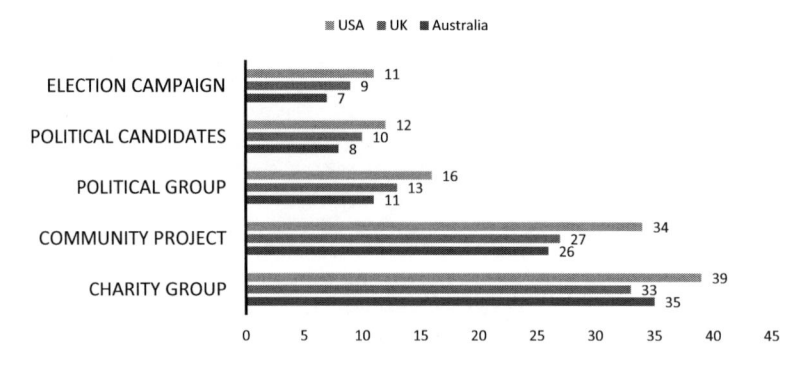

(USA, UK, Australia)

- DISCUSS POLITICS: 47, 41, 39
- RAISE MONEY: 46, 49, 46
- BUYCOTT PRODUCT: 58, 55, 48
- ATTEND DEMONSTRATION: 48, 53, 50
- WEAR SYMBOL: 56, 54, 52
- MAKE DONATION: 65, 61, 54
- BOYCOTT PRODUCT: 61, 56, 56
- PERSUADE VOTE: 61, 52, 58
- CONTACT GOV'T: 74, 67, 65
- SIGN PETITION: 74, 73, 70
- WRITE TO MEDIA: 74, 67, 77
- SIGN UP FOR INFO: 83, 77, 80

FIGURE 20.3 Percent Involved in Collective Political Engagement.

(USA, UK, Australia)

- ELECTION CAMPAIGN: 11, 9, 7
- POLITICAL CANDIDATES: 12, 10, 8
- POLITICAL GROUP: 16, 13, 11
- COMMUNITY PROJECT: 34, 27, 26
- CHARITY GROUP: 39, 33, 35

over two thirds of young people who signed up for information, wrote to the media, signed a petition, and contacted government. There were only two acts that clearly remain offline for a majority of young people across all three countries: raising money and discussing politics. The majority preference to discuss politics mainly offline and in person is significant for thinking about how political talk occurs (or not) on social media platforms and within young people's networks. We will return to this in the next section. There were some national-level differences, such as that young Americans were more likely to go online for boycotting, "buycotting" (deliberately purchasing a company's or a country's products in support of their policies, or to counter a boycott), making donations, and contacting government; this could be attributed to the comparative better development and range of these consumer mechanisms that enable these acts online in the United States over the other two countries, especially Australia.

Our second political engagement measure was designed to capture activities that specifically involved working with others in organizations and groups. We labeled this *collective political engagement*. Similar to individual political engagement, we sought to capture a wide array of types of engagement, so included items related to "political groups or causes," "nonpolitical or charitable groups," and groups associated with political candidates or parties. In all, we asked participants whether they joined, worked, or volunteered, with five different kinds of groups, allowing them to count activities that may or may not have involved the Internet to varying degrees. Figure 20.3 shows that young people were less likely to have participated in collective political engagement than most of the individual acts; in fact, an average of 54% of young people across the three countries had not been involved in a group. Young people in all three countries were more likely to have been involved in a charity group or community project than a more explicitly political group, and young Americans were more likely to have been involved in all five groups than were Australians or Britons. Figure 20.4 shows whether Internet use featured in young people's collective political engagement, and interestingly the three more overtly political groups were much more likely than the charity group or a community project to involve the Internet.

We ran regression analyses on both individual and collective political engagement in the three countries to examine the extent to which both were related to social media use, new citizenship norms, and political socialization factors, while controlling for other known determinants of participation (for details on key measures, see Xenos, Vromen, & Loader, 2014). Overall, we confirmed that social media use is positively related to both kinds of engagement in all three countries. We also found other forms of active political interest, such as the frequency of political talk in respondents' homes and families during their childhoods, were significantly associated with individual political engagement across the three countries. We also found that the extent to which young people responded positively to survey items derived from theoretical work on new, actualizing civic norms (and subjected to standard reliability analysis) further predicted individual and group engagement. Overall, our results demonstrate that new norms of political engagement are of critical importance in understanding contemporary youth engagement. The clearest pattern was a positive relationship between newer, self-actualizing civic norms

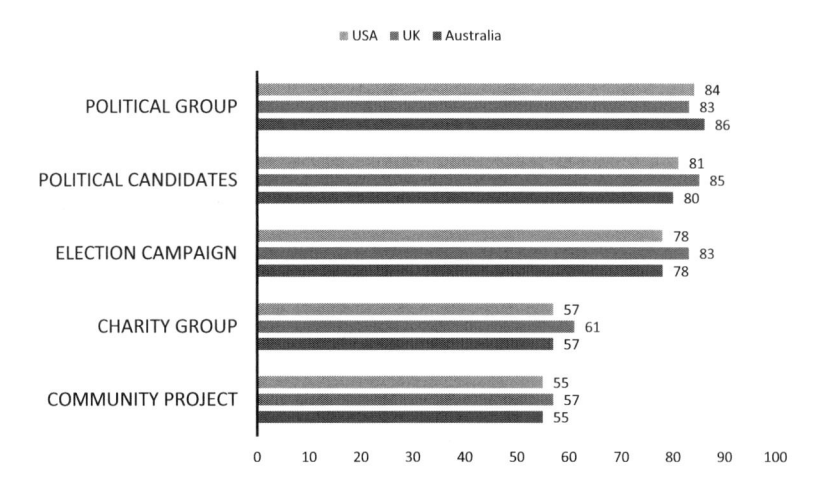

FIGURE 20.4 Percent of Collective Political Engagement Involving Some Internet Use.

and political engagement. The results were positive, significant, and consistent across the three countries for both individual political engagement and collective political engagement. Motivating our interest in doing this research was to identify whether socioeconomic resources, such as high levels of education and privileged backgrounds, were still the main predictors of subsequent political engagement; or whether widespread social media use was now having an equalizing effect. Overall, while we found, like most other studies of political participation, that prior interest in politics remains a key determinant of political engagement, our findings demonstrated that social media use is also a strong factor in youth political engagement, and that this relationship holds across different levels of socioeconomic status. The Internet and everyday social media use is helping to make engagement with politics accessible to an increasingly diverse range of young people in the three advanced democracies we studied (for more detail on these findings see Xenos et al., 2014).

Young People Use Social Media for Politics, in Symbolic, Expressive, and Active Ways but Are Also Wary of the Conflict That Politics Entails

The second stage of our study was an examination of how young people use social media to engage in politics. We argue that we need to see social media as a distinct space for undertaking politics, not only as an independent variable shaping subsequent offline forms of politics. As we have already shown above, the demarcation between offline and online forms of political engagement is rapidly dissolving for young people, with online being the first port of call for most ways of engaging. It is important to focus on explaining the politics that happens on social media and value it in of itself as active and expressive modes of engagement for young people. We particularly focused on Facebook, due to its near ubiquitous use by 90% of young people in our three countries. Here, we created a measure of Facebook-based political engagement built on nine indicators of Facebook use for politics that adapted measures used in Pew Internet Studies (see Rainie, Smith, Scholzman, Brady, & Verba, 2012).

Figure 20.5 shows a majority of young people in the three countries hear about, learn about, and follow links to news stories about politics via Facebook. That Facebook is the first port of call, for a

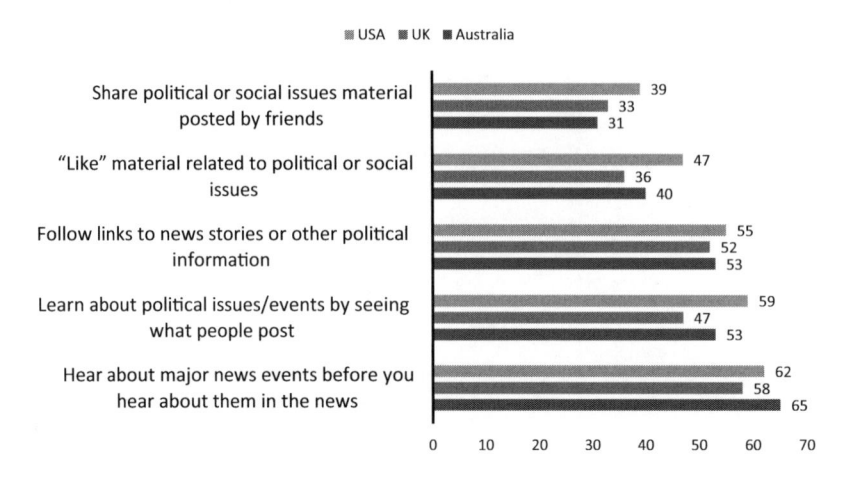

FIGURE 20.5 Using Facebook for Communicative Politics.

majority of young people, in finding out what is happening in the political world emphasizes its everyday ubiquity. It also highlights the importance of Thorson's (2014) social curators who provide links to news stories and share material posted by others within networks, for the majority to read and learn from. Figure 20.5 also demonstrates there is symbolic communicative importance for many young people in "liking" material their friends and connections post in their social networks. This simple act is politicized as it becomes the same as "sharing" and is visible in friends' newsfeeds, thus revealing both personalized social solidarity and networked political preferences.

Figure 20.6 on proactive forms of engagement includes using Facebook to enable offline forms of political action or online political debate. Overall, these more expressive and overt actions on Facebook are used less often by young people than the communicative and symbolic forms of political engagement in Figure 20.5. Between 34% and 40% comment about politics on social media; partisan electoral-based politics in particular appears to form only a small part of most young people's everyday experience on Facebook. The least common act of encouraging others how to vote suggests Facebook is not more conducive than traditional contexts as a space for young people's election-based discussion. That young people in the United States were most likely to do all of the Facebook-based political acts can probably be attributed to the 2012 presidential election having occurred in the year before the survey was in the field, rather than pointing to a greater level of politicization and dutiful norms among American youth. Nevertheless, that only 19% of young Australians encouraged others to vote may be due to compulsory electoral registration and voting in Australia, and less focus on turnout and mobilizing to "get out the vote."

Facebook has broad appeal as an avenue for youth engagement, and the communicative, symbolic, and expressive forms of Facebook-based politics are the most widespread acts. Only 6% of young people who use Facebook have *never* engaged in any of the nine acts in Figures 20.5 and 20.6. Considering just the proactive political acts on Facebook, we still find large majorities of young people have engaged in at least one of these, as only 27% have *never* done so. However, our qualitative data revealed that young people also have a considerable ambivalence about doing politics on Facebook, as highlighted below. This likely reflects the high levels of skepticism and feelings of exclusion many young people hold about formal, electoral politics, in many advanced democracies (see Henn & Foard, 2012; Amna & Ekman, 2013).

We ran regression analyses on a combined index of Facebook-based political engagement to see whether everyday making citizenship norms, prior forms of political socialization, political interest, or

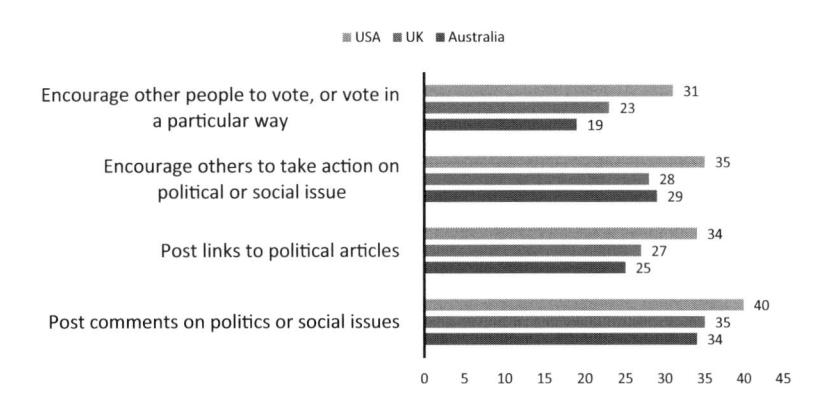

■ USA ■ UK ■ Australia

Act	USA	UK	Australia
Encourage other people to vote, or vote in a particular way	31	23	19
Encourage others to take action on political or social issue	35	28	29
Post links to political articles	34	27	25
Post comments on politics or social issues	40	35	34

FIGURE 20.6 Using Facebook for Proactive Political Engagement.

individual demographics were having direct effects on young people's social media-based participation (for full data analysis see Vromen et al., 2016). Overall, our results suggest that demographic indicators, such as gender, ethnicity, and level of education, may not be as centrally important for explaining young people's use of Facebook for politics as they are for offline and other Internet-based forms of participation (see Gil de Zúñiga & Shahin, 2015; Henn & Foard, 2012). At the same time, our analysis confirms that prior political socialization experiences, such as talking about politics at home, and norm-based expressions of dutiful citizenship, operationalized as attention to politics and elections, remain important factors in explaining this form of social media-based political engagement (see Xenos et al., 2014; Gil de Zúñiga & Shahin, 2015). However, this finding is not straightforward, as it is not only a more dutiful orientation toward politics that influences Facebook-based political engagement. Everyday making citizenship norms—operationalized from attitudinal items that show creative, horizontal, and ad hoc forms of engagement with politics are preferable to young people—are also very good predictors of variance in the use of Facebook for politics in all three countries. Lastly, the more time spent on social media may lead to more Facebook-based political engagement. This is not surprising, as the social use of Facebook and its networked functionality relies on young people using it frequently and for fun. That the ongoing importance of dutiful norms of citizenship were found to be intertwined with emerging everyday maker norms suggests that we need to dig deeper into how young people themselves understand the benefits and limitations of using Facebook for politics. This could mean, for example, that young people who are interested in politics may relate to it on Facebook in a nondutiful way, instead using humor and creativity with localized, personalized experiences to reflexively understand and communicate about politics.

The frequencies and regression analysis all demonstrated that social media provides a new way of engaging with politics, and it is clearly an important space for all kinds of young people who are already paying attention to politics and appreciate the horizontal affordances that social media use provides, including a permanent connection to their social networks (see Vorderer et al., 2016). Yet, young people were less likely to express themselves through proactive social media–based engagement than more symbolic or information-based uses of Facebook. Why is this the case? To find out, we used qualitative online discussion groups with young people in the three countries, recruiting participants from our original survey samples who were above or below average in their levels of political engagement, and from high versus low socioeconomic status groups. In response to our set of questions, it became clear that a majority of the young people participating in the online discussion groups were negative about engaging in politics on social media. Politics was simply equated with conflict, but was not based on a partisan reading of politics. Indeed, politicians and parties featured rarely in their explanation, as would be expected of those with dutiful citizenship norms. Their disquiet was instead about the level of public disagreement with friends and family on a range of political issues; others were concerned about saying something that was "wrong," some were just interested in social media remaining purely social, thus seeing politics as something distinct and separate from their everyday lives. For example, the quote below reveals a skeptical viewpoint, suggesting that politics is better done in person where there is less chance of misunderstanding or conflict:

> I am fairly willing to put my views out there, but generally I don't go out of my ways to. When people were changing their profile pictures to the equal sign for marriage equality, that was something I was willing to do, maybe with a quote or something. After Obama won his second term I definitely had some cheery tweets about it, but nothing that could really piss anyone off. I try to express my views more in real life than online because I don't think people are able to handle

those conversations maturely and people end up getting in fights that have nothing to do with politics and a lot more to do with name calling.

(female, US)

While clearly in the minority, some young people were more positive about using social media for politics, as it was a useful source of information and an important space for political expression. For example:

I do think it is good. Many people my age (early twenties) have switched off the traditional media, and it is rare to meet somebody who regularly watches the news or reads a newspaper. It is therefore important to spark their engagement in other ways. If they are actively reading, engaging, and being informed by conversations on social media sites, then it creates a more informed public.

(female, Australia)

Overall, our survey of young people in three advanced democracies demonstrated that social media, particularly Facebook, has become an everyday source of news and information on politics and is increasingly used by young people to show a personalized, symbolic solidarity with political issues. These findings underpin our argument that youth engagement through social media platforms is a form of political participation worthy of attention, and further point to the utility of theoretical frameworks that focus on the emergence of new citizenship norms for interpreting and understanding this growing phenomenon. In contrast, substantially fewer young people in all three countries were willing or had experiences of engaging in a more dutiful or traditional mode of political engagement by taking more proactive stances on Facebook that encouraged others to take political action or vote. This was also reflected in our online focus groups, in which young people were reluctant to actively do politics on Facebook for fear of conflict or being corrected (see Vromen et al., 2016 for further analysis). This further reinforced our finding in Figures 20.1 and 20.2 that discussing politics with others is the key participatory act that young people still tend to do offline rather than online (similarly see Ekstrom, 2016).

Despite their own reluctance, the young people who participated in our qualitative research still saw promise in using social media to connect them to broader processes of formal politics. Perhaps somewhat unexpectedly, when asked the question, "What do you think about politicians using Facebook and Twitter?" our participants were generally favorable in their responses. There was little surprise that politicians were adopting social media, and many respondents considered it essential for them to use such communication channels as a means of keeping up to date. As one person remarked, "if politicians do not connect through social media then they don't connect at all" (male, Australia). This was especially evident where they believed that it helped politicians to "connect" with young people. For example,

[Social media] does, in fact, have the potential for getting the "audience" to give feedback and have discussions, even if it is just among themselves. They can reply to posts and then to each other's replies to get a good discussion going that way.

(female, US)

While there was a strong expectation of a normalization of the use of Facebook and Twitter by politicians, with the possibility for two-way interactive engagement, there was also a concern about the capacity of politicians to use social media appropriately. Our respondents were, for example, aware that politicians rarely answered online queries personally or posted content themselves, nor did respondents realistically expect them to always do so. What they tended to object to was that they received no replies, that politicians never engaged in discussions in person, or that they appeared unaware of the interactive and participatory capacities of social media platforms (see Loader et al., 2016 for further analysis).

Conclusion: Future of Political Participation Will Be Online but . . . We Also Need to Focus on the Opportunities Politics Provides for Young People

This chapter on The Civic Network project provides ample evidence that young people in Australia, the United States, and the United Kingdom are not apathetic or disaffected from broader ideals of civic and political engagement. They engage in individual acts of political participation online, and particularly via new communicative political acts facilitated by social media platforms like Facebook. Horizontal, easily accessible, everyday social networks that make them permanently online and connected are making it easier than ever before for young people to have a political voice. There also remains an important interplay between the emergence of new, engaged, and actualizing norms of citizenship that foster individualized participation, *with* the maintenance of the ideal dutiful citizen. Thus, we caution against generalizations of the new turn to online political engagement to include all young people, as significant barriers to engagement remain that have much to do with the structure, openness, and appeal of broader political systems. Young people in our online focus groups expressed a reluctance to actively engage in political talk for fear of conflict within their broader social networks; this also reflects the lack of openness and responsiveness that young people perceive both in political systems and the everyday networks they sit within. If we want the "networked young citizen" to feel efficacious, that their voices are heard, and that their actions matter, then fundamental changes to the adversarial and hierarchical nature of formal politics itself will need to occur.

References

Amna, E., & Ekman, J. (2013). Standby citizens: Diverse faces of political passivity. *European Political Science Review*, *6*(2), 261–281.

Bakker, T. P., and Vreese, C. H. de (2011). Good news for the future? Young people, good news for the future? Young people, Internet use, and political participation. *Communication Research*, *38*(4), 451–470.

Bang, H. (2005). Among everyday makers and expert citizens. In J. Newman (Ed.), *Remaking governance* (pp. 159–179). Bristol: The Policy Press.

Beck, U. (1992). *Risk society: Towards a new modernity*. London: Sage.

Benkler, Y. (2006). *The wealth of networks: How social production transforms markets and freedom*. New Haven, CT: Yale University Press.

Bennett, L. (1998). The uncivic culture: Communication, identity, and the rise of lifestyle politics. *PS: Political Science and Politics*, *31*(4), 740–761.

Bennett, W. L., Wells, C., & Rank, A. (2009). Young citizens and civic learning: Two paradigms of citizenship in the digital age. *Citizenship Studies*, *13*(2), 105–120.

Cammaerts, B., Bruter, M., Banaji, S., Harrison, S., & Anstead, N. (2014). The myth of youth apathy: Young European's critical attitudes towards democratic life. *American Behavioral Scientist*, *58*(5), 645–664.

Collin, P. (2015). *Young citizens and political participation in a digital society: Addressing the democratic disconnect*. Basingstoke: Palgrave Macmillan.

Dalton, R. J. (2008). Citizenship norms and the expansion of political participation. *Political Studies*, *56*(1), 76–98.

Ekstrom, M. (2016). Young people's everyday political talk: A social achievement of democratic engagement. *Journal of Youth Studies*, *19*(1), 1–19.

Fieldhouse, E., Tranmer, M., & Russell, A. (2007). Something about young people or something about elections? Electoral participation of young people in Europe: Evidence from a multilevel analysis of the European social survey. *European Journal of Political Research*, *46*(6), 797–822.

Gil de Zúñiga, H., Jung, N., & Valenzuela, S. (2012). Social media use for news and individuals' social capital, civic engagement and political participation. *Journal of Computer-Mediated Communication*, *17*(3), 319–336.

Gil de Zúñiga, H., & Shahin, S. (2015). Social media and their impact on civic participation. In H. Gil de Zúñiga (Ed.), *New technologies and civic engagement: New agendas in communication* (pp. 78–90). New York: Routledge.

Henn, M., & Foard, N. (2012) Young people, political participation and trust in Britain. *Parliamentary Affairs*, 65(1), 47–67. doi:10.1093/pa/gsr046

Jenkins, H. (2006). *Convergence culture: Where old and new media collide*. New York: New York University Press.

Kahne, J., Lee, N., & Feezell, J. T. (2013). The civic and political significance of online participatory cultures among youth transitioning to adulthood. *Journal of Information Technology & Politics*, *10*(1), 1–20.

Loader, B. L., Vromen, A., Xenos, M. A. (2014). The networked young citizen: Social media, political participation and civic engagement. *Information, Communication and Society*, *17*(2), 143–150.

Loader, B. L., Vromen, A., Xenos, M. A. (2016). Performing for the young networked citizen? Celebrity politics, social networking and the political engagement of young people. *Media, Culture and Society*, *38*(3), 400–419.

Norris, P. (2002). *Democratic phoenix: Reinventing democratic activism*. Cambridge: Cambridge University Press.

Perrin, A. (2015, October 8). *Social media usage 2005–2015*. Pew Research Centre. Retrieved from file:///Users/ariadnevromen/Downloads/PI_2015–10–08_Social-Networking-Usage-2005–2015_FINAL.pdf

Poushter, J. (2016, February 22). *Smartphone ownership and Internet usage continues to climb in emerging economies*. Pew Research Centre. Retrieved from file:///Users/ariadnevromen/Downloads/pew_research_center_global_technology_report_final_february_22__2016.pdf

Rainie, L., Smith, A., Schlozman, K. L., Brady, H., & Verba, S. (2012). *Social media and political engagement*. Retrieved from www.pewInternet.org/files/old-media//Files/Reports/2012/PIP_SocialMediaAndPoliticalEngagement_PDF.pdf

Rainie, L., & Wellman, B. (2012). *Networked: The new social operating system*. Cambridge, MA: MIT Press.

Schlozman, K.L, Verba, S., & Brady, H. E. (2010). Weapon of the strong? Participatory inequality and the Internet. *Perspectives on Politics*, *8*(2), 487–509.

Stoker, G. (2006). *Why politics matters: Making democracy work*. Basingstoke: Palgrave.

Thorson, K. (2014). Facing an uncertain reception: Young citizens and political interaction on Facebook. *Information, Communication and Society*, *17*(2), 203–216.

Van Biezen, I., Mair, P., & Poguntke, T. (2012). Going, going, ... gone? The decline of party membership in contemporary Europe. *European Journal of Political Research*, *51*(1), 24–56.

Vorderer, P., Krömer, N., & Schneider, F. M. (2016). Permanently online—permanently connected: Explorations into university students' use of social media and mobile smart devices. *Computers in Human Behavior*, *63*, 694–703. doi:10.1016/j.chb.2016.05.085

Vromen, A., Loader, B. L., Xenos, M. A., & Bailo, F. (2016). Everyday making through Facebook engagement: Young citizens' political interactions in Australia, UK and USA. *Political Studies*, *64*(3), 513–533.

Xenos, M. A., Vromen, A., & Loader, B. L. (2014). The great equalizer? Patterns of social media use and youth political engagement. *Information, Communication and Society*, *17*(2), 151–167.

Zukin, C., Keeter, S., Andolina, M., Jenkins, K., & Delli Carpini, M. X. (2006). *A new engagement? Political participation, civic life, and the changing American citizen*. New York: Oxford University Press.

21
Permanent Entertainment and Political Behavior

R. Lance Holbert, Carina Weinmann, and Nicholas Robinson

As an area of study, political entertainment research is still in its infant stages. Nevertheless, over the past decade, it has become a rapidly growing, multifaceted endeavor focused on a variety of media outlets and formats (for overviews see Compton, 2011; Gray, Jones, & Thompson, 2009). Although scholars have called for a more systematic, well-organized approach to better understanding political entertainment media (Holbert & Young, 2013), no one dominant theoretical foundation has taken hold, and a strong argument can be made that a good percentage of this research is best defined as atheoretical (Holbert, Hill, & Lee, 2014). The lack of strong theoretical and empirical foundations prior to the rise of today's permanently online, permanently connected (POPC) existence (see Vorderer, Krömer, & Schneider, 2016) creates challenges and opportunities for studying political entertainment content and its impact on political behavior. Political entertainment is pervasive across a wide range of digital, social, and mobile media platforms. As a result, it has become more unwieldy but also of greater potential significance as the media environment has evolved. This chapter will detail the current state of political entertainment media research and make an argument for the need to develop multiple research agendas grounded in the study of enjoyment and appreciation. Building on this line of reasoning, an overview of the changing nature of political entertainment media consumption in a POPC environment is posited. The proposed effects offered in this work derive from empirical questions that can serve as a foundation for future research.

Conceptualizing Citizens' Motivations to Engage With Political Entertainment

Political entertainment media researchers need a better understanding of the explanatory principles underlying their research agendas. Clarifying these principles may be of significant epistemological value by offering the possibility to organize the field theoretically (Holbert et al., 2014; Pavitt, 2010). In particular, these explanatory principles indicate scholars' views concerning citizens as users of political entertainment media—how audience motivations define the nature and expectations of someone's media consumption. Properly conceptualizing these motivations is a necessary, but not sufficient, condition for explaining and evaluating the effects of political entertainment in a POPC environment.

The Traditional View: Understanding and Consistency

A majority of early research on political entertainment media adopted explanatory principles (e.g., understanding, consistency) that are anchors for the study of news (Holbert et al., 2014). Understanding refers to the basic human motivation to make sense of the environment in order to maximize utility (i.e., achieve their goals) within it. A dominant understanding-based theory in political communication is agenda setting (see McCombs, 2005). Obviously, this motivation is closely related to the acquisition of knowledge and information. Numerous extant political entertainment research efforts embrace this explanatory principle. For example, studies that look at political knowledge as the outcome of political satire consumption match this profile (e.g., Cao, 2008; Hollander, 2005; Xenos & Becker, 2009). Understanding-based research of this kind was driven by a desire to reveal the normative value of political entertainment media to generate positive democratic processes and outcomes.

The principle of consistency denotes humans' tendency to approach a given phenomenon, react to that phenomenon, and make decisions in accordance with pre-existing values and worldviews (cf. Cialdini, Trost, & Newsom, 1995). One prominent consistency-based theory used widely in political communication is cognition dissonance (Festinger, 1957). Much research on partisan selective exposure and avoidance of specific media content (e.g., Stroud, 2008) is best defined as addressing consistency-oriented questions (see Knobloch-Westerwick, 2014). Many political entertainment studies have explored the role of political ideology on the consumption and processing of political entertainment programs (e.g., Hmielowski, Holbert, & Lee, 2011; LaMarre, Landreville, & Beam, 2009). The consistency orientation has been most often used to reveal the potential for political entertainment media to produce differential, persuasion-oriented effects (e.g., biased processing producing distinct interpretations of content) within an electorate.

These two principles demonstrate scholars' view of the political entertainment media audience as consisting of either information seekers or consistency-driven consumers. While understanding and consistency have proven valuable perspectives for this area of study, political entertainment engagement and its effects cannot be explained in full by either of the two explanatory principles. This realization is all the more evident in a POPC information environment. More specifically, citizens' motivations for understanding and consistency set a clear focus on the "political" portion of political entertainment but neglect the latter "entertainment" component that is integral to understanding *political entertainment* media influence. Equal value should be given to the former and latter terms. To focus too much on understanding and consistency leads to treating political entertainment as a functional equivalent of news (i.e., the same processes that define news influence define political entertainment effects), and the field would be well served to shift away from this mindset given that it is offering an incomplete picture of why citizens engage political media.

An Expansion of Explanatory Principles: Enjoyment and Appreciation

Individuals' motivations to use entertaining media content, their experiences during exposure, and the possible effects of this exposure have been the subject of entertainment theory and research for several decades (see Bryant & Vorderer, 2006; Zillmann & Vorderer, 2000). This area of research is most clearly located within mass communication and media psychology, not political communication. However, scholars have started to introduce this perspective into research on media that retains a decidedly political bent (e.g., Bartsch & Schneider, 2014; Roth, Weinmann, Schneider, Hopp, & Vorderer, 2014; Weinmann, 2017).

In contrast to the principles of understanding and consistency, entertainment-based research adopts a perspective that is more affective than cognitive. From this vantage point, media users are conceptualized as entertainment-seeking creatures who use media in order to increase or maintain their well-being. Following recent theoretical conceptualizations, this well-being during media exposure may be described in terms of two different processes, enjoyment and appreciation (e.g., Lewis, Tamborini, & Weber, 2014; Oliver & Bartsch, 2010; Wirth, Hofer, & Schramm, 2012). The first seeks a positive affective state and involves experiences such as fun, pleasure, relaxation, or suspense (e.g., Vorderer, Klimmt, & Ritterfeld, 2004). Thus, the motivation behind this type of well-being, which is mostly referred to as "enjoyment," is purely hedonic. The second process is characterized by mixed emotions and driven by eudaimonic motivations, like the desire to gain deeper insights and to experience a sense of meaningfulness based on the fulfilment of human virtues (see Oliver, 2008; Oliver & Bartsch, 2010). Alternative explanations of how experiences of appreciation may be explained refer to the fulfilment of the intrinsic needs (e.g., autonomy, competence, relatedness) suggested by self-determination theory (Deci & Ryan, 2000; Ryan & Deci, 2000; Vorderer & Ritterfeld, 2009).

Applying these explanatory principles to citizens' consumption of political entertainment media allows for the "entertainment" to be brought into the fold of this area of research. This approach defines citizens' political entertainment engagement less by a desire for information or cognitive consistency and more by a desire to have fun and pleasure and/or to feel autonomous, competent, and socially connected. Both types of experiences have been found to play a distinctive role in citizens' engagement with political entertainment media (e.g., Mattheiß et al., 2013; Roth, 2015; Roth et al., 2014; Weinmann, 2017), not only in terms of their occurrence, but also their predictive value concerning further effects such as interest in political issues. Thus, taking these experiences into account may generate greater predictive power above and beyond understanding- and consistency-driven questions. The adoption of the mass communication-based, entertainment perspective provides heuristic value in that new and innovative questions may be raised by political communication researchers. In addition, this shift may hold distinct predictive utility when seeking to better understand what is leading citizens to engage political content in a POPC world.

Enjoyment- and Appreciation-Seeking Motivations and Media Use as Political Behavior

Relaxation, amusement, forgetting about one's problems, passing time, and other purely hedonic factors have been identified as predictors of exposure to political comedy and late-night political talk shows (Baum, 2002, 2005; Brewer & Cao, 2006; Browning & Sweetser, 2014; Diddi & LaRose, 2006). Viewers of a range of "soft news" US television programs, from *Oprah* to *The Daily Show* to *Leno*, report their primary motivation for watching is (hedonic) entertainment, not learning (Brewer & Cao, 2006; Diddi & LaRose, 2006). Pure hedonism, however, does not fully explain the use of entertainment media in general (Bartsch, 2012; Knobloch-Westerwick et al., 2012; Oliver & Raney, 2011) or political entertainment in particular (Mattheiß et al., 2013; Roth et al., 2014). Eudaimonic motivation offers a more parsimonious explanation for political entertainment use: audiences tune into programs like *The Daily Show* in the United States or the *heute-show* in Germany in pursuit of both enjoyment and what Oliver and Bartsch (2010) describe as "deeper meaning ... and the motivation to elaborate thoughts and feelings" (p. 76). Having fun is an important factor determining exposure to political entertainment, but the kind of entertainment experience that best predicts exposure is more eudaimonic than hedonic. For example, political talk show audiences in Germany identified information, provoking thoughts, and social interaction as their primary motivations for watching. Purely hedonic motivations like relaxation and escapism were among the least frequently cited (Roth et al., 2014). Experimental evidence has found that exposure to soft news triggers emotional responses characteristic of other eudaimonic entertainment experiences, and that such involvement can lead to increased reflection on and interest in political issues (Bartsch & Schneider, 2014). While hedonic tendencies do explain a portion of the popularity of soft news, audiences are also seeking more meaningful experiences from political entertainment.

Enjoyment, Appreciation, and Traditional Political Media Use

The same hedonic desires associated with watching movies, listening to music, and consuming political entertainment are at least sometimes predictive of hard news use (Diddi & LaRose, 2006; Roth et al., 2014). Escapism, the use of media to cheer up, relax, and forget about stressors, was significantly related to both comedic news and cable TV news viewing (Diddi & LaRose, 2006). Similarly, viewers of political talk shows in Germany were more likely to have hedonic experiences, even when these shows are generally regarded as rather serious and informative (Roth et al., 2014). But, as with political entertainment, hedonic motivations do not tell the whole story behind hard news use.

The eudaimonic drive for a "sense of insight, meaning, and social connectedness" motivates hard news consumption on both traditional and online platforms (Bartsch & Oliver, 2017, p. 81). Social utility, especially the desire to prepare for political discussions with others, appears to be a particularly powerful motivation (Johnson & Kaye, 2003; Kaye & Johnson, 2002). Individuals who frequently discuss politics with their family, friends, and coworkers are more likely to consume political news (Norris, 2000) and are more likely to watch televised debates (Kenski & Jamieson, 2011; Thorson et al., 2015). Additionally, watching televised debates with others is associated with greater appreciation of the experience and a greater likelihood to watch debates in the future (Thorson et al., 2015). The link between political discussion and traditional news use holds for online hard news as well. Kaye and Johnson's (2004) survey of Internet users found that entertainment and social interaction was the second most important predictor of accessing political information online, exceeding general political information seeking and trailing only guidance about specific political issues and particular politician's stances. Together, these findings suggest that while the desire to be informed is a motivator for hard news use, information seeking occurs partly in service of a larger eudaimonic goal. Citizens watch the news and read the paper to facilitate discussions of current events and politics with meaningful others in their lives. Given the ease of forging and maintaining social ties over the Internet, the role of social interaction as a motivator for political media use is a particularly important locus of research. And social interactions of this kind are grounded and best understood from enjoyment and appreciation perspectives.

Enjoyment, Appreciation, and New Media Use

Social media platforms like Facebook, Twitter, blogs, and YouTube are not merely entertaining diversions from work or school. Increasingly, they are a source of political news and a venue for political discussion (Gil de Zúñiga, Jung, & Valenzuela, 2012; Kushin & Kitchener, 2009; Robertson, Vatrapu, & Medina, 2010; Vitak et al., 2011). With the widespread adoption of smartphones and other mobile, Internet-connected devices, social media now offers opportunities to engage with political content all day and every day. As with political entertainment and hard news, information-seeking and consistency-seeking predict a portion of users' engagement with political content (Bobkowski, 2015; Gil de Zúñiga, Jung, &

Valenzuela, 2012; Macafee, 2013). However, patterns of use of social media as a tool for political engagement underscores the importance of hedonic and eudaimonic motivations as well.

Information- and consistency-seeking explanations are relatively poor approaches for studying political engagement on social media, compared to analyzing hard news. If citizens look to social media for information, their postings should include questions about policy stances and political ideology. If they are seeking consistency, their posts should exhibit discussions about policy and ideology. But in practice, conversations on candidates' social media pages are dominated by personal questions (Ancu & Cozma, 2009; Sweetser & Weaver-Lariscy, 2007). Citizens are much more likely to ask about a candidate's hobbies than his or her position on tax policy, for example. Furthermore, candidates do not seem inclined to use social media to engage in political debates. Their postings on SNSs tend toward soft, noncontroversial topics like music, sports, and hobbies (Bronstein, 2013; Holbert et al., 2007). When they do discuss political issues on social media, campaigns tend to stick to less controversial subjects (Bronstein, 2013).

Entertainment-seeking motivation, especially the eudaimonic drive for social connection, offers a stronger explanation for this type of political engagement through social media. Macafee (2013) probed Facebook users' motivations for engaging in four types of online political activity: posting political comments on others' pages, posting political news stories, posting political status updates, and liking candidates and parties. Principle components analysis revealed social motivations like engaging in discussion and finding out what others have to say were present in the dominant factors explaining three of the four activities. For liking candidates and parties pages, self-presentation (i.e., the desire to demonstrate knowledge to others) was the dominant factor. Notably, information and entertainment were also significant factors for all four activities (Macafee, 2013), reflecting the convergence of information-seeking, hedonic, and eudaimonic motivations.

Similar results reflecting the importance of social motivations have emerged from qualitative and quantitative research across diverse social media platforms including Facebook (Levin & Barak-Brandes, 2014), Twitter (Park, 2013; Thorson et al., 2015), and blogs (Chen, 2015; Grueling & Kilian, 2014), as well as in predecessors of social media like online discussion boards and chat rooms (Kaye & Johnson, 2006). The desire for social connection is a common thread connecting engagement with online political content. In some cases, this eudaimonic motivation appears more powerful than seeking information or consistency. Users of political message boards and chat rooms reported social interaction as a primary motivation for engagement (Kaye & Johnson, 2006). More recently, Grueling and Kilian's analysis of bloggers found that "social interaction with other blog users is the *main* motivation for blogging on German political blogs," (2014, p. 221) exceeding the desire for information and self-expression. Posting, sharing, and viewing political information on social media cannot be interpreted as an exclusively *informational* activity—the *social* portion of social media matters.

The ability to use social media in conjunction with traditional media forms may be increasing the importance of social connection motivations for engaging political content. More than 70% of Internet users report multitasking while online, with television viewing and listening to the radio rating as the most common associated activities (Pilotta & Schultz, 2005). Debates are an appealing focal point for political multitasking research, because they function as both political and social events (Gottfried, Hardy, Holbert, Winneg, & Jamieson, in press; Houston, Hawthorne, Spialek, Greenwood, & McKinney, 2013; McKinney, Houston, & Hawthorne, 2014). Before the 2012 US presidential debates, almost two thirds of Americans said they planned to watch while multitasking with a web-enabled device. The popularity of watching debates while discussing them on social media suggests audiences are enhancing the eudaimonic experience of political media with social interaction, and survey research supports this conclusion. Individuals who use Facebook and Twitter while watching debates report higher levels of enjoyment and appreciation, and Twitter users are likely to watch more debates and stay tuned into each debate longer (Thorson et al., 2015). Furthermore, the most prolific debate tweeters are those with the greatest interest in campaigns, reinforcing the connection between eudaimonic motivation (i.e., interest in politics) and social media use (McKinney, Houston, & Hawthorne, 2014).

POPC Political Entertainment Media Engagement

When viewing political media from the explanatory principles of enjoyment and appreciation, a more focused picture emerges for how citizens engage politics in a POPC information environment. Being permanently online and permanently connected affords citizens an opportunity to *supplement traditional political media experiences* (e.g., news, debates, political advertisements) with digital, social, and mobile political media content that may provide some enjoyment or appreciation value not offered through the traditional media outlets. Citizens can turn to their mobile digital platforms to engage their social networks in commentary on the traditional political media content they are consuming, see how elites are reacting on Twitter to the traditional political media messages, or engage related, but more whimsical, political content on YouTube or some other content aggregator while still viewing the more sober, stilted traditional political media content. A POPC environment allows citizens to produce their own political entertainment media experiences that allow them to achieve the levels of enjoyment and appreciation they desire, even when their traditional media outlets are producing content that retains clear ceiling effects for these types of gratifications.

Being fully ensconced in a POPC environment also allows citizens to *consume as much entertainment-driven political content as they desire*. While many of the most well-known and consumed forms of political entertainment content are distributed primarily through traditional media forms (e.g., cable television), this material can be found in complete and segmented form through a variety of digital platforms. Prior (2007) has argued that a high-choice, post-broadcast media environment has created not only a larger percentage of news avoiders, but also a devoted minority (12–15% of the population) of what he defines as "news junkies." News junkies are individuals who consume a great deal of traditional news content and are afforded an opportunity to do so in a POPC environment. The same POPC environment offers those citizens with a proclivity for political entertainment to consume as much of it as desired. As a result, there may exist something akin to a class of "political entertainment media junkies" in the population. The percentage of individuals who reflect this classification is most likely smaller than the percentage of news junkies, but may be an important subpopulation worth better understanding.

A POPC environment also allows citizens an opportunity to *create their own political entertainment media content*. Even those citizens with only modest technological skills have the ability to create mashups from their various political media experiences or to generate memes focusing on current office holders, those seeking to be elected, and the major social issues of the day. Not only are citizens able to consume political entertainment media content anywhere and at any time they desire, but they can create their own content and distribute their messages digitally for all the world to see. Enjoyment and appreciation is generated not only from the creation and dissemination of this material, but also from the feedback provided by a broad range of others, both known and unknown.

The combination of *supplementing traditional political media experiences, consuming as much entertainment-driven political content as desired*, and *creating user-generated political entertainment media content* serves to create heightened expectations for experiencing enjoyment and appreciation when engaging political media. Citizens socialized to politics in a POPC environment are more likely to associate enjoyment- and appreciation-based gratifications with their politics. For the POPC citizen, politics is not just about the normative ideal of being a well-informed individual who can make quality decisions in the voting booth, nor is politics just about being a loyal partisan who supports the in-group at the expense of the out-group. Instead, there is a playfulness to their politics, and this play can be reflected in base forms of enjoyment or more complex eudaimonic experiences that can produce self-actualization. As we have stated, citizens' engagement of politics through media may have always included some elements of enjoyment and appreciation. However, we may never know because we only rarely asked these types of empirical questions in past research. Regardless of the role of enjoyment and appreciation in a traditional media world, we are confident in arguing for their enhanced value in a POPC information world. Nevertheless, this is an empirical question we can attempt to address over time.

Future Research

Adopting a more mass communication–based lens and treating citizens as enjoyment- and appreciation-seeking creatures who retain hedonic and eudaimonic motivations for the consumption of political media is heuristically provocative. In addition, we argue that the adoption of such an approach is more ecologically valid in a POPC information environment. Embracing this perspective, researchers would be well served to focus on addressing four issues: (1) the continued expansion of bringing formal mass communication theory into the fold of political communication research. Many of the outcomes of political entertainment media consumption studied to date are the same types of effects addressed in relation to traditional political media (e.g., hard news, debates), but new dependent variables may emerge with an infusion of new theory from a likeminded subfield; (2) the development of new theories or process models that are specific to the study of entertainment and political media, perhaps building off theoretical advancements offered across the social sciences (e.g., Hurley, Dennett, & Adams, 2011); (3) the creation and use of novel political entertainment stimuli that will allow researchers the type of control needed to isolate specific messages effects (see Boukes, Boomgaarden, Moorman, & DeVreese, 2014; Holbert, Tchernev, Esralew, Walther, & Benski, 2013); and (4) the development of a better understanding of the complexities of various types of political entertainment messages. Humor is a multifaceted, deeply varied message type (Meyer, 2000). The field simply does not have a strong understanding of the message components of sarcasm versus irony versus parody, and with this lack of understanding has come an inability to isolate the effects of specific content elements. It does not help in the age of big data and computer-aided content analyses that many forms of humor (e.g., sarcasm, irony) have proven difficult to analyze via these methods. In the end, we are arguing that with the formation of a POPC information environment comes a need for researchers to return to the basics of message and what leads audience members to want to consume, engage, transmit, and create political content that provides some sense of enjoyment and appreciation.

References

Ancu, M., & Cozma, R. (2009). MySpace politics: Uses and gratifications of befriending candidates. *Journal of Broadcasting & Electronic Media, 53*, 567–583. doi:10.1080/08838150903333064

Bartsch, A. (2012). Emotional gratification in entertainment experience: Why viewers of movies and television series find it rewarding to experience emotions. *Media Psychology, 15*, 267–302. doi:10.1080/15213269.2012.693811.

Bartsch, A., & Olver, M. B. (2017). Appreciation of meaningful entertainment expereinces and eudaimonic well-being. In L. Reinecke & M. B. Oliver (Eds.), *The Routledge handbook of media use and well-being* (pp. 80–92). New York: Routledge.

Bartsch, A., & Schneider, F. M. (2014). Entertainment and politics revisited: How non-escapist forms of entertainment can stimulate political interest and information seeking. *Journal of Communication, 64,* 369–396. doi:10.1111/jcom.12095

Baum, M. A. (2002). Sex, lies and war: How soft news brings foreign policy to the inattentive public. *The American Political Science Review, 96,* 91–109. doi:10.1017/S0003055402004252

Baum, M. A. (2005). Talking the vote: Why presidential candidates hit the talk show circuit. *American Journal of Political Science, 49,* 946–959. doi:10.1111/j.0092-5853.2005.t01-1-00119.x

Bobkowski, P. S. (2015). Sharing the news: Effects of informational utility and opinion leadership on online news sharing. *Journalism & Mass Communication Quarterly, 92,* 320–345. doi:10.1177/1077699015573194.

Boukes, M., Boomgaarden, H. G., Moorman, M., & DeVreese, C. H. (2014). At odds: Laughing and thinking? The appreciation, processing, and persuasiveness of political satire. *Journal of Communication, 65,* 721–744. doi:10.1111/jcom.12173

Brewer, P. R., & Cao, X. (2006). Candidate appearances on soft news shows and public knowledge about primary campaigns. *Journal of Broadcasting & Electronic Media, 50,* 18–35. doi:10.1207/s15506878jobem5001_2

Bronstein, J. (2013). Like me! Analyzing the 2012 presidential candidates' Facebook pages. *Online Information Review, 37,* 173–192. doi:10.1108/OIR-01-2013-0002

Browning, N., & Sweetser, K. D. (2014). The let down effect: Satisfaction, motivation, and credibility assessments of political infotainment. *American Behavioral Scientist, 58,* 810–826. doi:10.1177/0002764213515227.

Bryant, J., & Vorderer, P. (Eds.). (2006). *Psychology of entertainment.* Mahwah, NJ: Lawrence Erlbaum.

Cao, X. (2008). Political comedy shows and knowledge about primary campaigns: The moderating effects of age and education. *Mass Communication and Society, 11,* 43–61. doi:10.1080/15205430701585028

Chen, G. M. (2015). Why do women bloggers use social media? Recreation and information motivations outweigh engagement motivations. *New Media & Society, 17,* 24–40. doi:10.1177/1461444813504269.

Cialdini, R. B., Trost, M. R., & Newsom, J. T. (1995). Preference for consistency: The development of a valid measure and the discovery of surprising behavioral implications. *Journal of Personality and Social Psychology, 69,* 318–328. doi:10.1037/0022-3514.69.2.318

Compton, J. (2011). Introduction: Surveying scholarship on *The Daily Show* and *The Colbert Report.* In A. Amarasingam (Ed.), *The Stewart/Colbert effect: Essays on the real impacts of fake news* (pp. 9–24). Jefferson, NC: McFarland & Company.

Deci, E. L., & Ryan, R. M. (2000). The "what" and "why" of goal pursuits: Human needs and the self-determination of behavior. *Psychological Inquiry, 11,* 227–268. doi:10.1207/S15327965PLI1104_01

Diddi, A., & LaRose, R. (2006). Getting hooked on news: Uses and gratifications and the formation of news habits among college students in an Internet environment. *Journal of Broadcasting & Electronic Media, 50,* 193–210. doi:10.1207/s15506878jobem5002_2

Festinger, L. (1957). *A theory of cognitive dissonance.* Stanford, CA: Stanford University Press.

Gil de Zúñiga, H., Jung, N., & Valenzuela, S. (2012). Social media use for news and individuals' social capital, civic engagement, and political participation. *Journal of Computer-Mediated Communication, 17,* 319–336. doi:10.1111/j.1083-6101.2012.01574.x.

Gottfried, J. A., Hardy, B. W., Holbert, R. L., Winneg, K. M., & Jamieson, K. H. (in press). The changing nature of political debate consumption: Social media, multitasking, and knowledge acquisition. *Political Communication.* doi:10.1080/10584609.2016.1154120

Gray, J., Jones, J. P., & Thompson, E. (Eds.). (2009). *Satire TV: Politics and comedy in the post-network era.* New York, NY: New York University Press.

Grueling, K., & Kilian, T. (2014). Motives for active participation in political blogs: A qualitative and quantitative analysis of eight German blogs. *Social Science Computer Review, 32,* 221–237. doi:10.1177/0894439313508611.

Hmielowski, J. D., Holbert, R. L., & Lee, J. (2011). Predicting the consumption of political TV satire: Affinity for political humor, *The Daily Show*, and *The Colbert Report*. *Communication Monographs, 78*, 96–114. doi:10.1080/03637751.2010.542579

Holbert, R. L., Hill, M. R., & Lee, J. (2014). The political relevance of entertainment media. In C. Reinemann (Ed.), *Political communication* (pp. 427–446). Berlin, Germany: De Gruyter.

Holbert, R. L., Lambe, J. L., Dudo, A. D., & Carlton, K. A. (2007). Primacy effects of *The Daily Show* and national TV news viewing: Young viewers, political gratifications, and internal political self-efficacy. *Journal of Broadcasting & Electronic Media, 51*, 20–38. doi:10.1080/08838150701308002.

Holbert, R. L., Tchernev, J. T., Walther, W. O., Esralew, S. E., & Benski, K. (2013). Young voter perceptions of political satire as persuasion: A focus on perceived influence, persuasive intent, and message strength. *Journal of Broadcasting & Electronic Media, 57*, 170–186. doi:10.1080/08838151.2013.787075

Holbert, R. L., & Young, D. G. (2013). Exploring relations between political entertainment media and traditional political communication information outlets. In E. Scharrer (Ed.), *The international encyclopedia of media studies: Vol. 5. Media effects/media psychology* (pp. 484–504). Boston, MA: Wiley-Blackwell.

Hollander, B. A. (2005). Late-night learning: Do entertainment programs increase political campaign knowledge for young viewers? *Journal of Broadcasting & Electronic Media, 49*, 402–415. doi:10.1207/s15506878jobem4904_3

Houston, J. B., Hawthorne, J., Spialek, M. L., Greenwood, M., & McKinney, M. S. (2013). Tweeting during presidential debates: Effect on candidate evaluations and debate attitudes. *Argumentation and Advocacy, 49*, 301–311. doi:10.1080/00028533.2013.11821804

Hurley, M. M., Dennett, D. C., & Adams, R. B. (2011). *Inside jokes: Using humor to reverse-engineer the mind*. Cambridge, MA: MIT Press.

Johnson, T. J., & Kaye, B. K. (2003). Around the World Wide Web in 80 ways: How motives for going online are linked to Internet activities among politically interested Internet users. *Social Science Computer Review, 21*, 304–325. doi:10.1177/0894439303253976.

Kaye, B. K., & Johnson, T. J. (2002). Online and in the know: Uses and gratifications of the web for political information. *Journal of Broadcasting and Electronic Media, 46*, 54–71. doi:10.1207/s15506878jobem4601_4

Kaye, B. K., & Johnson, T. J. (2004). A Web for all reasons: Uses and gratifications of Internet components for political information. *Telematics and Informatics, 21*, 197–223. doi:10.1016/S0736-5853(03)00037-6.

Kaye, B. K., & Johnson, T. J. (2006). The age of reasons: Motives for using different components of the Internet for political information. In A. P. Williams & J. C. Tedesco (Eds.), *The Internet election: Perspectives on the role of the Web in campaign 2004* (pp. 147–167). Lanham, MD: Rowman & Littlefield.

Kenski, K., & Jamieson, K. H. (2011). Presidential and vice presidential debates in 2008: A profile of audience composition. *American Behavioral Scientist, 55*, 307–324. doi:10.1177/0002764210392166

Knobloch-Westerwick, S. (2014). Selection, perception, and processing of political messages. In C. Reinemann (Ed.), *Political communication* (pp. 507–526). Berlin, Germany: De Gruyter.

Knobloch-Westerwick, S., Gong, Y., Hagner, H., & Kerbeykian, L. (2012). Tragedy viewers count their blessings: Feeling low on fiction leads to feeling high on life. *Communication Research, 40*, 747–766. doi:10.1177/0093650212437758.

Kushin, M., & Kitchener, K. (2009). Getting political on social network sites: Exploring online political discourse on Facebook. *First Monday, 14*(11). doi:10.5210/fm.v14i11.2645.

LaMarre, H. L., Landreville, K. D., & Beam, M. A. (2009). The irony of satire: Political ideology and the motivation to see what you want to see in *The Colbert Report*. *The International Journal of Press/Politics, 14*, 212–231. doi:10.1177/1940161208330904

Levin, D., & Barak-Brandes, S. (2014). Gabriel Tarde's model and online protest in the eyes of Jewish Israeli teenage girls. In B. Patrut & M. Patrut (Eds.), *Social media in politics: Case studies on the political power of social media*. New York, NY: Springer.

Lewis, R. J., Tamborini, R., & Weber, R. (2014). Testing a dual-process model of media enjoyment and appreciation. *Journal of Communication, 64*, 397–416. doi:10.1111/jcom.12101

Macafee, T. (2013). Some of these things are not like the others: Examining motivations and political predispositions among political Facebook activity. *Computers in Human Behavior, 29*, 2766–2775. doi:10.1016/j.chb.2013.07.019

Mattheiß, T., Weinmann, C., Löb, C., Rauhe, K., Bartsch, K., Roth, F., . . . Vorderer, P. (2013). Political learning through entertainment—Only an illusion? How the motivation for watching political talk shows influences viewers' experience. *Journal of Media Psychology, 25*, 171–179. doi:10.1027/1864-1105/a000100

McCombs, M. (2005). A look at agenda-setting: Past, present, and future. *Journalism Studies, 6*, 543–557. doi:10.1080/14616700500250438

McKinney, M. S., Houston, J. B., & Hawthorne, J. (2014). Social watching a 2012 Republican presidential primary debate. *American Behavioral Scientist, 58*, 556–573. doi:10.1177/0002764213506211.

Meyer, J. C. (2000). Humor as a double-edged sword: Four functions of humor in communication. *Communication Theory, 10*, 310–331. doi:10.1111/j.1468-2885.2000.tb00194.x

Norris, P. (2000). *A virtuous circle: Political communications in postindustrial societies*. Cambridge, UK: Cambridge University Press.

Oliver, M. B. (2008). Tender affective states as predictors of entertainment preference. *Journal of Communication, 58*, 40–61. doi:10.1111/j.1460-2466.2007.00373.x

Oliver, M. B., & Bartsch, A. (2010). Appreciation as audience response: Exploring entertainment gratifications beyond hedonism. *Human Communication Research, 36*, 53–81. doi:10.1111/j.1468-2958.2009.01368.x

Oliver, M. B., & Raney, A. A. (2011). Entertainment as pleasurable and meaningful: Identifying hedonic and eudaimonic motivations for entertainment consumption. *Journal of Communication, 61*, 984–1004. doi:10.1111/j.1460-2466.2011.01585.x.

Park, C. S. (2013). Does Twitter motivate involvement in politics? Tweeting, opinion leadership and political engagement. *Computers in Human Behavior, 29*, 1641–1648. doi:10.1016/j.chb.2013.01.044.

Pavitt, C. (2010). Alternative approaches to theorizing in communication science. In C. R. Berger, M. E. Roloff, & D. R. Roskos-Ewoldsen (Eds.), *The handbook of communication science* (2nd ed., pp. 37–54). Los Angeles, CA: Sage.

Pilotta, J. J., & Schultz, D. (2005). Simultaneous media experience and synesthesia. *Journal of Advertising Research, 45*, 19–25. doi:10.1017/S0021849905050087

Prior, M. (2007). *Post-broadcast democracy: How media choice increases inequality in political involvement and polarizes elections*. Cambridge, UK: Cambridge University Press.

Robertson, S. P., Vatrapu, R. K., & Medina, R. (2010). Online video "friends" social networking: Overlapping online public spheres in the 2008 U.S. Presidential election. *Journal of Information Technology & Politics, 7*, 182–201. doi:10.1080/19331681003753420

Roth, F. S. (2015). *Die Rezeption politischer Talkshows im Fernsehen: Der Einfluss des Unterhaltungserlebens auf die Informationsverarbeitung [The watching of political talk shows on TV: The influence of the entertainment experience on the information processing]*. Wiesbaden, Germany: Springer VS Forschung.

Roth, F. S., Weinmann, C., Schneider, F. M., Hopp, F. R., & Vorderer, P. (2014). Seriously entertained: Antecedents and consequences of hedonic and eudaimonic entertainment experiences with political talk shows on TV. *Mass Communication and Society, 17*, 379–399. doi:10.1080/15205436.2014.891135

Ryan, R. M., & Deci, E. L. (2000). Self-determination theory and the facilitation of intrinsic motivation, social development, and well-being. *American Psychologist, 55*, 68–78. doi:10.1037/0003-066X.55.1.68

Stroud, N. J. (2008). Media use and political predispositions: Revisiting the concept of selective exposure. *Political Behavior, 30*, 341–366. doi:10.1007/s11109-007-9050-9

Sweetser, K. D., & Weaver-Lariscy, R. (2007). Candidates make good friends: An analysis of candidates' uses of Facebook. *International Journal of Strategic Communication, 2*, 175–198. doi:10.1080/15531180802178687

Thorson, E., Hawthorne, J., Swasy, A., & McKinney, M. S. (2015). Co-viewing, Tweeting, and Facebooking the 2012 presidential debates. *Electronic News, 9*, 195–214. doi:10.1177/1931243115593320.

Vitak, J., Zube, P., Smock, A., Carr, C. T., Ellison, N., & Lampe, L. (2011). It's complicated: Facebook users' political participation in the 2008 election. *Cyberpsychology, Behavior, and Social Networking, 14*, 107–114. doi:10.1089/cyber.2009.0226

Vorderer, P., Klimmt, C., & Ritterfeld, U. (2004). Enjoyment: At the heart of media entertainment. *Communication Theory, 14*, 388–408. doi:10.1111/j.1468-2885.2004.tb00321.x

Vorderer, P., Krömer, N., & Schneider, F. M. (2016). Permanently online-permanently connected: Explorations into university students' use of social media and mobile smart devices. *Computers in Human Behavior, 63*, 694–703. doi:10.1016/j.chb.2016.05.085

Vorderer, P., & Ritterfeld, U. (2009). Digital games. In R. L. Nabi & M. B. Oliver (Eds.), *Handbook of media effects* (pp. 455–467). London, UK: Sage.

Weinmann, C. (2017). Feeling political interest while being entertained? Explaining the emotional experience of interest in politics in the context of political entertainment programs. *Psychology of Popular Media Culture, 6,* 123–141. doi:10.1037/ppm0000091

Wirth, W., Hofer, M., & Schramm, H. (2012). Beyond pleasure: Exploring the eudaimonic entertainment experience. *Human Communication Research, 38,* 406–428. doi:10.1111/j.1468–2958.2012.01434.x

Xenos, M. A., & Becker, A. B. (2009). Moments of Zen: Effects of *The Daily Show* on information seeking and political learning. *Political Communication, 26,* 317–332. doi:10.1080/10584600903053569

Zillmann, D., & Vorderer, P. (2000). *Media entertainment: The psychology of its appeal.* Mahwah, NJ: Lawrence Erlbaum.

PART VI
Brave New World
Networked Life and Well-Being

22
POPC and Well-Being
A Risk-Benefit Analysis

Leonard Reinecke

The key role of media use for our psychological health and well-being is hard to overlook: Media shape the way we see the world and ourselves, how we structure our time and daily routines, and how we communicate and interact with our social environment (for an overview, see Reinecke & Oliver, 2017). Media use can have short-term effects and make us happy or sad in the here and now when we laugh about a funny YouTube video or feel sorry for a Facebook friend who has shared a negative life event. But media use can also have long-term repercussions on our happiness and life satisfaction when it provides positive role models or social support in times of crisis. While the relevance of media use for well-being was evident even before the advent of social media and mobile Internet access, the growing prevalence of a "permanently online and permanently connected" (POPC) lifestyle (Vorderer & Kohring, 2013; Vorderer, Krömer, & Schneider, 2016) makes a comprehensive understanding of how media use in general and online content and communication in particular affect our well-being ever more pressing. Not only do smartphones, tablets, and other mobile devices make the Internet accessible at any time and any place, thus intensifying the presence of media use in our lives and its impact on our well-being. The constant availability of online access also changes the cognitions, expectations, and perception of users (see Klimmt, Hefner, Reinecke, Rieger, and Vorderer, this volume). Yet, how this POPC lifestyle affects psychological health and well-being remains largely unclear. How do users cope with the challenges arising from navigating through an "always on" environment and what chances and risks arise from a POPC mind-set?

The central goal of this chapter is to provide a first overview of the potential consequences of POPC for psychological health and well-being. After a short introduction to the theoretical concepts of hedonic and eudaimonic well-being, the chapter will first review the existing research on the effects of "traditional" Internet and social media use on well-being. Based on this overview of recent research, the potential changes that come along with a POPC lifestyle and the resulting consequences for the effects of Internet use on well-being will be discussed along with open questions for future research.

What Is Well-Being?

The question of what constitutes the "good life" or the nature of happiness is probably as old as humankind. In psychology, the theoretical concept of happiness has received growing attention since the 1960s and the advent of the "positive psychology" movement (Diener, Suh, Lucas, & Smith, 1999). Today, psychological research on well-being is dominated by two different "schools" representing different conceptualizations of well-being (Huta, 2017).

The concept of *hedonic well-being* defines well-being as a hedonically pleasant affective state. Research in this tradition usually distinguishes between three components of well-being: the presence of positive affect, the absence of negative affect, and a positive cognitive evaluation of life circumstance represented by high levels of life satisfaction (Diener et al., 1999). In contrast to this hedonic view on well-being, the concept of *eudaimonic well-being* goes beyond pleasure and positive affect and proposes a more complex perspective on well-being. The eudaimonic research tradition defines well-being in broader terms, such as psychological growth, meaning and purpose in life, moral elevation, or authenticity (Huta, 2017). As a consequence of its complexity, a unified or integrative theoretical model of eudaimonic well-being does not exist, and the research field is characterized by the multiplicity of co-existing definitions, theoretical approaches, and operationalizations (Huta & Waterman, 2014).

The theoretical and empirical relationship between hedonic and eudaimonic well-being is subject to ongoing scholarly debate (Huta & Waterman, 2014; Ryan & Deci, 2001). Factor-analytic approaches suggest that the experiential components of well-being do in fact show a two-factor structure, with feelings such as elevation, meaning, and self-connectedness establishing a eudaimonic well-being factor and feelings of positive affect, carefreeness, and low negative affect representing a hedonic well-being factor (Huta, 2017). However, other central variables, such as satisfaction with life or intrinsic need satisfaction, are not clearly accounted for by any of the two factors and suggest that hedonic and eudaimonic well-being may not be fully independent constructs but are instead connected through process and outcome variables incorporating both hedonic and eudaimonic facets.

Internet Use and Well-Being: Benefits and Risks

Since the early days of the Internet, communication scholars and media psychologists have been fascinated by the question of how online content and communication affect key processes and outcomes in the daily lives of users. Early research in this field was strongly dominated by a risk perspective suggesting, for example, that the Internet promotes isolation, a lack of offline interaction, and impaired psychological well-being (Kraut et al., 1998). Over the last two decades, however, a broad and steadily growing body of research has identified various processes and mechanisms that connect Internet use and well-being, providing a far more nuanced picture of the risks and benefits of Internet use (Vorderer, 2016). While a comprehensive review of this research field goes far beyond the scope of this chapter, the following sections will provide a short overview of the most relevant concepts and variables connecting Internet use and well-being.

Media Enjoyment

Probably the most apparent connection between Internet use and well-being is established by processes of media enjoyment. Media enjoyment is typically defined as a pleasurable affective reaction to media content (e.g., Vorderer, Klimmt, & Ritterfeld, 2004) and thus shows strong connections to the positive affect component of subjective well-being. Not only do online platforms such as YouTube or Spotify provide new channels for the distribution of "traditional" audiovisual entertaining media content. The interactive nature of the Social Web has also created new sources of media enjoyment. The extant research clearly demonstrates, for example, that enjoyment is one of the key gratifications of and motivations for social media use (e.g., Reinecke, Vorderer, & Knop, 2014; Smock, Ellison, Lampe, & Wohn, 2011), thus clearly characterizing it as an important source of hedonic well-being.

Social Capital and Social Support

Communication and social interaction have been two of the core drivers of Internet use early on. It is no surprise, then, that the interpersonal outcomes of online communication and the resulting effects belong to the most intensively researched processes in the context of Internet use and well-being (for an overview, see Trepte & Scharkow, 2017). The existing research in this context suggests that social media use, in particular, can act as an important social resource by increasing the availability of social capital and social support (Ellison, Steinfield, & Lampe, 2007; Trepte, Dienlin, & Reinecke, 2015). A number of studies have found that higher levels of online social capital and perceived online social support are positively related to well-being indicators, such as higher levels of life satisfaction (Burke, Marlow, & Lento, 2010) and lower levels of stress (Nabi, Prestin, & So, 2013). However, the existing research also suggests that the online context is not an equally effective source of all forms of social support. While the breadth and heterogeneity of online friend networks facilitate the availability of informational support (e.g., advice giving), other forms such as emotional support (e.g., giving solace, providing affirmation) and tangible support (e.g., concrete transactions of goods or services) are less easily provided online (Trepte et al., 2015). As a consequence, previous research has found stronger beneficial effects of offline friends and offline social support on psychological well-being compared to their online counterparts (Trepte et al., 2015).

Self-Affirmation and Social Sharing of Emotions

Besides social interaction with other users, the self-expressive functions of online communication have also received considerable scholarly attention and appear highly relevant in the context of well-being. Social media such as Facebook or Instagram provide new avenues for self-presentation through user profiles, status updates, or the sharing of pictures and videos. Crucial for the resulting effects on well-being is the fact that the majority of users tend to present themselves in a positive light, emphasizing or selectively presenting primarily the attractive and desirable facets of the self (for an overview, see Toma, 2017). This opens up new opportunities for self-affirmation (Toma, 2017; Toma & Hancock, 2013). Self-affirmation refers to the "process of bringing to awareness positive and cherished aspects of self" (Toma, 2017, p. 173) as a response to self-threat (e.g., negative performance feedback). As many users carefully curate a positive self-presentation on social media platforms, exposure to that content after a self-threatening situation should increase well-being. In fact, recent research confirms this assumption: Participants examining their own Facebook profile after negative self-relevant feedback showed higher levels of positive affect than participants examining the nonaffirming profile of a stranger (Toma & Hancock, 2013). In addition to its self-affirming functions, online self-presentation can also have a beneficial effect on well-being through the social sharing of emotions. Recent research suggests that sharing positive experiences and emotions online increases affective well-being through capitalization (Choi & Toma, 2014): Positive feelings are intensified by public sharing because personal expression increases the salience and memorability of the respective events and experiences. The downside of this, however, is that the same mechanisms also apply to negative emotion. Accordingly, sharing negative experiences online has been linked to decreased well-being (Choi & Toma, 2014).

Social Comparison

The well-being of Internet users is not only affected by their own online self-presentation. Exposure to the self-presentation of other users and the resulting processes of social comparison are another relevant factor of influence (Toma, 2017). The effects of social comparison with other users can be twofold: Downward social comparison (i.e., social comparison with other users who fare worse on a given dimension of comparison) may be an effective mood management strategy (Johnson & Knobloch-Westerwick, 2014). Upward social comparison (i.e., social comparison with other users who fare better on a given dimension of comparison), in contrast, may result in self-discrepancies and reduced satisfaction with the self (Haferkamp & Krämer, 2011). While both positive and negative effects of online social comparison are plausible, the existing research suggests that negative effects are more prevalent (Toma, 2017).

Deficiently Self-Regulated and Excessive Internet Use

Finally, a growing number of studies have addressed deficiently self-regulated Internet and social media use as a source of impaired well-being. One branch of research has characterized online content and communication as a frequent source of distraction and a challenge to self-control in everyday life (for an overview, see Hofmann, Reinecke, & Meier, 2017). Pleasurable online content is more and more ubiquitously available and can be a tempting alternative in situations where users are confronted with less hedonically attractive tasks and obligations. In line with this reasoning, recent research demonstrates that the use of online content for procrastination (i.e., dysfunctional task delay) is a common phenomenon, particularly among younger users, and has detrimental consequences for psychological health and well-being (Meier, Reinecke, & Meltzer, 2016; Reinecke, Meier et al., 2016). Besides such everyday self-control challenges of normal Internet use, a large body of research has addressed pathological forms of excessive and uncontrolled Internet use and Internet addiction (for an overview, see Müller, Dreier, & Wölfing, 2017). This line of research suggests that the relationship between psychological health and well-being is reciprocal: On the one hand, problematic Internet use and Internet addiction can be conceptualized as a form of dysfunctional coping with stress, personal deficits, and impaired well-being. On the other hand, Internet addiction is frequently discussed as a source of impaired well-being and has been linked to negative consequences in various life domains, lower levels of interpersonal functioning, and psychopathological symptoms (Müller et al., 2017).

POPC and Well-Being: Old Wine in New Bottles?

The research reviewed in the previous sections clearly demonstrates that the effects of Internet use on well-being have received considerable scholarly attention long before the POPC era. Online content and communication have already been strongly related to psychological well-being before the advent of the "always on" society, inducing both chances and risks in the everyday lives of Internet users. How has this situation changed with the new developments that come along with a POPC lifestyle? Is POPC a "game changer" for the effects of Internet use on well-being or merely "more of the same"? While the mechanisms linking Internet use and well-being discussed above seem to be easily transferable to the POPC context, the POPC lifestyle is also likely to create new challenges and opportunities for users. In the following sections, POPC is thus discussed as an amplifier that intensifies traditional effects of Internet use on well-being, as well as a source of new mechanisms connecting Internet use and well-being.

POPC as an Amplifier

POPC is likely to have consequences for all the mechanisms linking Internet use and well-being discussed above. The technological changes that enable POPC behavior—that is, ubiquitous access to online content and communication via mobile Internet connections, smartphones, and mobile devices—are likely to intensify the impact of Internet use on well-being in the daily lives of users. This significantly increases the chances Internet use provides for increased well-being, since many processes and mechanisms that are beneficial to well-being, such as mood management via media enjoyment, self-affirmation, or social support, are now constantly available and can be used flexibly whenever they are needed. The same intensifying effect should also apply, however, to the detrimental effects of Internet use on well-being. The constant presence of the online environment makes it hard to get a break from the challenging and potentially straining effects of Internet use. Users may more and more constantly feel exposed to social surveillance or permanently engage in toxic forms of social comparison. The constant availability of online content and communication may further intensify the self-control challenges arising from the temptations of hedonically pleasant forms of use that conflict with the responsibilities and long-term goals of the individual user (see van Koningsbruggen, Hartmann, and Du, this volume) as well as the risk of pathological forms of Internet addiction (see Klimmt and Brand, this volume).

Besides these technological and behavioral facets of POPC, the cognitive dimensions of the POPC mindset may have an even stronger influence on well-being. In other words, users not only "are POPC" more and more frequently, they also tend to "think POPC" and see their offline environment against the backdrop of their cognitive orientation toward the online world. The different dimensions of this "online vigilance" (see Klimmt, Hefner, Reinecke, Rieger, and Vorderer, this volume) work in unison with the increased technological availability of online content and further increase the potential positive and negative impact of the online environment on the individual user. Not only do mobile Internet connections and smartphones increase the technical availability of online communication; due to their high levels of *reactibility*, users are also constantly willing to react to external "connection cues," such as ringtones or notifications for incoming messages (Bayer, Campbell, & Ling, 2016), and to engage in online communication whenever they are contacted by their online network. This constant willingness to communicate should significantly support the availability of social capital and online social support, but it also increases the risk of frequent disruptions and distractions by online communication. The personal disposition for *monitoring* (i.e., constantly checking the online environment for news and relevant [social] events), creates a new level of constant connectedness to the online sphere. This should open up new chances for increased well-being, for example, new opportunities for mood management as users with a strong POPC mindset are unlikely to miss hedonically pleasant online content (e.g., memes, cat videos, or the latest gossip) posted and shared by their online friends. However, it also increases the risk of negative effects, for example, when monitoring results in a constant stream of self-relevant information triggering dysfunctional forms of social comparison with online peers. Finally, the permanent *salience* of the online environment should support users in reaping the benefits on online interaction. When the online environment becomes a permanent additional layer within the individual's information processing routines, the offline environment is constantly evaluated with regard to its relevance for future online behavior. Offline events or social interactions, for example, may be constantly checked for their "selfie" potential, their newsworthiness, and their usefulness for online self-presentation. This could make the online environment an even more effective context for self-affirmation, while the mere act of documenting (e.g., taking a picture) and sharing an event online could augment the offline setting by intensifying the engagement with and enjoyment of the offline experience (Diehl, Zauberman, & Barasch, 2016). However, the salience of the online environment may make users not only more aware of and attentive to the positive potentials and opportunities provided by online interaction, but may also result in a problematic preoccupation with the online world that increases the risks of Internet addiction and endangers the healthy functioning of the individual (see Klimmt and Brand, this volume).

POPC and New Challenges for Well-Being

As discussed above, both the behavioral and the psychological components of POPC can amplify the effects of Internet use on well-being. Additionally, however, the "always on" environment also creates new impacts on well-being that go beyond those traditionally found and investigated in the pre-POPC era. The new combination of permanent accessibility of online content and communication and growing levels of online vigilance confront users with both new cognitive strains and new social challenges.

The increasing amount and constant flow of online messages and notifications create unprecedented demands on the users' attention and information-processing resources (for an overview, see Hefner & Vorderer, 2017). Not only does the ever-growing number of online contacts, apps, and subscriptions to online services, platforms, and networks increase the overall amount of messages; thanks to mobile Internet connections, these messages are also immediately delivered directly to the users' smartphones. Furthermore, the cognitive strains created by this constant stream of communication are amplified by the mechanisms of online vigilance: Users with a POPC mindset are almost constantly willing to immediately react to incoming messages. This reactibility, in turn, further increases the amount of sent and received messages, creating a self-reinforcing spiral of communication. The constant monitoring of the online environment ensures the immediate detection and cognitive processing of relevant events and online interactions and thus increases the cognitive load created by online communication even in moments when no incoming messages or notifications demand the attention of the user. Furthermore, both reactibility and monitoring increase the likelihood of media multitasking (see also Xu and Wang, as well as David, this volume) when users cognitively engage with their smartphones to react to or proactively check for online communication in situations where they are already dealing with another primary activity (e.g., working, driving, eating, etc.). Finally, the permanent salience of online content creates additional cognitive strain and demands cognitive resources, even in situations where users are not actively using their phone or are offline. In combination, the constant flow of online content and communication, the frequent engagement in media multitasking, and the permanent online vigilance typical for Internet users who are POPC should dramatically increase the prevalence of digital stress (Hefner & Vorderer, 2017). In fact, recent research has identified the number of sent and received online messages, the subjective urge to check for new messages, and Internet multitasking (i.e., the concurrent use of the Internet and other activities) as significant sources of stress and impaired psychological health (Reinecke, Aufenanger et al., 2017).

Besides new strains in the form of digital stress, POPC also creates new interpersonal tensions (see Utz, this volume). In the era of stationary Internet access, the risks of potential conflicts between online communication and an ongoing offline interaction were relatively small. In those days, Internet use afforded more preparation and active planning (e.g., going to a place with Internet access, switching on the computer, etc.) and was thus less likely to interfere with an ongoing social interaction. The constant technical connection to online content in combination with high levels of online vigilance has changed this situation dramatically. Both reactibility and monitoring significantly increase the risk that users engage in online communication either reactively or proactively while they are simultaneously in a social offline interaction. Such "phubbing" behavior (a neologism derived from the words "phone" and "snubbing," see for example Roberts & David, 2016) comes at considerable costs. Recent research demonstrates that the mere presence of a mobile phone can decrease conversation quality in a dyadic setting (Przybylski & Weinstein, 2012), and that phubbing can have detrimental effects on relationship satisfaction and psychological well-being (Roberts & David, 2016). Besides such interpersonal conflicts, POPC can also produce other forms of conflict by increasing the permeability of different spheres of life. A good example of these processes are the effects of POPC at the work–home interface (Sonnentag & Pundt, 2017): Through the constant availability resulting from POPC, employees are facing an increased risk of encountering setting-inconsistent online interactions, for example, when they receive private messages at work or work-related messages during leisure time. While such forms of setting-inconsistent technology use can provide chances for well-being (e.g., the opportunity to cope with private problems during working hours), they can also create role conflict and tensions between the spheres of work and leisure.

Conclusion: POPC and Well-Being—A Question of Autonomy?

The preceding section clearly demonstrates that POPC comes with both considerable chances and risks for the well-being of users. But what do these partly opposing effects of POPC mean for an overall assessment of the "net effect" of POPC on well-being? Is the new "always on" culture a blessing or a curse? I want to conclude this chapter with the suggestion that chances and risks of POPC for psychological well-being heavily depend on a central variable: autonomy.

Autonomy has been discussed as a main factor of influence on psychological well-being (Ryan & Deci, 2000) and an important precondition for psychological growth and flourishing (Ryan & Deci, 2001). According to self-determination theory (Ryan & Deci, 2000), intrinsic motivation is a central source of well-being (Ryan & Deci, 2001). In contrast to extrinsically motivated activities that are performed "to attain some separable outcome" (e.g., a reward or the avoidance of punishment), intrinsically motivated behavior is performed "for the inherent satisfaction of the activity itself" (Ryan & Deci, 2000, p. 71) and thus represents the autonomous goals of the individual rather than external pressures, or expectations. Consequently, perceived autonomy is an inseparable component of intrinsic motivation.

So how does this continuum of internal versus external motivation and the key role of autonomy for psychological well-being relate to the phenomenon of POPC? I propose that POPC behavior and online vigilance possess both autonomy-enhancing as well as autonomy-inhibiting features. Prior research clearly demonstrates that online communication and interaction are a significant source of intrinsic need satisfaction and can thus represent a self-determined and intrinsically motivated form of behavior (Reinecke et al., 2014; Sheldon, Abad, & Hinsch, 2011). POPC behavior in conjunction with high levels of online vigilance should increase the autonomy perceived in the context of Internet use and online communication: The technological advances of the last few years have made the intrinsic rewards of Internet use ubiquitously accessible. Never before were users more autonomous in their decision of when and where to use online content and communication. The perceived autonomy resulting from this ubiquitous technical accessibility of online content is intensified by the psychological components of the POPC mindset. For users possessing high levels of online vigilance, permanently evaluating their offline environment against the backdrop of their online environment, reacting to incoming online communication instantaneously, and constantly monitoring the online environment for new events and information represents their natural action tendencies. For these users, "acting"

POPC feels just natural and is an expression of self-determination and their individual dispositions. Such autonomy-enhancing forms of POPC should have a positive effect on well-being.

In many instances and situations, however, online communication in general and POPC behavior in particular seem to be much less self-determined and autonomously controlled and more a product of external pressures. In the POPC era, the constant technical possibility to be reached via online communication has created new social expectations. Permanent availability has thus become a collectively shared internalized connection norm (Bayer, Campbell et al., 2016). Recent research supports this notion and demonstrates that users of social media and instant messaging platforms experience considerable levels of social pressure to be available and to react to incoming messages as fast as possible (Mai, Freudenthaler, Schneider, & Vorderer, 2015; Reinecke, Aufenanger et al., 2017; Reinecke et al., 2014). Rather than being an expression of intrinsic motivation, such forms of POPC behavior are driven by social pressure and the fear of being ostracized and thus represent externally controlled behavior. Previous research clearly demonstrates that social pressure significantly reduces the autonomy perceived during online interaction, resulting in impaired enjoyment and lower levels of positive affect (Reinecke et al., 2014).

Finally, the perceived pressures leading to extrinsically motivated forms of POPC behavior may not only have social origins, but may also reside within the individual user. Recent research suggests that the fear of missing out (FOMO) on rewarding social activities and events is a significant driver of social media use and online communication (Przybylski, Murayama, DeHaan, & Gladwell, 2013; Reinecke, Aufenanger et al., 2017). Rather than using the Internet autonomously and based on genuine intrinsic motivation, online interactions driven by FOMO represent the attempt to prevent the assumed negative consequence of not being online and thus, once more, are a form of extrinsically motivated behavior. The detrimental effects of Internet used driven by FOMO are underlined by recent research that has linked FOMO to higher levels of communication load and multitasking, resulting in increased digital stress (Reinecke, Aufenanger et al., 2017).

Overall, these findings strongly suggest that the chances and risks of living in the "always on" society not so much depend on *whether* an individual is POPC but *how and why*. On the one hand, being POPC offers intriguing opportunities for enhanced well-being, particularly when it represents a form of intrinsically motivated, self-determined, and autonomy-enhancing behavior. On the other hand, POPC may increase the vulnerability of Internet users and result in impaired well-being when it is driven by external forces or internal fears and thus represents an externally motivated and autonomy-impeding behavior.

What implications arise from this risk-benefit analysis for future research on POPC and well-being? While the relevance of the behavioral and cognitive dimensions of POPC for the quality of life and the psychological well-being of users is indisputable, numerous questions remain unanswered. As discussed above, the basic mechanisms linking general Internet use to well-being seem to be easily applicable to the POPC environment. How the specific facets of POPC behavior and the three dimensions of online vigilance (salience, reactivity, and monitoring; cf. Klimmt et al., this volume) interact with these mechanisms, however, has not been empirically tested so far. For now, the role of POPC as an amplifier of previously studied effects of Internet use on well-being and as a source of new challenges and opportunities thus remains speculative. An important precondition for an exploration of the effects of POPC on well-being will be the development of reliable and valid measures of POPC (also see Schneider, Reich, and Reinecke, this volume). Furthermore, previous research on Internet use and well-being has been limited by its strong focus on indicators of hedonic well-being, whereas the effects of the use of information and communication technology on eudaimonic well-being have received very little attention so far. Given the strong potential of POPC to both enhance and impede personal autonomy, the question of how POPC affects other dimensions of eudaimonic well-being, such as personal growth, meaning in life, or self-realization, appears more pressing than ever before. Finally, a central challenge for future research on the well-being implications of POPC is a more advanced understanding of the psychological origins of the partly contradictory effects of Internet use: Why is it that individuals engage in Internet usage patterns that impair their well-being instead of foraging only for the benefits of the POPC environment? Besides the external pressures discussed above, information processing and decision-making mechanisms are likely to play an important role. For a long time, communication research has addressed media use from a rational choice perspective, with research traditions such as the uses-and-gratifications approach (see Malka, Ariel, Avidar, and Cohen, this volume) characterizing media selection as a form of functional behavior. The dichotomy of positive versus negative effects of Internet use on well-being suggests a different perspective: In many situations, users seem to have great difficulties in critically evaluating the well-being implications of their usage decision. Dual systems models of information processing and self-control (e.g., Hofmann, Friese, & Strack, 2009; Kahneman, 2003) may provide valuable insights in this context. These models suggest that information processing and decision-making are driven by two different systems: fast, effortless, and impulsive processes on the one hand and effortful, deliberate, and reflective processes on the other. Recent research demonstrates that POPC-related behavior such as texting is initiated largely automatically, rather than on the basis of conscious and deliberative action control (Bayer, Dal Cin, Campbell, & Panek, 2016). This suggests that in many situations, Internet use circumvents deliberate processing and decision-making and represents the users' situational impulses to approach the immediate gratifications of Internet use without considering the costs and consequences. As a result, such instances of technology use may conflict with the long-term goals of the individual (also see van Koningsbruggen et al., this volume) and have detrimental effects on well-being. A better understanding of the role of impulsive and reflective processes for well-being in a POPC environment thus represents an important task for future research.

Addressing the questions and challenges discussed above will unquestionably provide us with new insights into the complex interactions of Internet use and well-being and a more comprehensive understanding of the individual and societal repercussions of a POPC lifestyle.

References

Bayer, J. B., Campbell, S. W., & Ling, R. (2016). Connection cues: Activating the norms and habits of social connectedness. *Communication Theory, 26,* 128–149. doi:10.1111/comt.12090

Bayer, J. B., Dal Cin, S., Campbell, S. W., & Panek, E. (2016). Consciousness and self-regulation in mobile communication. *Human Communication Research, 42,* 71–97. doi:10.1111/hcre.12067

Burke, M., Marlow, C., & Lento, T. (2010). Social network activity and social well-being. Paper presented at the *CHI 2010,* April 10–15, Atlanta, Georgia.

Choi, M., & Toma, C. L. (2014). Social sharing through interpersonal media: Patterns and effects on emotional well-being. *Computers in Human Behavior, 36,* 530–541. doi:10.1016/j.chb.2014.04.026

Diehl, K., Zauberman, G., & Barasch, A. (2016). How taking photos increases enjoyment of experiences. *Journal of Personality and Social Psychology, 111,* 119–140. doi:10.1037/pspa0000055

Diener, E., Suh, E. M., Lucas, R. E., & Smith, H. L. (1999). Subjective well-being: Three decades of progress. *Psychological Bulletin, 125,* 276–302. doi:10.1037/0033-2909.125.2.276

Ellison, N. B., Steinfield, C., & Lampe, C. (2007). The benefits of Facebook "friends": Social capital and college students' use of online social network sites. *Journal of Computer-Mediated Communication, 12,* 1143–1168. doi:10.1111/j.1083-6101.2007.00367.x

Haferkamp, N., & Krämer, N. C. (2011). Social comparison 2.0: Examining the effects of online profiles on social-networking sites. *Cyberpsychology, Behavior, and Social Networking, 14*(5), 309–314. doi:10.1089/cyber.2010.0120

Hefner, D., & Vorderer, P. (2017). Digital stress: Permanent connectedness and multitasking. In L. Reinecke & M. B. Oliver (Eds.), *The Routledge handbook of media use and well-being: International perspectives on theory and research on positive media effects* (pp. 237–249). New York: Routledge.

Hofmann, W., Friese, M., & Strack, F. (2009). Impulse and self-control from a dual-systems perspective. *Perspectives on Psychological Science, 4*, 162–176. doi:10.1111/j.1745-6924.2009.01116.x

Hofmann, W., Reinecke, L., & Meier, A. (2017). Of sweet temptations and bitter aftertaste: Self-control as a moderator of the effects of media use on well-being. In L. Reinecke & M. B. Oliver (Eds.), *The Routledge handbook of media use and well-being: International perspectives on theory and research on positive media effects* (pp. 211–222). New York: Routledge.

Huta, V. (2017). An overview of hedonic and eudaimonic well-being concepts. In L. Reinecke & M. B. Oliver (Eds.), *The Routledge handbook of media use and well-being: International perspectives on theory and research on positive media effects* (pp. 14–33). New York: Routledge.

Huta, V., & Waterman, A. S. (2014). Eudaimonia and its distinction from hedonia: Developing a classification and terminology for understanding conceptual and operational definitions. *Journal of Happiness Studies, 15*, 1425–1456. doi:10.1007/s10902-013-9485-0

Johnson, B. K., & Knobloch-Westerwick, S. (2014). Glancing up or down: Mood management and selective social comparisons on social networking sites. *Computers in Human Behavior, 41*, 33–39. doi:10.1016/j.chb.2014.09.009

Kahneman, D. (2003). A perspective on judgment and choice: Mapping bounded rationality. *American Psychologist, 58*, 697–720. doi:10.1037/0003-066X.58.9.697

Kraut, R., Patterson, M., Lundmark, V., Kiesler, S., Mukophadhyay, T., & Scherlis, W. (1998). Internet paradox: A social technology that reduces social involvement and psychological well-being? *American Psychologist, 53*, 1017–1031. doi:10.1037/0003-066X.53.9.1017

Mai, L. M., Freudenthaler, R., Schneider, F. M., & Vorderer, P. (2015). "I know you've seen it!" Individual and social factors for users' chatting behavior on Facebook. *Computers in Human Behavior, 49*, 296–302. doi:10.1016/j.chb.2015.01.074

Meier, A., Reinecke, L., & Meltzer, C. E. (2016). "Facebocrastination"? Predictors of using Facebook for procrastination and its effects on students' well-being. *Computers in Human Behavior, 64*, 65–76. doi:10.1016/j.chb.2016.06.011

Müller, K. W., Dreier, M., & Wölfing, K. (2017). Excessive and addictive use of the Internet: Prevalence, related contents, predictors, and psychological consequences In L. Reinecke & M. B. Oliver (Eds.), *The Routledge handbook of media use and well-being: International perspectives on theory and research on positive media effects* (pp. 223–236). New York: Routledge.

Nabi, R. L., Prestin, A., & So, J. (2013). Facebook friends with (health) benefits? Exploring social network site use and perceptions of social support, stress, and well-being. *Cyberpsychology, Behavior, and Social Networking, 16*(1), 721–727. doi:10.1089/cyber.2012.0521

Przybylski, A. K., Murayama, K., DeHaan, C. R., & Gladwell, V. (2013). Motivational, emotional, and behavioral correlates of fear of missing out. *Computers in Human Behavior, 29*, 1841–1848. doi:10.1016/j.chb.2013.02.014

Przybylski, A. K., & Weinstein, N. (2012). Can you connect with me now? How the presence of mobile communication technology influences face-to-face conversation quality. *Journal of Social and Personal Relationships, 30*(3), 237–246. doi:10.1177/0265407512453827

Reinecke, L., Aufenanger, S., Beutel, M. E., Dreier, M., Quiring, O., Stark, B., . . . Müller, K. W. (2017). Digital stress over the life span: The effects of communication load and Internet multitasking on perceived stress and psychological health impairments in a German probability sample. *Media Psychology, 20*, 90–115. doi:10.1080/15213269.2015.1121832

Reinecke, L., Meier, A., Aufenanger, S., Beutel, M. E., Dreier, M., Quiring, O., . . . Müller, K. W. (2016). Permanently online and permanently procrastinating? The mediating role of Internet use for the effects of trait procrastination on psychological health and well-being. *New Media & Society*, online first. doi:10.1177/1461444816675437

Reinecke, L., & Oliver, M. B. (Eds.). (2017). *The Routledge handbook of media use and well-being: International perspectives on theory and research on positive media effects*. New York: Routledge.

Reinecke, L., Vorderer, P., & Knop, K. (2014). Entertainment 2.0? The role of intrinsic and extrinsic need satisfaction for the enjoyment of Facebook use. *Journal of Communication, 64,* 417–438. doi:10.1111/jcom.12099

Roberts, J. A., & David, M. E. (2016). My life has become a major distraction from my cell phone: Partner phubbing and relationship satisfaction among romantic partners. *Computers in Human Behavior, 54,* 134–141. doi:10.1016/j.chb.2015.07.058

Ryan, R. M., & Deci, E. L. (2000). Self-determination theory and the facilitation of intrinsic motivation, social development, and well-being. *American Psychologist, 55,* 68–78. doi:10.1037110003-066X.55.1.68

Ryan, R. M., & Deci, E. L. (2001). On happiness and human potentials: A review of research on hedonic and eudaimonic well-being. *Annual Review of Psychology, 52,* 141–166. doi:10.1146/annurev.psych.52.1.141

Sheldon, K. M., Abad, N., & Hinsch, C. (2011). A two-process view of Facebook use and relatedness need-satisfaction: Disconnection drives use, and connection rewards it. *Journal of Personality and Social Psychology, 100*(4), 766–775. doi:10.1037/a0022407

Smock, A. D., Ellison, N. B., Lampe, C., & Wohn, D. Y. (2011). Facebook as a toolkit: A uses and gratification approach to unbundling feature use. *Computers in Human Behavior, 27,* 2322–2329. doi:10.1016/j.chb.2011.07.011

Sonnentag, S., & Pundt, A. (2017). Media use and well-being at the work-home interface. In L. Reinecke & M. B. Oliver (Eds.), *The Routledge handbook of media use and well-being: International perspectives on theory and research on positive media effects* (pp. 341–354). New York: Routledge.

Toma, C. L. (2017). Taking the good with the bad. Effects of Facebook self-presentation on emotional well-being. In L. Reinecke & M. B. Oliver (Eds.), *The Routledge handbook of media use and well-being: International perspectives on theory and research on positive media effects* (pp. 170–182). New York: Routledge.

Toma, C. L., & Hancock, J. T. (2013). Self-affirmation underlies Facebook use. *Personality and Social Psychology Bulletin, 39,* 321–331. doi:10.1177/0146167212474694

Trepte, S., Dienlin, T., & Reinecke, L. (2015). The influence of social support received in online and offline contexts on satisfaction with social support and satisfaction with life: A longitudinal study. *Media Psychology, 18,* 75–105. doi:10.1080/15213269.2013.838904

Trepte, S., & Scharkow, M. (2017). Friends and lifesavers: How social capital and social support received in media environments contribute to well-being. In L. Reinecke & M. B. Oliver (Eds.), *The Routledge handbook of media use and well-being: International perspectives on theory and research on positive media effects* (pp. 304–316). New York: Routledge.

Vorderer, P. (2016). Communication and the good life: Why and how our discipline should make a difference. *Journal of Communication, 66,* 1–12. doi:10.1111/jcom.12194

Vorderer, P., Klimmt, C., & Ritterfeld, U. (2004). Enjoyment: At the heart of media entertainment. *Communication Theory, 14,* 388–408. doi:10.1111/j.1468-2885.2004.tb00321.x

Vorderer, P., & Kohring, M. (2013). Permanently online: A challenge for media and communication research. *International Journal of Communication, 7,* 188–196.

Vorderer, P., Krömer, N., & Schneider, F. M. (2016). Permanently online—permanently connected: Explorations into university students' use of social media and mobile smart devices. *Computers in Human Behavior, 63,* 694–703. doi:10.1016/j.chb.2016.05.085

23
Being Permanently Online and Being Permanently Connected at Work

A Demands–Resources Perspective

Sabine Sonnentag

Introduction

Vorderer and his coworkers have described that during recent years, more and more people are "permanently online and permanently connected" (Vorderer, Krömer, & Schneider, 2016, p. 695; Vorderer & Kohring, 2013) via online media. Being permanently online and being permanently connected refers to overt media-use behavior over extended periods and being in a "psychological state of permanent communicative vigilance" (p. 695). This trend, which can be attributed to the increased availability of mobile devices and broadband connectivity, has many advantages in daily life, but may also contribute to a state of being "always-on," potentially leading to information overload, perceived stress, and symptoms of impaired well-being (Hefner & Vorderer, 2017; Reinecke et al., 2017).

Many workplaces have become "permanently online/permanently connected" (POPC) settings as well: On the job, employees rely on communication technology to accomplish their tasks online and to stay connected with their supervisors, coworkers, and customers (Mazmanian, 2013; Wajcman & Rose, 2011). Mobile and other Internet-based technologies help them continue working and stay connected with others even when not in the office, but also when at home and while traveling. To address potential consequences of job-related POPC, research has focused on the well-being implications of job-related technology use in the non-work domain (Boswell & Olson-Buchanan, 2007; Ohly & Latour, 2014). Large parts of the organizational literature, however, have largely neglected the impact of POPC technologies and work arrangements within the work domain itself (Barley, 2015; Orlikowski & Scott, 2008). Studies that did address these technologies and arrangements have revealed quite complex or even paradoxical findings (Borges & Joia, 2013; Fonner & Roloff, 2012).

In this chapter, I aim to extend this literature by discussing the implications of POPC work settings for employee well-being from a demands–resources perspective. Generally, well-being refers to individuals' "optimal psychological functioning and experience" (Ryan & Deci, 2001, p. 142) in various life settings. Research on work-related well-being mainly addresses affective and psychosomatic well-being (Fisher, 2010; Nixon, Mazzola, Bauer, Krueger, & Spector, 2011), capturing experiences such as positive affect, negative affect, or fatigue as short-term well-being indicators, as well as exhaustion, psychosomatic complaints, or other impairments of psychological health as longer-term consequences

(Sonnentag, 2015). During the past one or two decades, research has paid particular attention to work engagement (i.e., being vigorous, dedicated, and absorbed while working) as a positive well-being indicator (Schaufeli & Bakker, 2004).

When discussing the well-being implications of POPC work settings, I will use the POPC concept broadly, referring both to specific technologies (e.g., smartphones, tablets, and work stations that provide online connectivity) and to working arrangements in which these technologies are used to get work done (e.g., virtual team work settings where team members staying at different locations are permanently connected via a messenger system). Thus, it is not only the specific hardware and software technology, but also the work processes these technologies support that constitute POPC work.

In this chapter, I will first present the broader demands–resources perspective developed within organizational psychology. I will then apply this perspective to POPC work settings and describe three key features of POPC work that can be both a demand and a resource: constant availability, access to information, and multiple-goal pursuit. In the final section, I will discuss factors that can increase the demand aspect of POPC and emphasize the resource aspect of POPC, respectively.

The Demands–Resources Perspective

Job demands and job resources are two important dimensions that describe most jobs (Bakker, Demerouti, & Sanz-Vergel, 2014). Job demands are "physical, social, or organizational aspects of the job that require sustained physical or mental effort and are therefore associated with certain physiological and psychological costs" (Demerouti, Nachreiner, Bakker, & Schaufeli, 2001, p. 501). Job resources are those aspects of a job that help the employee to achieve his or her work goals (Halbesleben, Neveu, Paustian-Underdahl, & Westman, 2014). Research has shown that high job demands are associated with symptoms of poor well-being (e.g., exhaustion), whereas high job resources are associated with indicators of positive well-being (e.g., work engagement; Christian, Garza, Slaughter, 2011; Crawford, LePine, & Rich, 2010).

Scholars have started to discuss information and communication technologies (ICTs) from a demands–resources perspective (Day, Scott, & Kelloway, 2010; Demerouti, Derks, ten Brummelhuis, & Bakker, 2014; ter Hoeven, van Zoonen, & Fonner, 2016). Day et al. described some aspects of ICT as particularly demanding. For instance, ICT malfunctions, having to deal with incompatible technologies, and data security requirements are typical demands that can create hassles, resulting in strain. Moreover, the need for continuous learning can also be perceived as a demand (Day et al., 2010). Furthermore, Day et al. described that ICTs provide resources such as control over when and where to work, access to information that helps with problem solving, means for increased efficiency, and faster or better communication. In addition to these specific demands and resources, Day et al. identified some features of ICTs that are a resource and a demand at the same time. For instance, increased availability for work and access to information are both a demand and a resource.

Demand and Resource Aspects of POPC Technology and POPC Work Arrangements

Similar to ICT in general, POPC technology in particular increases availability and access to information. Moreover, POPC technology and POPC work arrangements facilitate the pursuit of multiple goals within short periods of time. These three features of POPC work are both a demand and a resource.

Day et al. (2010) described that ICTs make employees more available to others at work and make work matters more available to employees, even when they are not at the workplace in a physical sense. This increased availability is a demand, because it is often coupled with the expectation that employees are accessible and responsive to work issues also during non-work hours. However, this increased availability can be a resource as well, because it provides employees with more discretion and flexibility in planning their non-work time since they know that they can be reached if this turns out to be necessary (e.g., in case of on-call work).

Day et al. (2010) discussed availability mainly with respect to the interface between work and non-work. POPC technology and work arrangements increase availability also *at work*. Employees can be reached when they are in a meeting or on a business trip, or when they work on a task that needs concentration and focus. This increased availability is primarily a resource for others (team members, supervisors, subordinates, customers) because they can get quick responses to burning questions and can receive other input for problem solving, even when the person is not present in a physical sense. Being available might also be a resource for the person him- or herself, because POPC technology makes it possible to stay informed about ongoing processes and to join conversations even when in a remote location (Orlikowski, Mazmanian, & Yates, 2005). For instance, Middleton (2007, p. 170) reported that Blackberry users gained "a sense of security" by monitoring what was going on in projects or situations where they could not be physically present. Moreover, being available via POPC technology allows for getting work done during times that cannot be used otherwise (e.g., while waiting; MacCormick, Dery, & Kolb, 2012).

Increased availability at work, however, is also a demand. It implies frequent interruptions (Fonner & Roloff, 2012) that are associated with an increase in stress (Mark, Gudith, & Klocke, 2008), feelings of being overwhelmed (Chesley, 2014), and a more fragmented workday (Rose, 2014). Being available and responding to interruptions requires shifting attention quickly to a different topic and being aware of all background information that is needed to join a conversation or make a decision. Moreover, resuming the interrupted primary activity needs additional effort (Bailey & Konstan, 2006). Importantly, interruptions may not only be external, but may also be self-initiated (Adler & Benbunan-Fich, 2013; Mark, Iqbal, Czerwinski, Johns, & Sano, 2016). Along these lines, Bittman, Brown, and Wajcman (2009) reported that using mobile phones while working is associated with higher time pressure. This finding might indicate that being constantly available shortens the time for getting other work done; however, it might also reflect that employees who face more time pressure in their jobs make more mobile calls, for instance, in an effort to use their time more efficiently.

First empirical studies on the role of accessibility and connectivity on well-being offer interesting insights. For instance, ter Hoeven et al. (2016) reported that employees' perceived accessibility (a construct similar to the availability concept) was negatively related to burnout and positively related to work engagement. Importantly, in their structural model, ter Hoeven controlled for interruptions. Using a daily-survey approach, ten Brummelhuis, Bakker, Hetland, and Keulemans (2012) found that on days when employees experienced more connectivity (a construct also closely related to availability) than they usually do, employees experienced less exhaustion and more work engagement. Again, also in this study, the degree of interruptions was controlled for. Although the constructs of accessibility and connectivity used in these two studies incorporate a more active component than the availability concept, these two studies suggest that the mere availability can be an energizing experience, particularly when statistically removing the impact of interruptions from the availability experience.

POPC technology and POPC work settings enable access to information at all times and from all places. This ubiquitous access to information is a valuable resource, because in POPC work arrangements, information required for task accomplishment and decision-making can be retrieved at the very moment when it is needed. This easy access to information can contribute to improved problem solving and innovation (Dewett, 2003; Dewett & Jones, 2001). On the demand side, however, access to information implies that too much information might be available, resulting in information overload (Bellotti, Ducheneaut, Howard, Smith, & Grinter, 2005; Eppler & Mengis, 2004).

Importantly, it is a core feature of POPC work arrangements that they enable users to pursue multiple goals within short time frames: With POPC technology, it is possible to work on different tasks and communicate with different other persons nearly at the same point in time. This feature of enabling multiple-goal pursuit makes POPC work arrangements potentially very resourceful, because it allows one to make progress on several goals simultaneously. For instance, when employees reach a temporary impasse with respect to one task, they can easily switch to a different task; they also may use waiting time for working on another task.

Multiple-goal situations, however, can result in conflicts between competing goals that in turn may lead to increased stress or lack of goal attainment (Unsworth, Yeo, & Beck, 2014). Addressing multiple goals at the same point in time can result in multitasking behavior that can contribute to feelings of being overwhelmed (Chesley, 2014) and to physiological stress reactions (Wetherell & Carter, 2014). For instance, Kirchberg, Roe, and van Eerde (2015) showed that on days when employees engaged in high levels of multitasking behavior at work, they reported lower levels of affective well-being at the end of the workday. This association between multitasking behavior and impaired affect was particularly strong for those employees with low levels of polychronicity, that is, for those who preferred to focus on one task at a time.

To deal with goal conflicts, employees need to prioritize some goals over others and need to protect the pursuit of the most important goals from being disrupted by other goals (for a discussion of the implications of POPC for self-control and goal conflicts, see also van Koningsbruggen, Hartmann, and Du, this volume). Deciding among competing goals can be demanding in itself (Vohs et al., 2008). Inhibiting thoughts about less important goals so that they do not interfere with the pursuit of important goals needs some degree of self-regulation (Lord, Diefendorff, Schmidt, & Hall, 2010). Exerting too much self-regulation may lead to exhaustion.

Factors That Turn POPC Technology and POPC Work Arrangements Into Demands Versus Resources

Core features of POPC work settings (availability, access to information, pursuit of multiple goals) can be experienced as demands and as resources. In this section, I will discuss factors that influence whether a POPC technology or work arrangement is predominantly perceived as a demand or a resource. I will address factors in the organizational work environment, as well as individual factors.

With respect to the organizational work environment, the specific task environment, control over technology use, and organizational expectations around technology use could be relevant. First, the task environment is important in shaping how employees perceive POPC technology and POPC work arrangements. The more POPC technology is used for accomplishing core tasks (as opposed to peripheral tasks), the more the technology will be a resource. Core tasks are those that are central for a person's occupational role and contribute largely to the person's overall job performance level (Campbell, Gasser, & Oswald, 1996). When POPC technology is needed for the core tasks, it is difficult to imagine how to achieve one's work goals without using the technology. When, however, POPC technology is only needed for the less important peripheral tasks, the gain of using this technology is more limited and the demanding aspect may be dominant: Using POPC technology for peripheral tasks may distract from focusing on the core tasks, which in turn makes it more difficult to get the core tasks accomplished. Lack in goal progress, in turn, will be related to poor well-being (Williams & Alliger, 1994). In addition, with respect to access to information, the degree to which POPC technology is a resource will increase when real-time information is crucial for getting one's core tasks done. When it is less important to have access to real-time information, the advantage of POPC technology decreases.

Second, control over when and how to use POPC technology is crucial. The more employees can decide themselves about when and where to be available, when and where to access which kind of information, and which goals to pursue, the more they will see this POPC technology as a resource. When they do not have control over their availability, the timing of incoming information, and the scheduling of their goals, however, the more they will perceive the technology as a demand. Empirical research showed that when employees have control over when and where they use technology, they experience less physical and psychological symptoms and less burnout, and enjoy a better sleep quality (Barber & Santuzzi, 2015; Day, Paquet, Scott, & Hambley, 2012).

Third, organizational expectations around POPC technology use might also be important. For instance, high organizational expectations to be available at all times and to respond immediately to incoming messages have the potential to make POPC environments demanding. While the organizations' and customers' expectations to respond promptly seem to be widespread (Matusik & Mickel, 2011), empirical evidence on the well-being consequences of these expectations is mixed. For instance, Brown, Duck, and Jimmieson (2014) found that normative pressure to respond quickly to e-mails was positively related to the burnout dimension of emotional exhaustion (even when controlling for a range of other variables, including negative affectivity and e-mail quantity). Other studies, however, did not find significant associations between response expectations and burnout indicators (Barber & Santuzzi, 2015; Day et al., 2012). It might be that although normative response expectations are demanding, employees often find effective ways to deal with them so that well-being indicators remain within acceptable ranges.

When it comes to individual factors, a person's skills and knowledge, personality, and also active approach to influence his or her work situation (i.e., job crafting) will be important. First, skills and knowledge relevant for effectively working in a POPC setting will help employees to perceive POPC technology and POPC arrangements as a resource. For instance, the broader literature on ICT use reported that perceived ease of use of a specific technology is positively related to the perceived usefulness of this technology (Schepers & Wetzels, 2007), corresponding to the perception that the technology is a resource. The relationship between perceived ease of use and perceived usefulness is particularly strong for Internet technologies (King & He, 2006). Although perceived ease of use depends on multiple factors, without a minimum level of skills and knowledge it will be impossible to perceive ease of use. In addition to skills and knowledge about how to use a specific technological system, self-regulatory skills may also be highly important for perceiving POPC systems as a resource and not as a time-consuming demand. Because dealing with multiple goals requires goal prioritization and goal shielding (Unsworth et al., 2014), expertise on how to prioritize tasks and how to focus on them during specific periods (Macan, 1994) will be highly valuable.

Second, in addition to skills and knowledge, a person's personality might also play a role. Among the broad Big Five personality dimensions, neuroticism and extraversion are probably most influential here. Persons high in neuroticism might see POPC arrangements more as a stressful demand, because they focus more on negative experiences and respond more negatively to negative aspects of a situation

(Bolger & Zuckerman, 1995). Accordingly, they will perceive the negative features of POPC arrangements as a stressful demand. Empirical evidence supports this view. Brown et al. (2014) reported that negative affectivity—an individual characteristic closely related to neuroticism—predicted e-mail overload appraisals. The higher the employees' negative affectivity, the more likely they were to agree with statements such as "I find dealing with the amount of e-mails I receive stressful."

Persons high in extraversion might tend to see POPC arrangements as a resource, because these persons tend to focus more on positive experiences (Costa & McCrae, 1980) and react more positively to appetitive stimuli when pursuing goals (Smillie, Cooper, Wilt, & Revelle, 2012). Accordingly, more extraverted persons will perceive the positive features of POPC arrangements more as a resource. In addition, extraverts also will appreciate that POPC technology enables spontaneous communication processes.

Also, more specific individual differences could be important. For instance, polychronicity (i.e., the degree to which a person prefers "to be engaged in two or more tasks or events simultaneously" and believes that this "preference is the best way to do things"; Bluedorn, Kalliath, Strube, & Martin, 1999, p. 207) might be important. Because POPC work arrangements enable employees to attend to multiple goals within a short period of time, persons who prefer a polychromous working style will welcome the multiple-goal pursuit feature as a resource, whereas persons with lower levels of polychronicity will be easily overtaxed in a POPC environment and will see the multiple-goal feature more as a demand.

Third, not only skills and knowledge or personality will influence how employees perceive their POPC environment. Employees may not only *react* to a given POPC technology or work arrangement and evaluate it as more or less demanding or more or less resourceful. Research on job crafting suggests that people may also actively change their work settings, for instance, by redefining their tasks, by accomplishing their tasks with a specific focus, and by re-creating social interactions at work (Wrzesniewski & Dutton, 2001). Such job-crafting efforts can address job demands and job resources (Tims, Bakker, & Derks, 2012). Employees may decrease those job demands they perceive as negative, and increase those job demands they perceive as challenging as well as their job resources. In the context of POPC work arrangements, such job-crafting activities could imply a reduction in the demanding aspects of POPC use, for instance, by negotiating time when one is not available and should not be interrupted. It might also imply—if organizational procedures allow—disabling specific types of demanding applications on specific devices. Increasing the resourcefulness of POPC technologies and work arrangement would mean to use more efficient tools or to customize devices or applications so that they better match one's personal working style.

Conclusion

The conceptualization of POPC technologies and POPC work arrangements as demands and resources offers interesting avenues for empirical research. First, the interrelations between the demand and resource aspect of being permanently online and permanently connected with other constructs should be examined. Such studies addressing the convergent and divergent validity of the construct of POPC demands and POPC resources could include other job demands (e.g., workload, emotional demands), other job resources (e.g., job control, social support), well-being indicators (e.g., exhaustion, work engagement), job attitudes (e.g., job satisfaction), and job performance as potential correlates of the POPC constructs. Second, POPC demands and POPC resources might not only be directly related to well-being, attitudinal, or performance outcomes. It could also be that they interact with other demands and resources in predicting well-being, job attitudes, and performance. Third, the construct of POPC demands and POPC resources itself needs more attention. For instance, it would be interesting to investigate stable versus more dynamic aspects of this construct. It might be that seeing POPC technologies and POPC work arrangements as a demand or a resource is not a stable feature that employees perceive in or attribute to POPC work settings. The perceptions might fluctuate, depending on technological features, the organizational environment, and even momentary states such as fatigue or excitement.

Of course, not only when using online media at work, but also when using them off the job, availability, access to information, and simultaneous pursuit of multiple goals are typical features of being POPC. Accordingly, the associations between these features on the one hand and being POPC as a demand versus a resource on the other hand cannot only be observed in a job setting, but also in other life domains. Whereas off-the-job people may start using online media and being POPC mainly out of the expectation that specific media and their online behavior are a resource that benefits their life (Cheung, Chiu, & Lee, 2011; Ellison, Steinfield, & Lampe, 2007), recent research has highlighted the demand aspect of POPC as well (also see Reinecke, this volume). For instance, information overload resulting from ubiquitous access to information and multitasking being associated with the pursuit of multiple goals were found to be associated with increased stress in students and in the general population (Misra & Stokols, 2012; Reinecke et al., 2017; for a review, Hefner & Vorderer, 2017). It would be interesting to see when and how the positive outlook on POPC turns into a demanding experience. Therefore, future research should strive to capture both the resource and the demand aspects of being POPC also outside of job settings. Probably, it is typical for technology use outside work to be less regulated by external factors than it is on the job, providing people with more decision-making latitude about when to be online and connected and when not. At the same time, however, more self-regulation is probably needed to protect well-being (Hofmann, Reinecke, & Meier, 2017).

References

Adler, R. F., & Benbunan-Fich, R. (2013). Self-interruptions in discretionary multitasking. *Computers in Human Behavior, 29,* 1441–1449. doi:10.1016/j.chb.2013.01.040

Bailey, B. P., & Konstan, J. A. (2006). On the need for attention-aware systems: Measuring effects of interruption on task performance, error rate, and affective state. *Computers in Human Behavior, 22,* 685–708. doi:10.1016/j.chb.2005.12.009

Bakker, A. B., Demerouti, E., & Sanz-Vergel, A. I. (2014). Burnout and work engagement: The JD-R approach. *Annual Review of Organizational Psychology and Organizational Behavior, 1,* 389–411. doi:10.1146/annurev-orgpsych-031413-091235

Barber, L. K., & Santuzzi, A. M. (2015). Please respond ASAP: Workplace telepressure and employee recovery. *Journal of Occupational Health Psychology, 20,* 172–189. doi:10.1037/a0038278

Barley, S. R. (2015). Why the Internet makes buying a car less loathsome: How technologies change role relations. *Academy of Management Discoveries, 1,* 31–60. doi:10.5465/amd.2013.0016

Bellotti, V., Ducheneaut, N., Howard, M., Smith, I., & Grinter, R. E. (2005). Quality versus quantity: E-mail-centric tasks management and its relation with overload. *Human-Computer Interaction, 20,* 89–138. doi:10.1207/s15327051hci2001&2_4

Bittman, M., Brown, J. E., & Wajcman, J. (2009). The mobile phone, perpetual contact and time pressure. *Work, Employment and Society, 23,* 673–691. doi:10.1177/0950017009344910

Bluedorn, A., Kalliath, T. J., Strube, M. J., & Martin, G. D. (1999). Polychronicity and the Inventory of Polychronic Values (IPV): The development of an instrument to measure a fundamental dimension of organizational culture. *Journal of Managerial Psychology, 14,* 205–230. doi:10.1108/02683949910263747

Bolger, N., & Zuckerman, A. (1995). A framework for studying personality in the stress process. *Journal of Personality and Social Psychology, 69*, 890–902. doi:10.1037/0022-3514.69.5.890

Borges, A. P., & Joia, L. A. (2013). Executives and smartphones: An ambiguous relationship. *Management Research Review, 36*, 1167–1182. doi:10.1108/MRR-09-2012-0204

Boswell, W. R., & Olson-Buchanan, J. B. (2007). The use of communications technologies after hours: The role of work attitudes and work-life conflict. *Journal of Management, 33*, 592–610. doi:10.1177/0149206307302552

Brown, R., Duck, J., & Jimmieson, N. (2014). E-mail in the workplace: The role of stress appraisals and normative response pressure in the relationship between e-mail stressors and employee strain. *International Journal of Stress Management, 21*, 325–347. doi:10.1037/a0037464

Campbell, J. P., Gasser, M. B., & Oswald, F. L. (1996). The substantive nature of job performance variability. In K. R. Murphy (Ed.), *Individual differences and behavior in organizations* (pp. 258–299). San Francisco, CA: Jossey-Bass.

Chesley, N. (2014). Information and communication technology use, work intensification and employee strain and distress. *Work, Employment and Society, 28*, 589–610. doi:10.1177/0950017013500112

Cheung, C. M. K., Chiu, P.-Y., & Lee, M. K. O. (2011). Online social networks: Why do students use Facebook? *Computers in Human Behavior, 27*, 1337–1343. doi:10.1016/j.chb.2010.07.028

Christian, M. S., Garza, A. S., & Slaughter, J. E. (2011). Work engagement: A quantitative review and test of its relations with task and contextual performance. *Personnel Psychology, 64*, 89–136. doi:10.1111/j.1744-6570.2010.01203.x

Costa, P. T., & McCrae, R. R. (1980). Influence of extraversion and neuroticism on subjective well-being: Happy and unhappy people. *Journal of Personality and Social Psychology, 38*, 668–678. doi:10.1037/0022-3514.38.4.668

Crawford, E. R., LePine, J. A., & Rich, B. L. (2010). Linking job demands and resources to employee engagement and burnout: A theoretical extension and meta-analytic test. *Journal of Applied Psychology, 95*, 834–848. doi:10.1037/a0019364

Day, A., Paquet, S., Scott, N., & Hambley, L. (2012). Perceived information and communication technology (ICT) demands on employee outcomes: The moderating effect of organizational ICT support. *Journal of Occupational Health Psychology, 17*, 473–491. doi:10.1037/a0029837

Day, A., Scott, N., & Kelloway, E. K. (2010). Information and communication technology: Implications for job stress and employee well-being. In P. Perrewe & D. Ganster (Eds.), *New developments in theoretical and conceptual approaches to job stress: Research in occupational stress and well-being* (Vol. 8, pp. 317–350). Burlington, VT: Emerald.

Demerouti, E., Bakker, A. B., Nachreiner, F., & Schaufeli, W. B. (2001). Job demands–resources model of burnout. *Journal of Applied Psychology, 86*, 499–512. doi:10.1037//0021-9010.86.3.499

Demerouti, E., Derks, D., ten Brummelhuis, L. L., & Bakker, A. B. (2014). New ways of working: Impact on working conditions, work-family balance, and well-being. In C. Korunka & P. Hoonakker (Eds.), *The impact of ICT on quality of working life* (pp. 123–142). Dordrecht: Springer.

Dewett, T. (2003). Understanding the relationship between information technology and creativity in organizations. *Creativity Research Journal, 15*, 167–182.

Dewett, T., & Jones, G. R. (2001). The role of information technology in the organization: A review, model, and assessment. *Journal of Management, 27*, 313–346. doi:10.1177/014920630102700306

Ellison, N. B., Steinfield, C., & Lampe, C. (2007). The benefits of Facebook "friends": Social capital and college students' use of online social network sites. *Journal of Computer-Mediated Communication, 12*, 1143–1168. doi:10.1111/j.1083-6101.2007.00367.x

Eppler, M. J., & Mengis, J. (2004). The concept of information overload: A review of literature from organization science, accounting, marketing, MIS, and related disciplines. *The Information Society, 20*, 325–344. doi:10.1080/01972240490507974

Fisher, C. D. (2010). Happiness at work. *International Journal of Management Reviews, 12*, 384–412. doi:10.1111/j.1468-2370.2009.00270.x

Fonner, K. L., & Roloff, M. E. (2012). Testing the connectivity paradox: Linking teleworkers' communication media use to social presence, stress from interruptions, and organizational identification. *Communication Monographs, 79*, 205–231. doi:10.1080/03637751.2012.673000

Halbesleben, J. R. R., Neveu, J.-P., Paustian-Underdahl, S. C., & Westman, M. (2014). Getting to the "COR": Understanding the role of resources in conservation of resources theory. *Journal of Management, 40*, 1334–1364. doi:10.1177/0149206314527130

Hefner, D., & Vorderer, P. (2017). Digital stress: Permanent connectedness and multitasking. In L. Reinecke & M.-B. Oliver (Eds.), *The Routledge handbook of media use and well-being: International perspectives on theory and research on positive media effects* (pp. 237–249). New York: Routledge.

Hofmann, W., Reinecke, L., & Meier, A. (2017). Of sweet temptations and bitter aftertaste: Self-control as a moderator of the effects of media use on well-being. In L. Reinecke & M.-B. Oliver (Eds.), *The Routledge handbook of media use and well-being: International perspectives on theory and research on positive media effects* (pp. 211–222). New York: Routledge.

King, W. R., & He, J. (2006). A meta-analysis of the technology acceptance model. *Information & Management, 43*, 740–755. doi:10.1016/j.im.2006.05.003

Kirchberg, D. M., Roe, R. A., & van Eerde, W. (2015). Polychronicity and multitasking: A diary study at work. *Human Performance, 28*, 112–136. doi:10.1080/08959285.2014.976706

Lord, R. G., Diefendorff, J. M., Schmidt, A. M., & Hall, R. J. (2010). Self-regulation at work. *Annual Review of Psychology, 61*, 543–568. doi:10.1146/annurev.psych.093008.100314

Macan, T. H. (1994). Time management: Test of a process model. *Journal of Applied Psychology, 79*, 381–391. doi:10.1037/0021-9010.79.3.381

MacCormick, J. S., Dery, K., & Kolb, D. G. (2012). Engaged or just connected? Smartphones and employee engagement. *Organizational Dynamics, 41*, 194–201. doi:10.1016/j.orgdyn.2012.03.007

Mark, G., Gudith, D., & Klocke, U. (2008). The cost of interrupted work: More speed and stress. In *CHI '08. Proceedings of the SIGCHI Conference on Human Factors in Computing Systems* (pp. 107–110).

Mark, G., Iqbal, S. T., Czerwinski, M., Johns, P., & Sano, A. (2016). Email duration, batching and self-interruptions: Patterns of email use on productivity and stress. In *CHI'16, May 07–12, San Jose, CA*. doi:10.1145/2858036.2858262

Matusik, S. F., & Mickel, A. E. (2011). Embracing or embattled by converged mobile devices? Users' experiences with a contemporary connectivity technology. *Human Relations, 64*, 1001–1030. doi:10.1177/0018726711405552

Mazmanian, M. A. (2013). Avoiding the trap of constant connectivity: When congruent frames allow for heterogeneous practices. *Academy of Management Journal, 56*, 1225–1250. doi:10.5465/amj.2010.0787

Mazmanian, M. A., Orlikowski, W. J., & Yates, J. A. (2005). Crackberries: The social implications of ubiquitous wireless e-mail devices. In C. Sorensen, Y. Yoo, K. Lyytinen, & J. I. DeGross (Eds.), *Designing ubiquitous information environments: Socio-technical issues and challenges* (pp. 337–343). New York: Springer.

Middleton, C. A. (2007). Illusions of balance and control in an always-on environment: A case study of BlackBerry users. *Continuum: Journal of Media & Cultural Studies, 21*, 165–178. doi:10.1080/10304310701268695

Misra, S., & Stokols, D. (2012). Psychological health outcomes of perceived information overload. *Environment and Behavior, 44*, 737–759. doi:10.1177/0013916511404408

Nixon, A. E., Mazzola, J. J., Bauer, J., Krueger, J. R., & Spector, P. E. (2011). Can work make you sick? A meta-analysis of the relationships between job stressors and physical symptoms. *Work & Stress, 25*, 1–22. doi:10.1080/02678373.2011.569175

Ohly, S., & Latour, A. (2014). Use of smartphones for work and well-being in the evening: The role of autonomous and controlled motivation. *Journal of Personnel Psychology, 13*, 174–183. doi:10.1027/1866-5888/a000114

Orlikowski, W. J., & Scott, S. V. (2008). Sociomateriality: Challenging the separation of technology, work and organization. *The Academy of Management Annals, 2*, 433–474. doi:10.1080/19416520802211644

Reinecke, L., Aufenanger, S., Beutel, M. E., Dreier, M., Quiring, O., Stark, B., . . . Müller, K. W. (2017). Digital stress over the life span: The effects of communication load and Internet multitasking on perceived stress and psychological health impairments in a German probability sample. *Media Psychology, 20*, 90–115. doi:10.1080/15213269.2015.1121832

Rose, E. (2014). Who's controlling who? Personal communication devices and work. *Sociology Compass, 8*, 1004–1017. doi:10.1111/soc4.12194

Ryan, R. M., & Deci, E. L. (2001). On happiness and human potentials: A review of research on hedonic and eudaimonic well-being. *Annual Review of Psychology, 52*, 141–166. doi:10.1146/annurev.psych.52.1.141

Schaufeli, W. B., & Bakker, A. B. (2004). Job demands, job resources, and their relationship with burnout and engagement: A multi-sample study. *Journal of Organizational Behavior, 25*, 293–315. doi:10.1002/job.248

Schepers, J., & Wetzels, M. (2007). A meta-analysis of the technology acceptance model: Investigating subjective norm and moderation effects. *Information & Management, 44*, 90–103. doi:10.1016/j.im.2006.10.007

Smillie, L. D., Cooper, A. J., Wilt, J., & Revelle, W. (2012). Do extraverts get more bang for the buck? Refining the affective-reactivity hypothesis of extraversion. *Journal of Personality and Social Psychology, 103*, 306–326. doi:10.1037/a0028372

Sonnentag, S. (2015). Dynamics of well-being. *Annual Review of Organizational Psychology and Organizational Behavior, 2*, 261–293. doi:10.1146/annurev-orgpsych-032414-111347

ten Brummelhuis, L. L., Bakker, A. B., Hetland, J., & Keulemans, L. (2012). Do new ways of working foster work engagement? *Psicothema, 24*, 113–120.

ter Hoeven, C. L., van Zoonen, W., & Fonner, K. L. (2016). The practical paradox of technology: The influence of communication technology use on employee burnout and engagement. *Communication Monographs, 83*, 239–263. doi:10.1080/03637751.2015.1133920

Tims, M., Bakker, A. B., & Derks, D. (2012). Development and validation of the job crafting scale. *Journal of Vocational Behavior, 80*, 173–186. doi:10.1016/j.jvb.2011.05.009

Unsworth, K., Yeo, G., & Beck, J. (2014). Multiple goals: A review and derivation of general principles. *Journal of Organizational Behavior, 35*, 1064–1078. doi:10.1002/job.1963

Vohs, K. D., Baumeister, R. F., Schmeichel, B. J., Twenge, J. M., Nelson, N. M., & Tice, D. M. (2008). Making choices impairs subsequent self-control: A limited-resource account of decision making, self-regulation, and active initiative. *Journal of Personality and Social Psychology, 94*, 883–898. doi:10.1037/0022-3514.94.5.883

Vorderer, P., & Kohring, M. (2013). Permanently online: A challenge for media and communication research. *International Journal of Communication, 7*, 188–196.

Vorderer, P., Krömer, N., & Schneider, F. M. (2016). Permanently online—permanently connected: Explorations into university students' use of social media and mobile smart devices. *Computers in Human Behavior, 63*, 694–703. doi:10.1016/j.chb.2016.05.085

Wajcman, J., & Rose, E. (2011). Constant connectivity: Rethinking interruptions at work. *Organization Science, 32*, 941–961. doi:10.1177/0170840611410829

Wetherell, M. A., & Carter, K. (2014). The multitasking framework: The effects of increasing workload on acute psychobiological stress reactivity. *Stress and Health, 30*, 103–109. doi:10.1002/smi.2496

Williams, K. J., & Alliger, G. M. (1994). Role stressors, mood spillover, and perceptions of work-family conflict in employed parents. *Academy of Management Journal, 37*, 837–868. doi:10.2307/256602

Wrzesniewski, A., & Dutton, J. E. (2001). Crafting a job: Revisioning employees as active crafters of their work. *Academy of Management Review, 26*, 179–201. doi:10.5465/AMR.2001.4378011

24

The Dose Makes the Poison

Theoretical Considerations and Challenges of Health-Related POPC

Jutta Mata and Eva Baumann

Introduction

A century ago, the main causes of death were infectious diseases. Today, most individuals die of chronic degenerative diseases, mainly caused by unhealthy lifestyles such as an unbalanced diet or physical inactivity (Centers for Disease Control and Prevention, 2015). Not surprisingly, health behavior change and maintenance have been proposed as one of the major challenges of this century (Benjamin, 2014). In the past, health or fitness coaching was a privilege for the few well off enough to afford it. Today's mobile health technology, *mHealth*, promises easily accessible and individually customizable health and fitness coaching for everyone. mHealth possibilities range from text message reminders, to fitness apps for use on mobile phones or tablets, to real-time user-generated data from wearable sensors (Miyamoto, Henderson, Young, Pande, & Han, 2016). Compared to illness-related topics—such as diseases, medicines, and pharmaceuticals—fitness, exercise, diet, and nutrition are of major interest for young people, also indicated by their health-information-seeking behavior on the Internet (Escoffery et al., 2005). Social media offer numerous health-related platforms that can serve as ongoing motivators for healthy behaviors through social reinforcement, support, inspiration, or information (Vaterlaus, Patten, Roche, & Young, 2015). For example, social media and the Internet are used as health information sources to receive and provide information about what one is eating, restaurant reviews, recipes, or pictures of food (McKinley & Wright, 2014).

The popularity of using technology, social network sites, and other online and electronic media such as mobile apps or smartwatches for health-related activities has risen dramatically (Kim, Park, & Eysenbach, 2012). In 2012, already one third of the cell phone and half of the smartphone owners in the United States used their devices for health purposes (Fox & Duggan, 2012). In 2015, more than 100,000 health apps were available (Research2Guidance, 2015); other estimates have counted up to 400,000 applications (Kramer, 2015). Health apps can support quitting harmful behaviors, enhance health-promoting behaviors, or monitor risk factors of chronic illness. Health-promoting behaviors such as physical activity or balanced nutrition are common goals of health applications (Kim, 2014).

Importantly, many such health-promoting behaviors occur often and repeatedly across the day, for example, eating or walking. Other behaviors are boosted by social comparisons, including publicly showcasing the achievement of one's exercise goals. Thus, efficient monitoring of health behaviors and use of social networks and mHealth applications to support changes in lifestyle behaviors often require being permanently online and permanently connected (POPC; Vorderer & Kohring, 2013; Vorderer et al., 2015). Being POPC describes both, a permanence in communication—as an overt behavior of persistently using online media—and a psychological state of permanent communicative vigilance (Vorderer, Krömer, & Schneider, 2016). That is to say, a person can be permanently connected by actually engaging in an online social activity as well as by thinking about online activities, such as incoming messages or updates on activities of social partners while not currently interacting online. Thus, being POPC or having a "POPC mindset" (Klimmt, Hefner, Reinecke, Rieger, & Vorderer, this volume) does not only entail actual behaviors, such as monitoring what is going on online or quickly responding to messages and events, but also entails salience of online contents during offline times.

In this chapter, we aim at exploring the link between effective—i.e., health promoting—usages of mHealth tools and being POPC. While most of our theoretical arguments and examples in this chapter refer to mHealth tools, often smartphone applications, we believe that they also apply to other forms of health-related media, including social networks, blogs, or online channels for health-related topics.

Health-Related POPC

Self-monitoring or self-tracking—i.e., recording of a person's behaviors, feelings, and thoughts—is a central tool in behavioral psychology, medicine, and health provision serving both behavioral assessment and treatment functions (Korotitsch & Nelson-Gray, 1999). Mobile applications provide an easily accessible, permanently available, and economic opportunity to track individual data on health and fitness, which has become quite popular (Choe, Lee, Lee, Pratt, & Kientz, 2014). In 2012, about every fifth smartphone owner had at least one health app installed—preferably an exercise, diet, or weight app (Fox & Duggan, 2012). In Germany, 11% to 17% of the population currently use apps and services for fitness, tracking, and self-monitoring, with a higher proportion among young people (Albrecht, Höhn, & von Jan, 2016; BMJV [The Federal Ministry of Justice and Consumer Protection], 2016). However, the health apps market is described as chaotic, fragmented, and confusing (Research-2Guidance, 2015). Profound basic research on users and determinants of use is lacking. Most current research on the topic was conducted by commercial market companies and not designed for scientific purposes.

If and how mHealth technologies are used depends on user characteristics and motivations. Overall, health-related self-tracking is common particularly among young people up to 35 years. The potential of mHealth devices to sustainably support health behavior changes is high for those who are either already motivated to improve their health, are regular mobile technology or tracking device users, or both. For most people, increasing their motivation to start using mHealth tools represents the main challenge (Patel, Asch, & Volpp, 2015). Thus, apps and wearables facilitate, but cannot directly drive or trigger, health behavior changes. To make use of mHealth technology for health promotion, at least two preconditions need to be met (Patel et al., 2015): (1) People need to be motivated to acquire such a device *and* actually use it. Among those who own an activity tracker, more than half do not engage in long-term use, one third stops using it during the first six months after acquisition (Ledger & McCaffrey, 2014). (2) Long-term engagement in mHealth use such as activity tracking requires the formation of new behavioral habits, strong motivation, and experience of success and progress toward defined goals (Ledger & McCaffrey, 2014). Therefore, information should be tailored to individual profiles and has to be fed back to the user in an understandable and motivating way (Patel et al., 2015).

mHealth technology allows constant tracking of health indicators and behaviors as well as monitoring of activities within one's health-related social network, for example, exercise performance of fitness buddies. A POPC mindset with its facets salience and monitoring of online content (e.g., data on health indicators of oneself and others), as well as reactibility to messages and content (e.g., social support concerning exercise performance), is not only a prerequisite but also potentially increases adherence to mHealth. Whether a POPC mindset for health-related purposes leads to long-term health behavior change and successive health improvement likely depends on a number of factors, which we discuss below.

Modeling the Relationship of POPC, Use, and Effects of mHealth Devices

A precondition to being POPC for health-related purposes is using mHealth technology. In the following section, we will summarize conceptual models of determinants of using mHealth technology and discuss how being POPC and mHealth interact for changing health-promoting behaviors in the long term.

Determinants of Using mHealth Devices

The intention to use and the actual use mHealth applications are often explored based on the technology acceptance model (TAM; Davis, Bagozzi, & Warshaw, 1989) and the unified theory of acceptance and use of technology (UTAUT; Venkatesh, Morris, Davis, & Davis, 2003). The UTAUT is an extension of the TAM that also integrates factors focusing on human and social change processes (Legris, Ingham, & Collerette, 2003). In both models, the user's perception of technological devices, corresponding expectations, and attitudes toward technology and its context are major determinants of the intention and actual usage of technology. As an alternative, Wirth, von Pape, and Karnowski (2008) proposed the mobile phone appropriation model that predicts the adoption of new technology, particularly smartphones, which are central to the mHealth context. The model has started to be used in the field of health behavior change (e.g., Stehr, Rossmann, & Karnowski, 2016). Sun and colleagues provided a comprehensive integration of technology acceptance models and health behavior theories, adding psychological factors such as subjective norm and self-efficacy (Sun, Wang, Guo, & Peng, 2013). Generally, one of the conceptual challenges in the context of mHealth is adjusting existing models to the specific aspects and determinants of using technology for *health*-promoting purposes. In one of the first studies, Yoganathan and Kajanan (2014) tested predictors of the adoption of fitness app use. Next to predictors of technology acceptance, psychological factors, such as intrinsic motivation for physical activity, were particularly important.

Taken together, the individual decision to use and adopt mHealth technology is not an automatic consequence of providing health apps or wearables—even if they are offered for free. The first important step to facilitate mHealth use is reaching potential users and motivating them to not only buy or install a tool, but also to use it in a specific, health-promoting way. In the next section, we describe how being POPC could facilitate the long-term adoption of mHealth devices and, in turn, affect health-related outcomes.

Effective Use of mHealth Devices: The Role of Being POPC

Over the last years, several theoretically relevant aspects of health-promoting technologies have been discussed, including the scarcity or even lack of evidence-based behavior change techniques used in mHealth tools (e.g., Azar et al., 2013; Breton, Fuemmeler, & Abroms, 2011) or the use of helpful features to make mHealth persuasive (e.g., Fogg, 2009). In our view, POPC could promote long-term health behavior change by making the following three evidence-based strategies more effective: (1) the duration of using an mHealth tool, (2) the potential for real-time monitoring of activities and the interactive character facilitating immediate feedback or reinforcement, and (3) the connectedness to other users for social support or social comparison.

Duration

Despite many theoretical and practical advances in health behavior change interventions, long-term changes in health behaviors, such as physical activity or balanced nutrition, remain a big challenge. A number of studies in behavioral weight loss have suggested that longer treatment duration increases intervention success (e.g., Levy et al., 2010; Perri et al., 2001). mHealth technology offers a cost-effective solution, because it can be used for very long periods of time without significant additional costs. Importantly, a POPC mindset (including salience and monitoring of as well as reactibility to online content) could facilitate long-term adherence to weight loss interventions. The effects of a POPC mindset have not been investigated in the context of duration or adherence to health behavior interventions. Technological solutions, particularly mHealth, have been rarely examined in randomized controlled trials targeting health outcomes such as long-term weight control (Gilmartin & Murphy, 2015). Several systematic reviews concluded that these studies have important limitations, and underlying mechanisms have not been studied (Mateo, Granado-Font, Ferré-Grau, & Montaña-Carreras, 2015; Allen, Stephens, & Patel, 2014). In sum, to date few randomized controlled trials targeting long-term health behavior change have taken advantage of the potential of mHealth solutions for longer duration of interventions. The potential facilitating role of a POPC mindset is yet unexplored.

Real-Time Monitoring and Interaction

A second important feature of mHealth technology with implications for POPC is the interactive character of mHealth applications (Noar & Harrington, 2012) and the potential of real-time monitoring. Real-time monitoring of activities has been facilitated and in some cases was made possible only through the latest technological developments. Today's smartphones integrate measures of step count and distance walked, calorie consumption, heart rate, and much more, often requiring only a few clicks. Two major advantages of real-time monitoring include eliminating common memory biases for (health) behaviors (e.g., Shiffman et al., 1997) and teaching individuals to make better, more accurate estimates of their health behavior (Rosenthal, McCormick, Guzman, Villamaory, & Orellano, 2003). Based on real-time monitoring, users can receive immediate feedback on their performance, which is an evidence-based, effective technique for behavior change (Michie et al., 2013). The interactive character of mHealth devices, that is, enabling information exchange between user, the app, and other users, offers immediate feedback on one's performance. Such feedback is extremely rewarding and reinforcing (Hattie & Timperley, 2007), helps self-regulation (e.g., Ilies & Judge, 2005), and most likely triggers high levels of being POPC. At the same time, high levels of monitoring of and reactibility to online content make performance-related feedback immediately available and could increase its effectiveness. Importantly, a recent analysis of over 3,000 paid health apps showed that while reinforcement is one of the key psychological factors to drive behavior change, only about 6% of paid apps were reinforcing (Becker et al., 2014) and thus made use of one major advantage of mHealth.

Social Support and Social Comparison

Being part of a social network comprised of users with similar goals using the same mHealth technology is a third important aspect in the context of POPC and mHealth. Social support by other users, for example, through praise for achievements or cheering and encouragement in the face of failure as well as social comparison and competition are important elements of many mHealth tools. Feeling connected with others is a central human need and a prerequisite for intrinsic motivation, which in turn is the basis of long-term behavior change (Ryan & Deci, 2000; Teixeira et al., 2010). Social control is associated with engaging in more healthy behaviors (e.g., Lewis & Rook, 1999). Social comparison can be very motivating (particularly when performing better than one's reference group; e.g., Deci, 1971) and for the same reasons can be demotivating (when performing worse than one's reference group). Importantly, knowing that relevant others are monitoring one's health behaviors, commenting on (non-)performance, and attempting to outperform one's achievements likely increases the desire to be POPC. More frequently monitoring comments and behaviors of others in a social network allows reacting and using these social mHealth features to their full potential. At the same time, not all social support is beneficial (Berkman, Glass, Brissette, & Seeman, 2000) and of induced stressors, social stressors are arguably the most stressful (e.g., Heinrichs, Baumgartner, Kirschbaum, & Ehlert, 2003). Consequently, monitoring one's social network—also for health-related purposes—might be the strongest motivator for being POPC (cf. Vorderer et al., 2016).

POPC, mHealth, and Their Potential for Health Promotion

As we described above, central features and advances of mHealth technology are likely more effective the more often users are online and feel connected. Importantly, based on evolutionary theory on enhancement, predictions can be deduced about when POPC likely enhances the benefits of mHealth technology, social networks, or other health-related Internet sources, such as blogs, Instagram, or YouTube channels, for engaging in healthy behaviors and when it diminishes them. Every performance enhancement is associated with tradeoffs, with a vast majority of studies suggesting an inverted U-shaped performance function (Hills & Hertwig, 2011). That is, too little or too much performance enhancement can have undesirable side effects. For example, both lower- and considerably higher-than-recommended levels of physical activity are associated with lower well-being compared to medium levels (e.g., Merglen, Flatz, Bélanger, Michaud, & Suris, 2014). Concerning the use of social media, young adults reported perceiving both advantages and disadvantages for their health behaviors (Vaterlaus et al., 2015). For example, social media could be a motivator for exercise, for example, through social support and at the same time a barrier due to intense screen-based media use leading to more sedentary time (Finne, Bucksch, Lampert, & Kolip, 2013). It is likely that the engagement in health-related POPC is related to its effectiveness for enhancing health promotion. Generally, very high levels of health-related POPC behavior potentially lead to conflicts with other health-related behaviors, because POPC takes up time planned for other activities. Also, being in a POPC mindset could additionally lead to stress and distraction from socially engaging with physically present others or procrastination of important but long-term goal behaviors, such as studying or physical exercise, with potential negative consequences for health and well-being (for a discussion of POPC and goal conflicts also see van Koningsbruggen, Hartmann, & Du, this volume). Therefore, we propose an inverted U-shaped relation between POPC behavior for health-promoting purposes and mental and physical health and well-being (Figure 24.1).

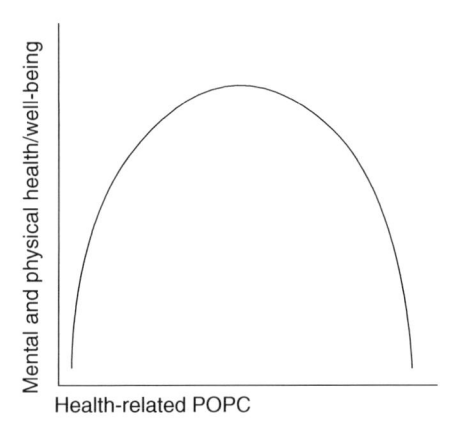

FIGURE 24.1 Relation Between the Individual's Engagement in Being POPC for Health-Related Purposes and Health Promotion.

Additionally, individual differences in the effectiveness of health promotion through being POPC can be assumed. Studies on cognitive enhancement showed that primarily individuals with lower baseline capabilities improved after drug treatment, while effects on individuals of normal or above-average cognitive ability showed negligible improvements or even decrements in performance (de Jongh, Bolt, Schermer, & Olivier, 2008). Similar patterns could be hypothesized for health behaviors: Physically very active persons might show a smaller relative benefit of a health-related POPC mindset than less active individuals might.

Conclusions, Implications, and Future Perspectives

In this chapter, we have described different forms and determinants of mHealth use and how it relates to behaviors triggered by a POPC mindset. We argue that a POPC mindset could increase effectiveness of health promotion through mHealth and other electronic media devices. In our view, at least two main conclusions can be drawn based on the state of the current research reviewed above.

First, effective use of mHealth technology and other online media for health promotion is determined by at least two different factors: (A) affinity to information and communication technology (as prerequisite for being POPC), and (B) motivation for a healthy lifestyle. People in Group A can build on their technology interest and could profit from triggers toward healthy lifestyles. People in Group B are already looking for tools to improve health behaviors and would benefit from technology that can support them to achieve these goals. Mobile online media, such as mHealth tools or social networks, show great promise to support users in achieving healthy lifestyles and thus promise to be an important part of the big challenge to improve health in the long term (Noar & Harrington, 2012).

Second, as we outlined in this chapter, an *adequate dose* of being POPC could be an important prerequisite for using mHealth and other social media tools to their full potential and, thus, more effectively. Such effective use could be associated with higher levels of mental and physical health and well-being (see also Figure 24.1). Importantly, mHealth and other mobile media tools provide answers to previous challenges such as longer duration of health behavior change interventions, real-time monitoring that can replace cumbersome analogue tracking and biased memories of health activities, immediate rewarding feedback, and social connectedness with others in the same situation or with similar goals. These functions hold the promise to make a healthier lifestyle more accessible and sustainable. At the same time, the relation between being POPC—both as a determinant of technology adoption and a consequence of (mobile) technology use—and the effectiveness of mHealth use has not been explored yet. It is likely that a POPC mindset affects the different ingredients of effective behavior change differently: An increase in the duration of health behavior change based on mobile technology is probably the result of an even share of the POPC mindset dimension of salience, monitoring, and reactivity to online content. For receiving performance feedback on health behaviors, monitoring could be the most important POPC facet, whereas both particularly high levels of reactivity and monitoring might be central to receive social support from others. As none of these relationships has been tested yet, however, these assumptions remain hypothetical. The general lack of theoretical delineations and empirical evidence of the effects of a POPC mindset in the context of health purposes is somewhat surprising, given the profound impact of technological advances and related POPC behavior on everyday life, communication, and well-being of individuals in our modern society (Becker et al., 2014).

Many open questions remain. As discussed above, for example, the right level of being POPC seems to be crucial for successful mHealth. However, what that means in everyday life remains largely unclear. According to previous research, too much use of online media is associated with lower physical activity (Bélanger, Akre, Berchtold, & Michaud, 2011)—but can this also be transferred to health-related use of (mobile) online media such as mHealth? Future research needs to address how being POPC and effective health promotion work together most effectively. To further explore this relationship empirically and theoretically, we finally want to emphasize another challenge that an integrated, process-oriented theoretical model of health-related POPC faces: Instead of focusing on single sequences of uses and effects, chains or cascades of multiple and interacting determinants of use and effects should be taken into account (see also Schneider, Reich, & Reinecke, this volume). Considering the interplay between determinants could help explain why mHealth supports only some people in improving health sustainably while others use devices only for a short period but do not benefit in the long run. Thus, a longitudinal perspective of both theoretical and empirical delineations of health-related POPC is essential in future research.

Being POPC is probably highly intertwined with the (effective) use of health-related mobile media and likely follows the same pattern as many other behaviors: The dose makes the poison. More research is profoundly needed to better understand how POPC, as one important facet of our modern and media-saturated world, influences health promotion and well-being. The current state of research suggests that the importance of mobile online media such as mHealth is increasing both for medical applications as well as for a healthy lifestyle. A POPC mindset and online media tools could be an important part of the puzzle to understand one of the major challenges of this century—health behavior change and maintenance.

References

Albrecht, U.-V., Höhn, M., & von Jan, U. (2016). Kapitel 2. Gesundheits-Apps und Markt [Chapter 2. Health apps and the market]. In U.-V. Albrecht (Ed.), *Chancen und Risiken von Gesundheits-Apps (CHARISMHA)* [Chances and risks of health apps] (pp. 62–82). Hannover: Medizinische Hochschule Hannover.

Allen, J. K., Stephens, J., & Patel, A. (2014). Technology-assisted weight management interventions: Systematic review of clinical trials. *Telemedicine and e-Health, 20*, 1103–1120.

Azar, K. M. J., Lesser, L. I., Laing, B. Y., Stephens, J., Aurora, M. S., Burke, L. E., & Palaniappan. L. P. (2013). Mobile applications for weight management: Theory-based content analysis. *American Journal of Preventive Medicine, 45*, 583–589.

Becker, S., Miron-Shatz, T., Schumacher, N., Krocza, J., Diamantidis, C., & Albrecht, U.-V. (2014). mHealth 2.0: Experiences, possibilities, and perspectives. *JMIR mHealth and uHealth, 2*, e24.

Bélanger, R. E., Akre, C., Berchtold, A., & Michaud, P.-A. (2011). A U-shaped association between intensity of Internet use and adolescent health. *Pediatrics, 127*, e330–e335.

Benjamin, L. (2014). *A brief history of modern psychology* (2nd ed.). New York: John Wiley & Sons Inc.

Berkman, L. F., Glass, T., Brissette, I., & Seeman, T. E. (2000). From social integration to health: Durkheim in the new millennium. *Social Science & Medicine, 51*, 843–857.

BMJV [Bundesministerium für Justiz und für Verbraucherschutz; The Federal Ministry of Justice and Consumer Protection] (2016, February 9). *Wearables und Gesundheits-Apps. Verbraucherbefragung im Auftrag des Bundesministeriums der Justiz und für Verbraucherschutz* [Wearables and health apps. Consumer research on behalf of the German Federal Ministry of Justice and Consumer Protection]. Retrieved from www.bmjv.de/DE/Ministerium/Veranstaltungen/SaferInternetDay/YouGov.pdf;jsessionid=A31888202E4A6918AEB880FA0F1F6084.1_cid297?__blob=publicationFile&v=4

Breton, E. R., Fuemmeler. B. F., & Abroms, L. C. (2011). Weight loss—there is an app for that! But does it adhere to evidence-informed practices? *Translational Behavioral Medicine, 1*, 523–529.

Centers for Disease Control and Prevention. (2015). *Leading causes of death, 1900–1998*. Retrieved from www.cdc.gov/nchs/data/dvs/lead1900_98.pdf

Choe, E. K., Lee, N. B., Lee, B., Pratt, W., & Kientz, J. A. (2014). Understanding quantified-selfers' practices in collecting and exploring personal data. In *CHI '14 Proceedings of the SIGCHI Conference on Human Factors in Computing Systems* (pp. 1143–1152).

Davis, F. D., Bagozzi, R. P., & Warshaw, P. R. (1989). User acceptance of computer technology: A comparison of two theoretical models. *Management Science, 35*, 982–1003.

Deci, E. L. (1971). Effects of externally mediated rewards on intrinsic motivation. *Journal of Personality and Social Psychology, 18*, 105–115.

de Jongh, R., Bolt, I., Schermer, M. H. N., & Olivier, B. (2008). Botox for the brain: Enhancement of cognition, mood and pro-social behavior and blunting of unwanted memories. *Neuroscience & Biobehavioral Reviews, 32*, 760–776.

Escoffery, C., Miner, K. R., Adame, D. D., Butler, S., McCormick, L., & Mendell, E. (2005). Internet use for health information among college students. *Journal of American College Health, 53*, 183–188.

Finne, E., Bucksch, J., Lampert, T., & Kolip, P. (2013). Physical activity and screen-based media use: Cross-sectional associations with health-related quality of life and the role of body satisfaction in a representative sample of German adolescents. *Health Psychology and Behavioral Medicine, 1*, 15–30.

Fogg, B. (2009). *A behavior model for persuasive design*. Retrieved from www.bjfogg.com/fbm_files/page4_1.pdf

Fox, S., & Duggan, M. (Pew Research Center's Internet & American Life Project, Ed.). (2012, November 8). *Mobile health 2012*. Retrieved from www.pewInternet.org/~/media/Files/Reports/2012/PIP_MobileHealth2012_FINAL.pdf

Gilmartin, J., & Murphy, M. (2015). The effects of contemporary behavioural weight loss maintenance interventions for long term weight loss: A systematic review. *Journal of Research in Nursing, 20*, 481–496.

Hattie, J., & Timperley, H. (2007). The power of feedback. *Review of Educational Research, 77*, 81–112.

Heinrichs, M., Baumgartner, T., Kirschbaum, C., & Ehlert, U. (2003). Social support and oxytocin interact to suppress cortisol and subjective responses to psychosocial stress. *Biological Psychiatry, 54*, 1389–1398.

Hills, T., & Hertwig, R. (2011). Why aren't we smarter already: Evolutionary trade-offs and cognitive enhancements. *Current Directions in Psychological Science, 20*, 373–377.

Ilies, R., & Judge, T. A. (2005). Goal regulation across time: The effects of feedback and affect. *Journal of Applied Psychology, 90*, 453–467.

Kim, J. (2014). Analysis of health consumers' behavior using self-tracker for activity, sleep, and diet. *Telemedicine Journal and e-Health, 20*, 552–558.

Kim, J., Park, H.-A., & Eysenbach, G. (2012). Development of a health information technology acceptance model using consumers' health behavior intention. *Journal of Medical Internet Research, 14*, e133.

Korotitsch, W. J., & Nelson-Gray, R. O. (1999). An overview of self-monitoring research in assessment and treatment. *Psychological Assessment, 11*, 415–425.

Kramer, U. (2015). *Gesundheits- & Versorgungs-Apps. Report 2015: Einsatzgebiete, Qualität, Trends und Orientierungshilfen für Verbraucher* [Health and health provision apps. Report 2015: Areas of application, quality, trends, and orientation guidance for consumers]. Retrieved from www.tk.de/centaurus/servlet/contentblob/724458/Datei/83809/TK-Pressemappe-Digitale-Gesundheit-Praesentation-Dr-Kramer.pdf

Ledger, D., & McCaffrey, D. (2014). *Inside wearables: How the science of human behavior change offers the secret to long-term engagement. Endeavour Partners Report*. Retrieved from http://endeavourpartners.net/assets/Endeavour-Partners-Wearables-and-the-Science-of-Human-Behavior-Change-Part-1-January-20141.pdf

Legris, P., Ingham, J., & Collerette, P. (2003). Why do people use information technology? A critical review of the technology acceptance model. *Information & Management, 40*, 191–204.

Levy, R. L., Jeffery, R. W., Langer, S. L., Graham, D. J., Welsch, E. M., . . . Yatsuya, H. (2010). Maintenance-tailored therapy vs. standard behavior therapy for 30-month maintenance of weight loss. *Preventive Medicine, 51*, 457–459.

Lewis, M. A., & Rook, K. S. (1999). Social control in personal relationships: Impact on health behaviors and psychological distress. *Health Psychology, 18*, 63–71.

Mateo, G. F., Granado-Font, E., Ferré-Grau, C., & Montaña-Carreras, X. (2015). Mobile phone apps to promote weight loss and increase physical activity: A systematic review and meta-analysis. *Journal of Medical Internet Research, 17*, e253.

McKinley, C. J., & Wright, P. J. (2014). Informational social support and online health information seeking: Examining the association between factors contributing to healthy eating behavior. *Computers in Human Behavior, 37*, 107–116.

Merglen, A., Flatz, A., Bélanger, R. E., Michaud, P.-A., & Suris, J.-C. (2014). Weekly sport practice and adolescent well-being. *Archives of Disease in Childhood, 99*, 208–210.

Michie, S., Richardson, M., Johnston, M., Abraham, C., Francis, J., . . . Cane, J. (2013). The Behavior Change Technique Taxonomy (v1) of 93 hierarchically clustered techniques: Building an international consensus for the reporting of behavior change interventions. *Annals of Behavioral Medicine, 46*, 81–95. https://doi.org/10.1007/s12160-013-9486-6

Miyamoto, S. W., Henderson, S., Young, H. M., Pande, A., & Han, J. J. (2016). Tracking health data is not enough: A qualitative exploration of the role of healthcare partnerships and mHealth technology to promote physical activity and to sustain behavior change. *JMIR mHealth and uHealth, 4*(1), e5.

Noar, S. M., & Harrington, N. G. (2012). eHealth applications: An introduction and overview. In S. M. Noar & N. G. Harrington (Eds.), *eHealth applications: Promising strategies for health behavior change* (pp. 3–16). New York: Routledge.

Patel, M. S., Asch, D. A., & Volpp, K. G. (2015). Wearable devices as facilitators, not drivers, of health behavior change. *JAMA, 313*, 459–460.

Perri, M. G., Nezu, A. M., McKelvey, W. F., Shermer, R. L., Renjilian, D. A., & Viegener, B. J. (2001). Relapse prevention training and problem-solving therapy in the long-term management of obesity. *Journal of Consulting & Clinical Psychology, 69*, 722–726.

Research2guidance. (2015). *mHealth app developer economics 2015. The current status and trends of the mHealth app market*. Retrieved from http://research2guidance.com/r2g/r2g-mHealth-App-Developer-Economics-2015.pdf

Rosenthal, V. D., McCormick, R. D., Guzman, S., Villamaory, C., & Orellano, P. W. (2003). Effect of education and performance feedback on handwashing: The benefit of administrative support in Argentinean hospitals. *American Journal of Infection Control, 31*, 85–92.

Ryan, R. M., & Deci, E. L. (2000). Self-determination theory and the facilitation of intrinsic motivation, social development, and well-being. *American Psychologist, 55*, 68–78.

Shiffman, S., Hufford, M., Hickcox, M., Paty, J. A., Gnys, M., & Kassel, J. D. (1997). Remember that? A comparison of real-time versus retrospective recall of smoking lapses. *Journal of Consulting and Clinical Psychology, 65*, 292–300.

Stehr, P., Rossmann, C., & Karnowski, V. (2016, June). The multi-faceted usage patterns of nutrition apps: A survey on the appropriation of nutrition apps among German users. Paper presented at the *66th ICA Conference*, Fukuoka, Japan.

Sun, Y., Wang, N., Guo, X., & Peng, Z. (2013). Understanding the acceptance of mobile health services: A comparison and integration of alternative models. *Journal of Electronic Commerce Research, 14*, 183–200.

Teixeira, P. J., Silva, M. N., Coutinho, S. R., Palmeira, A. L., Mata, J., . . . Sardinha, L. B. (2010). Mediators of weight loss and weight loss maintenance in middle-aged women. *Obesity, 18*, 725–735.

Vaterlaus, J. M., Patten, E. V., Roche, C., & Young, J. A. (2015). #Gettinghealthy: The perceived influence of social media on young adult health behaviors. *Computers in Human Behavior, 45*, 151–157.

Venkatesh, V., Morris, M. G., Davis, G. B., & Davis, F. D. (2003). User acceptance of information technology: Toward a unified view. *MIS Quarterly, 27*, 425–478.

Vorderer, P., Klimmt, C., Rieger, D., Baumann, E., Hefner, D., Knop, K., . . . Wessler, H. (2015). Der mediatisierte Lebenswandel: Permanently online, permanently connected [The media-based lifestyle: Permanently online, permanently connected]. *Publizistik—Vierteljahreshefte für Kommunikationsforschung, 60*, 259–276.

Vorderer, P., & Kohring, M. (2013). Permanently online: A challenge for media and communication research. *International Journal of Communication, 7*, 188–196.

Vorderer, P., Krömer, N., & Schneider, F. M. (2016). Permanently online—permanently connected: Explorations into university students' use of social media and mobile smart devices. *Computers in Human Behavior, 63*, 694–703.

Wirth, W., von Pape, T. & Karnowski, V. (2008). An integrative model of mobile phone appropriation. *Journal of Computer-Mediated Communication, 13*, 593–617.

Yoganathan, D., & Kajanan, S. (2014). What drives fitness apps usage? An empirical evaluation. In B. Bergvall-Kåreborn & P. A. Nielsen (Eds.), *Creating value for all through IT (IFIP Advances in Information and Communication Technology, 429*, 179–196). Berlin, Heidelberg: Springer.

INDEX

Note: Italicized page numbers indicate a figure on the corresponding page.

academic performance and multitasking 168
addiction-facilitating cognitions 63
adolescents and media use *see* early adolescence and media use; mindfully connected adolescents; networked young citizens
affect misattribution procedure (AMP) 54
affordances in smartphone use 21
Airbnb 14
Amazon MTurk 118
amplification dynamics of POPC 65
anxiously-attached individuals 157
Apple watch 97–8
appreciation-seeking with political entertainment 222–5
apps (applications) for smartphones *see* specific apps
artificial tellers and meaning 101–3
attachment styles in relationships 156–7
attention and multitasking 85–7
attention-processing resources 238
audacious (chutzpadic) temperament 191
Auto-Awesome Movies 103
autonomy and social roles 166
autonomy and well-being 239–41
averse states, avoidability 24–5
avoidant-attached individuals 156–7

behavioral components: continuum of behaviors 73–4; coping behaviors 63; dual-systems models of behavior 51; dysfunctional partner behavior 155; meaningfulness and privacy 110–11; *meiwaku* (bothersome) behavior 190; phubbing behavior 239; of POPC 32, 77; qualities of 189; unobtrusive assessment 31

Bluetooth proximity 35
bond-based groups 131–2
boycotting/buycotting online 212–13
breaking up and permanent connectivity 155–6
Bump app 15

central bottleneck theories 74, 85–7
Chinese *guanxiwang* manners 190
The Civic Network project 210
cloud-based services 16
cognition and media 85, 168–9
cognitive resource theories 118
cognitive structures in smartphone use: default expectations with smartphones 23–5; empowerment *vs.* overwhelm 25–7, *26*; human reasoning and smartphones 19–23; introduction 18–19
collective political engagement 213–14
collective self-stabilization 67
common bond/identity 131, 134
Communication and Mass Media Complete (CMMC) 29
computer-mediated communication (CMC) 141
consistency-driven consumers 221
continuum of behaviors 73–4
coping behaviors 63
core social group 13
cosmopolitanism index 192
co-tellership 101–3
cross-cultural differences: intercultural linkages 192–4; introduction to 188–9; overview of 189–92; research perspectives 193
crowd sourcing 14–15
cultural identities 189

customizing apps 6
cyberloafing 56

demands–resources perspective 244–9
dichotic listening tasks 85
digital communication observations/reflection 181
divided attention theories 85–7
dual-systems models of behavior 51
dutiful norms of citizenship 209
dyadic relationships 6
dysfunctional partner behavior 155

early adolescence and media use: developmental characteristics 168–71; identity development and 169–70; importance of studying 165–7; introduction to 165; media and cognition 168–9; overview of 167; peer context and 170–1; summary of 172; *see also* mindfully connected adolescents
email technologies 248
embeddedness 99
emergent goals 90
emotional content 77
emotional privacy 111
emotional sharing and well-being 235
empowerment *vs.* overwhelm 25–7, *26*
engagement with narrative 120
enjoyment-seeking with political entertainment 222–5
ethical concerns 34–5
eudaimonic well-being 234, 240
EU Kids Online network 167
excessive online use 62
experience sampling method (ESM) 32, 33

Facebook: cross-cultural connections 192; limitations in using 100; media enjoyment 109; memorial/R.I.P pages 124; political engagement on 214–16, *215*; politician use of 217–18; reflective-impulsive model 53; self-presentation with 253; smartphone access to 143; vibrating notifications 122
face-to-face (FTF) communication: intoxication of 154; overview of 140–1, 145; perception of the value of 194
facial feature analysis 79
fandom 123–4
fan fiction 118–19
fear of missing out (FOMO) 145, 240
filter theory 85
focused attention 85
fourth age of political communication 199
"friending" a third party 151
functional magnetic resonance imaging (fMRI) 74

general Internet addiction (GIA) 62–3, 68; *see also* Internet addiction
generation M 73
geographic (landline) addressability 12

Global Positioning System (GPS) 31, 35
goals and multitasking 78, 89–91
Google+ Story album 103
GPS functionality 15
gratifications in smartphone use 21
group affiliation needs 177
group co-presence 134
group dynamics of POPC: effects of 135; group attachment 130–3; introduction to 7, 129–30; mobile instant messaging applications 129–36; norms in 133–5; overview 130; summary of 135–6
group norms 133–5
guanxiwang manners 190

habitualized reactibility 21
habituation of online use 65–6
Hall, G. Stanley 166
health-related technology *see* mHealth (mobile health technology)
hedonic well-being 98, 234, 240
high-context communication 190
human reasoning and smartphones 19–23

identity-based groups 132
identity development and media 169–70
impulsive influences on media use: conflicts over 55–6; examples of 56–7; further studies on 57–8; introduction to 51–2; overview 52–5; summary of 58
independent multitasking 122
individual addressability *see* mobile communication
individual political engagement *211–12*, 211–13
informational privacy 111
information and communication technologies (ICTs) 53–4, 202, 245–6
information flow 76–7
information modality 76
information-processing resources 238
information utility model 51
Instagram app 168–9, 235
instant meaningfulness 98–103
intercultural linkages 192–4
internalized connectedness 179
International Telecommunications Union 10
Internet addiction (IA): availability and appeal concerns 64–5; chances for prevention and intervention 67–8; collective self-stabilization 67; defined 62–3; habituation of online use 65–6; introduction to 61; normalization of heavy online use 66–7; POPC connection to 64–7; research challenges 68–9; well-being and 237
Internet gaming disorder 62
Internet of Things 16
Internet use and well-being 234–6
interpersonal tensions 238
interstitial communication 141–2

intimate relationships with permanent connectivity: anxiety *vs.* control 151–2; attachment styles 156–7; breaking up 155–6; introduction to 149–50; jealousy concerns 154–5; online dating, effort *vs.* risk 151; positive aspects of POPC 152–4; stage of relationship formation 150–2; summary of 157–8
I-PACE (interaction of person-affect-cognition-execution) model 62–3

jealousy concerns 154–5
job-crafting efforts 249
journalistic news content 201

landline addressability 12
linearity 99
"live video" feature 97
living in the moment: artificial tellers and meaning 101–3; instant meaningfulness 98–103; introduction 97–8; perspectives on 103–5; self-narratives 99–101
low-context communication 190

macro developments 7
maintenance in romantic relationships 142–3
Maitland, Donald (Maitland Commission) 10–11
mass communication 221
meaningfulness and privacy: calculus of needs for 112–13; communication as entertainment 108–9; foundational theories 109–10; introduction 6, 107; POPC behaviors 110–11; social media use 107–8; summary of 113
media exposure: cognition and 168–9; enjoyment of 234–5; identity development and 169–70; measurements of 34; peer context and 170–1; psychology of 221; *see also* early adolescence and media use; impulsive influences on media use; social media
meiwaku (bothersome) behavior 190
memes on social media 134
messaging groups 14
mHealth (mobile health technology): determinants using 256; effective use of 256–8; introduction to 254–5; overview of 255; promotion of 258–9, *259*; real-time monitoring 257; social support/comparison 258; summary of 259–60; treatment durations 257
microcoordination 13–14
mindfully connected adolescents: adolescents as connection seekers 177–8; challenges of 178–80; characteristics of mobile phone use 181; content created by others 180; encountering of challenges 180–3; introduction to 6–7, 176–7; online *vs.* offline integration 178–9; self-created content 179–80; summary of 183; *see also* early adolescence and media use
mobile communication: characteristics of 181; geographic to individual addressability 12–13;

Internet of Things 16; introduction to 10–12; microcoordination and 13–14; smartphone development 14; social spheres of 14–16; summary of 16; *see also* cognitive structures in smartphone use
mobile instant messaging applications (MIMAs) 129–36
mobile phones in Global North 11
monitoring concept 19, 22, 237
moral stance 99
motivation and multitasking 90–1
multidimensional framework of multitasking 76–7
multiple-goal situations 247
multiple resources theories 74, 86
multiscreening 117–18
multitasking: academic performance and 168; attention and 85–7; competing theories on 74; continuum of behaviors 73–4; goals and motivation 89–91; goals of 78; independent multitasking 122; introduction to 72–3, 83–4; level of analysis 77–9; modalities and features 78–9; multidimensional framework 76–7; narrative experiences 117–22, *119*; political information and 202–3; social multitasking 121–2; summary of 79–80, 92; task switching *vs.* 84–5; threaded cognition 74–5, *87*, 87–9, *89*, 91–2; time and 79

narrative experiences of online environments: introduction to 116–17; multitasking and 117–22, *119*; POPC and 122–4; summary of 124–5
networked young citizens: introduction to 208–10; political conflict and *214*, 214–18, *215*; political engagement of 210–14, *211–12*, *213*; summary of 218
news finds me (NFM) expectation 202
normalization of heavy online use 66–7

objectification theory 170
offline activities 20
one-sided liking 123
one-to-one communications 14
online dating, effort *vs.* risk 151
online procrastination 56, 65
online vigilance 19, 29, 113, 237
online *vs.* offline integration 178–9
origin-oriented migrants 193

parental hovering 6–7
peer context and media 170–1
permanently online and permanently connected (POPC): availability and appeal 64–5; behavioral qualities 189; characteristics of 200–1; defined 29–30; disruptive shift of 4–5; as double-edged sword 145; downside of 144–5; ethical concerns 34–5; future challenges with 5–8; intercultural linkages 192–4; introduction to 29, 199–200; meaningfulness and privacy 110–11; methodological

challenges 33–5; mindset of 3, *26*, 26–7; as mood amplifier 237–8; obstacles and opportunities 30–3; political information exposure 201–4; positive aspects of 152–4; relationship-building function of 143–4; remedies and solutions to 35–6; research methods 29–33; summary of 47–8, 204–5; well-being and 236–9; *see also* group dynamics of POPC; Internet addiction; multitasking; workplace POPC
persuasion-oriented effects 221
Pew Internet Studies 214
Pew Research Center 210
Phatic communication signals 143
phubbing behavior 239
political engagement: conflict with *214*, 214–18, *215*; information exposure 201–4; networked young citizens 210–14, *211–12*, *213*; summary of 218
political entertainment: citizen engagement with 220–6; enjoyment-/appreciation-seeking with 222–5; explanatory principles 221–2; future research 226; introduction to 220; media engagement with 225–6; traditional view of 221
POPC *see* permanently online and permanently connected
privacy concerns *see* meaningfulness and privacy
procedural resource manager 88–9
process-oriented approach 52
procrastination online 56, 65
PRP (psychological refractory period) paradigm 86
psychological refractory paradigm (PRP) 74
psychological state of vigilance 29

qualities of POPC behaviors 189

reactibility concept 19, 20–2, 237
real-time notification 24
reflective-impulsive model 51, 52, 53–5
relational communication 141
relationship-building function of POPC 143–4
resource theory 86–7

salience concept 19, 20
selective attention 85
self-affirmation and well-being 235
self-control concerns with media use 55–6
self-disclosure in social groups 134, 142
self-efficacy 6
self-esteem concerns 178
self-narratives 99–101
self-objectification 170
self-regulation: addiction and 64–5, 67–8; of digital communication 181–3; impulsiveness and 57–8; Internet/social media use 236; reactibility and 238
self-report questionnaires 32, 52
self-worth and meaning making 99
sequential processing 75
shared modality 76
sharing economy 14–15

Skype 193
smartphones: apps for 43–8; averse states, avoidability 24–5; default expectations with 23–5; development of 14; disadvantages of 140; human reasoning and 19–23; member communication 24; monitoring concept 19, 22; multitasking behavior 76; online vigilance concept 19; reactibility concept 19, 20–2; real-time notification 24; salience concept 19, 20; social network accessibility 23; social network observation 24; summary of usage 22–3, 25; technology and software features of 69; *see also* cognitive structures in smartphone use
Snapchat 100, 104
soccer mom multitasking 79
social assurance needs 177–8
social capital/support 235
social cohesion 13–14
social comparison online 256
social identity of couples 153
social media: communication as entertainment 108–9; memes on 134; POPC with 107–8; Twitter 122, 217–18; well-being and 236; while doing homework 72; YouTube 109; *see also* Facebook
social multitasking 121–2
social network sites (SNS) 29, 36, 108; accessibility 23; context of using 191; encounters with news bits 204; observation of 24; political information on 199; relationship maintenance 143–4
social penetration theory 142
social-psychological perspective 200
social relationships: connected presence and interstitial communication 141–2; downside of POPC 144–5; introduction 140–1; relationship-building function of POPC 143–4; role of communication in 142–3; summary of 145–6
standardized psychological tests 32
sturm und drang (storm and stress) 166
subjective well-being 98
synchronous narrative 120

tailoring apps 6
Tanzanians telecommunications 11
task contiguity 76
task output 77
task relations 77
task relevance 76
task switching *vs.* multitasking 84–5
technological tellers 102–3
telephony in Global South 10
tellability 99
temporarily expanded boundaries of the self model (TEBOTS) 121, 124
texts/texting during breakups 155
threaded cognition: multitasking and *87*, 87–9, *89*, 91–2; overview of 74–5
time and multitasking 77, 79
Twitter 122, 217–18

Uber 14–15
uncontrolled online use 62
understanding-based theory 221
unobtrusive assessment of usage behavior 31
user experiences 108–9
uses and gratifications (U&G) research 44, 48, 51

value and meaning making 99
videoconferencing technologies 188
video-stream platforms 142

well-being: defined 233–4; enjoyment of media 234–5; Internet use and 234–6; introduction to 233; POPC and 236–9; self-affirmation and emotional sharing 235; self-regulated Internet/social media use 236; social capital/support 235; social comparison online 256; summary of 239–41
WhatsApp 45–8, 104, 193
wireless-based connectivity 10
workplace POPC: demands-resources perspective 244, 245–9; information and communication technologies 245–6; introduction to 244–5; summary of 249–50

young citizens *see* networked young citizens
YouTube 109